THE BIRDS
SWITHLAND RESERVOIR

and some thoughts and memories
of a birdwatcher

IAN GAMBLE

*For since the creation of the world God's invisable qualities – his
eternal power and divine nature – have been clearly seen, being understood
from what has been made, so that men are without excuse.*

Romans ch.1 vs. 20

Loughborough Naturalists' Club
and
KAIROS PRESS
2001

Copyright © Ian Gamble, 2001

ISBN 1-871344-27-1

First Edition, 2001

Layout by Robin Stevenson, Kairos Press
Body text in Aldine 721 BT 10.0pt & 9.0pt
Imagesetting by dotperfect, Leicester
Printed in Great Britain by Norwood Press, Anstey, Leics.

Cover painting by Ernest Leahy:
Ducks on northern section of Swithland Reservoir from Kinchley Lane.

KAIROS PRESS
552 Bradgate Road,
Newtown Linford
Leicester LE6 0HB
Great Britain.

Contents

4

Paintings by Ernest Leahy

Maps

Photographs

Archive photographs (No.s 2, 3 and 4) used by permission of Severn Trent Water.
Frontispiece photograph by Robin Stevenson. All other photographs by Peter and Ian Gamble.

Foreword

Swithland Reservoir is a part of one of Leicestershire's most beautiful areas, the Charnwood Forest, and it is a great attraction not only to people but also to birds – birds of much variety and interest. Ian Gamble is ideally qualified to write about this lovely site, having grown up in the shadow of Buddon Hill with the reservoir at its feet, and been nurtured in his love of birds by his naturalist father, Peter.

Ian's early interest, awakened by bird books shown to him as an infant, has led him beyond the shore of Swithland Reservoir to each of the world's continents except Antarctica and his experiences, both at home and abroad, are related with infectious enthusiasm.

Under the heading "Charnwood a thousand years of change" Ian reveals a deep understanding of the changes that have fashioned our countryside and its wildlife and which will affect it in future years. The largest section is the systematic account of birds recorded at the reservoir, in which their distribution, local and national status, habits and appearance are well described.

A section showing the movements of some of the ringed birds associated with Swithland Reservoir illustrate another aspect of its importance.

This book is a welcome result of Ian's considerable experience and meticulous research.

Gerald Felstead, July 2001.

The LNC would like to thank the following for making possible the publication of this book through their generous donations:–

The Helen Jean Cope Trust

together with
Owen Black's Memorial Fund
Mr C.B. and Lady Byford
Charnwood Borough Council
Charnwood Wildlife
Peter and Margaret Gamble
Ian and Pamela Gamble
Lafarge Aggregates Limited
Leicestershire County Council
The Squire de Lisle
Angela Marmot
Severn Trent Water plc

Acknowledgements

Firstly I would like to thank Severn Trent Water Authority for allowing me onto the Swithland Reservoir site in order to study its diverse natural history and Colin Green, the former Estates Manager for his help and support during the study period.

I would also like to pay tribute to the many dedicated birdwatchers from both the Loughborough Naturalists' Club and the Leicestershire and Rutland Ornithological Society who have spent hours birdwatching at Swithland Reservoir and without whose records this book would not have been possible. I would like to thank the Leicestershire and Rutland Ornithological Society for allowing me to use their records and for the support they offered.

Other records that were greatly appreciated are a detailed breeding bird survey carried out by Harry Ball and Peter Jones and also the bird ringing information from Jeff Higgott and Gerald Felstead. Gerald was my bird ringing trainer, a man of infinite patience with a great knowledge of our local birdlife. We spent hours bird ringing in the field together and I learnt a great deal about birds from him. I would also like to mention Kingsley Lloyd with whom I shared many enjoyable birdwatching expeditions, and it was Kingsley who enabled me to travel to many exciting birding localities in my youth.

I am indebted to the British Trust for Ornithology and the European Bird Census Council for allowing me to use their figures from their respective publications *The State of the U.K.s Birds 1999* and *The EBCC Atlas of European Breeding Birds*. The rare breeding bird numbers for 1997 were reproduced by kind permission from the monthly journal *British Birds*.

I have received a great deal of help with the compilation of this book and would particularly like to thank the following people: John Ward, Gerald Felstead, Brenda Hudson, Michael Stanley, Rose Warner and Katherin Ward for their time spent proof reading the work and giving their advice on the written text. Gerald also wrote the foreword. Dr Ian Keil who very kindly read through the Heritage chapter and who made some valuable additions to the original text. Finally to Mike Caldwell who gave of his technical expertise in computing and photography.

Ernest Leahy very kindly agreed to do the paintings for the book. One cannot but admire his skill when you look at his work.

In the final months before going to print, the members of Loughborough Naturalists' Club publications committee put in a great deal of time and effort which I much value.

My family have helped me considerably with this book. My father Peter Gamble wrote the Introduction and the chapter on the topography and vegetation of Swithland Reservoir. He also supplied many of the photographs and I received a lot of help and advice from him with regard to the written text. My mother Margaret has supported me and given me encouragement through this venture. Lastly a very special thank you must go to my wife Pamela who has put up with me, supported me and helped me in nearly every aspect of producing this work. Thank you to you all!

Author's Preface

One May morning some twenty years ago I walked from my house in Quorn along the Buddon Brook, around the margins of Swithland Reservoir and returned home the same way. I saw a total of 87 species of bird in my four mile walk which lasted about three hours. There are very few places in Britain that could better that total given the distance travelled and the time spent in the field. In fact some 218 species have been recorded here in the last 60 years and some 92 species have bred at Swithland Reservoir and in the adjacent area including Buddon Wood; another five species have been suspected of breeding. However, after stating that, it does not matter how good any individual site is, even if its bio-diversity is extremely rich, for no area can sustain a large number of bird species on its own. The many and varied bird species that visit the reservoir require a large range of habitats in which to breed and feed during the year and some travel thousands of miles to obtain one of these. A few birds are only transitory visitors to the reservoir, others spend the summer or winter months with us, but very few are completely sedentary. So what happens in other areas of our country or world can directly affect the status of birds at Swithland Reservoir.

For me birdwatching has very seldom been boring. At times it can be predictable. At certain times of the year you will probably have a good idea of the species you will come across on an outing to your local patch. Species like the Swallow or Cuckoo will normally arrive back to the same area within a few days of when they were first recorded the previous year. Occasionally, however, birds can be unpredictable. Some can be found miles outside their normal range or you might spot a bird behaving in an unusual manner. All these things add to the excitement of birdwatching. Some birds are very beautiful, others graceful in their behaviour, while some species have a certain amount of mystery surrounding their life-style. Given all these facets you have a hobby of which you will never tire. In this book I have not only given scientific facts and figures but I have also tried to help the birdwatcher and non-birdwatcher alike understand more about the birds that have visited Swithland Reservoir showing their behaviour, distribution, favoured habitat and how to identify each species.

As we stood on the threshold of a new millennium I also wanted to put into perspective the state of our local bird population and how national and international trends are affecting them. Throughout the 20th century our birdlife has changed dramatically and once common species like the Corncrake and Barn Owl are now absent from large areas of our land. Over the last 28 years of the last century major declines were noted in 37 of our commonest species and some of them might be lost from Swithland Reservoir and even the county or country in the future. Whoever would have imagined that the House Sparrow or Starling could be under threat, but both have had their populations decimated, falling by 58% between 1970 and 1998?

The Americans of the mid-19th century probably thought their commonest bird, the Passenger Pigeon, whose flocks numbered millions of birds could never be lost but because of habitat change and persecution it became extinct in four decades, the last one surviving until 1914. Our natural heritage is important and if birds are not to survive on their own beauty and charm alone then let us turn around our greed which is causing their decline and realise that it is the natural diversity of our planet that ultimately enables mankind to survive.

Introduction
by
Peter Gamble

It has long been intended to produce a Unit Survey Report for Swithland Reservoir (unit survey No. 19) and to make available some 40 years of Loughborough Naturalists' Club fauna and flora notes for this important Site of Special Scientific Interest. However, in total, these records are so comprehensive that to produce them in a single survey report would have necessitated the information appearing in little more than list form for the many separate groups covered, a production which would have had little interest other than for the specialist. Consequently when Ian offered to write a report on the Bird Fauna, the most popular and intensively observed group, it was decided to accept his offer with the intention of following this later with other reports covering the various other groups.

Between its being built in 1896 and the formation of the Leicestershire and Rutland Ornithological Section of the Literary and Philosophical Society in 1941, little appears to have been written down on the birds at this favourite locality and it is intriguing, though sad, to think of what may have bred or visited the reservoir in its early years, especially considering the unspoilt nature of the reservoir and its environs and the many species which were much more common and widespread at this time.

In the early years of the last century a Mr. Frisby of Quorn, the local representative of the British Empire Naturalists' Association, (now the British Naturalists' Association), did frequently visit the site, sometimes accompanied by scholars and the Head of the local school. In an article in the Quorn Parish Magazine dated July 1906, he reports on watching Black Terns on spring and autumn passage, Common and Arctic Terns fishing here and Little Grebe and Great Crested Grebe (8 pairs of the latter). He also mentioned Common Sandpiper and Common Snipe and a variety of duck species, including Wigeon, Pintail, Teal, Pochard, Tufted Duck and Goldeneye, all species frequently observed today. The Canada Goose was plentiful even then and frequently accompanied by goslings.

Many of the records used, especially of the less common species, were gleaned from the bulletins and reports of the Leicestershire and Rutland Ornithological Society, as also were the wildfowl count figures and we wish to record our thanks for the use of these records.

This locality is a favourite place for many bird-watchers; a place of precious memories, though sadly not the peaceful place it once was. Today it is not regarded as one of the best places to see rare birds but few if any other local sites could show the same diversity of breeding species.

Swithland Reservoir: the view from Kinchley Lane

1. SEASONS AND MEMORIES

I was born in Quorn in 1956 and at a very early age I started birdwatching. My father, instead of reading me stories, would sit me on his knee and we would look through a large volume of British Birds by Kirkman and Jourdain. Many of the lovely illustrated plates had been painted by the well known bird artists, Seaby and Lodge. Some of the birds in this book held a mythical status for a young boy: Great Grey Shrike, Waxwing, Hoopoe, Roller and Golden Oriole to mention but a few.

My sister Jane and I would alternate with each other on Sundays to go out birdwatching with my father and one of his close friends. When it was my turn I would sit in the back of his bricklayer's van with his little dog Sherry and we would go to one of Charnwood's many and varied habitats. It would often be Swithland Reservoir which at this time was a quiet place and if you ever met a birdwatcher you would be sure to know him or her. Birdwatching in the early 1960s was not the fashionable pastime that it has become today.

In October 1962 on one of my Sunday expeditions I was taken to an area near Groby where I saw my first male Ring Ouzel sitting on a pile of rocks directly in front of me. A little later in the morning I was shown a Woodlark singing. Both of those species were very unusual birds for Leicestershire – my twitching days had started; I had got the bug!

By the age of seven my identification skills were improving and as I walked down the garden from the bird trap I announced to my father that we had caught a Brambling! To his astonishment we had and after ringing the bird we released it. During my early childhood my father held a ringing licence that allowed him to catch wild birds. After the birds were caught they were aged and sexed and then an individual ring was fixed around their legs. The ring held a number similar to that found on a car number plate and the address of the British Natural History Museum. Over the years dedicated bird ringers have collected a huge amount of valuable information about our wild birds.

The downside to birdwatching hit me hard in 1965 when on one of my sister's outings she was shown the first Bearded Reedlings to be seen in the county last century at Wanlip Gravel Pits – my dipping out days had come! In birdwatching parlance that means I missed seeing the bird.

In 1974 I became a trainee bird ringer and my trainer was a close family friend. He gained permission for us to ring at Swithland Reservoir and at some gravel pits in the Wreake Valley. It was exactly ten years since I had missed seeing the Bearded Reedling at Wanlip Gravel Pits that I at last literally got to grips with them. While bird ringing in the Wreake Valley during March 1975 we caught a pair that were subsequently controlled (re-captured) over a year later at Fordwich, Canterbury, Kent. Then in the winter of 1977/78 we caught 17 more Bearded Reedlings at the same site and this still remains the largest number ever recorded in Leicestershire.

I spent hours outside, birdwatching and bird ringing during the next fifteen years and learnt much about our local birdlife. Swithland Reservoir was one of my favourite haunts and I soon knew which areas certain species favoured and I got to know the site so intimately that it almost became a part of my life.

Swithland Reservoir is one of Leicestershire's most scenic areas with its mature margins and the backdrop of Buddon Wood. Over the past two decades however the summit of Buddon Hill has been quarried away, leaving the hill truncated and the ancient woodland site but a remnant of its former glory. This is nevertheless still one of the county's most important ornithological areas and a species list of over two hundred confirms this.

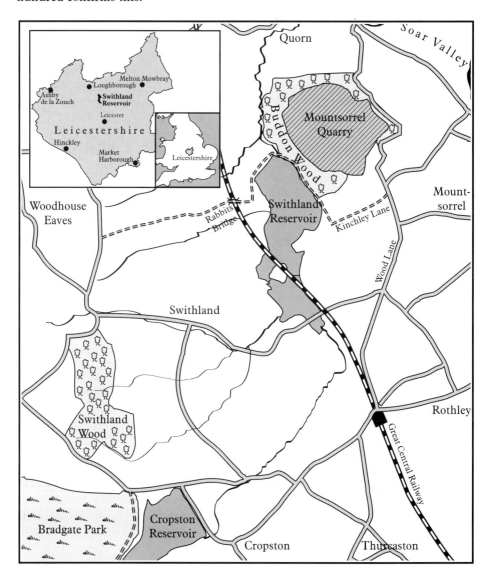

A good observation point for viewing birds is where the water comes close to the railings at the bottom of Kinchley Hill. A stop here on a typical winter's day will certainly produce a good variety of duck species, the males being colourful but their partners looking rather drab. During January the ducks are generally in their best plumages and the males can be easily identified.

Of the diving ducks, the Pochard with its chestnut head, black front and grey body, and the Tufted Duck with its drooping crest, black upper parts and white flanks are the most common and easily spotted. Both these species occur in large numbers, sometimes in flocks of several hundred. The next in frequency is the Ruddy Duck which over the past few winters has been present in flocks well in excess of a hundred. The Ruddy Duck is an introduced species and a native of North America. It started to breed in the feral state in Britain in 1960 and was seen in Leicestershire a year later. It is smaller than the two previous species with white cheeks, brown body and stiff, erect tail, while in breeding plumage it has a bright blue bill making this little bird very distinctive. The last of the more frequent diving ducks to be seen is the Goldeneye, a visitor from Northern Europe which stays with us all winter. Its numbers vary, rarely getting any higher than 50 and they normally remain well scattered in ones and twos over the whole reservoir, though before leaving in the early spring gather together to indulge in courtship display. The male is a fine duck with its bottle-green head, white spot behind bill, white body and black and white back making it obvious at several hundred yards. Other species of diving duck are uncommon but do occur and are well worth looking for.

Of the dabbling ducks, the Mallard is the most frequent but the Wigeon can be here in large numbers on occasions, although Swithland is not as good as some waters for this species because it lacks open areas of short grass for the birds to graze. Wigeon, in flocks of several hundred, have occurred from time to time especially in recent winters. The male looks superficially similar to the Pochard, it has a chestnut head but with a bright yellowish crown stripe, grey back and a white line along the wing. When large numbers are on the water they normally give their presence away by their evocative "whee-oo" whistle and when airborne the white chevron patches on their wings make them distinctive. The Teal and Shoveler both occur in small numbers though occasionally in hundreds and feed in the reedy shallows, the Teal being readily identified by its small size, chestnut head with curving green eye-patch, grey body and white stripe along the wing; the Shoveler by its large shovel-shaped bill, bottle-green head, chestnut flanks, white breast and pale blue on the wing. Another good identification feature for this species is its head-down attitude which can be noted at a distance. The only other dabbling duck that is a regular visitor and now breeds annually is the Gadwall but this usually occurs only in small numbers. This species is similar in size and shape to the Mallard. The male can easily be identified by its grey body, black undertail coverts and white on the wing which is very distinctive in flight. Pintail are seen on occasions and are worth looking for, especially among the large flocks of Wigeon and must be one of our most elegant duck species.

In addition to the duck, other waterfowl species present on Swithland include large numbers of Coot while around the edges of the reservoir Moorhen can be seen swimming in and out of the vegetation and if you are very fortunate you may hear a squeal and get brief views of the elusive Water Rail as it moves stealthily through the reeds.

Occasionally Little Grebe can be spotted just out from the reeds and on the main body of water their bigger relative, the Great Crested Grebe, with elegant long white neck, dark cap and mantle and pinkish bill can be seen swimming buoyantly or diving. These birds are here in fairly good numbers but like the Goldeneye, they are well scattered. It is worth keeping an eye out for Red-necked, Slavonian and Black-necked Grebe that turn up from time to time. The occasional Red-throated Diver can be found and very rarely Great Northern and Black-throated. In recent years the similar looking Cormorant can be seen on most visits to the reservoir often perched upright with outstretched wings on the anchored raft in the middle of the large north section of the reservoir. These now even stop to breed. Sometimes all you can see of the Cormorant is its long neck and head protruding like a periscope above the water and you get a brief glimpse of its partially submerged body as it slides effortlessly beneath the surface out of sight.

There are generally one or two Mute Swans to be seen and also the odd Canada Goose. Flocks of a hundred Canadas do occur but they do not normally remain long and in recent years Greylag Geese have become much more frequent. Occasionally other goose species can be found in these flocks, but their origin is suspect for most tend to be escapes from wildfowl collections. You could also be lucky enough to see either of the wild species of swan, the Whooper and Bewick's, which call here briefly on their travels.

Close examination of the shoreline may produce a Heron standing statuesquely waiting for its prey. Herons are one of the earliest species to breed and by February they are returning to their nest sites. Several pairs now breed annually in the tall trees on the edge of the reservoir but not in a large communal heronry that is normally the case.

During the winter months Merlins have been seen occasionally and my father and I saw a female in January 1983. The Merlin is Britain's smallest falcon and it has a swift low flight when hunting and feeds mainly on small birds. Unfortunately because of its hunting manner only brief views are normally obtained before it darts out of sight.

As the day moves on squadrons of gulls wing their way in chevron or open formation to roost, in what seems a never-ending stream. They come in and circle above the water then tumble down like snowflakes onto the surface where a white blanket of up to 15000 birds forms. It is at this time you may be fortunate enough to see a Peregrine stoop into the gull roost in an attempt to catch its prey. The mayhem that ensues is something to be seen. Since the national recovery of this species in the early 1980s this has been a not infrequent sight. All the common species of gull occur in the roost but by far the most numerous is the Black-headed Gull which accounts for two thirds of the birds. Three Black-headed Gulls have been found at the reservoir bearing foreign rings. Two were ringed as nestlings, one in Denmark in 1982 and one in Lithuania in 1988 and another was ringed as an adult in the Netherlands in 1979. Most of the Black-headed Gulls that visit the reservoir in the winter originate from the Baltic. The gull roost is well worth close observation and a diligent birdwatcher may record rarer species! Mediterranean and Yellow-legged Gulls from southern Europe, Glaucous Gull which breeds north of the Arctic Circle,

Iceland Gull from Arctic America and Greenland and the Ring-billed Gulls from North America have all been found. I wonder what new species will be next on the list.

In February 1983 my father and I were walking towards the roadbridge at the southern end of the reservoir when we noticed a small group of gulls flying around close to the shore. They were feeding on bread being thrown out onto the water by people feeding the ducks. My father pointed out a gull that was larger than the associated Black-headed and Common Gulls. The gull had white primaries, a pale grey mantle, white underparts and tail; it was an adult Iceland Gull.

Now let us turn to the birds that can be found during the winter in the mature woodland of the waterworks grounds, the landscaped area around the filter beds, the stream and its margins.

A walk into the woodland will generally produce a nomadic flock of tits; this is normally made up of either large numbers of Blue, Great or Long-tailed Tits and sometimes has in association with it the odd Marsh, Willow or Coal Tit. Other species will forage about with these flocks, Treecreeper, Goldcrest and Nuthatch and on occasions I have seen Lesser Spotted Woodpecker. The last is well worth searching for in this area and can be seen quite regularly. Its larger relative the Great Spotted Woodpecker is also frequent here, nearly always drawing attention to itself by its loud "tchic tchic" alarm call.

Lower down on the woodland floor Blackbirds grub about and the occasional Pheasant can be flushed from the thickets. As you walk along amongst the bushes and trees on either side of the path, the clockwork "churr" of the Wren may be heard or the mournful winter song of the Robin or the "pink, pink" call of the Chaffinch. Dunnock are also quite frequent here and as you walk further into the wood away from the road, Wood Pigeon will soon be disturbed from their high perches and the harsh cries of the Jay might be heard, then as you look up you might get brief glimpses of the white rump and pink body as it disappears through the trees.

One part of the woodland is quite moist with springs rising to form rivulets of water that flow down into the overflow channel. It is here that the Woodcock might be flushed from its feeding area, showing off its long bill, brown mottled body and russet rump as it goes, the bird being no sooner seen than gone as it quickly and quietly makes off dodging between the trees.

At the edges of the woodland there are several Alder trees where Siskin and Redpoll flocks can often be found feeding. They hang upside down and use all their acrobatic skills to extract the seeds from the cones.

On frequent occasions since the early 1980s, the alarm calls of small birds have drawn attention to the presence of a hunting Sparrowhawk and you may get a glimpse of the bird as it dashes silently on its mission of death, twisting and turning at speed as it flies low through the trees. This species was nearly exterminated throughout the eastern counties of England during the 1960s and '70s due to the use of chlorinated hydrocarbon pesticides in agriculture, which led to a weakness in the shell of its eggs which were then easily broken during incubation and also because predators, being at the end of the food chain, build up chemical residues in their bodies.

On reaching the stream at the bottom of the overflow channel, frequent Coot and Moorhen can be seen feeding and a Heron often rises as you approach. This is the best area for seeing Grey Wagtail with its grey mantle and bright lemon-yellow underparts. During very severe weather when the reservoir is iced up, Snipe, Jack Snipe and Woodcock feed along this stretch of stream and I have even seen Dunlin. If you sit quietly on the bank it will not be long before you see an iridescent flash of blue and hear the shrill whistle of the Kingfisher as it passes by.

On the west side of the overflow channel is an area of woodland including several large beech trees and under these large numbers of Redwing can occasionally be found foraging about in the leaf litter to find food. During particularly frosty weather when pastureland is frozen Redwing can often be found feeding under mature deciduous trees. This Arctic breeding thrush is smaller than the Song Thrush with a creamy eye-stripe and reddish chestnut flanks. Another species which breeds in the Taiga Forests of Northern Europe and also comes to feed under the beeches during good beechmast years is the Brambling, the northern counterpart of the Chaffinch, differing from the Chaffinch in its orange-buff breast and shoulders, dark head and mantle and white rump.

There are a few Holly and Hawthorn bushes hereabouts and Blackbird, Song Thrush, Fieldfare and Mistle Thrush feed hungrily on the berries; the last tend to monopolise the Holly bushes, frightening away any bird that encroaches upon their territory. These bushes sometimes hold roosting Goldfinch and up to two hundred have been counted arriving at dusk.

The two cooling ponds at the back of the waterworks grounds have Coot, Moorhen and Mallard on them regularly and on occasions Little Grebe. The small pond, largely covered by bulrush, sometimes holds a Water Rail, while on one of the last occasions I walked up to the edge of it in early March 1987, a Bittern flew out! – its brown mottled body, dagger-like bill and green trailing legs giving me an unforgettable experience. One bird wintered around the reservoir's margins over several years during the late 1980s. In recent years the Bittern has become a nationally threatened species and fears remain that we might lose it as a breeding species.

The main area of the waterworks grounds has filter beds and plantings of coniferous and other ornamental trees with large open stretches of grass. It is here you often hear the laughing call of the Green Woodpecker or see a bird feeding on the grassy areas, trying to procure ants with its enormous tongue, while in the tops of the surrounding trees Magpies perch sentinel-like. The Kestrel frequently hunts across this area and in several winters the Great Grey Shrike has been observed. The Great Grey Shrike is similar in size to a Blackbird, with ash grey head and back, a black highwayman's mask stretching from its beak to well beyond its eye, black wings which show a white wingbar and a long black tail with white edgings. Some sights stay in one's memory. The first time I saw a Great Grey Shrike was in November 1968 when my father and I found one perched on telegraph lines while walking along the railway line between Rabbits Bridge and the reservoir. I also clearly recall a day in January 1971 when one flew across in front of me looking very clumsy as it clutched a Redpoll in its feet! Most Great Grey Shrike which visit Britain come from Northern Europe and its Latin name *excubitor* comes from its habit of perching in exposed positions, such as the topmost branch of a tree or a high post where it can keep a watchful eye for prey.

The trees round about hold an assortment of common species, most of which have already been mentioned. The Goldcrest is especially notable here and quite numerous among the ornamental conifers. These energetic little birds are well worth a close look because on one occasion I found their rarer cousin the Firecrest in the reservoir grounds. It was feeding with a nomadic flock of tits – this was in March 1985. Similar in size and shape to the Goldcrest it differs in having a black eye-stripe, white supercilium and bronze shoulder patches.

Formerly, as you walked towards the two houses in the grounds close to the entrance you would have come to some dense Rhododendron bushes and here, towards dusk, large numbers of Greenfinch and Chaffinch gathered to roost, but in recent years these have been much reduced and the bushes have been cut hard back. Blackbirds could also be seen and heard as they made their way to their favourite roosting sites in the area.

So much for winter! Let us now turn to one of the most exciting times of year – the spring migration. An extraordinary event took place in early March 1988. As a friend and I watched a large number of gulls feeding over the water at the northern end of the reservoir, we suddenly realised they were adult Kittiwakes! About 89 were present. These birds are superficially similar to several other species of gull but have a

small yellow bill and their wingtips look as though they have been dipped in ink. This species is a pelagic (oceanic) species and a true seagull and is normally seen inland only after storms and gales and then in ones and twos. At the same time large numbers of Kittiwakes were reported throughout the Midland region, and it appears that the birds had been grounded by a stationary weather front.

At the end of March the first summer migrants arrive. These are normally the little brown and white Sand Martin that sweep hurriedly, low across the water surface catching the few insects that are available at this time of the year. Unfortunately this species declined dramatically during the 1970s and 1980s to fewer than 10% of its former numbers, supposedly as a direct result of the drought in the Sahel region of Africa where the species spends the winter. Recently, however, it has shown signs of some recovery.

Bittern flying over bulrushes.

Also about this time a look across adjacent ploughed fields may give you a glimpse of a Wheatear with its erect stance and distinctive white rump in flight. A walk along the road on the dam may give you your first sighting of a returning wader. You need to look very carefully over the wall onto the dam itself, and then you might see the Little Ringed Plover, its yellow eye-ring and lack of wingbar distinguishing it from the larger but similar Ringed Plover. The Little Ringed Plovers have occasionally remained throughout the summer, breeding along the reservoir shore or if the water levels are too high, supposedly in the adjacent quarry on Buddon Hill. The Little Ringed Plover started to breed in Britain only in 1938 but soon colonised most of England. My father found the first nest in Leicestershire in 1954 at Hemington Sand Pits and now the species breeds in several areas within the county where the habitat is suitable.

The woodlands are now beginning to echo with the resident bird songs as the frenzied activity of establishing a territory goes on and soon the first migrants start to add their voices to the volume of song. The first is the Chiffchaff, a small green warbler with dark legs whose song repeats its name, "chiff-chaff", "chiff-chaff". Some of these birds will immediately take up territory and start to breed.

As the year progresses into April, migrant numbers increase, Swallows then House Martins joining the Sand Martins in their quest for insects over the water. Blackcaps and Garden Warblers sing their similar melodic songs from bramble thickets and trees and the Willow Warblers are everywhere with their lovely descending cadence. Whitethroats start to sing their scratchy song in the more scrubby areas and the Lesser Whitethroat sings from its favourite Hawthorn thicket on the edge of the railway line; first its strident song but as you approach it gives its alarm call which sounds like two stones being knocked together. It is sometimes hard to imagine where some of these small birds have spent the winter and the countries they have visited on their migration. One Garden Warbler that I caught and ringed while it was nesting on the margins of the reservoir in June 1982 was later killed by a young boy at Asesewa in Ghana, West Africa, in February 1989. The Swallow will have travelled even further – right down to the Cape Province of South Africa to winter. The first British recovery from there came in December 1911 when one was caught in a farmhouse in Utrecht, Natal, eighteen months after being ringed as a nesting adult in Britain.

Swallows, House Martins and Sand Martins feeding over the water.

A walk along the road adjacent to Buddon Wood at dusk in the 1970s and early 1980s would almost certainly have led to an encounter with a roding Woodcock but like so many things it is a rare sight here today. "Roding" is the term given to the male Woodcock's display flight. At twilight the birds fly low over the tree canopy uttering sharp "tsiwich" and croaking calls as they pass over, patrolling their regular beat. In April 1970, I was running through a wet spinney near the reservoir pumping station when a Woodcock startled me as it rose from beneath my feet. On looking down I saw its nest which was a small depression of flattened leaves and on them lay four brown-blotched eggs. As dusk gives way to night you will almost certainly hear the hoot of a Tawny Owl from the reservoir grounds or the adjacent woodland.

In early April 1969 I found my first female Black Redstart feeding on insects taken from the masonry wall of the overflow channel and road bridge. It was a very warm April and the insect life was prolific so that this lively dark-looking little bird with its rusty tail did not have to struggle for food and stayed several days in the same area. The Black Redstart is generally a passage migrant throughout Britain though some birds do over-winter in the southwest and it does breed in small numbers. Nesting was first recorded in Britain in 1923 and the species had a breeding boom just after the war when they took advantage of habitat provided by bomb sites.

If the water is low the reservoir will tend to produce a few waders but generally water levels are high in the spring and the dam wall is the only suitable feeding area. The Common Sandpiper is the most frequent species and as you walk along the dam it flies off low with its wings arched above the water uttering its shrill "twee-wee wee" call. The outflow stream often holds one or two Green Sandpipers that make a noisy retreat as you approach, showing off their white rumps and dark mantles as they fly up steeply into the sky. Other waders do occur from time to time and it makes the heart race to hear the wild call of the Curlew or Whimbrel as they head northwards.

On the grassy bank at the back of the dam and in the fields around the reservoir the canary coloured Yellow Wagtails have arrived and have started to vie for food with the resident Pied Wagtails. The bushes and trees at the bottom of the dam are worth watching because you may be fortunate enough to see a Redstart. The male in summer is stunning; it has a slate-grey head, back and wings, white forehead, black face and throat, orange underparts and rump, and a fiery-red tail. Another bird you could find is the Pied Flycatcher that also makes occasional brief stops here to feed on the abundant insects.

On the water courting groups of Goldeneye have gathered together. They will suddenly rise up and fly around in groups grunting as they go, their wings producing a distinctive whistling sound. They will soon land back on the water where the males start bobbing their heads up and down and then suddenly throw their heads back in an extravagant display. In a few days they will have left for breeding places in the far north.

Occasionally at this time of year, the small Garganey duck puts in an appearance and they are often already paired when they arrive. The drake is a handsome bird with brown head and a large broad, pale stripe over the eye, grey patterned flanks and pale blue on the wing. An old name for this small duck is Summer Teal.

The central area of the reservoir is the main breeding area for duck, probably because it is very quiet and not often disturbed. The Ruddy Duck first bred here in 1973 and has bred here in most years since. In recent years there has been great

Male White-headed Duck.

concern about the feral Ruddy Duck because it is thought that inter-breeding on a large scale with the very rare White-headed Duck that occurs in small colonies in the western and eastern Mediterranean may cause that species' extinction. This is not just speculation for there is evidence that the Ruddy Duck has already spread to continental Europe and crossed with the White-headed Duck and produced breeding young. Some conservationists now want to cull large numbers of Ruddy Duck but it looks like too little too late. The White-headed Duck is the only European member of the stiff-tail family to which the Ruddy Duck also belongs. Many of the species that man has introduced throughout the world whether plant, mammal or bird have caused major damage to delicately balanced environments and alien species account for a 20% threat to the world's birdlife. Can you imagine the surprise we had when my father and I found an adult male White-headed Duck displaying with the Ruddy Duck in early April 1982? It was larger than the Ruddy Duck and had a more hunched appearance. It had a more rounded head that was all white except on the top of the crown which was black. The bill was pale blue and noticeably swollen near the base. The back of the neck was black which spread along the sides of the neck forming a collar which faded into the rich chestnut of its breast and front area. The back, wings and flanks were paler chestnut than the front of the bird and only slightly paler in tone than the Ruddy Duck. The tail appeared dark and almost black.

While walking around the reservoir in late April 1986 I came across a striking male Red-crested Pochard, an uncommon visitor from the Continent, feeding with a group of Tufted and Common Pochard in the central section of the reservoir. As soon as the birds saw me on the shoreline they stopped diving and kept a nervous watch on me. The Red-crested Pochard kept its neck erect; it had a red bill, large chestnut head, black neck and breast, brown back and white flanks. It was a very skittish bird that after a few minutes flew, making me think it was a truly wild bird.

Towards the end of April the reeds begin to come alive with the harsh staccato sounds of Reed and Sedge Warblers that have just arrived from their wintering quarters in Africa, though like so many migrants their numbers have also declined in recent years. In the bushes at the edge of the reed swamp a black hooded Reed Bunting sings its repetitive song from the top of a Sallow.

Over the water, hundreds of hirundines – Swallows and martins – are joined by a few Swifts and by May this becomes a flood and it is amazing how they avoid a collision. The Swift is one of the most aerial of all species and they even mate on the wing. Shortly after they arrive they can be observed chasing each other and screaming whilst indulging in their courtship rituals. On cold days a large mixed flock of Swifts, Swallows and martins feeds low over the water but if you watch them for a long period you may suddenly see them all fly upwards and form a massed throng in the sky high overhead; at this point keep a close watch because the scythe-shaped Hobby could be hunting close by.

May normally brings the terns, sometimes in large numbers, the most frequent species being Common and Arctic looking like giant white swallows with their black caps and long tail streamers. The Arctic Tern has the longest migration of any bird going from one polar region to the other annually. The oldest ringed Arctic Tern lived for 27 years. In its life it would have travelled 500,000 miles in direct migration alone but as it is a very mobile species it probably travelled in excess of 3,000,000 miles. Other tern species do occur from time to time but the only other regular visitor is the Black Tern. As its name suggests it has black plumage but only during the breeding season. It is slightly smaller than the other two species already mentioned and lacks their long tail streamers. All the terns quarter the reservoir in elegant fashion and on occasions the Common and Arctic Tern can be seen to plummet into the water and pull out a small fish. At times the Little Gull accompanies the terns; this is also an elegant bird. The adults have a wholly black head, pale mantle and pearl grey underwings, the last being one of the most distinctive features. In recent years a few of the Common Terns will have remained to breed on the specially constructed pontoons that have been placed on the northern side of the reservoir.

You may also have the good fortune to catch a sight of the majestic Osprey as it breaks its journey northwards. A memory I have as a young lad is watching one hovering over the water, diving in feet first to take a large fish then battling with it for

Osprey in flight.

a few minutes, flapping and being dragged under the water before having to release it because it was so heavy! That bird stayed throughout May 1967 and towards the end of the month another bird joined it. Hopes grew that the birds might remain to breed but unfortunately they both left a few days later. The last time I saw an Osprey at Swithland Reservoir was in early May 1983. For a few days an individual took up residence in the waterworks grounds and fed on Perch taken from the large cooling pond. It would then spend long periods of time sitting in a Larch digesting its prey.

In a tree above the reeds a female Cuckoo sits watching for some unwary Reed Warbler to leave her nest before she flies quickly down and deposits her slightly larger egg amongst the others, removing one of the Warbler's eggs before flying away, never to return!

The Spotted Flycatcher is also starting to breed by the end of May, finding a nest site either in the ivy or on top of a wall bracket. This rather neat, plain bird will fly from a branch, hover, twist and turn in the air in a constant effort to catch insects, before returning usually to the same perch.

We tend to take our summer migrants for granted but in recent years their numbers have been falling steadily. Some species such as Spotted Flycatcher and Turtle Dove are causing real concern because they have both suffered a 50% population decrease in the last two decades and the local decrease is greater than this. These population collapses could have been brought about by several factors: predation by the now abundant Grey Squirrel, the drought in the Sahel region of Africa, over-hunting on migration (100,000-200,000 Turtle Doves are thought to be shot annually in Malta alone), the changing of habitats in Britain and in their wintering areas in Africa, or a combination of all five. It was in the early 1970s that I found my last Turtle Dove's nest in the reservoir grounds. It was situated five feet up in a small Norwegian Spruce, small, fragile and made of fine twigs and had two small pure white eggs laid on top.

These are a few sights of spring and the migration period but as passage ends, birds settle down to breeding and the site becomes a lot quieter and with the developing foliage and undergrowth birds become harder to see.

Several of our once common resident species have also declined markedly over the last two decades. The local species that have been hit the hardest are:
– Grey Partridge, Lapwing, Song Thrush, Skylark, Marsh Tit, Willow Tit, House Sparrow, Tree Sparrow, Bullfinch, Linnet, Redpoll, Yellowhammer, Reed Bunting, and Corn Bunting. These declines could have been brought about by agricultural changes but at present we just don't know for certain!

Spotted Flycatcher and young.

Pochard's nest and eggs with one Ruddy Duck's egg.

By late May and early June all but a few duck have departed – a few Tufted, Gadwall, Ruddy Duck, Mallard and occasionally Shoveler and Pochard remain to breed, some in the reed swamp and lush shoreline vegetation and others quite a way from the water. I recorded the first nest of Pochard for the reservoir at the end of May 1984 in some lush reed swamp vegetation in deepish water. It contained seven eggs plus one Ruddy Duck egg. It is not unusual for some North American diving ducks to be parasitic, laying their eggs in the nests of other ducks. By the beginning of May some of the earlier breeding Mallard duck can already be seen escorting their offspring across the water.

Great Crested and Little Grebe will have built their nests of accumulated plant debris among the reed swamp vegetation and again some of the early breeding Great Crested Grebe will already have young and the parents can be seen ferrying them round on their backs.

Moorhen and Coot are everywhere, their nests being built under every available overhanging willow. Only the odd pair or two of Mute Swan normally breed; the female will sit for weeks on top of her large nest mound while the male swims about, taking some delight in seeing off other birds that venture near. Canada Geese also breed but again only in small numbers.

In the woodland all the more common species are breeding and the Sparrowhawk keeps a watchful eye from its nest high in a pine or larch, while on the ground a bunch of nettles may hold a Red-legged Partridge sitting on eggs.

As the summer wears on bird song becomes less and less and it gives way to hungry calls of young birds waiting to be fed. Family parties of tits and other small birds can be found in the woods and around the margins of the reservoir. On the water young Coot and Moorhen as well as the ducklings are growing rapidly and starting to acquire their feathers. Some of the summer migrants will now be leaving on their long journeys south, swift, cuckoo and some warblers starting to move early in August.

In July and August it is a good idea to check carefully through the birds assembled on the water because at this time of year Common Scoter and Black-necked Grebe have been recorded frequently. The Common Scoter males are all black with an orange patch on the bill and the females are all brown with pale cheek patches. Scoters are diving ducks that are generally found at sea during the winter. The Black-necked Grebe tend to be in breeding plumage at this time of year showing a black body with chestnut flanks and the distinctive golden-yellow cheek plumes and at close range a bright red eye. Black-necked Grebes have been recorded during every month and breeding remains an exciting possibility.

During late August duck numbers start to build up but they look drab as they go into "eclipse" and moult their feathers. Return migration starts again and all the summer visitors are leaving and the passage migrants move through, terns, gulls, waders, ducks and warblers. Identification of the birds becomes more difficult now because a lot of the returning birds are the young of that year and juvenile and sub-adult plumages can be very misleading.

The Greenshank is frequent and makes brief appearances most autumns as it heads south. They are normally very vocal birds, with long green legs, greyish bodies, white backs and long, upturned bills. At this time of year almost anything can turn up.

In September the summer roost of Lesser Black-backed Gull has reached a climax with one or two thousand birds being present. Gradually throughout the month the other species of gull become more numerous. As the nights get colder the remaining summer visitors start preparing for their long return trips. Large numbers of Swallows and martins come together in pre-dispersal flocks but by early October all but a few have departed.

October also brings the returning Goldeneye and Wigeon from their northern breeding grounds, likewise the Fieldfares and Redwings that can now be seen in flocks flying overhead. The duck start to regain their handsome full plumage and the gull roost builds up again.

Strong winds and storms can be a feature of October and November. It was after one such storm in October 1987 that two Grey Phalarope appeared. One was eaten by a Pike, but the next day I saw the remaining bird feeding close to the dam wall, where it was picking up food off the water's surface. It was a lovely little wader with a white head and blue-grey mantle and a small thickset bill. These birds are normally pelagic outside the breeding season. A visit to the reservoir is always recommended after storms and gales and several other interesting seabirds have been recorded over the years.

Can you imagine my surprise when in November 1975 I stopped and looked over the railings near Kinchley Hill only to see on the shoreline a very large ringed plover with a double breast band and reddish-orange rump? It was an American species, a Killdeer Plover, named after its repetitive 'kill-dee, kill-dee' call and was only the nineteenth British record.

By Christmas the nights have drawn in and at dusk the calls of Mallard, Wigeon and Teal can be heard as the birds leave the reservoir to feed in the Soar Valley. In one week another year will commence and another year's cycle will start again.

Killdeer Plover.

These were just a few of my memories along with a glimpse of a year in the life of Swithland Reservoir. My memories, however, are not unique, other birdwatchers having seen equally interesting species at Swithland including Alpine Swift, Avocet, Eider, Leach's Storm-petrel, Little Auk, Red-necked Phalarope and Spoonbill, to mention but a few. But let us not forget the more usual occurrences either, the sight of a Great Crested Grebe ferrying its stripy young on its back, or the brief view of a Kingfisher. Each one will remain a treasured memory for the observer.

As I write this chapter I have just heard of another exceptional record for the reservoir: a Crag Martin which if accepted will be only the fifth British Record. It was found on the northern side of the reservoir on April 17th 1999. So, you really do not know what you might find on your next trip to this outstanding site!

Although much remains the same, the years have taken their toll on our birdlife. As mentioned previously, there is real concern for some of our commonest species. Areas like Swithland are a precious resource that must be conserved. Some areas must be kept private and free from disturbance so that birds can breed and shy birds reside. This will enable large numbers of people to enjoy the diverse and abundant birdlife of the reservoir well into the future from the many public vantage points.

Great Crested Grebe and young.

2. CHARNWOOD A THOUSAND YEARS OF CHANGE

I grew up in the rural setting of Quorn where Swallows, House Martins and Spotted Flycatchers were common and the unmistakable calls of the Cuckoo were a feature of May walks across the local fields. Now only small numbers of these once common species breed in the village. On the other hand, Sparrowhawks were extremely rare in the 1960s and 1970s and yet a few hours spent in surrounding countryside today would almost certainly lead to a glimpse of this small hawk. A century ago to see a gull in Leicestershire would have been an unusual experience but today hundreds pass over the village each winter evening on their way to roost

Cuckoo on a fence post.

on the Charnwood reservoirs. The small village is now not so small and recent visits home make me realise that change is an inevitable process in life and my past memories are now part of history.

As I have already stated Swithland Reservoir cannot remain as an island, because it is part of a much bigger picture and as long as it remains in its present state it will always attract some birds. Over the centuries man has fashioned the world in which we live, but it was only in the last century that he obtained the capability to destroy it completely. With our knowledge and skill, however, we can also create good environments for birds working with nature and not against it. My great grandfather helped construct Swithland Reservoir. He lived in Loughborough and was paid walking time from the cemetery to the reservoir site two and a half miles away providing he arrived at the cemetery by 06.30 a.m., which made it a good job to have in the mid-1890s. Although the reservoir was built to give water to the quickly expanding industry in the city of Leicester it has in more recent years become one of Charnwood's most attractive areas and has given pleasure to generations of naturalists and country lovers. I am sure my great grandfather would have been proud of that. Now the question has to be asked "What are we going to leave our children and future generations?"

First of all we need to identify the problems our world faces and the reasons why they exist. At present there are between 9,236 and 9,951 species of bird in the world (depending on which taxonomist is referred to). To some people that might seem like quite a disparity in numbers but, as our knowledge and understanding grow, birds which were once considered as sub-species are now given full specific status. At present about 1000 species of birds are on the verge of extinction or their populations are so restricted that any slight change to their habitat could bring about their demise. At no time in man's history have plants and animals become extinct at their present rate and although we realise there is a problem, extinctions are accelerating year after year. The main reason for the mass of extinctions is habitat loss, followed by hunting and the predation and competition from introduced species.

It is frequently said that the majority of endangered species come from the world's rainforests; as they are felled so the life within them dies out. Over 40% of the world's rainforests have been lost in the last 30 years. It is very easy for us living in a temperate, affluent society to think that the major problems with our planet lie in the Third World. The world, however, can be likened to the human body if one limb is injured the whole body hurts. In some ways we can feel so helpless with major events taking place thousands of miles away and it is very easy to say, "What can I do about that"? We can, however, use practical initiatives to save the tropical forest by not buying furniture made from tropical hardwoods other than that bearing the Forest Stewardship Council logo, in other words stop the demand for such wood except where verified as grown in sustainable forest. We can also try to get the debts of poorer countries cut so they are not forced to use up their natural resources to pay off loans. Many of the third world countries are just developing and going through events similar to those that Britain went through centuries ago.

Let us now examine some of the events that have fashioned Charnwood Forest and made it into the landscape we know today. Let us also look at our local environment today and see how it is standing up to the economic pressures that are still being placed upon it by an ever expanding population and by continued technological change. What legacy will we take through into the new Millennium and will our natural heritage be part of our thinking?

One of the problems of Charnwood Forest is that it never had precise boundaries until for the convenience of 20th century Town and Country Planning the area began to be defined. Historically, Charnwood was never legally a forest since it was not an area subject to the Forest Law, first enacted by the Normans. Moreover, it was never a private forest like Savernake in Wiltshire that belonged to one landowner. Thus the boundaries were fluid.

During the Saxon period Charnwood was split up into four manors, Groby, Whitwick, Shepshed and Barrow. After the Norman Conquest the multiple ownership of Charnwood allowed the piecemeal settlement of the area. Thus, for example, Newtown Linford was created in the 12th century. At the same time it explains the sprawling ancient parish boundaries, whose centres were all outside the core area of the Forest – Shepshed, Loughborough, Barrow-on-Soar and so on round to Whitwick. This absence of direct controls made the creation of the hunting parks easier.

Parks for hunting were a statement of privilege and wealth during the late 12th and early 13th century. During this period and continuing into the early 14th century several large hunting parks were set up on Charnwood Forest. These were situated at Quorn (known as Barrow Park), Loughborough, Bradgate, Groby, Whitwick, Garendon Park (probably at Dishley), Beaumanor, Rothley, Shepshed and Burley. The hunting parks were used mainly for the hunting of Red and Fallow Deer, although Roe Deer was mentioned on one occasion. Other animals mentioned during this period included Wild Cat but there is no mention of Wolf or Wild Boar. Hunting parks declined after the mid-14th century when plagues wiped out large numbers of people and enclosed land could be farmed more profitably. By the middle of the 16th century only Bradgate survived as a hunting park.

Male Black Grouse displaying.

Charnwood had been changing gradually over the centuries and from Norman times the predominant oak woodland was gradually being replaced by grassland, moorland, heathland and scrub. The timber was being taken for building, fencing and charcoal. The regeneration of woodland was kept at bay by burning and grazing.

During the 12th and 13th centuries three religious orders set up establishments on the forest. Augustinian Canons started Ulverscroft Priory in 1134, followed by Cistercian Monks at Garendon Abbey in 1135 and Augustinian Canonesses at Grace Dieu Priory somewhere around 1239. These religious orders were often gifted less productive land by lay landowners. These establishments had a great effect on the landscape and economy of Charnwood Forest. Ulverscroft Priory for example, remained until its dissolution in the 1530s. The monks were very good at farming and by the end of the 14th century they had enclosed a large area of the waste ground around the two houses. Before the dissolution of the priory, the monks owned 1000 acres of land and held rights over another 700 acres. The priory's land was used mainly to pasture 300 cattle, 1000 sheep and 50 pigs. In its last 60 years the priory kitchen, brewhouse and bakehouse used large amounts of wood. The priory employed seven men to fell trees and these woodsmen collected between four and eight cart-loads daily!

During the 16th century large areas of Charnwood were being over-grazed and it became a stark, almost barren wilderness with its dark crags of Precambrian rocks. As human populations grew during the 16th and 17th centuries there were further encroachments of enclosure for agricultural purposes.

Parts of Charnwood Forest core were enclosed by several Acts, the last taking effect in 1820s. This produced the straight roads and field divisions easily seen in the Charley and Beacon areas. Enclosure saw the planting of hedges, building of walls, and the digging of ditches for drainage, the landscape of Charnwood was changed dramatically in a fairly short period of time. Within a few years of enclosure several breeding species of bird were lost to the county or became only rare or sporadic breeders. These included Red Kite, Hen Harrier, Buzzard, Peregrine, Red Grouse, Black Grouse, Quail, Curlew, Long-eared Owl, Wryneck, Woodlark, Dipper, Wheatear, Ring Ouzel and Raven. The Red-backed Shrike was also well distributed on Charnwood prior to its enclosure and bred sporadically in the area until 1906, where the last known pair bred near Quorn Station. Before the end of the 20th century the Red-backed Shrike had disappeared completely from England as a breeding species. Unfortunately we know little or nothing about our birdlife prior to the 19th century.

The 19th century saw the greatest changes on the Charnwood Forest and the emergence of the landscape we recognize today. Between 1810 and 1900 the population of Leicestershire excluding Leicester rose from approximately 280,000 to 430,000 and that of the city of Leicester from 23,000 to 210,000. This population explosion and the need for food and water brought many pressures on Charnwood Forest.

Prior to the industrial revolution farming was hard labour. Farmers used oxen to pull the plough. Sowing, weeding, harvesting and threshing were done by hand with the help of the sickle, scythe and flail. The grain was crushed into flour by watermill and windmill. Watermills could be found at Rothley, Quorn and Swithland (the Swithland watermill was situated on the edge of the reservoir on the south-western side) and windmills at Rothley, Bradgate and Woodhouse Eaves. Major changes took place in the 19th century. By 1850 horses had taken over from oxen for ploughing. The first horse-drawn reaper was produced in 1820 and binder in 1879; these two inventions saved thousands of man-hours' of work. Steam threshing machines were in use by 1850 and continued to be used on the Forest until the late 1950s and early 1960s.

Agricultural improvements were also made after the enclosure. Many hedges were planted and walls built although some old hedges were already in place on the old monastic lands of Ulverscroft and these boundaries changed little. Stones and boulders were removed from fields and the acid nature of the soil was changed by the use of lime. Many of the boggy and marshy areas were also drained during this period. It was during the mid-19th century that the use of chemicals in agriculture was first being explored. Good husbandry was also encouraged and from 1808 farmers used a six-course rotation of crops. Turnips would be planted in the first year followed by swedes, barley and legumes, ley, ley and wheat. Some farmers, however, grew corn, corn and corn that exhausted the soil of all its nutrients and after several years the land was spent. This land was normally returned to grassland.

In these days of readily available oil, coal and electricity it is not easy to appreciate the importance of hay to our forefathers. But it was in fact hay that kept their transport in the shape of horse drawn traffic moving through the winter months and fed the animals, horses and oxen, which pulled the ploughs. It was for these reasons that hay meadows had a high value placed on them in years gone by – in some instances three times the value of other fields. How different today when many meadows are neglected or destroyed!

The Corn Laws of 1697 and 1815 were an effort to regulate the price of Wheat, the principle bread grain. However, I wonder whether the Charnwood farmers would have preferred to grow Barley and Oats for which there were good expanding markets, namely for brewing beer at Burton-on-Trent and for feeding the ubiquitous horse so necessary for road transport. The price of Wheat remained high after the repeal of the Corn Laws in 1846 due to a series of bad harvests and an increased demand. After 1840 many farmers changed from pastureland to arable. The price of grain remained good for farmers until the early 1870s when a series of bad harvests ruined crops and quantities of cheap grain were imported at low prices from overseas, especially the U.S.A. and Canada. Charnwood Forest became a mosaic of mixed farmland that would have been rich in birdlife. The Corncrake was still a common bird on the Forest at this time.

During the enclosure period from 1808 onwards, areas with rocky or poor soils were often planted with trees and afforestation continued on Charnwood until 1875. It appears that most of the trees planted were Pedunculate or Common Oak, Scots Pine and Larch. It was also during this period that Rhododendrons were planted in the new woodlands. Well-known areas that were planted with trees at this time included Roecliffe; The Brand; an area between Swanimote and The Oaks; Longcliffe, Nanpantan; Grace Dieu and Gisborne's Gorse. In the hedgerows large numbers of hardwoods were planted with a preference for ash and oak. Hedges were not only considered as boundaries but a valuable resource for timber-brushwood, light poles and even nuts and fruit for human consumption. These large scale plantings must have had a major effect on the distribution of some species of woodland birds such as woodpeckers, Nuthatches and tits. A large invasion of

Male Lesser Spotted
Woodpecker at nest.

Crossbill occurred between 1839-40 and during 1839 the first record of a breeding pair in Leicestershire came from Bradgate. These birds would have almost certainly been aided by the recent plantings of conifers. Because the Rhododendrons are evergreen they too have had a major effect on birdlife giving wintering thrushes and finches warm roosting sites but at the same time they have been very damaging to much of our native flora.

During the 18th century quarrying expanded on Charnwood Forest. Slate was produced at quarries at Swithland and Woodhouse Eaves but extraction ended in 1888. Lime was also dug at Barrow from the Lower Lias and at Grace Dieu in the Carboniferous Limestone deposits and by 1800 Breedon Hill was being worked. Coal mining was undertaken on the western edge of the Charnwood Forest and this greatly impacted upon the area, especially with the growth of urban development around the mines. Clay for making bricks and tiles was found in the Carboniferous Coal Measures at Coalville, Whitwick and Desford and from Mercian Mudstone (Keuper Marl) deposits at Hathern, Shepshed and Loughborough. The bricks that were produced made possible a great deal of urban growth in the Midlands and beyond.

Charnwood's hard rock had been largely unused since Roman times but with the introduction of the macadam process of road surfacing in 1760 came a demand for hard stone. In about 1800 the first surfacing took place of what was to become the A6 using granite from Mountsorrel and it was very successful. In 1840 the workings at Mountsorrel expanded and by 1858 Bardon Quarry was being developed. The high demand for hard rock saw quarries open at Shepshed, Whitwick, Cliff Hill and Groby. Sand was also extracted from pits at Rothley and during the 18th century sand and gravel were extracted from several sites in the Soar valley. It takes a long period of time for quarries and gravel workings to become mature enough to support a wide variety of organisms, but some species that favour a sparsely vegetated environment will colonise almost immediately.

The railways impacted Charnwood as they did so many areas of Britain during the 19th century. The Charnwood Forest Branch Line was constructed in 1882 and followed the route of the Charnwood Forest Canal for some of its way between Loughborough and Coalville on the Nuneaton -Loughborough line. It carried both passengers and goods. It was formally closed down in 1965. The Great Central Railway Line that bisects Swithland Reservoir was opened on the 25th July, 1898, and it ran between London and Sheffield. It was closed in 1967, but in 1969 a short section of track between Loughborough Central Station and Rothley was leased to the Main Line Steam Trust. This line is now used for recreation, and runs steam trains with fare paying passengers on the short journey from Loughborough to Birstall on the recent track extension. The cuttings and embankments that have been left by the railways have matured over the years and have become a haven for many species of wildlife.

Charnwood Forest is drained by a series of small streams and brooks. Grace Dieu Brook rises on Bardon Hill just to the north of Shepshed while the Black Brook is formed by the union of several small brooks rising near Lower Bawdon, Charley Hill, Cat Hill and Charnwood Lodge, eventually flowing down the valley to feed Blackbrook Reservoir, then passing west and north of Shepshed and past Thorpe Acre, crossing the A6 at Dishley Mill and on into the River Soar near Dishley Pool.

The Wood Brook rises near Whittle Hill and West Beacon Farm, passing Buck Hill to feed the small reservoir at Nanpantan, then on through Loughborough to join the Summerpool Brook and thence into the River Soar on the north side of Loughborough Meadows. The Ulverscroft Brook rises in Copt Oak Wood and Fox Covert on the Ulverscroft Nature Reserve. It becomes known as the River Lyn when it flows through Newtown Linford and Bradgate Park and later, downstream, the Buddon Brook and the Quorn Brook before it reaches the River Soar at Quorn.

The only large area of apparently natural water on the Charnwood Forest prior to the building of the first reservoirs was Groby Pool and this site has always held a wealth of waterfowl. The first Blackbrook Reservoir was built in 1796 to feed the Charnwood Forest Canal but unfortunately the canal and the reservoir were a failure. In 1804 the reservoir was dismantled because its dam had burst. The present Blackbrook Reservoir was completed in 1906 to supply Loughborough. The need for water to run Leicester's industries prompted the building of Charnwood's other reservoirs. Thornton was completed in 1853, Cropston by 1870 and Swithland by 1896. These large expanses of open water had a major effect on the waterfowl and other water birds on Charnwood Forest. Before the end of the 19th century Cropston had recorded rarities such as Osprey, Lesser Black-backed Gull, Little Gull, Bittern, Pomarine Skua and Spoonbill.

During the period of the enclosure of Charnwood almost seven thousand acres were added to the lands in the area owned by the then Earl of Stamford which gave the Earl controlling interests over three- quarters of Charnwood Forest. He and his descendants were wealthy men and high up in Victorian society. The fashion of the day was hunting and shooting and friends would often come to Charnwood for a few days' sport. By 1820 the estate had a team of gamekeepers for rearing game and destroying vermin. The bag for twelve seasons of shooting included 40,201 Pheasants, 7,088 partridges and 75,736 Rabbits. The seasons started in October and continued through to January and up to thirteen guns went out daily. The list of so called vermin killed between 1827 and 1834 was 46 Herons, 2,222 Jays, 1,443 crows, 1,382 Magpies, 843 hawks and owls, (the majority were hawks because in five years out of seven only 31 owls were killed. We don't have a breakdown for the other two years) 98 Stoats, 180 Polecats, 1,454 Weasels, 724 cats and 4 dogs.

Another influence on the area came from Thomas Boothby who on his death in 1762 left a pack of foxhounds to his son in law, Hugo Meynell, who was probably responsible more than anyone else, for the start of fox hunting as it is known today. He was a horse breeder and hunting was his passion. He was master of the Quorn Hunt that hunted on the open land on the edges of Charnwood Forest and the sport became very popular among the nobility. In 1791 the elite from all over the country gathered in the Quorn area for hospitality and hunting and on some days over three hundred horsemen took part. Hugo Meynell gave up mastership of the Quorn Hunt in 1800. With the coming of enclosures, hunting changed and the horses had to be able to gallop and jump. Throughout the 19th century fox hunting remained popular among the nobility of Britain.

In 1856 the 7th Earl of Stamford, who had large houses in Shropshire and Cheshire, became Master of the Quorn Hunt after which he built a new mansion at Steward's Hay near Groby and renamed it Bradgate House. The 7th Earl died childless in 1883. The Leicestershire estates were not inherited with the title and according to his will they passed on his wife's death in 1905 to his niece.

Changes in farming practice were slow in coming during the 20th century and remained much as they had done since the middle of the 19th century. There had been a slump in grain prices, largely due to cheap grain imports. Planting grain would only become profitable again with the outbreak of war in 1939. Farming was in a depression and old crafts such as hedge laying, which required many hours of manual labour, died out because they were too costly. The result on the countryside was overgrown unkempt hedgerows and large areas of formerly arable land being returned to grassland. Horses were still in widespread use, especially for ploughing, until the outbreak of the Second World War. The First World War saw some areas turned back to arable but because of the lack of resources this was very limited. With the outbreak of the Second World War, however, came the requirement for as much home-grown food as possible. Large areas of previously uncultivated land on Charnwood were put to the plough. Many old pastures with their associated flora and fauna were lost at this time.

The period from 1939 through to the 1950s saw most of Charnwood's remaining upland heath and moorland drained to disappear under the plough. Areas where upland heath and moorland were lost were at High Sharpley, Warren Hills and

Timberwood Hill and once they were ploughed a rich upland flora was lost. Between 1939 and 1945 farming became mechanised. Within a decade of the Second World War finishing most horses had been replaced by machines. The tractor had taken over from the horse and within a few years almost half the farmland in Leicestershire had become arable. The Agriculture Act of 1947 gave stability to the industry and when Britain joined the E.E.C. in 1973 more subsidies were available to the farming community. The E.C. Common Agricultural Policy made cereal growing more profitable than keeping dairy cows and thus produced massive changes. Since the war, mechanisation, transportation, chemicals, energy (electricity, gas and oil) and new technology have hastened the boom in farming. Within a few years of mechanisation during the 1940s the Corncrake had died out as a breeding species in Leicestershire and also from much of Britain. In the 1950s the use of organochlorine pesticides nearly caused the extermination of the Sparrowhawk,

Calling Corncrake.

Peregrine and Barn Owl. Since their ban the Sparrowhawk and Peregrine have bounced back. Unfortunately the Barn Owl had lost the pastureland over which it hunted for prey and many have been killed on the roads by the upsurge in fast motor vehicles.

Another change in farming practice that must have had an adverse effect on ground nesting birds was the change from hay to silage in the 1960s. By the time the hay was cut in late June or July most ground nesting species, such as Skylark, Yellow Wagtail and Grey Partridge would have reared a first brood but with the change to silage often cut in May, this was not possible. Additional crops of silage, stimulated into rapid growth by fertilizers, are cut in July and September further reducing the chances of ground nesting birds successfully rearing any young. Other harmful factors are the dense nature of silage crops and the lack of insects compared with the old hay meadows.

Over the final 45 years of the 20th century many hedges were removed. Their removal accelerated particularly in the 1960s and 70s and most of the hedges that remained were periodically slashed and cut by machinery. Also during this period many ponds and ditches were filled in. Intensive prairie farming took over in many areas, land was ploughed to the edge of the fields and large amounts of herbicides, pesticides, insecticides and fertilisers were used. During the late summer and early autumn after the harvest, further crops are increasingly sown so that the stubble fields on which many birds fed have disappeared. For the farmer, however, this method, known as minimal cultivation had the advantage of taking extra land without any extra labour which because of the availability of new breeds of autumn cereals could be sown in less time than ploughing would take. A further advantage on heavy clay soils, was the ability of growing a heavy yielding crop without the risk of a wet spring preventing sowing in March and April as often would be the case. However, this has left little or no place for many specialised farmland birds and if no action is taken Grey Partridge, Lapwing, Turtle Dove, Cuckoo, Skylark, Swallow, Linnet, House Sparrow, Tree Sparrow, Yellowhammer, Reed Bunting and Corn Bunting could be lost from much of Britain as breeding birds or reduced to very low numbers. One species that probably favours the more open farmland is the Hobby and it has increased greatly in the last 28 years.

A Forestry Commission Survey carried out between 1947 and 1949 showed that Leicestershire had only 2.3% of its land surface taken up by woodlands of five acres and over. Only four counties in England and Wales had less. The demands for timber largely brought about by two world wars was considerable on Charnwood's woodlands. Between 1914 and 1950 most of the oak woodland that remained on ancient forest sites was clear-felled. The Outwoods, Benscliffe, Blakeshay, Lea Wood, Poultney Wood, Bardon Hill and Buddon Wood were all badly affected. Buddon Wood had been largely a sandy oak woodland and it had a very rich associated flora and fauna. It was one of the richest natural woodlands in the Midland region. Only a few woods such as Grace Dieu, Swithland Wood, Piper and Oakley Woods escaped the felling and it is not surprising that these woods, have a rich flora and fauna. Over 50 species of bird have bred within the Swithland Wood and The Brand complex. Swithland Wood is one of Leicestershire's natural amenities and open to the public. Large numbers of people and dogs visit the area attracted by the two car parks bringing many pressures upon its wildlife and in due course the variety of plants and animals to be found within the wood will diminish.

Natural forest, wherever it occurs, is always the richest in bio-diversity because it is the primary covering providing the long-term stability and continuity essential to many organisms. Many species associated with old woodland are now becoming scarce on the Charnwood Forest. These include Woodcock, Lesser Spotted Woodpecker, Redstart, Wood Warbler and Hawfinch. In the years following clear-felling the Nightjar took advantage of the devastation left and bred at several old woodland sites on Charnwood. Blakeshay, Benscliffe and Lea Wood, all originally old oak woods, were replanted with conifers which lack the diversity of natural broad-leaved woodland and eventually create heavy shade and increased acidity. Large plantings of conifers in Britain, however, have enabled certain specialised species of birds to spread their range. These include the Crossbill, Goldcrest, Coal Tit and Siskin and I think it will not be many years before the last is proved to breed in Leicestershire.

The 20th century saw a continued expansion in mineral extraction, mainly of hard metamorphic rocks on the Charnwood Forest, and with modern machinery and ever better technology huge amounts of land were taken. What would earlier have taken several generations to achieve was happening in a few years. Bardon Quarry was considerably expanded and a new quarry was opened at Whitwick. Buddon had not gone unnoticed as a granite resource and in 1974 the new workings were officially opened. By the end of the century little remained of the 131 metre hill and its unique habitat. Prior to the wood disappearing a team of naturalists surveyed the site and recorded many of the rare plants and animals known to occur here prior to clear felling and quarrying. Quarries or holes in the ground are valuable commodities and very few are allowed to return to nature. The vast hardrock quarry at Mountsorrel has been a rubbish tip for many years and this can bring its own hazards. Early quarries that have returned to nature such as the old slate quarries in Swithland Woods and The Brand have now become a feature of the landscape. The Cocklow Quarry on the edge of Buddon Wood in Quorn was an old quarry that had been allowed to go back to nature. It was good for orchids and I remember being taken in there as a lad and shown both the Bee and two species of marsh orchids. Two bird species which have taken advantage of the hardrock quarries in recent times are the Peregrine which bred in 1994 for the first time in Leicestershire for over a century and the Little Ringed Plover which occasionally breeds in the granite quarries but favours mainly gravel pits.

Gravel and sand extraction has boomed during the 20th century and had a marked effect on the landscape of the Soar Valley. The local gravel pits at Quorn, Cossington and Wanlip have become excellent places for birds. Unusual and rare birds are occasionally recorded. In 1965 the first Bearded Reedlings to be seen in Leicestershire for nearly a century were seen at Wanlip and in 1975 a Black-winged Pratincole was recorded there. Because large areas of shingle are exposed at these sites some species have found new breeding habitats. The Ringed Plover bred for the first time in Leicestershire at Wanlip in 1965 and other county firsts included Oystercatcher in 1970 and Common Tern at Cossington in 1979. The Little Ringed Plover first bred in Leicestershire at Hemmington Gravel Pits in 1954 but it has bred regularly at the Soar Valley gravel pits since.

The stream and river valleys have all been impoverished during the 20th century, losing many of the old grassland meadows, marsh and boggy areas. The lower Soar Valley has undergone a flood alleviation scheme. This has done away with areas of flooded grassland that are important in winter for feeding Wigeon, Teal and Snipe. In summer Lapwing, Redshank and Snipe bred on marshy ground along the streams and river

Nightjar in flight at dusk.

valleys, but in recent years they are becoming increasingly uncommon. Groby Pool has remained an important area for waterfowl and still unusual birds turn up there from time to time. The first Mandarin Duck bred at this site in 1985. The reservoirs have matured throughout the 20th century and become extremely rich in both flora and fauna. The higher altitude and deeper reservoirs at Blackbrook and Thornton have never attracted such large numbers of birds as the lower altitude and shallower reservoirs, like Cropston and Swithland. The last two reservoirs play host to hundreds of wintering duck and thousands of gulls roost on them during the winter months. Because Swithland has mature margins and plenty of emergent vegetation many species of waterfowl have bred there over the years and because reservoirs are often frequented by birdwatchers, many rare and unusual species have also been recorded.

Hunting and shooting continued in much the same vein at the beginning of the 20th century as it had finished the 19th. Changes started to take place during the First World War when many gamekeepers went off to fight. This gave many birds of prey a respite from persecution and some made a brief recovery. There were massive changes after the war, both politically and socially, and the ruling elite also faced pressures. With the onset of the Second World War the gamekeepers left the estates once again and the birds of prey again took advantage and their numbers rose. After the war many of the large estates were broken up and now very few gamekeepers are left and shooting, though still too much, is less widespread than it once was. Fox hunting, however, has managed to survive throughout the 20th century although, it has to be said, not on the scale it once was and in certain areas it is becoming politically unpopular. The greatest threat to the British bird populations by shooting and trapping now comes from overseas. Many thousands of migrating birds are killed each year on their travels through southern Europe and that is a tragedy of our time!

Several large areas of Charnwood Forest are now open to the public mainly through very generous gifts. Unfortunately as our population grows, more pressure is brought to bear on these natural sites. Some areas are experiencing erosion and the wildlife in all of them is suffering from disturbance. Bradgate Park was donated to the City and County of Leicester by Charles Bennion in 1928. Species such as Whinchat and Redstart bred on Bradgate in good numbers until recently but unfortunately they no longer breed regularly and Meadow Pipit, Tree Pipit, Grasshopper Warbler, Reed Bunting and Yellowhammer are also now becoming less common. Most of the ground-nesting species would find it difficult, being disturbed both by people and their dogs. Similar comments can be made about Beacon Hill which was purchased by Leicestershire County Council in 1947 and Broombriggs that was donated to the Council in 1970. One recent highlight, however, was the breeding of the Pied Flycatcher at Broombriggs Country Park in 1996 and males took up territory at Beacon Hill in 1997 and 1998. In 1931, Swithland Wood was gifted to the City and County of Leicester by the Rotary Club of Leicester. The Outwoods was opened to the public following three gifts. The first was to the then Loughborough Corporation in 1946 by Mr Alan Moss and a year later another area was donated to Loughborough Borough Council by Mr George Harry Bowler. In 1977 an area was donated to Leicester County Council by Mrs A.I. Cope to commemorate Queen Elizabeth I I's Silver Jubilee and this is known as Jubilee Wood.

The Leicestershire and Rutland Trust for Nature Conservation was set up in 1956 and now holds several large tracts of land on Charnwood Forest. The largest reserve is Charnwood Lodge and Charley Woods which comprises 230.7 hectares (570 acres) of woodland, rough grassland, moorland and arable farmland. The second in size is at Ulverscroft which contains woodland, heath, meadow and marsh. Further down the valley is the Lea Meadows Nature Reserve that encompasses a large area of herb-rich meadow and marsh. Over the last 50 years of the 20th century Charnwood Forest has been well surveyed and its natural wealth is well known. Knowledge, however, does not save sites, not even those with S.S.S.I. designation: Buddon Wood bears testament to that. If our plants and animals are to be kept for future generations then financial gain cannot be the only criterion used.

Several alien species have found their way onto Charnwood Forest. I am only going to mention those that are having a direct effect on our birdlife. The Grey Squirrel was introduced into England and Wales from the U.S.A.. It was released at thirty sites between 1876 and 1929. Introductions were made in Scotland and Ireland in 1948. The indigenous Red Squirrels were being hit by disease during the first half of the 20th century. Competition from the Grey Squirrel that was just getting a foothold spelt its demise. The Red Squirrel is now restricted to the coniferous woodlands of Britain which are not favoured by the Grey Squirrel. In recent years the numbers of Grey Squirrels have risen enormously largely due to a lack of natural predators and persecution. They have also found a major source of food during the winter months at bird tables and the relatively mild winters in the last decade have meant low mortality. Many birdwatching organisations do not consider that the Grey Squirrel poses any great threat to our songbird population, but I disagree. With the unnaturally high numbers and the scarcity of food in the spring, it is only natural that they should turn to feed on protein-rich birds' eggs. I shall never forget the Spotted Flycatchers which built their nests annually in the open nestbox on the back of our house constantly dive-bombing the squirrels as they tried to get to their nest. They obviously perceived the threat. Eventually they would not nest in the nestbox but bred on top of an old blackbird's nest placed behind the swan neck of the downpipe near to the gutter and the squirrels nearly got to that too.

The American Mink was also introduced into Britain from North America but this time not so deliberately as in the case of the Grey Squirrel. The American Mink was brought into Britain in the 1920s for fur farming but it soon escaped. Some animals were turned loose by fur farmers when trade was bad and others were illegally released by animal liberation groups and they are now widespread across the country. The American Mink is almost certainly responsible for the demise of the Water Vole from our waterways and it probably will not be long before that species becomes extinct in these isles. The American Mink is semi-aquatic and has slightly webbed feet. It feeds at dusk and during the night and that is probably why it is seldom seen. Its food is waterfowl, fish, rodents and crustacea. Like the Grey Squirrel it has no natural predators in Britain. It seems more than likely that the recent fall in Little Grebe and Moorhen numbers along our smaller streams and rivers is due to this species. The real effect of what these two species are doing or have done to our wildlife will become apparent only after detailed research and time.

The 20th century saw the expansion of our cities, towns and villages. Birds had to come to terms with the changing landscape. With large numbers of people coming together in conurbations it was inevitable that they would produce vast quantities of waste. Gulls and crows took advantage of the regular food sources provided by rubbish tips. The gull population exploded and they became regular visitors inland. Prior to this period they were rare in Leicestershire. Old style sewage works also became a haven for birds and attracted many waders and the two small sewage farms close to Swithland Reservoir held breeding Redshank and Snipe. Ornamental parks and gardens were soon colonised by birds and Blackbirds, Song Thrushs, Dunnocks, Robins, Blue Tits, House Sparrows, Starlings, Greenfinchs etc. became commonplace. Many buildings produced nest sites for House Martins, Swifts, House Sparrows etc., with their pitched roofs, overhanging eaves and wide soffits. However, with the changing style of architecture during the middle of the 20th century very few holes were left on buildings for birds to exploit and species like the Swift found it increasingly difficult to find nest sites.

With so much natural habitat disappearing over much of Britain, gardens have become very important to wildlife. The varied and often dense vegetation to be found in gardens can make them oases for wildlife even in the centre of towns and cities. Many people became interested in natural history with the birth of wildlife programmes on the television in the 1960s. The garden feeding of birds has gone on for many years but it was only after the Second World War that most people had the money to devote specifically to specialised bird food. Now thousands, if not millions of people feed birds. How many of us have sat back and thought about the effects this could be having on our wildlife? I am not going to say whether feeding birds is a good or bad thing. I want to highlight some observations I have made over the past thirty years.

When we attract birds into the garden they immediately meet one predator that is common in urban and suburban areas alike: the cat. Although I have never owned a cat I have seen them kill many birds in our garden and if that is mirrored throughout the country mortality by them alone must be very high.

Feeding birds in one localised area also makes them vulnerable to other predators such as the Sparrowhawk, which will soon realise where the birds congregate and make regular patrols of the area. The Sparrowhawk might be having a major impact on our songbirds. It is the most widespread bird of prey and 88% of its prey are small birds. For nearly 20 years from the late 1950s until the 1970s it was virtually extinct over large areas of eastern England. Prior to this period it was heavily persecuted by gamekeepers and now it is probably as common as it has ever been in Britain. The highest density of this species in Europe now occurs in Britain with 348 breeding pairs per 50 kilometres square. Each Sparrowhawk requires 53 grams of food a day, which is equivalent to three sparrows. Over a year a pair of Sparrowhawks eats 2000 – 2200 birds. In these days when small birds are declining through a variety of other reasons the numbers taken by Sparrowhawks could be significant.

Bird tables and feeding areas are used month after month and if they are not regularly cleaned they can harbour bacteria, which can kill. This is not helped by the large quantities of food that is now available to a dwindling bird population. Food on bird tables also gets wet and stays uneaten for days that also helps bacteria to develop. In a wild environment this would seldom happen because once a food source had been exploited the birds would move on to pastures new.

With large amounts of food being put out a certain amount will be eaten by mammals. Species such as Foxes, Grey Squirrel, mice and Rats will take advantage of this easy food source. The larger species such as Foxes and Grey Squirrel nowadays have few natural predators. Given a regular and easy food supply and the relatively mild winters of recent years their populations must be very high at present. Each of the species mentioned can have devastating effects on breeding birds, taking both eggs and young.

Peanuts are not a natural food for birds in Britain but they are put out in millions of gardens every year. What effect is a continued diet of peanuts having on our native bird life, being rich as they are in protein and fat? Recently it has been realised that peanuts kept in warm temperatures with high humidity produce a deadly poison called aflatoxin. The poison is produced by a mould found naturally in peanuts and is undetectable without analysis. How many of our garden birds have been killed by contaminated peanuts? We are now encouraged to feed birds throughout the year and I have known of several cases where young Blue Tits have been choked and killed by peanuts. It is far better during the summer months to allow birds to eat their more natural insectivorous diet.

In the 1990s the Magpie appeared as the twelfth most frequent visitor at feeding sites. The Magpie is a very successful species that must have a drastic effect on breeding songbirds. Between 1965 and 1990 its numbers rose enormously almost tripling its population according to the Common Bird Census. Again we are told it is having little or no effect on our birdlife. This year I have watched a pair of Magpies systematically work the hedges and bushes of the local gardens and so far I have not seen any young birds. In a five-year survey in a suburban area of Braunschweig in northern Germany Magpies took 100% of eggs and young of some species in a 10 hectare area. The overall total was 64% of open nesters and 1.3% of hole nesters. Is something different happening in Britain; or is the overall effect Magpies and other Corvids are having on our birdlife being underestimated?

So far I have only discussed the more negative aspect of encouraging wild birds into our gardens. Over the last three decades much has changed in the countryside, hedges have been removed and there has been a general tidying up of the natural landscape. There is now little room left for what most people call "waste ground", but such areas supported a rich and diverse wildlife. Our gardens, therefore, can be made into "natural" oases and help in some way to redress the balance. I suggest planting your garden with a few native trees and shrubs. Native species are the best because they will support a far wider variety of organisms than foreign plants. Species that are good for producing berries include Hawthorn, Rowan, Holly, Honeysuckle, Bramble, Guelder-rose, Yew and Ivy and will attract warblers, thrushes, finches and, if you are fortunate Waxwing into your garden. The Ivy is a very important shrub because as it is evergreen, it supports hibernating butterflies through the winter and provides good roosting and nesting sites for birds. It also flowers in the autumn when most plants have died back and provides nectar for late flying butterflies, moths and other insects that in turn attract insectivorous birds. Its berries ripen in February, March and early April and are a vital food source when most natural foods are in short supply and Wood Pigeons, thrushes and Blackcaps come to gorge themselves on their fruit. Other species worthy of note include Silver Birch, Goat Willow and, if you have a damp garden, Alder. Many species of birds will come to feed on the seeds and cones produced by Birch and Alder including the Siskin and Redpoll. Goat Willow flowers, an important early nectar source, attract insects in March and early April which are much sought after by newly arrived warblers.

Nesting sites for birds can be in short supply. Old trees with holes in them are often removed and buildings are kept in better condition than they once were and so hole nesting species find it increasingly difficult to find nesting sites. Putting a wide range of nestboxes around a garden in safe places will certainly be advantageous and will probably result in you coming into closer contact with several species. Open fronted nestboxes will attract Robins and Spotted Flycatchers while those with a 30mm hole drilled in the front or side will favour tits, Nuthatches and sparrows. For those who are more ambitious and want to attract larger birds:- take four planks of wood 750mm long and 200mm wide and screw them together into an elongated box and fix in a bottom with drainage holes adding on top a handful of sawdust. Position the box with straps to the underside of a branch at an angle of about 30 degrees. This box may attract a pair of Stock Doves, Jackdaws or even Tawny Owls. Be careful, however, if the Tawny Owls take up residence as they are liable to attack any intruder including humans!

We can also provide birds with clean fresh water in a bird bath and this will attract a number of species. A wide variety of food can be put out for birds: – nuts of various sorts, cooked meat, fat, seeds and fruit such as apples and pears. Make sure that feeding areas are kept clean and in the case of bird tables occasionally disinfected. Where food is put out on a bird table or on the ground make sure that the birds have a large open area so that predators cannot sneak up on them unawares. Try also to limit the quantity of food put out so that stale food does not remain for days. Do not put out any food containing salt as this has a harmful effect on birds. I would also limit the amount of feeding during the spring and summer months as birds are better served bringing their chicks up on a natural insectivorous diet.

Since 1955 many thousands of birds have been ringed at my parents' house in Quorn. Over the years some 57 species have been caught in the garden. I now visit my parents on only a few occasions in the year, but since the late 1980s I have seen a sharp decline in the birds visiting the garden. Most species are lower in numbers than previously recorded and the overall bird population has dropped quite dramatically in the last 25 years. The local habitat has changed little in that time and birds are still fed regularly during the winter months. Could the drop in numbers correspond to the overall rise in garden feeding in the local area? I now live in Hertfordshire and set up a bird table in the large rural grounds where I work. The staff keep the bird table well stocked with peanuts and seed but in two years I have still to see a Greenfinch take advantage of the food and the number of tits visiting is very small. I can only guess at the reason for the apparent decline in our garden birds but it is very worrying.

One of the greatest changes during the 20th century has been that of transport. The motor car has had a huge impact upon our society. As the population has grown the motor car has become the preferred form of transport for most people. With congestion came the pressures to build more roads. In 1965 Charnwood Forest was split in two by the M1 and large areas of land were lost to this enterprise. It cut through Martinshaw Wood and Longcliffe Plantation and it took the edge of Piper Wood and Garendon Park. Before the end of the century other large roads were built across parts of the Charnwood Forest and down the Soar Valley. Roads can have a devastating effect on our wildlife, especially when areas of woodland are split in two. Many large animals such as Badger and Deer are slaughtered trying to cross them. Roads are also particularly bad for nocturnal predators such as owls, which get dazzled by headlights and sucked into the path of vehicles and killed. The unfortunate thing is that owls are drawn to the roadside verges because they are one of the few areas of ancient turf and obviously rich in voles. The Kestrel is a feature of motorway travel, but its hunting method of hovering seldom brings it into contact with the car. Other species particularly susceptible to the car are species like Blackbird and Whitethroat. The Blackbird has a tendency to fly low and the Whitethroat breeds in tall herbage and scrub adjacent to the roads where its dancing song flight can take it into the path of vehicles. Many thousands of birds must die on our roads each year but also what effect are roads having on our insect life, particularly moths?

If you are old enough, you can look back and see that our climate has changed. In the 1960s we had long periods of frost which we seldom get now. The last prolonged period of severe weather in the Midland region happened in the winter of 1981-82. Over the last two decades of the 20th century, however, we did see abnormal weather patterns resulting in far more gales, floods, late frosts, warm winters etc. For many species of our wildlife that live and die, breed and migrate by the seasons this must have a very disturbing effect. It is now generally recognised that Global Warming is taking place and this is going to have either a beneficial or catastrophic effect on every creature on the planet. The greenhouse effect has been brought about by the large amounts of carbon dioxide and carbon monoxide being liberated into the atmosphere, either

Firecrest

from the burning of fossil fuels or the burning of the rainforests. Already we are seeing the effects on our birdlife with the colonisation of Britain by such southern species as Cetti's Warbler, Firecrest and Little Egret. I am sure these are the vanguard of the great changes that Global Warming will bring and many of them may not be so beneficial.

In the last ten years some birds that were once considered as rare vagrants are now becoming annual and others that were of rare occurrence are being recorded annually in fairly large numbers. If thirty years ago you had been told that over 600 Yellow-browed Warblers from the Eastern Palearctic or 25 Red-eyed Vireos from the Nearctic would be recorded in a single autumn in Britain it would not have been believed. Could it be that birds are more susceptible to climatic conditions than we at present understand, and is increased vagrancy the start of range expansion or populations moving due to climatic change? Migrating birds will find it difficult travelling during severe weather and some will be thrown off course and major changes in the position of pressure systems could also adversely affect migration. All records are interesting, even of vagrants, and it will be intriguing to see how birds cope with the climatic changes ahead. Vagrants of the past included Little Egrets with only twelve sightings in Britain up to 1952 and Cetti's Warbler which were not recorded prior to 1961. Now they are both resident breeding species.

More localised weather disruptions can also seriously affect our local bird populations. Towards the end of the 1960s and the beginning of the 1970s the Sahel region of Africa suffered a severe drought. Many of our long distance migrants that wintered in that area of west Africa were affected. Some species suffered only partial losses while others were more severely hit and in certain cases the entire population of British breeding birds was halved. In the mid-1980s more droughts occurred, reducing yet again already depleted populations. Species that suffered in one way or another included Turtle Dove, Sand Martin, Yellow Wagtail, Wheatear, Redstart, Sedge Warbler and Common Whitethroat.

Many of man's other inventions and so-called scientific advancements could affect our environment catastrophically. If we don't have the knowledge to be able to control all the effects of our scientific advancements then we should query their use, and this is particularly true about genetic engineering and nuclear power. The Chernobyl legacy will be left for generations to come and if genetically modified plants do cause major problems could we stop the spread of pollen once it is in the biosphere?

I have tried to show some of the main hazards that have affected our local birdlife and other factors that might be a problem in the future. Our birds face enormous pressures and they are being attacked from every quarter. If we still want to have the pleasure of seeing a wide range of species and enjoying the melodies of a dawn chorus then we need to act quickly to preserve them.

Our Creator gave us a wonderful planet to sustain us and give us enjoyment. Nature has a wonderful way to heal itself. We need to give it time and encouragement to regenerate and stop exploiting it for short-term profit. When the exploitable resources run out we still have to live or die on this planet.

3. PHYSICAL FEATURES, HISTORY AND VEGETATION

by Peter Gamble

Swithland Reservoir lies within four parishes, Swithland, Woodhouse, Quorn and Rothley. It was built by the Leicester Corporation to supplement supplies of water from the Cropston and Thornton Reservoirs. The water gravitated from the reservoir through a series of sand filters and was eventually pumped into the supply via the steam-driven pumps at the pump house. The old steam pumps were removed in the 1950s and replaced by electrically driven pumps, since when further, updated, electric pumps have been installed. Today major problems are occurring with water quality through nutrient enrichment probably caused by fertilizer run-off and the large gull roost (plate 58).

The reservoir, formed by damming the shallow valley adjacent to Buddon Wood, is fed by two streams, the larger being the stream which also feeds Cropston Reservoir, upstream from Swithland Reservoir. This delightful stream, known as Bradgate Brook where it flows into the southern part of the reservoir, rises from two sources in the upper Ulverscroft Valley; at Copt Oak Wood and on the Ulverscroft Nature Reserve at Fox Covert. It flows by the Priory, past Nowell Spring Wood, Lea Wood, and, before passing Ulverscroft Mill, is joined by several lesser streams, eventually reaching Newtown Linford and on through Bradgate Park as the River Lin before flowing into Cropston Reservoir.

The smaller of the two feeder streams, which enters Swithland Reservoir in the south-west near the lagoon and marsh, is the result of two streams coming together, one of which rises on the north side of Bradgate Park, passes through the south end of Swithland Wood along its south-east boundary and then flows across the Swithland Hall Estate whilst the other rises near Roecliffe Farm and then flows through the northern end of Roecliffe Spinney and through The Brand and Swithland village as the Swithland Brook to where the two join near the Church.

When full the water level is 58 metres (190 feet) above sea-level and the whole Severn-Trent complex occupies 68.7 hectares (170 acres) including some 52.6 hectares (130 acres) of open water. At the centre of the dam the water is 8 metres (26 feet) deep when full but owing to the shallow nature of the valley the depth of water over much of the area is less than 3 metres (10 feet). Near the road bridge at the southern inflow, large areas are now quite shallow as a result of the accumulated deposition of silt which must have resulted in its holding capacity being considerably less than the 490 million gallons it was built to hold.

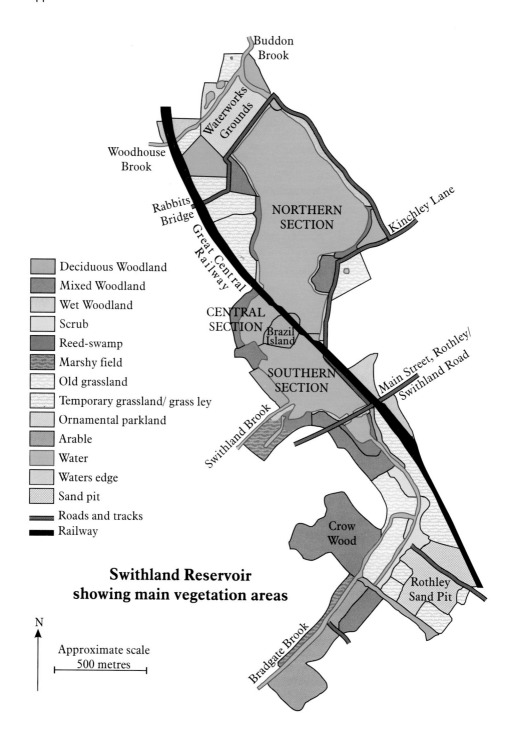

Buddon
Brook

Waterworks
Grounds

Woodhouse
Brook

Rabbits
Bridge

Great Central
Railway

NORTHERN
SECTION

Kinchley Lane

CENTRAL
SECTION

Brazil
Island

SOUTHERN
SECTION

Main Street, Rothley/
Swithland Road

Swithland Brook

Crow
Wood

Rothley
Sand Pit

Bradgate Brook

Deciduous Woodland
Mixed Woodland
Wet Woodland
Scrub
Reed-swamp
Marshy field
Old grassland
Temporary grassland/ grass ley
Ornamental parkland
Arable
Water
Waters edge
Sand pit
Roads and tracks
Railway

**Swithland Reservoir
showing main vegetation areas**

N

Approximate scale
500 metres

As is usual with reservoirs used for drinking water the whole of the inflow section in the south is cut off as a settling area, the division at Swithland being effected by Brazil "Island" and two weirs, the tops of which are one foot below the surface when the reservoir is full. Because of these weirs the southern section of the reservoir normally shows little fluctuation of water-level. The reservoir is also divided by the embankments and viaducts of the old Great Central Railway Line (now a Steam Trust tourist attraction) which crosses the reservoir adjacent to Brazil Wood (plates 18 and 19).

The Reservoir was completed in 1896 and its construction necessitated the felling of large numbers of Sessile Oaks and Alders. Prior to its construction the ancient woodland at Buddon Wood continued further down towards where the brook meandered through the valley and it seems more than likely that rare plants such as the Alternate-leaved Golden Saxifrage, Marsh Cinquefoil, Grass of Parnassus, Marsh Helleborine and Autumn Lady's-tresses, formerly recorded for the environs of Buddon Wood by early botanists such as Dr. Pulteney, grew in the marshes, meadows and wet woodland here. One uncommon species, the Brookweed, has managed to survive on the sandy shore of the northern section's south-east corner. Other rare and local plants such as Shoreweed, Needle Spike-rush and Orange Foxtail also grow along the shore here.

Swithland Reservoir is accessed by a good road down Kinchley Lane off Wood Lane, between Quorn and Rothley. The lane turns sharp right on reaching the bottom of the hill, continuing along the south-west side of Buddon Wood to the dam and overflow channel. A good viewing point occurs half way along the road, adjacent to Buddon Wood, where the reservoir water comes close to the boundary wall and

Plate 1. Aerial view of Swithland Reservoir from the south, September 1968.

Plate 2. The dam and overspill, nearing completion in 1896. **Plate 3 (below).** Also from 1896. Beyond the newly built dam wall can be seen the fresh scar of 'The Crag', which had provided the granite for construction of the dam.

rocky outcrops and where the view is not obscured by trees. The dam footpath also provides good viewing over the stone wall across the large north water. At the south-west end of the dam, a partially surfaced road continues over Rabbits Bridge past Rushey Fields Farm to the Brand Lane between Woodhouse and Swithland. A private gated road passes down the eastern side of the reservoir to join the Rothley to Swithland road which crosses the south end of the water giving good views of the southern section of the Reservoir.

Until a few years ago the reservoir was overlooked by the 122 metres (400 feet) rounded hill of Buddon Wood, sadly, now largely destroyed by quarrying, and my most abiding memory of this locality is of listening to Nightjars' "churring" and watching their display flight in the summit area during warm summer evenings in the late 1940s and 1950 whilst hundreds of bats disported themselves, often in company with Swifts, over the nearby reservoir, large Noctules high up and several smaller species at lower levels.

Further away, some three miles to the west, the reservoir is overlooked by the Charnian hills which form a fine backcloth, especially during colourful sunsets.

It is proposed now to look briefly at the all-important vegetation of the reservoir grounds, and firstly around that of the large north section situated to the north of the railway.

The Waterworks Grounds

In the extreme north, below the dam, lie the Pumping Station Grounds housing the pump station buildings and symmetrically laid out filter beds and clear water-tank, none of which are now in use (see plates 4 and 5). This area somewhat resembles a park, or arboretum, with numerous specimen trees, some native but also many exotic species, including conifers. Other areas are closely planted with both deciduous and coniferous species. Much of the central area consists of open managed grassland, probably of old turf judging by the rich mix of wildflowers such as Lady's-mantle, Cowslip, Devil's-bit Scabious and Betony which have appeared on occasions when left uncut. The whole area supports a varied flora. A small stream which rises near Woodhouse Eaves flows through the north section of the grounds from south-west to north-east (plate 6) where it enters the Buddon Brook near the bottom of the overflow channel and beyond this, near the north boundary, are a cooling pond and a settling pond, the latter colonised by Lesser Bulrush and both supporting an interesting flora and fauna.

With its varied tree cover, its plentiful drinking places, abundant insect life and its sheltered position below the dam this is an excellent site for song birds.

Plate 4. In 1896 the Victorians laid out the filter-beds like a formal garden. Buddon Wood can also be seen before it was clear-felled in the 1940s and later quarried for roadstone.

48

Plate 5 (above). The Waterworks Grounds. October, 2000. The original formal planting has gone. The filter beds are no longer required and the surrounding trees are now mature mixed woodland
Plate 6 (below). The Woodhouse Brook running through the Waterworks Grounds, 1983. The stream provides a favourite feeding area for the Grey Wagtail.

Plate 7 (above). The overflow channel in full spate. May 1983.

Plate 8. (below) The reservoir overflow. October 2000.

The Main Northern Section

Immediately to the east of the Pumping Station Grounds is the overflow channel, or byewash (plates 2 and 7), with stone walls and stone, now well vegetated base and a significant flora including some local and uncommon species. The channel falls quickly down to the point where it becomes the Buddon Brook and the more level area south of the road, near the spill-over is a good place to see Little Ringed Plovers (plate 51) and Grey Wagtails.

The dam itself is a fine structure, faced with locally quarried granodiorite now becoming well vegetated with aquatic and marginal species at the high water mark and the stone walls here and elsewhere around the reservoir, are built of the same local stone. The dam is a good place to observe waders such as Common Sandpiper and Greenshank, especially when water levels are high, as has often tended to be the case in recent years.

The area of Sessile Oak and Silver Birch woodland lying between the overflow channel and Buddon Wood (formerly part of Buddon Wood) is particularly important as it supports these and other tree and shrub species and a ground flora characteristic of Buddon Wood itself, as well as many of the special invertebrates long known to occur there. A small streamlet, originating from a spring, which flows across the woodland into the overflow channel is a good spot to find Woodcock, especially during periods of hard weather. The high cliff here, often called 'The Crag', (plate 9) is a breeding site for Stock Doves and is sometimes frequented by Kestrel while the adjacent steep Heather-covered bank is an excellent site for observing Purple Hairstreak butterflies in July and August. The acid grassland below 'The Crag' supports a number of Buddon's special plants such as Slender St. John's-wort, Cow-wheat and Hairy Wood-rush.

The narrow strip of woodland along the north-east margin of the reservoir, close to Buddon Wood, consists of frequent Alder, Sessile Oak, Wych Elm, Ash, Sycamore and Norwegian Maple and occasional Black Pine and Larch; the Wych Elm probably originating from sucker growth from old weeping elms which used to grow at intervals along the margins here. The Sycamore and Norwegian Maple are currently being removed to prevent them seeding into neighbouring areas. Crack, Grey and Goat Willows, and Osiers fringe the waterside and when water-levels drop a stony shore is revealed (plate 11).

A small stream piped under the road enters the reservoir in the north-east bay where the sandy and muddy shore supports well developed reed-swamp with both Bulrush and Lesser Bulrush, Yellow Iris, Greater Pond-sedge and Slender Tufted-sedge, Common Club-rush, Reed Canary-grass and many other herbaceous species, besides bushes of Common Sallow and Osier. This is one of the regular breeding sites for Reed Warbler. During periods of low water Shore-weed and Needle Spike-rush can be seen here.

Situated on the drier ground in this north-east corner is the triangular shaped Ash plantation with tall trees and a varied ground flora, including plenty of Burdock whose seeds are much sought after by Marsh and Willow Tits and flocks of Goldfinch. Grey Willow and occasional Goat Willow and Alder fringe the high water mark.

The Kinchley Promontory, accessed by the private road lined with Cricket-bat Willows, has trees of various ages, including Common Oak, Silver Birch, Wych Elm and a variety of planted aliens, including some Red Oak, Norway Spruce and Larch. The Wych Elms support varying numbers of White-letter Hairstreak butterflies during July and August. The more open areas are dominated by tall herbaceous species including thistles, willow-herbs and umbelliferous species providing nesting habitat for various warblers. Much of the shoreline here is rocky as a result of intrusive igneous rocks and during periods of low water a rocky peninsula (plate 15) stretches well out into the reservoir where it becomes a favourite resting site for Cormorants, gulls, terns and on occasions wading birds. A narrow strip of reed-swamp, best developed in the south occurs around the high-water mark on the promontory.

Kinchley Farm, which once stood on the promontory became unviable with the loss of most of its land with the flooding of the valley; it fell into disrepair and was finally demolished around 1975. Some of the garden flowers and shrubs associated with the farm still survive here.

Adjacent to, and to the east of the promontory is the site of the old Kinchley Hill Quarry and an interesting field of acid grassland. The old quarry site has some large old Hawthorns and plenty of Gorse and in places with low vegetation, Storksbill, Sand Spurrey, Knotted Clover, Birds-foot and Early Hair-grass. These Gorse covered areas were always good for Linnets and Yellowhammers although these are much less common today.

The narrow strip of reservoir margin lying between the Kinchley Promontory and the railway alongside the private road, has Wych Elm and five willow-sallow species and a strip of herb-rich grass verge with Great Burnet, Betony, Bird's-foot-trefoil, Bush Vetch, etc., although it is currently being overgrown by shrubs.

The railway margins and embankment on the southern boundary of the large north section of the reservoir provide nesting sites for waterfowl and support a large variety of plant species. The waterside on the west bank immediately north of the railway has a few Alders and a line of pollarded willows runs northwards into where the margins broaden and contain a variety of trees, including Common Oak, Silver Birch, Ash and Scots Pine, the latter frequently used by nesting Kestrel. Underneath the trees grow Field Rose and a variety of herbaceous species. On the water's edge a naturalised colony of Bridewort has been used in the past by breeding Reed Warblers and to the north there is a broadening area of reed-swamp (plate 13) with Bulrush, Branched Bur-reed, Meadowsweet, Purple Loosestrife, Lesser Pond-sedge, Slender Tufted-sedge, Reed Sweet-grass, etc., and bushes of Grey Willow. In past years numbers of Harvest Mice have been discovered here and in other areas with well-developed reed-swamp around the reservoir. A low hedgerow forms the boundary of these western margins, and beyond this, grass-ley. The gently sloping shore here, yields extensive areas of muddy shore during periods of low water levels when it becomes a favourite place for waders.

Further north, towards the dam, a steep bank and deeper water prevents the development of much reed-swamp and on the bank, close to the water, is a planting of Norwegian Spruce. To the west of the track here a line of large, mature Black Pines runs parallel to the reservoir-margins and west of this a mature Ash plantation reaches the west end of the dam in the north and borders the road to Rabbits Bridge

52

Plate 9 (top). Overflow channel and granite cliff, April 1981. The cliff is home to pairs of Stock Dove.

Plate 10 (middle). Northern section showing the dam and overflow. June 1987.

Plate 11 (bottom). The eastern shoreline near Buddon Wood, northern section, October 1989. Occassionally, when this stony shoreline is exposed during spring, the Little Ringed Plover will breed here.

Plate 12 (top). A view from Kinchley Promontory towards Buddon Hill, September 1999.
Plate 13 (middle). Reed swamp on the western shore, northern section. May 1982.
Plate 14 (below). Muddy shoreline on the western edge of the northern section, August 1984. When the mud is exposed it often attracts numbers of gulls and the occassional wader.

as far as the track next to the open area of grass-ley in the south. To the north and west and on the opposite side of the road, south of the dam, is a Sycamore plantation with mature Common Oaks on its south, west and north boundary whilst on its north-east side lie the Pumping Station Grounds. Because of the heavy shade factor this plantation has little ground flora.

The Main Southern Section

We turn to look next at the margins of the main southern section (plate 20) and firstly at Brazil Wood in the north. This wooded hill, adjoining the railway embankment, forms one of the main features of the reservoir and prior to the flooding of the valley was considerably larger than today and a habitat, of two rare plant species, the Lily of the Valley and the Nettle-leaved Bellflower, neither of which appear to be present today.

It is located on an intrusion of igneous rock which forms a low hill, its highest part over 65 metres (213 feet) above sea-level, and considerably higher than the nearby railway embankment. The wood occupying some 2.4 hectares (6.0 acres) is covered with mature deciduous woodland (plate 19), including Pedunculate and Sessile Oaks, Silver and Downy Birch and occasional Ash, Wych Elm, Lime, Hazel and Elder. Fringing the water are Alder, Goat and Grey Willow and occasional Crack Willow.

Some of the Oaks are circa 200 years old and the wood on its rocky substrate bears a close resemblance to what Buddon Wood was like prior to wartime clear-felling. Interestingly, Red Wood Ants which used to be one of the specialities of Buddon Wood, before the felling and quarrying, sometimes established colonies here though apparently these were not permanent and seemed to be an overflow from Buddon. Though often called "Brazil Island" the wood joins up with the railway embankment and because of sparks from the passing steam engines has, on occasions, suffered undergrowth fires. In spring the eastern side of the wood is carpeted with Bluebells making an attractive and colourful feature for travellers using the railway. To the west the hill overlooks the small, largely hidden central section of the reservoir. Much of the woodland flora here is typical of acidic ground including plants such as Wood Sage, Foxglove, Great and Hairy Wood-rush and Wavy Hair-grass. The "island" constitutes an important breeding site for waterfowl and Shoveler (plate 38) have been known to breed here in the past. At present it is the main breeding site at the reservoir for Grey Herons. It also attracts good numbers of migrants whilst hirundines and Swifts often feed in large numbers over the treetops.

A fisherman's footpath runs along the foot of the south facing embankment from Brazil Wood to connect with the private road on the eastern side of the reservoir. This road, south of the blue brick railway bridge, where Stock Doves breed, is bounded by the railway and embankment to the east and a narrow strip of woodland fringing the reservoir to the west. The trees here consist of abundant Ash, frequent Sycamore and Wych Elm and occasional Larch whilst Alder, Crack Willow, Goat Willow and Osiers line the waterside. Marshy ground here has Common Valerian, Meadowsweet and Yellow Iris and the reed-swamp extending out into shallow water has Bulrush, Greater and Lesser Pond Sedge and Reed Sweet-grass. The quiet margins here offer good conditions for a variety of breeding waterfowl while the bushes and scrub along the nearby railway embankment offer breeding sites for Blackcaps, Garden Warblers and Whitethroats.

The narrow grassy margins alongside the Main Street near the road bridge, to the south of the large southern section, have several trees, White Poplar, Sycamore, Silver Birch and Lime and small herbaceous species including Wood Anemone, Celandine, Germander Speedwell and Common Dog-violet. A variety of waterfowl tend to gather here, and across the road, waiting to be fed by regular visitors who, misguidedly, daily bring bread with which to feed them.

To the west of the road bridge and north of the road the reservoir margins consist of mixed woodland and well developed reed-swamp. The trees consist of frequent Alder, Crack, White, Goat and Grey Willows, Norwegian Spruce and Hawthorn and occasional Sycamore and Pedunculate Oak while the reed-swamp supports Gypsywort, Water Mint, Yellow Iris, Bulrush, Lesser Pond Sedge and Reed Sweet-grass.

A derelict mill / boat house is located on the north of these wooded margins and old water courses which cross the area are doubtless connected with the old water-mill which ceased working around 1895.

To the west of this woodland lies a rapidly silting up lagoon, an area of wet woodland with plenty of Marsh Marigolds, a wet 2.6 hectare (7.0 acre) meadow/marsh and the Swithland Brook inflow stream. The lagoon is now largely separated from the main body of water by the spread of vegetation across its mouth. This secluded lagoon has long been an important feeding and resting place for dabbling ducks and waders such as the Green Sandpiper. The extensive reed-swamp here holds Purple Loosestrife, Hemp Agrimony, Bulrush, Yellow Iris, four species of rush, five species of sedge, including Brown Sedge and Cyperus Sedge and a large colony of Reed Sweet-grass which has, in the past, supported nesting colonies of Reed Warblers. Bushes of Osier, Goat and Grey Willow, Elder and Hawthorn occur here and Alders are plentiful along and around the mouth of the stream, a favourite breeding site for Lesser Spotted Woodpecker. A drainage channel carries water through the meadow into the lagoon marsh and the area to the south of the lagoon is the former site of a large mill pond. The feeder stream follows the meadows north-west boundary and enters the reservoir on the north side of the lagoon. The wet meadow/ marsh and the small area of woodland in this area have a diverse flora and some 105 flowering plant species have been recorded.

A rustic bridge crosses the stream allowing access to the 1.2 hectare (3.0 acre) Ash plantation. In addition to the dominant mature Ash, this area also has some Sycamore, Field Maple and Silver Birch, and Alder and Crack Willow on the waterside. Shrub growth here includes Hawthorn, Hazel, Holly and Guelder-rose and the plantation supports a varied ground flora including Yellow Pimpernel, Golden Saxifrage, Large Bitter-cress, Primrose, Wood Sanicle, Wood Sedge and Wood Melick.

The new, now well established colony of breeding Cormorants have their nests in trees in the north-east of this woodland and into the south-east of the adjacent woodland to the north. Being quiet and undisturbed the area provides good conditions for a variety of breeding birds.

To the north of here a wooded hill with some coppiced Pedunculate and Sessile Oaks used to be part of Brazil Wood which before the construction of the reservoir

Plate 15 (above). The Northern section has a promentory extending from the eastern shoreline, which is exposed when the water level is low. At such times it is a favourite resting place for cormorants, gulls and terns, with occasional waders. Photograph: August 1984.
Plate 16 (below). View from the quarry south mound on Buddon Wood, across the northern section to the viaduct and Brazil Island.

Plate 17 (above). Central section, May 1985.
Plate 18 (below). Central section looking towards the viaduct carrying the Great Central Railway, with Buddon Hill beyond. 1984. The central section provides a quiet backwater, disturbed only by periodic steam trains along the viaduct. It is an area of the reservoir favoured by breedfing waterfowl.

58

was twice its present size. The hardrock intrusion here has a vertical face and is the site of an old quarry. In addition to the two oaks, Silver and Downy Birch and Rowan occur here and also some planted Larch while the lower shoreline has some Alder and Grey Willow. A colony of Aspen adds interest to the north-west corner. Smaller woodland plants found here include Wood Anemone, Wood Speedwell, Figwort, Wood Sage, Greater Stitchwort, Foxglove, Heath Groundsel, Bluebell, Great Wood-rush, Wavy Hair-grass and Wood Millet. The northern shore has Purple Loosestrife, Pink Water-Speedwell, Yellow Iris and various other aquatic and marginal species and looks out over the small secluded section of the reservoir which lies to the west of Brazil Wood, south of the railway embankment and north of the dam which separates it from the large southern section.

The Secluded Central Section

This largely hidden section of the reservoir (plates 17 and 18) has long been an important feeding and breeding site for waterfowl and during dry years, with low water-levels has attracted waders to its areas of freshly exposed mud. In the past the drier grassy margins along the western side were cut regularly and supported an interesting variety of wildflowers, including Cowslip, Lady's Bedstraw, Zig-Zag Clover, Bush Vetch, Tufted Vetch, Meadow Vetchling and Betony but in recent years, with less regular cutting, some small species have declined markedly. Much of this area is wet and holds an extensive reed-swamp community with meadowsweet, Hairy Willow-herb, Marsh Bedstraw, Water Mint, Skullcap, Yellow Iris, Soft Rush, Reed Canary-grass and Reed Sweet-grass. During recent years the Crack Willows have been allowed to grow up and now dominate much of the reed-swamp and drier areas also hold large Hawthorns. Some years the shallow, open water is covered with masses of Amphibious Bistort and during periods of low water exposed areas become colonised, here and elsewhere, with unbroken colonies of richly coloured Golden Dock. The small rocky island whose igneous rocks have long been known to contain small garnets is now overgrown with *Salix* scrub. In past summers it has held healthy colonies of noisy Reed Warblers.

Some 82 species of flowering plants have been recorded in this section of the reservoir. In 1982 numbers of mating and egg-laying Migrant Hawker dragonflies were noted here for the first time; in 1983 a Ringlet made its first appearance at the reservoir here and in 1984 a Pochard bred here amongst the reed-swamp.

The Southern Inflow Section

As on the opposite side of the road a narrow grassy bank, each side of the road bridge, with occasional Silver Birch, Sycamore, Lime, Horse Chestnut and Black Pine forms the northern edge of this section and the bridge parapet makes a good look out point to scan this small reed fringed area of shallow water (plate 21), a favourite feeding site for dabbling ducks such as Mallard, Teal and Gadwall and occasionally, less common species such as Garganey. It is also a good spot to catch a glimpse of the elusive Water Rail.

A narrow strip of woodland with frequent Alder and Ash and occasional Crack and Grey Willows and Pedunculate Oaks and Hawthorns forms the eastern boundary to the water and reed-swamp areas and a varied herbaceous flora includes Meadowsweet, Red Campion, Herb Robert, Water forget-me-not, Common Hemp-nettle, Bearded Couch and Hairy Brome. Also Broad and Narrow Buckler Ferns.

At the south of the inflow woodland is a Crack Willow plantation, with most of the trees circa 60 years old but with occasional older trees circa 100 years old; also frequent Alders along the brook and occasional Ash and Pedunculate Oak while shrub growth consists of occasional Hazel, Hawthorn and Elder and a ground flora including Herb Robert, Red Campion, Wood Avens, Meadowsweet, Bittersweet, Wood Dock, Reed Canary-grass and Rough Meadow-grass. Much of the ground is, however, dominated by Common Nettle. To the south and west of this plantation lies herb-rich meadowland.

To the north-west is an Ash plantation with trees circa 70 years old; this extends from the meadow in the south to the Main Street in the north and from the marsh/reed-swamp westwards to the plantations western boundary. In addition to the Ash the plantation has some Sycamore, Norwegian Maple, Wych Elm, Silver Birch and Pedunculate Oak, including several ancient veteran, parkland type trees in the south-west, and plantings of Larch. Also Alder in some wetter areas. Shrubs include plenty of Bramble, Elder, Field Rose and Honeysuckle. Plants of the woodland floor include Wood Anemone, Goldilocks Buttercup, Common Dog-violet, Greater Stitchwort, Dog's Mercury, Herb Robert, Enchanters Nightshade, Angelica, Pignut, Bluebell, Lady-fern, Male-fern and Broad Buckler-fern. An open, grassy area on the edge of the marsh, which used to be periodically cut, formerly had a varied flora with Ragged Robin, Great Burnet, Fen Bedstraw, Betony, Sneezewort, Brown Sedge and Carnation Sedge, but some of these may have been lost as a result of a cessation of the mowing regime during recent years.

Much of the central area to the east, south and west of the open water is made up of reed-swamp and marsh and with constant silting up this has extended greatly during recent years. The marginal willows, sallows and osiers have also increased greatly in size and now dominate much of the wetter margins. The open areas of reed-swamp are dominated by Bulrush, Yellow Iris and Reed Sweet-grass and marshy areas have plenty of Meadowsweet, Hairy Willow-herb, Common Valerian, Water Chickweed, Water Figwort, Water Forget-me-not, Skullcap, Gypsywort, Marsh Bedstraw, Soft Rush and Lesser Pond Sedge, and occasional specimens of Black Currant and Greater Tussock-sedge.

This is an important area for insects and one of the main breeding sites for Reed Warblers.

Finally the southern inflow stream, the Bradgate Brook (plate 22), passes through the woodland and it is much frequented by Kingfishers (plate 34) and has some good colonies of Large Bitter-cress, Water Mint, Water Chickweed and Water Forget-me-not.

Plate 19 (above). Oak woodland on Brazil Island. May 1981. This small fragment of woodland is on a small granite hill, and is reminisent of what Buddon Wood itself looked like prior to its clear-felling in the 1940s.

Plate 20 (below). The southern section of the reservoir. February 1977. This is the view from the Rothley to Swithland road, so is the most accessible viewpoint across the reservoir. The large trees in the distance now hold breeding colonies of Cormorant and Grey Heron during spring and summer.

Plate 21 (above). Small southern inflow section of the reservoir. August 1973. The Rothley to Swithland road cuts off this extreme southern tip of the reservoir, creating an enclosed and richly vegetated pool. During the winter months Teal and occasionally Water Rail can be seen here, and in spring pairs of Garganey sometimes put in an appearance.

Plate 22 (below). Bradgate Brook, which is the main inflow brook to the reservoir. May 1982. This quiet section of brook is a favourite haunt of the Kingfisher.

Changes Past and Present

In the past 60 years, during which time the reservoir's bird life has been closely watched, some big changes have taken place to the surrounding countryside. By far the greatest change took place in the early 1940s – during the war years – when Buddon Wood was clear felled. As could be expected this had a huge effect on the birdlife of the whole region for the wood covered almost a square mile of hilly, rocky ground with mature Sessile Oaks, Silver and Downy Birch, Aspen and Small-leaved Limes with much dead wood and innumerable holes for hole-nesting birds and bats.

After the felling, regeneration soon got underway and for a period of years the area supported large numbers of song birds, Meadow and Tree Pipits some seven species of warbler, and Yellowhammers and Reed Buntings, etc. Sedge and Grasshopper Warblers and Reed Bunting nested on the western margins of the wood close to the reservoir.

By the 1960s regeneration was quickly converting the area back to woodland again and many woodland birds, including local species such as Woodcock and Wood Warbler, were again breeding there.

Regrettably during the 1970s any hopes we had of the woodland recovering to something like its former splendour were shattered when an old planning permission to quarry, granted in the 1940s, was taken up resulting in today's enormous hardrock quarry.

In the years following the Second World War changes also took place on the western side of the reservoir when several herb-rich fields with Spiny Restharrow, Green-winged Orchids and many other interesting wild flowers were lost and two small sewage farms, where Redshank and Snipe used to breed, one between Rabbits Bridge and Woodhouse and the other between Rabbits Bridge and Swithland were changed and lost most of their former interest. Until this time Redshank were much more frequent visitors than nowadays feeding on the reservoir margins.

Other management actions that must have brought about changes to the reservoir's birdlife were the introduction of conifer plantations to various parts of the margins. Such plantations are used by a variety of breeding warblers, Dunnocks, Chaffinch and Linnets when young, and Goldcrests, Coal Tits, Jays and Sparrowhawks later as they grow and become more mature.

The loss of many elms through Dutch Elm disease in the1970s also charged the appearance of the reservoir margins for many English and Wych Elms were lost and a very distinctive weeping variety of Wych Elm, which grew as standard trees in many places on the margins, was almost totally lost. These were favourite nesting sites for several species. Also, more recently lost through disease, except for an odd remaining tree, was the row of Lombardy Poplars which grew in the waterworks grounds at the base of the dam bank. These are known to have been used as nesting sites by Lesser Spotted Woodpecker on several occasions.

The tendency during recent years for there to have been constant high water levels, with little or no draw down, has resulted in there being little in the way of shore or muddy margins to attract waders. However, since the installation of an anchored raft by the Water Authority on the large north water in 1993 Common Terns have bred annually-something which would not have been deemed likely in the 1940s!

Compared with the 1940s and 1950s some predator species have undergone big increases, Grey Squirrels, Carrion Crows and Magpies are three such, and in their present numbers these must be having quite an impact on many bird species. Recent decades have also seen the arrival of the American Mink, an unwelcome introduction indeed especially as far as Water Voles and waterfowl are concerned. The Red Squirrel was still present in the area up until the early 1940s though almost certainly it was never anywhere near as plentiful as the Grey Squirrel now is and the Water Vole was common along the inflow and outflow brooks until the 1980s since when it declined rapidly and has not been seen for some years.

Also, less shooting has apparently taken place in recent years and this may well be the main reason for the successful establishment of breeding colonies of Grey Heron and Cormorant.

During the last decade Peregrine Falcons have shown an increasing inclination to winter in the neighbourhood, probably feeling much at home in the presence of the Buddon Wood Quarry with its extensive cliffs, and this last year, even more thrilling and unexpected, Ravens have also put in an appearance.

The lack of general management work during recent years has resulted in the decline of many small herbaceous species of open grassy areas whilst small woodland plants have declined or disappeared, in woodland areas as pathways have become overgrown. However, it must also be true that some bird species have benefited from the lack of disturbance during the breeding season.

At present management work being undertaken by Severn Trent Water in co-operation with the Leicestershire and Rutland Wildlife Trust and English Nature includes the removal of some Sycamores and Norwegian Maple from the north-east margins adjacent to Buddon Wood. This work is being carried out to prevent further colonisation of the S.S.S.I. by these two non-native species. It is also intended to continue the coppicing of willows and osiers around the margins. With Severn Trent Water and the conservation bodies working together at this site it will enable this rich biodiversity to continue into the future

In conclusion it should be stressed that the marked declines that many bird species have undergone during recent decades are only partly due to local changes in the environment but are often the result of national declines, or, as is frequently stated in the species accounts, because of climatic or other environmental changes in distant places.

Opposite page, clockwise from top left:–
Plate 23: Slender Tufted-sedge (*Carex acuta*). May 1977. This is a common constituent of the reed-swamp vegetation of the reservoir.
Plate 24: Greater Tussock Sedge *(Carex paniculata)* March 1980. It produces these spectacular tussocks but is restricted to the southern inflow section of the reservoir.
Plate 25: Cyperus Sedge (*Carex pseudocyperus*). July 1972. This handsome sedge is locally frequent on the south-western margins of the reservoir.
Plate 26: Large Bitter Cress (*Cardamine amara*). May 1982. This is locally frequent under the trees at the southern inflow section.
Plate 27: Marsh Marigolds (*Caltha palustris*). April 1988. These striking flowers are found in abundance in the wet alder/willow woodland near where the Swithland Brook enters the reservoir.
Plate 28: Brookweed (*Samolus valerandi*). September 1972. This is more commonly found along coastal salt marshes and is a rare plant of the Primula family. It was present in Buddon Wood before the reservoir was built and still survives on the north-east margins of the reservoir.

Right from top:–
Plate 29: When the water level is low, fresh water mussel shells can be found on the exposed mud.
Plate 30: A male Migrant Hawker dragonfly at the reservoir in October 1982. It was first recorded breeding there in 1982 and is now a common species, seen in numbers in late summer.
Plate 31: A female Purple Hairstreak butterfly, Buddon Wood, July 1975. An attractive species found in old oak woodland, it is locally common along the margins of the reservoir adjacent to Buddon Wood, where it can be seen flying in late July and August.
Plate 32: A White-letter Hairstreak butterfly. Quorn, July 1999. A local species, restricted here to colonies of English and Wych Elm on the Kinchley promontory. It can be seen on the wing in July and early August.

Plate 33 (above left). Grey Heron. Though a common resident, these large birds are always a dramatic sight, whether flying with great slow wing-beats, or as here, standing statuesque on the bank. Herons have been breeding at the reservoir most years in recent times.

Plate 34 (above right). Kingfisher: a shy and retiring resident breeder that is often overlooked.

Plate 35 (below). Great Crested Grebe's nest and eggs. Swithland Reservoir, May 1977.

Plate 36 (above). Mute Swan and cygnets at their nest site at Swithland Reservoir. May 1999. One or two pairs breed annually.

Plate 37 (below). Canada Goose at Swithland Reservoir. This is a common resident, with large numbers congregating at times in the winter, although only a few breed at the reservoir most years.

69

Plate 38 (top opposite). Male Shoveler: a common passage migrant and winter visitor to the reservoir, that breeds sporadically.

Plate 39 (middle opposite). Male Ferruginous Duck. This is a rare vagrant from central Europe that has been seen here only once, in 1990.

Plate 40 (bottom opposite). Male Goldeneye. These are common winter visitors, frequenting the reservoir from October to May, before heading north to their breeding grounds.

Plate 41 (top right). Male Smew. These are rare winter visitors to south-eastern Britain. Swithland Reservoir is at the northern limit of their winter range, and sightings are sporadic.

Plate 42 (middle right). Male Ruddy Duck, with its distinctive blue bill..

Plate 43 (bottom right). Ruddy Duck's nest and eggs. at Swithland Reservoir, May 1984.
The Ruddy Duck, is a native to the Americas, and the British ferel population only dates back to 1953, when it first escaped into the wild. It has bred at Swithland Reservoir most years since 1973 The species is now subject to culling due to interbreeding with the White-headed Duck, a threatened European native.

Plate 44 (above left). Male South African Shelduck on the dam wall. September 1999. This is one of several exotics to have appeared at the reservoir, having escaped from a wildfowl collection.

Plate 45 (above right). Male Chiloe Wigeon at Swithland Reservir in April 1998 – another escapee, this one native to South America.

Plate 46 (middle left). Male and female Gadwall. These are common winter visitors, but in recent years have also begun to breed regularly at the reservoir in small numbers

Plate 47 (below). Male Garganey. These ducks spend their summers below the Arctic circle, and winter in central Africa. Sightings at the reservoir are mainly of spring and autumn passage migrants. Very rarely a pair stays over the summer.

Plate 48 (above left). Male Kestrel caught for ringing in Quorn. This common resident breeds annually in small numbers in trees around the reservoir.

Plate 49 (above right). Osprey in the waterworks grounds in May 1983. This fish-eating bird of prey has been an extremely rare visitor to the reservoir. However, with successes in the re-introduction programme at Rutland Water there is a possibility of increased numbers throughout the region.

Plate 50 (middle left). Male Sparrowhawk. In the 1960s this species was nearly extinct in the area due to use of chlorinated hydrocarbon pesticides. Since 1980 it has recovered to become a common resident again.

Plate 51 (below left). Little Ringed Plover on the dam wall. This uncommon passage migrant has been known to breed at Swithland Reservoir, if low water levels provide suitable sites.

Plate 52 (below right). Greenshank on the Swithland dam wall. An uncommon but regular passage migrant.

72

Plate 53 (top). Newly hatched Lapwing chicks in a field adjacent to the reservoir in May 1993. Once a very common species throughout Britain, the Lapwing population has more than halved in the last 30 years, and it is doubtful if it now breeds in the Swithland Reservoir area.
Plate 54 (middle left). Snipe caught for ringing at Buddon Brook meadows in February 1991.
Plate 55 (bottom left). Snipe's nest and eggs at Ulverscroft in July 1972. Once a locally common breeding bird throughout Charnwood, it is now only a winter visitor in small numbers.
Plate 56 (middle right). Woodcock caught for ringing at Buddon Brook meadows in March 1986.
Plate 57 (bottom right). Woodcock's nest and eggs at Buddon Wood in April 1965. As with the Snipe, Britains Woodcock poulation has declined by 70% in 30 years, and there have been no recent signs of them breeding in the area.

Plate 58 (above). Gull roost in the reservoir's northern section. January 1985. These large gatherings of a mix of gull species are a familiar sight on winter evenings, with up to 15,000 birds being present on occasions.

Plate 59 (middle). Adult Little Gull. This is the world's smallest gull species, and can occasionally be seen at Swithland in the spring, when it has been known to visit along with terns on their spring journey northwards.

Plate 60 (below). Common Tern (left) and Arctic Tern (right) on the reservoir overflow. Both these species are regular passage migrants in varying numbers. Since 1993 small numbers of Common Tern have bred at Swithland Reservoir on specially constructed rafts.

Plate 61 (above). Turtle Dove taking a drink at the reservoir.

Plate 62 (left). Turtle Dove's nest and eggs, Kinchley Promontory. June 1972.

The Turtle Dove is a species in severe decline throughout the country, the population having dropped by 77% in the last 30 years. It was once a common breeding summer visitor to Swithland Reservoir, but there have been no positive breeding records since 1985.

Plate 63 (above left). Male Great Spotted Woodpecker – a common resident in the mature woodland around the reservoir..

Plate 64 (above right). Immature Green Woodpecker. This species can often be seen feeding in the grassy areas of the dam and the waterworks grounds.

Plate 65 (below). Male Lesser Spotted Woodpecker at nest along Buddon Brook . June 1975. This species is in severe decline throughout the country, The Swithland Reservoir area has always been a stronghold for it, but even here its population has fallen in recent times.

A number of the photographs are of birds in the hand. These birds have been caught for the purpose of ringing by trained and licenced ringers. When caught and handled correctly, the birds are completely safe, and undergo minimal disturbance before being released. Wild birds must not be caught except by suitably trained and licenced bird handlers.

The process of bird ringing involves the placing of an individually marked metal ring around a bird's leg. The rings are made in several sizes to fit different species – the smallest size for a Goldcrest and the largest for a Mute Swan. Bird ringing as we know it today was started by a Danish ornithologist, H.C. Mortensen in 1899. In Britain it began with two schemes in1909. Only the scheme run by Harry Forbes Witherby continued after the First World War and in 1937 this was handed over to the British Trust for Ornithology who now oversee the ringing scheme across Britain. Each individual ringer has to go through an intensive training programme and hold a current ringing licence. In 1963 the B.T.O. collaborated with other European ringing schemes to form E.U.R.I.N.G. – the European Ringing Committee. This body standardised all the information collected by the different national ringing schemes across Europe. Over the years somewhere in the region of 115 million birds have been ringed in Europe. The information gathered has given us an amazing insight into many aspects of birds' lives. Ringing data has been crucial in the conservation of certain species and their habitats.

Plate 66 (opposite top left). Reed Warbler's nest and eggs in Reed Sweet-grass at Swithland Reservoir, July 1972.

Plate 67 (opposite top right) Reed Warbler – a fairly common breeding bird and passage migrant at the reservoir.

Plate 68 (opposite bottom) Sedge Warbler – uncommon at Swithland Reservoir. A decline in numbers over recent years may have been caused by droughts in West Africa, where the birds spend the winter.

Plate 69 (Right). Male Common Redstart, caught for ringing at Buddon Brook meadows in April 1990.

Plate 70 (below) A Willow Tit (left) and Marsh Tit (right) – both these species have declined by half in the last 30 years.

Plate 71 (above left). Male Yellowhammer caught for ringing at Buddon Brook meadows. This is another species with a declining population, probably caused by changes in farming practice.
Plate 72 (above right). Yellowhammer's nest and eggs at Swithland Reservoir in May 1981. The Yellowhammer nests close to the ground amongst scrub or brambles.
Plate 73 (below) Lesser Whitethroat caught for ringing at Buddon Brook meadows. Although fairly common around Leicestershire, it breeds at Swithland Reservoir only occassionally.

4. A SYSTEMATIC ACCOUNT OF THE BIRDS OF SWITHLAND RESERVOIR

The following species are laid out in approximately the taxonomic order and using the scientific nomenclature as presented in the *'List of Recent Holarctic Bird Species'* (Voous 1977). The English names are those currently in general use and follow those in *'Palearctic Birds: a checklist of the Birds of Europe, North Africa and Asia north of the foothills of the Himalayas'* (Beaman, 1994). Several species have been split in recent years and where possible I have attempted to follow present thinking, but things are changing and they might be revised again in the future. Where possible I have given alternative or previously used English names, some of which are just for interest and some will help the reader understand which species is being referred to.

I have listed several escaped or feral species that have been seen on Swithland Reservoir, the reason for this being that their populations might make an impact on our avifauna in the future: e.g. Mandarin Duck; or their overall status might change: e.g. White-headed Duck.

Given with each species is an idea of its world-wide breeding distribution and breeding habitat, followed by its times of migration and winter distribution where applicable. There is a brief description of the adult bird and an outline of the occurrence and distribution in both Britain and Leicestershire. The last part covers the occurrence and distribution of the species with regard to Swithland Reservoir and the relevant records. Birds are never hemmed in by man-made boundaries, and when striving to understand fully why a species occurs in one particular small area every piece of knowledge is valuable even though this knowledge is far from perfect.

At the start of some sections – waterfowl, raptors, waders, gulls, owls, woodpeckers, chats and thrushes, and warblers – I have written about some of my own personal memories intertwined with some unusual facts, mainly about other members of the bird families I am about to write about in detail. These show how some species travel enormous distances on their migrations, how their habits help them survive, and how some families can be found world-wide. I hope these sections will give you as much enjoyment in reading them as they gave me in their writing and that it makes your interest and wonder in birds grow as a result.

The breeding population figures that are given to some individual species are taken mainly from the Rare Breeding Birds Panel 25th annual report: *Rare Breeding Birds in the United Kingdom in 1997* (Ogilvie, 1999): found in *British Birds Volume 92 No.7* and also from *The State of the Nation's Birds* (Mead, 2000).

Throughout the 20th century Britain's birdlife has undergone radical changes mainly due to the changing landscape brought about by agricultural changes and intensification. Some species have become more widespread and numerous while others have had their ranges contract and their numbers diminish. Unfortunately it is only in recent years that sufficient resources have been put into survey work. This allows us for the first time to have a clear picture of what is happening to Britain's birds and some of the findings are disturbing. In putting together each bird's profile I have tried to outline the historical population trend with the rather scant information that was available. To achieve this I used two main references: the *Handbook of the Birds of Europe the Middle East and North Africa: The Birds of the Western Palearctic* (Cramp, 1977-1994); and the *Breeding Birds of Britain and Ireland: A Historical Survey* (Parslow, 1973).

The recent population trends are shown in percentage increases or decreases and are those published jointly by the B.T.O. and the R.S.P.B. in *The State of the U.K.'s Birds, 1999* (Gregory, Campell and Gibbons, 2000) and cover the years from 1970 to 1998. These figures were mainly compiled from the B.T.O.'s Common Bird Census and the Waterways Bird Survey. To enlarge the picture into Europe I have also referred to the *EBCC Atlas of European Breeding Birds: Their Distribution and Abundance* (Hagemeijer and Blair, 1997).

Some of the comments regarding a species' decline are those that are widely held amongst ornithologists whilst others are my own beliefs. Today there are many pressures on our nation's birdlife such as habitat loss and pollution that are causing huge losses to our bird population and most authorities would agree on that. Given that bird numbers are already very low it is my personal opinion, however, that an ever increasing number of predators such as Sparrowhawks, Corvids, Fox, Mink and Grey Squirrels are inflicting a disproportionately large amount of damage on our bird populations.

The records of the birds of Swithland Reservoir come mainly from two sources, the published annual reports and bulletins of the Leicestershire and Rutland Ornithological Society (from 1941) and the Loughborough Naturalists' Club (from 1960). The records cover a period up to the year 2000 with only a few unusual additional records being added for that year. In most cases I have used only records of rare and unusual species that have been accepted by The Leicestershire and Rutland Referees' Committee or The British Birds Rarities Committee. On the few occasions when I have used records that have not gone through the verification process I have stated that fact in the text.

The wintering wildfowl counts were taken from the Leicestershire and Rutland Ornithological Society's Annual Reports and Bulletins. The Society's members have been carrying out these counts since 1947 for the National Wildfowl Counts organised by the Wildfowl Trust.

The status for each species seen in Leicestershire follows closely that used in *The Status of Birds in Britain and Ireland* (BOU 1971), but has two extra categories of 'Very rare' and 'Rare' as used in *The Leicestershire and Rutland Bird Report* 1998.

Very rare   Fewer than ten ever recorded.

Rare   More than ten ever recorded, but not of annual occurrence.

Scarce   Fewer than ten birds being recorded in a year or ten breeding
                 pairs annually.

Uncommon   Between ten and 100 birds occurring in a year or ten to 100
                 breeding pairs annually.

Fairly Common   Between 100 and 1000 birds occurring in a year or 100 to 1000
                 breeding pairs annually.

Common   Between 1000 and 10000 birds occurring in a year or 1000
                 to10000 breeding pairs annually.

Abundant   More than 10000 birds occurring in a year or more than 10000
                 breeding pairs annually.

DIVERS (or LOONS) Gaviidae

Red-throated Diver *Gavia stellata*

The Red-throated Diver breeds across northern Europe and Asia reaching Kamchatka and Sakhalin in the east and throughout northern North America to the coast of Greenland. In winter it is mainly a maritime species that can be found along the coast or in bays of eastern Asia, the Caspian and Black seas and around North America. It also occurs on the Great Lakes. European birds winter along the western seaboard, southward to the Mediterranean.

In Britain it nests on the quieter lochs of northern Scotland and in small numbers in northern Ireland. There was in the region of 935 breeding pairs in Britain in 1994. It is a common winter visitor and passage migrant around our coast. Passage takes place from April to June and September to November.

It breeds on lakes and pools on tundra and moorland. The nest is either a pile of aquatic vegetation and moss built in shallow water close to the water's edge or a shallow scrape on the shoreline close to the water.

The Red-throated Diver is the smallest of the loons and can easily be identified by its black up-tilted bill. In breeding plumage it has a rufous throat patch, grey face and foreneck, black and white lined nape and rear neck, white breast and grey body. It has dark legs and webbed feet. In winter the bird has grey upperparts with a pale face, throat and breast.

The Red-throated Diver is a rare winter visitor to Leicestershire's inland waters. On Swithland Reservoir it is an irregular and uncommon winter visitor that has been recorded on ten occasions since the first sighting in April 1944. All records came in a period from October to early May and all were of single birds except for one, two birds being seen between the 23rd and 26th March 1945.

Black-throated Diver *Gavia arctica*

The Black-throated Diver has a similar breeding distribution to the Red-throated Diver. It can be found throughout northern Asia, North America and Europe but it does not breed in Iceland and the more northerly Arctic Islands. In autumn the Black-throated Diver migrates south along the east coast of Asia, or to the Black and Caspian seas and in North America down the west coast. In Europe it winters along the western seaboard southward into the Mediterranean. During the winter it is found mainly on salt water and tends to be more gregarious than other Divers.

In Britain it nests in Scotland, Orkney and the Outer Hebrides but its population is probably no more than 170 pairs. During winter and on passage it can be found around our coasts in small numbers. It is a rare straggler to inland waters.

It generally breeds on large freshwater lakes. The nest is either a mound of aquatic vegetation or moss with a cup, built close to the shoreline in shallow water or a shallow depression on land close to the water's edge.

The Black-throated Diver is a good diver and dives of up to two minutes have been recorded. In breeding plumage it has a grey head, black throat patch and bordering black and white lines running down the neck, with a white breast. Its back is black with black and white chequering on the upper mantle. In winter it looks similar to the Red-throated Diver but it has a darker mantle and the bill is held more horizontally. It has a black bill and legs with webbed feet.

The Black-throated Diver is a rare winter visitor to Leicestershire. It is a rare vagrant to Swithland Reservoir that has been recorded only once. A single bird was present on the 3rd and 4th March 1962.

Great Northern Diver *Gavia immer*

The Great Northern Diver or Common Loon (as it is known in North America) breeds only in Iceland in Europe, where there are probably no more than 300 pairs. It also breeds across northern North America and on the coast of Greenland. In winter it can be found on both the east and west coast of North America and along Europe's western seaboard.

In Britain the Great Northern Diver has bred on two occasions, in Scotland in 1970 and 1997 but it is chiefly a winter visitor that is found around the coast. It is an uncommon visitor to inland waters.

It breeds on large freshwater lakes, the nest being usually on an island or a promontory. The nest can be either a shallow depression close to the water's edge or occasionally a mound of vegetation in reeds in shallow water.

The Great Northern Diver is a large bird about the size of a goose or Cormorant and it is superficially similar to the Black-throated Diver. In breeding plumage it has a dark head, white breast and black and white vertical striped areas on the neck and throat. Its body is dark with white chequering on the back. Like the smaller Black-throated Diver it has a horizontally-held dagger-like bill. The bill and legs are black and it has webbed feet. In winter plumage it is very similar to the Black-throated Diver but it is a more powerfully built bird and has a pale eye ring and a blackish half-collar. On their breeding grounds the birds are very vocal and keep you awake through the long summer evenings and into the short nights with their evocative mournful yodelling calls.

The Great Northern Diver is a rare winter visitor to Leicestershire. It is a rare straggler to Swithland Reservoir that has been seen on three occasions. Two birds were present on the 9th December 1933; one bird was recorded between 25th and 28th November 1944, and two were seen between the 8th and 22nd January 1956.

GREBES Podicipedidae

Little Grebe *Tachybaptus ruficollis*

The Little Grebe or Dabchick breeds across central and southern Europe and Asia eastwards to Japan and south to New Guinea and in Africa south of the Sahara. Only the most northerly and easterly populations are migratory, wintering within its southern breeding distribution.

In Britain it is a common resident and winter visitor. Some movement of resident birds does take place, especially during cold spells when birds will travel to rivers and tidal waters. Migrant birds arrive from the Continent from September to November and return again from March to early May.

The Little Grebe breeds on well-vegetated rivers, ponds and lakes. Its nest is a floating platform of aquatic vegetation that is often placed on the submerged branches of overhanging bushes or hidden in emergent vegetation.

It is a small squat bird with rich chestnut cheeks, small yellow-gaped black bill, dark brown mantle and buff flanks in breeding plumage. It has olive green legs with lobed toes. All grebes have lobed toes. This means they have flaps of skin along each side of the toe instead of having webbed feet. In winter it becomes paler brown around the neck and flanks and often shows a white stern.

The Little Grebe is an uncommon to fairly common resident breeding bird in Leicestershire. It was a common resident on Swithland Reservoir with two or three pairs breeding annually and there could have been more. This is a very secretive species and its numbers are hard to ascertain during the breeding season. The largest number of birds recorded at the reservoir was 30 on the 21st October 1961. In the last few years its numbers have fallen dramatically and it now breeds only intermittently. This decline could be linked to the occurrence of Mink on Swithland Reservoir.

Great Crested Grebe *Podiceps cristatus*

The Great Crested Grebe breeds across central and southern Europe southward to North Africa and throughout central Asia reaching the Sea of Japan. Scattered populations can also be found in Africa south of the Sahara, Australia and New Zealand. The northern populations are migratory, wintering just to the south of its breeding range. The northern European populations start to move south from September to November and return in March and April. Many birds move to coastal waters during prolonged periods of frost when inland waters are frozen.

British birds tend to be sedentary and pairs can be faithful to one site for long periods. During the 19th century this species was almost exterminated in Britain due to the milliner's trade. The soft thick satin breast plumage of these birds was used to adorn ladies' hats and it was given the name 'grebe fur'. In 1860 the British population was down to just 42 pairs and before the end of the 19th century it had the distinction of being the first bird to obtain statutory protection. A census taken in 1965 showed that the species had made a dramatic recovery and the British population was estimated to be 4,500 pairs. Today Britain holds somewhere in the region of 8,000 pairs. This recovery was probably due to the construction of reservoirs and gravel pits that afforded the birds large areas of breeding habitat.

It breeds on freshwater reed-fringed lakes in Europe, but in Asia it may breed on brackish or salt water. The nest is a large mound of aquatic vegetation placed in shallow water in reeds or on the submerged branches of bushes.

In breeding plumage the Great Crested Grebe is unmistakable with chestnut and black head and neck plumes, a long white-fronted slender neck and dark grey upperparts, long flattened body and brown flanks. In winter the head shows a dark cap, the face and foreneck are white and the rest of the body is dark, grey on the upperparts with brown flanks. The bill is long, slim and pinkish in colour and it has olive green legs.

The first breeding record came for Leicestershire in 1874 when a pair bred at Saddington Reservoir. The Great Crested Grebe is a common passage migrant and winter visitor to Leicestershire and an uncommon breeding bird. It is a common and noticeable resident on Swithland Reservoir. As many as eight pairs breed in some years but when the water is low and no suitable places can be found to make a nest, the birds struggle to raise a brood. In the early part of the year the amazing courtship displays can be observed with birds shaking their heads at each other while holding pond weed in their bills. Birds also swim towards each other, necks stretched out on top of the water, and as they reach each other rise up together breast to breast in synchronised display. The largest number of birds recorded on Swithland was 125 on the 27th July 1969.

Red-necked Grebe *Podiceps grisegena*

The Red-necked Grebe breeds across northern and central eastern Europe and into western Siberia nearly reaching the Ob River. It can also be found in Kazakhstan and Turkey. Other populations occur in eastern Asia from central Siberia eastwards to Kamchatka and southward to northern Japan and across northern North America. In winter birds are generally found on salt water. It winters along both coasts of North America and down the coast of eastern Asia southward to China. It can also be found on the Black and Caspian Seas. In Europe it winters mainly on the coast of the North and Baltic Seas and in parts of the Mediterranean. It is a more migratory species than the Great Crested Grebe and the European population moves westward and southward during the autumn.

Winter visitors can be seen in Britain from October to March but passage birds can be recorded as late as June or as early as August and it has attempted to breed in Scotland. In Britain it is found frequently in winter on the east coast, but appears to be scarce on western shores.

It breeds on small freshwater pools and lakes. The nest is a floating mound of aquatic vegetation with a depression on top built in shallow water, generally hidden among emergent growth.

The Red-necked Grebe is only slightly smaller than the Great Crested Grebe. In breeding plumage it has a yellow based black bill, black crown, white throat and cheeks, a thick-set chestnut neck and dark grey-brown mantle and white grey-washed flanks. The legs are dark with green tones. In winter plumage it is similar to the Great Crested Grebe but is more dusky around the head and neck and it retains the yellow base to the bill.

The Red-necked Grebe is a scarce passage migrant and winter visitor to Leicestershire. It is a scarce and irregular winter visitor and passage migrant to Swithland Reservoir. It was first recorded on Swithland Reservoir on the 6th March 1926 and has been noted on 16 occasions since. All the records except one fall in a period from September to April. The other record was of a bird in breeding plumage on the 12th May 1993.

Horned Grebe *Podiceps auritus*

The Horned Grebe or Slavonian Grebe breeds across northern Europe and Asia, reaching Kamchatka and Sakhalin in the east and over much of northern North America. It winters on the coast of eastern Asia, the Caspian and Black Seas and the west and east coasts of North America. In Europe it winters on western European coasts and reaches the Mediterranean in eastern Europe. Autumn passage starts in September and continues into November and return migration starts in April and finishes in June.

In Britain it breeds in small numbers in central Scotland. It was first discovered breeding in Invernessshire in 1908 and at present about 56 pairs breed annually in Scotland. It can be found in small numbers on inland waters and sea coasts during the winter months.

It breeds on small freshwater pools and shallow lakes surrounded by emergent vegetation. The nest is a heap of aquatic vegetation with a small depression on top built in shallow water, normally hidden amongst emergent growth.

The Horned Grebe is mid-way between the Little Grebe and Red-necked Grebe in size. In breeding plumage Horned Grebe show a stout straight bill, a black head, red eye, golden 'horns', chestnut neck and flanks and black back. At a distance this species can look almost black in summer dress. The bill and legs are grey with blue tones. In winter it is a very black and white bird, with a black cap, nape, hindneck and back, a white face, foreneck and breast and dusky flanks.

The Horned Grebe is a scarce winter visitor and passage migrant to Leicestershire. On Swithland Reservoir it is a rare and irregular winter visitor that has been recorded on 14 occasions. All but one of the records were of single birds and all except one fell in a period between September and March. The other bird appeared in April and was probably a passage migrant and two birds were present on the 21st November 1998.

Black-necked Grebe *Podiceps nigricollis*

The Black-necked Grebe or Eared Grebe breeds across central and southern Europe eastwards into Western Siberia and southwards in scattered populations over Asia Minor with a small population occurring in north-east China. It can also be found in central North America and in scattered populations in south and east Africa. It winters on sea coasts and inland on lakes and reservoirs. In winter it can be found over much of the western United States, Asia Minor and on the coast of eastern Asia from northern Japan south to Hong Kong and over central and southern Europe, reaching North Africa.

In Britain it is a winter visitor and passage migrant with small numbers remaining to breed. Passage begins in March and goes on into mid-May and the return movement starts again in July and goes through to September. It breeds regularly in central Scotland but only isolated pairs nest elsewhere in Britain and probably no more than 46 pairs now breed annually. In most of Britain they have proved sporadic breeders, colonising an area in good numbers then, if conditions vary, disappearing. A good example of this was in Ireland between 1929 and 1932 when about 250 pairs bred annually on Lough Funshinagh in Roscommon. This species now no longer nests in Ireland.

It often breeds in colonies and prefers shallow well-vegetated freshwater lakes. The nest is a mound of aquatic vegetation built in shallow water generally in the cover of emergent vegetation.

The Black-necked Grebe is smaller and more slender than the Horned Grebe, with a finer bill. The lower mandible is angled upward giving the bill an up-tilted appearance. The bill and legs are black. In breeding plumage it shows a black head, neck, breast and back with chestnut flanks but its most distinctive feature is the yellow fan of feathers behind its red eye. Like the Horned Grebe these birds look completely black at a distance. In winter plumage it is very similar to the Horned Grebe but it is more dusky around the cheeks and neck.

It is a rare winter visitor and uncommon passage migrant and summer visitor to Leicestershire. It is an uncommon and irregular visitor to Swithland Reservoir that has been seen in every month except June. A pair were seen displaying on the 31st May 1980. Birds were present in May, July and August in 1983 and some display was also noted. It remains an exciting prospect that some day this species might breed on Swithland Reservoir. The largest number recorded in spring were four birds in breeding plumage on the 15th April 1944. The highest autumn counts came in 1997 when seven birds were present on the 21st September with six remaining at the reservoir throughout October rising to eight on the 18th October 1997. This is the largest number ever recorded at Swithland.

SHEARWATERS and PETRELS Procellariiformes

STORM-PETRELS *Hydrobatidae*

Leach's Storm-petrel *Oceanodroma leucorhoa*

The Leach's Storm-petrel breeds on oceanic islands in the north Atlantic and Pacific and winters in the subtropical waters of the southern oceans.

It nests in burrows and crevices on rocky coasts. In Britain it breeds on the Outer Hebrides and Shetland.

The Leach's Storm-petrel is a small fork-tailed bird that has blackish-brown plumage with a grey wing stripe and a white rump divided by a dark line. It has a black bill and legs. Birds migrating south in the autumn occasionally get caught up in strong westerly gales. Many hundreds of birds can be blown off course and swept inland and such movements are given the name 'wrecks'.

The last major 'wreck' to affect this species in Britain happened in the autumn of 1978 and one bird ended up at Swithland Reservoir. It was seen on the 2nd of October.

CORMORANTS Phalacrocoracidae

Great Cormorant *Phalacrocorax carbo*

The Great Cormorant has a wide but fragmented distribution breeding on the coasts of the north Atlantic from eastern Canada to Greenland, Iceland and northern Norway southward to France. It can also be found in central and southern Europe and Asia eastward to Japan. Populations also occur on the coast of west Africa and inland east Africa southward to the Cape and in Australia and New Zealand. It winters on the coasts of eastern Canada, central and southern Europe to North Africa and throughout much of southern and eastern Asia. It is resident in Africa, India eastward to China and in Australia and New Zealand.

In Britain it breeds around our coasts. Recently it has started to breed more frequently inland and numbers are increasing.

It is a colonial breeder that nests on sea cliffs or rocky islets and by inland freshwater lakes in trees. In trees the nest is usually made of sticks and lined with plant material while on cliff ledges on the coast it is a mound of seaweed and sticks.

The Cormorant is a large bird with a hefty hooked bill and a long, usually bent neck. It can often be observed swimming low in the water reminiscent of a loon or drying its outstretched wings on a promontory. The adults are generally dark all over with yellow basal skin to the lower mandible, the rest of the bill being greyish. It has a white throat and black legs.

It is a common resident and an uncommon breeding bird in Leicestershire. Records have increased dramatically in Leicestershire over the past decade. This is almost certainly due to the colonisation of Rutland Water. It first bred at Rutland Water in 1992 when five pairs raised seven young. By 1993, 12 pairs were breeding and the enormous total of 825 birds was counted on the 25th September that year. In 1996 the number of breeding pairs had risen to 36. It is not surprising that with such large numbers being present in the region, Swithland Reservoir's records would also have increased. Birds can now be seen throughout the year at Swithland Reservoir and in 1997 two pairs bred raising two young and a count of 124 birds was noted on the 21st October 1997. Breeding continued in 1998 when two pairs nested raising at least three young and the largest count for this water was made on the 14th October 1998 when 163 birds were present. Seventeen pairs bred in 1999 raising a total of 38 young and 134 birds were present on the 24th October 1999. Eighteen pairs bred in 2000 raising a total of 55 young. Prior to the 1990s the Cormorant was mainly a winter visitor and passage migrant in small numbers. Birds showing characteristics of the Continental race *Phalacrocorax carbo sinensis*, showing more white on the neck, have been recorded in four years since their first appearance in 1980 and all have been in a period from February to April.

European Shag *Phalacrocorax aristotelis*

The European Shag is confined as a breeding species to the coasts of Europe, the Black Sea and North Africa. In winter the most northerly populations move south but all winter on coasts within the species' breeding range.

In Britain it breeds on rocky cliffs or boulder-strewn shores around our coasts. The nest is a mound of seaweed and other vegetation with a small depression lined with finer material. The largest concentrations are on the western seaboard. It is a more marine species than the Cormorant and only occasionally wanders inland. Most of the records inland have a bias towards the autumn and winter and involve mainly immature birds.

The Shag is slightly smaller and slimmer than the Cormorant and differs in winter plumage in having a yellow bill and less white on the throat. In breeding plumage it has a distinctive crest, the black plumage has a glossy green sheen and it has a dark bill and legs.

The Shag is a scarce autumn and winter visitor to Leicestershire that was first recorded in the county in 1946. It is a rare autumn and winter visitor to Swithland Reservoir that has been recorded on seven occasions. All the records were in a period from August to February and all but one were of single birds. Two birds were present on the 4th and 5th February 1961.

HERONS, STORKS and IBISES Ciconiiformes
HERONS *Ardeidae*

Great Bittern *Botaurus stellaris*
The Bittern breeds throughout central and southern Europe reaching North Africa and across central Asia as far as Sakhalin and Japan in the east. A small population can also be found in southern Africa. It winters in central and southern Europe and from Pakistan across northern India to Bangladesh and eastwards through south-east China and in scattered parts of southern Africa.

It has a patchy distribution over most of Europe and the more northerly breeding birds move south and west during the winter, arriving in Britain during November and returning in February and March. In Britain the Bittern became extinct as a breeding species in the latter part of the 19th century. It re-colonised East Anglia early in the 20th century and numbers rose until there were over 100 booming males in the early 1960s. The severe winter of 1963 cut the population back dramatically. In the spring male Bitterns announce that they have taken up territory with a booming call that can carry for over a mile. In Britain today the Bittern still remains a rare winter visitor from continental Europe with birds arriving from November to February. The breeding numbers still continue to decrease. In 1999 only 13-14 individuals were heard booming in the whole of the country and the majority of these were in the bird's stronghold of East Anglia. The main threat to the Bittern over much of its range appears to be habitat destruction. It is a very secretive species and seldom seen.

The Bittern is a bird of swamps and wetlands with extensive reedbeds of *Phragmites* or bulrush *Typha*. The nest is placed in dense reedswamp and consists of a mound of dead reeds and other vegetation with a depression that is lined with finer material.

The Bittern is a large brown and buff heron with dark mottling and streaking. It has a dark cap and black moustachial stripes, a large yellow bill and green legs. In flight it could easily be mistaken for an owl with its brown mottled plumage.

The Bittern is a rare winter visitor to Leicestershire. It is also a rare winter visitor to Swithland Reservoir that has been seen on eight occasions. These birds could have been either immigrants from the continent or British birds that had dispersed during the winter. Single birds were recorded in 1947, 1970 and 1983. There were two records in 1986 - one at the beginning of the year and the other at the latter end, the bird arriving in December and leaving in March 1987. One was present from November 1988 until February 1989 and another from December 1989 until February 1990. The last record came from Swithland in January 1991. All the records from 1986 onwards could relate to the same bird returning in successive winters.

Grey Heron *Ardea cinerea*
The Grey Heron breeds throughout much of Europe and across central and southern Asia eastwards to Japan and southward to Java. It also occurs in southern and eastern Africa. It winters in western and southern Europe, southern Asia, western Africa and Africa south of the Sahara. Autumn migration starts in September and continues through October. Return movement takes place in February and March. Some of the northern and eastern European populations migrate south and west during the autumn and some winter as far south as northern Africa.

The Grey Heron is resident in Britain but there is a certain amount of immigration from continental Europe during the autumn and winter. Herons are susceptible to long periods of cold freezing conditions and during severe winters like 1963 their population can drop dramatically.

The Grey Heron usually nests in tall trees or occasionally on the ground, especially in reed beds. The nest is a platform of sticks with a shallow depression lined with twigs. They generally breed in colonies but on occasions they do nest singly or in small numbers.

The adult Grey Heron is a large bird with a long dagger-like yellow bill, white crown and face and black head plumes extending from the eye and down the nape. It has a grey back, long pale neck with black central streaking and white underparts and long yellow-grey legs.

The Grey Heron is an uncommon resident and breeding bird in Leicestershire. On Swithland Reservoir it is a resident in small numbers and in previous decades odd pairs occasionally bred with varying success. It has bred annually since 1995; three pairs nested in 1997, five pairs in 1999 raising at least six young, and eleven pairs in 2000. Prior to these records one or two pairs only had bred during any given year. The largest count for this water came on the 26th October 1996 when 24 birds were present.

SPOONBILLS Threskiornithidae

Eurasian Spoonbill *Platalea leucorodia*

The Spoonbill breeds in scattered colonies in central and southern Europe and Asia with a few birds breeding on islands in the Red Sea. It winters in southern Europe, North Africa and southern Asia, and is resident in India. It migrates in August and September and returns in February and March. The nearest major population to Britain is in Holland where 600 pairs breed annually.

In Britain it is an uncommon but regular visitor especially during spring and autumn migration. The vast majority of records are from the English east coast. It actually bred regularly in East Anglia until the middle of the 17th century. In 1998 a pair raised two young at a site in eastern England. This was the first successful breeding in Britain for over 300 years.

It is a bird of coastal lagoons, river deltas and marshes. They are colonial breeders and nest either on the ground or in trees. The nest is a platform of sticks and twigs lined with grass when in trees, or a mound of reeds when on the ground. This species is globally threatened mainly because of habitat destruction, pollution and disturbance.

The Spoonbill is roughly the same size as the Grey Heron and has a similar upright stance. In breeding plumage it is almost completely white except for a tinge of yellow on the short nape crest, a yellow half collar on the frontal part of the lower neck and small yellow areas on the throat and at the base and tip of the bill. The most distinctive feature about this bird, however, is its long dark broad bill that is spoon-shaped at the tip. The Spoonbill uses this amazing bill in a side-to-side sweeping action where it appears to hoover a section of shallow water to obtain a wide range of aquatic animals and insects. The legs are black.

It is a rare vagrant to Leicestershire that has been recorded once at Swithland Reservoir. An adult was seen on the 14th August 1989, and this constituted the 12th county record.

THE WATERFOWL Anatidae

Swithland Reservoir was built in 1896. This has given the margins over a hundred years to develop a rich reed-swamp shoreline and aquatic vegetation. Swithland is a reservoir at low altitude and is fairly shallow with a maximum depth of only forty feet. This allows the water to be degrees warmer than that in reservoirs situated at higher altitudes or of a greater depth. Consequently this has a propagation effect on the aquatic life, enabling it to grow faster and in greater profusion. The reservoir has now become very important for the numbers of breeding waterfowl and also for the considerable numbers and variety that occur during the winter. There are few sites in Leicestershire that can boast Great Crested Grebe, Little Grebe, Cormorant, Grey Heron, Mute Swan, Canada Goose, Tufted Duck, Pochard, Mallard, Gadwall, Teal, Shoveler and Ruddy Duck on their list of breeding birds.

When you see large flocks of duck on a reservoir, you probably wonder whether there is going to be sufficient food to sustain them, but when you study their actual feeding requirements you learn to appreciate how the water provides the necessary food.

Take, for instance, the two common diving ducks, the Tufted Duck and Pochard which associate in large mixed flocks and are closely related species, despite having quite different diets. The Tufted Duck feeds mainly on insect larvae, crustaceans and molluscs while the Pochard takes the leaves and stems of water plants. Another diving duck, the Goldeneye, also dives deeply to feed on molluscs and crustaceans and the newest arrival at Swithland Reservoir, the Ruddy Duck, although a diving duck, is wholly vegetarian, feeding on marginal sedges, bulrushes and various bottom growing plants. It must have found a niche because its numbers have increased steadily.

The various dabbling ducks tip upside-down to feed on plant and animal life so they are unable to reach the plants and animals that the diving ducks manage to find. Mallard and Teal feed on plant material as do the Gadwall although the latter will take insects. The Shoveler with its unique filtration system inside its bill takes in small animals and seeds that would be too small for other ducks to procure in sufficient quantity. The Wigeon is a grazing duck and so probably does not feed much on the reservoir. A lot of dabbling ducks leave the reservoir at night to feed on the flood meadows of the Soar Valley.

The sawbills, Red-breasted Merganser, Goosander and Smew are usually here in small numbers during the winter months and are of only occasional occurrence. They feed mainly on fish and larger animal life that they catch with the aid of a serrated bill.

The Mute Swan, with its long neck, feeds mainly on aquatic vegetation and can procure food further down than the dabbling ducks. Canada Geese, on the other hand, normally crop the vegetation on the edges of the reservoir and can occasionally be seen grazing in nearby fields.

Of the other common species of birds that spend their time on the open water, both the Great Crested Grebe and the Little Grebe feed mainly on fish although the Great Crested will take molluscs and insect larvae. The Cormorant is one of the reservoir's breeding newcomers and feeds predominantly on fish. Each bird requires a daily intake of 1.5 pounds. The Coot is abundant on the reservoir and these birds feed on grass and grain taken from the reservoir's margins. If you watch Coot over a period of time, you will see them dive in a fashion or plunge into the water to acquire aquatic vegetation or molluscs.

It is clear from this that through the different feeding habits and different food requirements, Swithland Reservoir can support a rich and varied wildfowl population.

During January the average number of wildfowl on the reservoir is about 1,200 birds and as many as 40 different wild species have been noted since the reservoir was built. These birds will have travelled here from as far afield as northern Scandinavia, Iceland, Arctic Russia, central and eastern Europe and parts of Russia which lie well into Asia. As many of the natural wetlands of Britain and much of Europe have been drained, the man-made reservoirs have become more and more important to the many birds which find refuge on them. Therefore, Swithland Reservoir should remain a sanctuary for its varied waterfowl and be protected at all costs.

SWANS Cygnus

Mute Swan *Cygnus olor*
In its true wild state the Mute Swan has a scattered distribution across central Asia from the Black and Caspian Seas to northern China. It winters on the shores of the Black and Caspian Seas, in parts of Greece

and Turkey and also in China. It has been introduced to much of central Europe, North America, South Africa, Australia and New Zealand. In Britain and Ireland the Mute Swan is mainly sedentary. Some of the northern and eastern populations in Europe are migratory and move south-west in winter, some occasionally reaching Britain.

The Mute Swan has long been semi-domesticated in Britain and this situation probably dates back to medieval times. The British population appears to be static at about 19,000 birds, although in recent years large numbers have succumbed to lead poisoning and pollution.

It can be found on freshwater ponds, rivers and lakes. It makes a very large nest mound that is composed of reed stems and other vegetation with a depression on top. The nest is placed in shallow water or close to the water's edge.

This species can be readily identified by its large size, white plumage and long curved neck. It has an orange bill with a black knob at its base and black legs. The male has a larger knob at the base of his bill than the female. The male is often called the 'Cob' while the female is known by the name 'Pen'. Juvenile birds are a dirty brown but they slowly attain their white plumage over their first year and they are nearly completely white by their second autumn.

The Mute Swan is a fairly common resident and an uncommon breeding bird in Leicestershire. It is a resident on Swithland Reservoir that occurs in varying numbers. The numbers are generally small during the summer months. Usually one or two pairs remain to breed with varying success. The largest breeding number recorded was in 1975 when the reservoir held four pairs. The highest number of birds recorded for this water was 40 on the 13th November 1994.

Bewick's Swan *Cygnus columbianus*

The Bewick's Swan or Tundra Swan is the smallest swan to visit Britain. It breeds across Arctic Siberia and North America. It winters in western Europe mainly in the Netherlands, Britain and Ireland and in eastern China, Korea and Japan. The sub-species Whistling Swan of North America migrates to the southern United States.

Nearly 90% of the European wintering population can be found at fifteen sites across the Netherlands, Britain and Ireland. Birds arrive in Britain in late October and November and leave in March or early April.

It nests on low lying tundra which has pools and lakes. The nest is a large heap of vegetation consisting of grasses, sedges, moss and lichens, with a depression on top. In winter it can be found on lakes, reservoirs and areas of flooded grassland.

The adult Bewick's Swan has white plumage and a black bill with a yellow base which often ends abruptly being either rounded or square ended, the yellow falling short of its nostrils. It also has black legs. It differs from the similar Whooper Swan in its smaller size, shorter neck and having less yellow on the bill. The juvenile is grey-brown and has a pink base to the bill.

The Bewick's Swan is an uncommon winter visitor and passage migrant to Leicestershire. It is a slightly more frequent visitor to Swithland than the Whooper Swan although it is still a scarce winter visitor. This species was first recorded at the reservoir by Montague Browne in 1904. The Bewick's Swan has been recorded on 30 occasions since. Most of the groups are small but double figure flocks have been recorded on eleven occasions. The largest number recorded was a flock of circa 48 birds on the 27th October 1991. All the records fall in a period from October to early April. As with the Whooper Swan, visits by this species are normally short.

Whooper Swan *Cygnus cygnus*

The Whooper Swan breeds across northern Europe and Asia from Iceland in the west to Kamchatka and Sakhalin in the east. It winters in western Europe and areas around the Black and Caspian Seas and also in eastern China, Korea and Japan.

Most of the birds that winter in Britain and Ireland come from Iceland and these spend the winter in Scotland and Ireland. Smaller numbers arrive from Scandinavia and Russia. They have their own defined wintering area in East Anglia and it is probably these birds that visit Swithland. Occasionally wild pairs nest in northern Scotland.

It nests on the edge of shallow lakes and pools in the taiga (northern coniferous forests) and more open lakes and pools in Iceland. Like the other swans' the nest is a large heap of reeds, sedges and other vegetation with a depression on top that is usually placed close to the water's edge. In winter it can be found along coasts and in areas of flooded grassland and it also feeds on agricultural land.

The Whooper Swan is a very large bird and is similar in size to the Mute Swan. This bird differs from the Mute Swan in having a straighter neck and a large wedge shaped bill that is mainly yellow. Like the other two swan species the adult has white plumage. It has a black-tipped yellow bill in which the yellow normally ends in a point just below the nostril. It has black legs. The juvenile is grey-brown with pink at the base of the bill. Both the Whooper Swan and Bewick's Swan are quite vocal giving calls more reminiscent of geese, unlike the Mute Swan that is generally silent except for the sound of its wing beats.

The Whooper Swan is a scarce winter visitor and passage migrant to Leicestershire. It is a scarce winter visitor to Swithland Reservoir with birds being recorded from October onwards with the last sightings coming in March. There have been 14 records since a flock of five was seen in January 1942. The largest number recorded on the reservoir was 19 birds, 17 adults and two first winter birds on the 28th October 1991. All the other sightings consisted of small groups not exceeding five birds. Like the Bewick's Swan these birds normally stay only a few hours before continuing on their journey. I have seen one record of 60 wild swans flying over the reservoir on the 21st February 1988 but unfortunately they could not be specifically identified.

GEESE Anser, Branta

Pink-footed Goose *Anser brachyrhynchus*

The Pink-footed Goose breeds in eastern Greenland, Iceland and Svalbard (Spitzbergen). It winters in western Europe, the Greenland and Iceland birds wintering in Britain and Ireland and the birds from Svalbard in the Netherlands, Belgium and Denmark.

It is a common winter visitor to Britain arriving in late September and October and leaving again in April and early May.

It nests on hummocks in tundra and also in rocky gorges and on cliff sides. The nest is a shallow depression lined with moss, lichen, plant material and down. The Pink-footed Goose often breeds in colonies. In winter it can be found on pastureland, stubble and arable land.

The adult Pink-footed Goose is a small goose. It has a grey mantle with pale feather edgings forming bars across the back, a short dark head and neck, brown breast and upper belly which shows a pink suffusion and dark, slightly pale-barred flanks. It has a white rear which extends from just behind the legs to the undertail coverts. It has a small dark triangular bill with a pink band across it and diagnostic pink legs. The juveniles are plainer and show buff-pink legs.

Wild Pink-footed Geese are scarce winter visitors to Leicestershire. It is a rare visitor to Swithland Reservoir that has been recorded on five occasions. On four of these occasions only single birds were recorded and it has to be more than likely that most, if not all, of these individuals were escapes from wildfowl collections. On the 10th February 1994 four birds flew south-east over the reservoir and these were probably genuinely wild birds considering a flock of 118 birds was noted flying over the Soar Valley and smaller flocks were seen in the Wreake Valley during the early part of that year.

Greater White-fronted Goose *Anser albifrons*

The White-fronted Goose breeds across Siberia, northern North America and Greenland. They winter in western and south-east Europe across to Turkey, the Black and Caspian Seas, Iran, China, Japan and the southern United States.

It is a winter visitor to Britain arriving in October and November and departing in March and April.

It breeds on tundra, either along the coast or inland on hilly areas and bogs. They often breed in large numbers near the nests of Rough-legged Buzzards, Merlin or Peregrine. The nest is a shallow depression lined with plant material and down.

The White-fronted Goose is a medium-sized grey goose. The adult has a dark grey-brown mantle with pale feather edging forming bars across the back. The head and neck are grey-brown but the breast and upper belly are paler, the latter showing black transverse lines. It has white extending from behind the legs through to the undertail coverts. The legs are orange and it has a white blaze around the base of its bill from which it gets its name. There are two separate races which winter in Britain: one with yellow bill *'flavirostris'* which breeds in Greenland and winters in Ireland, west Scotland and west Wales and the other with a pink bill *'albifrons'* which breeds on the Siberian Tundra and winters in Southern England and scattered areas throughout Europe. The juveniles are plainer looking, lacking the white blaze on the bill and black bars on the belly.

The truly wild White-fronted Goose is an uncommon winter visitor and passage migrant to Leicestershire. This species has been recorded on three occasions at Swithland Reservoir. Two of these records refer to single birds of unknown origin and were most likely escapes from captivity. The third record was on the 18th May 1962, when a flock of 90 birds was observed flying over the reservoir and judging from the date these were probably late passage migrants and were almost certainly wild birds..

Greylag Goose *Anser anser*

The Greylag Goose breeds in scattered populations in northern, central and south-eastern Europe. It occurs in a wide band across central Asia eastwards to the Sea of Japan. It winters in southern and western Europe, North Africa, and around the Black and Caspian Seas, northern India and eastern China.

Over a century ago, the wild Greylag Geese bred in many parts of Britain. In recent times, however, the only birds that are met with throughout much of Britain and Ireland are of introduced stock and the only wild breeding birds that can still be found are restricted to northern Scotland. During the 1980's the British feral breeding population increased by 13% per annum to a total of 19,500 birds by the middle of 1991. In winter the feral British population is augmented by wild birds from the continent but these move mainly to favoured sites in northern England, south-western Scotland and Ireland.

It nests near freshwater marshes, lakes, ponds and rivers with adjacent grassland or cultivation. The nest is usually a shallow depression sparsely lined with plant material and down. In wetter locations it makes a mound of sticks, reeds and other plant material. The nest is usually placed close to the water and often in the cover of reeds or bushes.

The Greylag Goose is a large bulky-looking bird. It has a grey-brown mantle and the pale feather edgings form bars across the back. The head, neck and belly are slightly paler grey-brown and like the other grey geese it has white extending from behind the legs to the undertail coverts. It has pink legs and an orange/pink bill. In flight it shows characteristic lavender-grey fore-wings and rump. The juveniles are more scaly looking on their backs.

Until the last few years this species was considered to be an uncommon and irregular visitor to Swithland Reservoir. Over the last decade, however, the Greylag Goose has started to breed in the feral state in Leicestershire and its numbers have risen dramatically. It is now a fairly common resident in Leicestershire but remains an uncommon breeding bird. It is a fairly regular visitor to Swithland Reservoir but their numbers are usually relatively small. Large numbers do, however, occur from time to time. The largest count I have for the reservoir is of 180 birds that were present during September 1995.

Snow Goose *Anser caerulescens*

The Snow Goose breeds in north-east Siberia and arctic North America and winters in the southern United States and Mexico.

Occasionally, genuine vagrants have been recorded in Britain and Ireland, especially in the company of Greenland White-fronted Geese in Scotland and Ireland and with Pink-footed Geese in Scotland and northern England. In most cases odd birds turn up in the company of Canada Geese or Greylag Geese and they are probably escapes from captivity, or feral birds. In Britain escaped birds have started to inter-breed with grey geese and so hybrid birds can occasionally be seen. The feral population in Britain was estimated at about 250 birds in 1992, but as yet it is not considered to be a self-sustaining population although they do breed.

In the wild it nests on lowland wet and rocky tundra, generally close to water. The nest is a shallow depression that is lined with grass, plant material and down and is hidden in vegetation.

The Snow Goose is a small goose that has two colour forms. The white phase has white plumage with black primaries, reddish legs and bill. The blue phase has a grey/brown body and a white head and neck. The Snow Goose is a scarce resident feral species in Leicestershire that has been seen on Swithland Reservoir on two occasions: the 20th May 1975, and 7th February 1987.

Canada Goose *Branta canadensis*

The Canada Goose is a native of North America which, like the previous species, migrates down to the Gulf of Mexico to winter.

Feral birds can be found in Britain, Ireland and Scandinavia with smaller populations elsewhere in western Europe. Genuine vagrants, however, have been recorded in Britain but these are very rare and they are often seen in association with wild geese. The Canada Goose with which most of us are familiar was introduced and has now become a common sight throughout most of Britain. It was first recorded as being domesticated in Britain as early as 1678. In 1953 the British population was 2,500-4,000 birds that had risen to an estimated 64,000 birds by 1992.

It breeds from lowland tundra to freshwater lakes, rivers, reservoirs and gravel pits with well vegetated islands. It usually nests close to water under the cover of vegetation where it makes a low mound of leaves, grass and other plant material with a depression on top which is lined with down.

The Canada Goose is a large goose with a brown mantle that has pale edges to some feathers which form faint bars across its back. It has a long black neck and head, the black head broken only by a white bar which goes from behind the eye and under the chin. The breast and belly are paler brown but it has slightly darker flanks and white from behind the legs extending to the undertail coverts. It has a black bill and dark grey legs.

The Canada Goose is now a common resident and regular breeding bird in Leicestershire. It is a winter visitor to Swithland Reservoir and a resident in small numbers. The first breeding records came early in the 20th century shortly after the reservoir was completed. In recent times, however, it was not recorded breeding again until 1956 and it has bred in most years since. Two pairs have bred in some years. Occasionally very large flocks come to rest on the reservoir for short periods. The largest flock to be seen on this water was 1,040 on the 20th September 1992.

Barnacle Goose *Branta leucopsis*

The Barnacle Goose breeds in Svalbard (Spitzbergen), Greenland, Novaya Zemlya and Vaigach Island and, since about 1975, on islands in the Baltic. It winters on northern European shores mainly in Ireland, western Scotland and the Netherlands.

Birds arrive in Britain during late September and October and leave in March and April.

It nests on cliffs or on the ground and in some areas in close proximity to a breeding Gyr Falcon *Falco rusticolus* from which it gains protection from such animals as Arctic Fox *Alopex lagopus*. It is generally a colonial nester. Its nest is a low heap of grass and other plant material with the depression on top lined with down.

The adult Barnacle Goose is smaller than the Canada Goose with a shorter neck. It has grey upperparts, barred black with faint white feather edgings and white underparts with grey-barred flanks. The neck and cap are black and it has a characteristic white or yellow-tinged face. The bill and legs are black.

In Leicestershire the wild Barnacle Goose is a scarce winter visitor but occasionally odd birds turn up with Canada Geese and these are normally escapes from captivity. The Barnacle Goose has been seen at Swithland Reservoir on four occasions. In 1980 and 1981 single birds were seen with Canada Geese and in September 1994, two birds were present again in the company of Canada Geese. All these records probably refer to escapes from captivity. On the 3rd January 1993, three birds were seen flying over the reservoir and these were far more likely to have been of wild origin.

Bar-headed Goose *Anser indicus*

The Bar-headed Goose breeds in central Asia on high mountain plateaux up to 5000 metres. It winters in northern India and Pakistan on lakes, rivers and marshes. In recent years the world population has been much reduced and now stands at about 10,000 birds. A feral population established itself for a few years in southern Sweden around the 1930s.

It nests in colonies by saline lakes or on open wet ground. Like some other geese it often nests in close proximity to a raptor, in this case the Upland Buzzard *Buteo hemilasius*, from which it gains protection.

When seen in the company of other geese it looks very pale. The adult Bar-headed Goose has a pale grey mantle with the pale feather edgings forming bars across its back. It has a white head with two distinctive black bars across its nape from which it derives its name. The neck is dark grey with a white stripe running down the sides of the neck. The breast and belly are grey with darker barring on the flanks and it is white from behind the legs extending to the undertail coverts. The bill is yellow with a black tip and the legs are yellow-orange.

This species is kept commonly in wildfowl collections and escaped birds can be found from time to time in the company of Canada Geese or Greylag Geese. There has been one record of this species at Swithland Reservoir on the 26th October 1996.

SHELDUCKS Tadorna

Ruddy Shelduck *Tadorna ferruginea*

The Ruddy Shelduck breeds across central Asia as far as China with only a small population extending into the extreme south-east part of Europe. There is also another fragmented population in north-west Africa. In winter they move into southern Asia in an area stretching from Afghanistan east to southern China. It is a rare straggler to western Europe including Britain.

It breeds by brackish lakes, freshwater lakes and rivers in open country and like the Shelduck it nests in holes preferably in river banks or coastal cliffs. The nest is a shallow hollow, lined with down. It is generally an upland species in the summer, breeding at over 5,000 metres. They are nomadic in winter and can be found on lowland marshes.

The Ruddy Shelduck is the size of a small goose with a rusty orange plumage, black primaries, rump and tail and a paler buff head. The male differs from the female in having a black neck collar. The bill and legs are black. In flight it shows a black tail, rump, primaries and secondaries, the last showing a green sheen in good light, and a white forewing.

Like so many wildfowl, this species is frequently kept in captivity and most records refer to escaped birds. There have been three records on Swithland Reservoir and all involved single birds: 25th June 1977; 20th September 1985 and 5th January 1986.

Common Shelduck *Tadorna tadorna*

The Shelduck has two breeding populations. The European population breeds around the coast of southern Scandinavia, Britain and the Atlantic coast of France with isolated pockets in the Mediterranean. The Asiatic population extends from south-eastern Europe across Turkey through central Asia as far as China. In Asia birds favour salt lakes and are found less frequently on freshwater. After the breeding season a large proportion of the western European population of 180,000 birds moves to the Waddenzee in Germany to moult. In Europe birds winter on the central western coasts and around the Mediterranean and Black Seas. In Asia they winter in Asia Minor and south-eastern China.

The Shelduck is a common coastal and estuarine duck, breeding all around the British Isles. The breeding population of Britain is around 11,000 pairs. Passage takes place from February to mid-May and from mid-July to September. Winter visitors arrive from September onwards.

It derives its name from the word 'sheld' meaning 'pied'. An old name for this species was 'Burrow Duck' because it often nests in a rabbit hole. It breeds in a variety of holes and cavities from haystacks to holes in trees. The nest is a shallow hollow, sparsely lined with plant material and down. In Britain an important food source for this bird is the Spire-shell Snail *Hydrobia ulvae* which makes up over 80% of its diet.

The Shelduck is a large goose-like duck, very conspicuous with what appears to be, at a distance, completely black and white plumage. At close range the adult has a bottle green head and upper neck, chestnut breast band around the body, black line down the scapulars, black primaries, secondaries, tip of tail and belly stripe and buff undertail coverts. The rest of the plumage is white. It has pink legs and a red bill. The adult male has a large knob at the base of the bill.

In the past two decades the numbers of Shelduck seen in Leicestershire have risen probably because they started to breed at Rutland Water in 1977, and have now become resident there. In 1995 eight pairs raised at least 59 young. In Leicestershire it is now an uncommon passage migrant and winter visitor and a scarce breeding bird. This species is an irregular winter visitor and passage migrant to Swithland Reservoir. The largest counts made at the reservoir were of ten birds. This number has been seen on three occasions: 30th January 1972; 8th August 1989, and 5th September 1995.

PERCHING DUCKS Aix

Wood Duck *Aix sponsa*

The Wood Duck or Carolina Duck is a bird of central and southern North America, where it inhabits rivers and lakes and breeds in holes in trees in adjacent woodland. It winters in the southern part of its breeding range south to central Mexico.

In Britain it is commonly kept in wildfowl collections and escapes are found quite frequently. It was first introduced into England in the 1870s and there have been two small feral populations, one in the Lake District and the other in East Anglia but neither became fully established. More recently 24 pairs bred in Kent during 1996.

The male is unmistakable in breeding plumage with a large metallic green drooping crest bordered by a thin white line, black head, white throat-patch forming two distinct bars across the face, rufous breast, buff flanks bordered by white and iridescent blue and green upperparts and a black stern. The bill is red with a black central ridge and nail and a thin yellow line around its base. It has a red eye-ring and yellow legs. The female is similar in shape but greyer and has a less pronounced crest. It has a grey head, grey-brown upperparts, white throat and brown underparts mottled buff. It has a noticeable white eye-ring and eye-stripe, dark bill and dark legs with a yellow suffusion.

The first record for Swithland Reservoir came in 1982 and birds were recorded quite frequently during the next four years. Two birds were present on the 1st May 1983.

Mandarin Duck *Aix galericulata*

The Mandarin is a native of eastern Asia where it occurs in northern China, Japan and the extreme eastern Soviet Union. It winters in Japan and eastern China. It migrates from late August to November with return passage taking place from March to early May. Like the previous species they favour streams and lakes in secluded woodland where they nest in holes in trees. Unfortunately the wild population has declined significantly in recent years due to the destruction of habitat and large numbers being exported from China for wildfowl collections. Their numbers in the wild could be as low as 6,000 pairs.

The Mandarin was first introduced to Britain before 1745 but started to breed in the feral state only in 1971 and now there are as many as 3,500 pairs breeding in southern England, making this population very significant to this species' future.

The male is colourful and unmistakable in breeding plumage, having a red bill, large head with a slight crest, a black, blue-green and copper-purple shot iridescent crown, white head band, orange side-whiskers, dark purple breast with two vertical white and black stripes, white belly and buff flanks. The central tertials are large, forming the orange sails that protrude above the back. It has a long tail with white undertail coverts. The upperparts and tail are dark brown glossed green but it has white outer scapulars. The legs are yellow. The female is similar to the female Wood Duck being a drab grey-brown. It has a grey-brown head with a narrow white eye-ring and a thin eye-stripe which extends back towards the nape. The mantle and tail are olive grey-brown and it has a green speculum. The throat is white and it has a brown breast and flanks that are heavily spotted buff; the belly is white and the undertail coverts are buff. The female's bill is brown with yellow or pink tones and tipped pale yellow.

In Leicestershire it is a scarce visitor and a very rare breeding bird. The Mandarin is an uncommon and irregular visitor to Swithland Reservoir and was first recorded on 3rd November 1974. In 1985 one male and four females were present and display, courtship and mating were noted. The birds were present throughout the summer and breeding was probably attempted.

DABBLING DUCKS Anatini

Eurasian Wigeon *Anas penelope*

This Wigeon breeds in northern Europe and Asia from Iceland and Britain in the west to Kamchatka and Sakhalin in the east. It winters in western and southern Europe southward to North Africa and across southern Asia reaching Japan.

In Britain it breeds regularly in Scotland and sporadically in England, Wales and Ireland with 300-500 breeding pairs. Birds that are bred in Britain tend to be sedentary within these Isles. Large numbers of migrants come into Britain from as far afield as Iceland and Russia. Birds arrive in Britain from late September onwards and return passage takes place from March to May.

The Wigeon breeds on tundra pools, shallow freshwater lakes and pools with an open aspect and a profusion of aquatic vegetation, but not closed-in lakes that are surrounded by trees or reeds. The nest is a shallow hollow that is concealed in vegetation and lined with grass, leaves and down. Many Wigeon spend the winter around our coasts and it is chiefly a salt-water duck that feeds on the sea-grass *Zostera*.

The adult male Wigeon has a chestnut head with a bright yellowish crown stripe, pink breast, grey upperparts and flanks with a white and black stern and a white line along the wing. The female is similar in shape but is dull by comparison. It is either rufous-brown or grey-brown on the head, breast and flanks and has a white belly. The mantle is similar in colour to the rest of the body but heavily streaked black. The bill is blue-grey tipped black and it has dark blue-grey legs. The Wigeon often gives its presence away by its evocative "whee-oo" whistle and an old English name for the bird was the 'Whew Duck'.

The Wigeon is a common passage migrant and winter visitor to Leicestershire but it is uncommon in the summer months. It is a common winter visitor to Swithland Reservoir, although odd birds can be seen sporadically in almost any month. Wigeon tend to use Swithland as a resting place and can sometimes be present in very large numbers although they never stay long. Swithland Reservoir is poor feeding habitat for the Wigeon on account of the lack of adjacent short grassland and so birds staying for more than a few days will probably move into the Soar Valley to feed at night. The largest number of birds recorded at one time on the reservoir was 1,664 in February 1987.

Gadwall *Anas strepera*

The Gadwall breeds across Europe, central Asia and North America. It has a scattered distribution throughout much of Europe but is more widely distributed across central Asia as far as Lake Baikal with only scattered populations eastward to Kamchatka. In North America it is found mainly in central western North America with scattered populations in the east. It winters in western and southern Europe southward to North Africa and across southern Asia with scattered wintering areas from Turkey to eastern China. In America it winters in the southern United States southward to central Mexico.

The Gadwall was introduced into Britain as a breeding bird in 1850. The species then began to spread and breeding commenced in many counties in the first half of the 20th century. During the 1960s over 1,000 birds were released in Britain and this is thought to be the reason for the recent upsurge in numbers. In Britain a certain amount of migration from continental Europe does occur during the autumn and birds will remain with us throughout the winter months. Passage starts in late August but the majority of birds arrive in October and November and the return passage takes place in March and April.

It breeds generally on shallow freshwater lakes and pools with an open aspect and plenty of aquatic and emergent vegetation although it will on occasions use brackish water. The nest is a shallow depression lined with plant material and down which is normally hidden in dense cover.

The Gadwall is similar in size and shape to the Mallard. The male has a grey-brown head and neck, grey breast and flanks that are finely vermiculated and black undertail coverts. The mantle is grey with dark grey and buff scapulars and white speculum. In flight it shows a white speculum, black rump, chestnut wing coverts and a white belly. The bill is grey and the legs yellow-orange. The female is very similar to the female Mallard, being largely brown with black feather centres giving the bird a mottled appearance. It differs from the Mallard in having the white speculum and more orange on the bill.

The Gadwall is a common autumn and winter visitor to Leicestershire and a scarce breeding bird. This species has greatly increased in Leicestershire over the past two decades. In recent years Rutland Water has seen some of the largest counts ever made for this species in Europe with 2,181 being present on the 16th November 1987. This must have an effect on the Swithland population. The Gadwall is now a regular winter visitor to Swithland and has bred on several occasions since 1978. Three broods were reared during 1991 and it is now becoming an almost annual breeder. There have been four occasions when more than a hundred birds have been present: 101 birds on the 16th October 1995; 102 birds on the 23rd November 1996; 107 on the 5th October 1997, and 192 on the 15th October 1998. It is interesting to note that the numbers are still rising and that all the large counts come in successive years.

Common Teal *Anas crecca*

The Teal is a common breeding bird throughout northern Europe, Asia and North America. It breeds from Iceland and Britain in the west through to Kamchatka and northern Japan in the east. In North America it can be found from Alaska to Newfoundland. It winters across Europe reaching southward to northern and central Africa and across southern Asia from Turkey eastwards into the Indian subcontinent through to China. The North American birds winter across the southern United States south into Central South America.

It breeds throughout Britain and is most widespread in the upland areas of Scotland. It nests only sparingly in England and Wales. British bred Teal tend to be sedentary but in autumn large numbers move into Britain from northern and eastern Europe. Wintering birds start to arrive from August onwards and leave again during March and April.

It breeds in a wide variety of habitats using fresh and brackish water. It generally prefers shallow bodies of water with plenty of aquatic and emergent vegetation. The nest is a shallow depression lined with plant material and down that is hidden in dense vegetation.

The Teal or Green-winged Teal as it is known in North America (differing from the European Teal in having a white breast stripe and lacking the white stripe along the scapulars) is our smallest duck. The adult male Teal is identified by having a chestnut head with a curving green eye-patch that is lined by a thin buff stripe, buff breast which is spotted dark, grey upperparts and flanks which are finely vermiculated, a white stripe along the wing and yellow undertail coverts, bordered and divided by a black band. The female is like a small female Mallard with brown-grey plumage, heavily mottled with black, and has a distinctive white tail patch. In flight it shows a white wing bar and green speculum.

The Teal is a common passage migrant and winter visitor to Leicestershire and a rare breeding bird. On Swithland Reservoir it is a common winter visitor and an occasional breeder. It has been proved to breed in three years, 1947, 1949 and 1975, and has been suspected of breeding on other occasions. The largest count made on the reservoir was in January 1977, when 725 birds were present.

[Towards the end of 2000 the British Ornithologists' Union Records Committee split the Teal into two separate species. These are now the Common Teal *Anas crecca* of Eurasia and the Green-winged Teal *Anas carolinensis* of North America.]

Mallard *Anas platyrhynchos*

The Mallard breeds throughout Europe, much of northern and central Asia and North America. It breeds in every European country, being absent only from the high Arctic tundra and high altitude. It is resident and a winter visitor over central and southern Europe, Asia Minor and central North America. It winters in North Africa and in a broken band across southern Asia, and in the southern United States southward to Mexico. It has been introduced to southern Australia and New Zealand and parts of North America.

The Mallard or Wild Duck, as it used to be known, is a familiar and common sight on most waters throughout Britain and Ireland and it is the ancestor of the domestic duck. Large numbers move into Britain each autumn from northern Europe. Movement starts in late August but peak passage takes place from November to December and return migration is from February to May.

It breeds on a wide variety of waters and favours shallow, still freshwater lakes and ponds, but it will nest by brackish lagoons or even on sheltered coastal bays. The nest is placed under thick cover and is a shallow depression that is lined with plant material and down.

The adult male Mallard has a yellow bill, bottle green head and upper neck, white collar, purplish brown chest, grey body which is finely vermiculated, black stern with two curly black tail feathers, white edges to the tail and orange legs. In flight it shows a black rump and dark blue speculum bordered by white. The female, like the male, is a large duck with a brown and buff plumage heavily mottled with dark feather centres. It shows a buff throat, white sides to its tail and dull yellow bill.

The Mallard is a common resident breeding bird, passage migrant and winter visitor to Leicestershire. It breeds on Swithland Reservoir in fairly good numbers. In the past some birds have been introduced onto the reservoir to improve the stock for shooting. The locally bred Mallard tend to be sedentary but their numbers are reinforced during the winter by birds from continental Europe. The largest count made on the reservoir was in January 1947, when 900 birds were present. In the last few years it has been realised that the Mallard numbers have been declining throughout Britain and the reasons for this are not fully understood, but American Mink *Lutreola vison* predation could be the major factor.

Northern Pintail *Anas acuta*

The Pintail breeds throughout northern North America from Alaska to Newfoundland, and from Iceland and Britain in Europe across Asia to Kamchatka and Sakhalin. Birds winter in western and southern Europe southward to central Africa and in scattered areas across southern Asia from Turkey eastwards to southern Japan. It winters in the southern United States southwards through central South America.

In Britain it is a localised breeder with 33 pairs breeding in 1997. British bred birds tend to be sedentary. It is a winter visitor and passage migrant over much of Britain in small numbers. The majority of immigrants start arriving in Britain from mid-September and passage continues until November. Return passage takes place from late February through to April. Like the Wigeon, with which it often associates, it has a preference for sea coasts and estuaries.

It breeds in a variety of habitats including wet tundra, coastal lagoons, brackish marshes, freshwater lakes and shallow pools in lowland grassland. The nest is a shallow depression sparsely lined with plant material and down and is normally placed in low cover.

In Dorset and Hampshire it was given the local name of 'Sea Pheasant' because of its long tail. The adult male Pintail is an elegant bird with a long sleek neck and two long elongated central tail feathers. It has a black-topped slate grey bill, dark brown head and upper neck and two long white stripes which divide the brown and continue down the neck to merge with the white of the lower neck and breast. The flanks and back are grey and finely vermiculated but the secondaries on the wings are dark centred with buff edges that are quite striking. There is a buff area on the lower abdomen that contrasts markedly with the black undertail coverts. It has a long black pin tail and the legs are grey. In flight it has a very long silhouette and shows a green speculum bordered by a buff stripe and a white trailing edge. The belly is white. The female shows a white trailing edge to a brown speculum. The female is not unlike a female Mallard but is sleeker and has a long neck and a pointed tail which is much shorter than the male's. The overall colour of the plumage is brown but it has dark mottling on the upperparts and dark scalloping on the flanks and the undertail coverts are white with dark spotting.

The Pintail is an uncommon autumn and winter visitor to Leicestershire that can be common in some years. It is a regular visitor to Swithland Reservoir in small numbers. As with the Wigeon, this water is not really suitable for this species, lacking ideal feeding areas. The four highest recorded counts are 35 on the 7th and 14th February 1954; 14 on the 2nd February 1985; 19 on the 2nd September 1989, and 32 on the 16th February 1996. This species has been recorded on the reservoir in 52 out of the last 59 years and all have been seen in a period from September through to April.

Garganey *Anas querquedula*

The Garganey (or Summer Teal as it was known in East Anglia) breeds below the Arctic circle throughout the Palearctic in a wide band from Britain in the west to Sakhalin in the east with a small isolated population occurring in Kamchatka. It winters mainly in a band across central Africa, and in Asia in the Indian Subcontinent and Indo-China. In Africa they winter on flood pools and meadows adjacent to the Senegal and Niger Rivers close to Lake Chad where as many as 900,000 birds congregate. The Garganey population dropped dramatically in parts of Europe and Russia in the early 1970s, probably due to more intensive farming methods and drainage on the breeding grounds and flood alleviation schemes and the building of reservoirs where they winter.

In Britain it is a passage migrant and localised breeder with only 129 breeding pairs in 1997. Birds arrive during late March and April and leave again during September and October. Small numbers do, however, remain to winter in western and southern Europe.

When breeding it favours shallow freshwater pools and lakes and marshes with emergent vegetation. The nest is built in a shallow hollow that is hidden in dense cover and is lined with plant material and down.

The Garganey is only slightly larger than the Teal. The adult male Garganey has a dark grey bill, dark brown head, neck and breast with a large white stripe extending over the eye and curving down the nape; grey flanks which are finely vermiculated and brown dark-spotted stern. Its upperparts are brown with dark mottling and it has striking, elongated black and white scapulars. In flight it shows distinctive blue-grey wing coverts and green speculum edged on either side by white bars. The legs are grey. The female Garganey is very similar to the female Teal but it has a heavier, longer bill, paler face with dark lines across it, a pale spot at the base of the bill and an off-white throat.

In Leicestershire the Garganey is a scarce spring passage migrant and uncommon autumn visitor. It is a very rare breeding bird. On Swithland Reservoir it is a passage migrant that is not recorded every year.

Some birds that are seen in the spring are already paired when they arrive and they occasionally stay into the summer. In 1976 it was thought to have bred or at least attempted to do so. Swithland Reservoir has many quiet backwaters and it is often very difficult to get absolute proof of breeding. The largest numbers to be recorded have been in the late summer: 6 were present on the 18th August 1974, and 5 on the 22nd August 1995. In the spring 2 pairs were present on the 11th April 1947, and on the 21st April 1968. The Garganey has been seen on the reservoir in a period from March to November with one January record, a female being present on the 9th and 20th January 1977. This species has been recorded in 29 out of the last 59 years.

Northern Shoveler *Anas clypeata*

The Shoveler breeds in scattered populations across Europe, and in a wide band across northern and central Asia reaching Kamchatka and Sakhalin in the east. It also breeds across northern and central North America with the bulk of the population biased to the west. Birds winter throughout Europe southward to tropical Africa and in scattered areas across southern Asia from Turkey in the west to Japan in the east. In North America it winters in the southern United States southward through central South America

In Britain it occurs throughout the year, breeding in small numbers in suitable habitats with about 1,250 pairs, although it does not breed frequently in south-west England and large areas of Wales. Passage takes place, involving birds from continental Europe, from August to November and return migration is from March to May. At these times the largest numbers can be recorded in Britain. Smaller numbers do, however, remain throughout the winter months. The numbers of birds wintering in Britain fell sharply during the early 1960s but then recovered until the early 1970s. Since that time their numbers are falling again but not so rapidly. More recently the numbers of birds breeding in Britain appear to be falling.

It breeds on lowland freshwater lakes, water meadows and marshes with aquatic and emergent vegetation. The nest is a shallow depression that is lined with plant material and down. It is usually placed close to the water in an open area, in grass or other low vegetation.

The male Shoveler has a large shovel-shaped black bill, bottle-green head, white breast, chestnut flanks and white and black stern. The upperparts are black and white with striking elongated black and white scapulars. In flight it shows a pale blue forewing bordered by a white bar and a green speculum. The female is mottled brown like a female Mallard but it has the characteristic spatula-shaped yellow-brown bill, head-down attitude and a dark brown belly.

The Shoveler is a fairly common autumn passage migrant and winter visitor in Leicestershire and a scarce breeding bird. On Swithland Reservoir the Shoveler is a regular winter visitor and passage migrant with occasional birds staying to breed. Summer residents tend to arrive with passage migrants from the end of February to March and have left again by mid-August. Shoveler have been proved to breed on fourteen occasions with three pairs breeding in 1951, the last confirmed breeding being in 1991. The largest recorded number was on the 28th September 1991, when 291 birds were present; smaller numbers were recorded on the 17th September 1994, with 158 birds and 22nd October 1995, when 134 birds were recorded. More recent high counts were made on the 13th September 1999, when 184 birds were present, which then rose to 203 birds by the 10th October 1999.

DIVING DUCKS Netta, Aythya, Somateria, Melanitta, Clangula and Bucephala

Red-crested Pochard *Netta rufina*

The Red-crested Pochard has a patchy distribution throughout Central and Southern Europe extending eastwards into Asia Minor, but its main stronghold lies in a band through central Asia from the Black Sea eastwards into western Mongolia and north- western China. It winters in southern Europe, the Black and Caspian Seas and the Indian subcontinent eastwards into Burma.

It is a rare bird in Britain, and because of the number of birds escaped from captivity its true status is difficult to ascertain. It first bred in Britain in 1937 and then not again until 1958. Since 1968 it has become an annual breeding bird but all the birds involved are considered feral.

It breeds by lowland lakes, marshes and slow-flowing rivers with an abundance of aquatic and emergent vegetation. It nests close to the water in dense vegetation where it makes a shallow hollow, lined with plant material and down.

The adult male Red-crested Pochard has a large chestnut head, a red bill, long black neck and breast, brown back and white flanks with a black stern. The legs are red. In flight it shows a conspicuous broad white wing-bar and dark belly. The female is similar in shape to the male but has brown plumage and the most distinctive feature is its conspicuous pale cheek patches. It has a dark brown crown, nape and upperparts with paler brown on the breast and flanks. The bill is dark grey with a pink patch towards its tip and the legs are greyer than the male's.

The Red-crested Pochard is a scarce passage migrant and winter visitor to Leicestershire. It has been seen on five occasions on Swithland Reservoir and all have been male birds. There are two spring records, one on the 2nd April 1984, and another on the 23rd April 1986. The other three records were all in the autumn:- one on the 1st September 1974, one from the 8th-18th October 1992, and the last an immature bird on the 19th November 1994. There is the possibility that some of these birds were escapes from captivity, although the times of year when these sightings were made would fall into the right period for genuinely wild birds.

Common Pochard *Aythya ferina*

The Pochard breeds throughout much of Europe with a patchy distribution in the western and southern parts of its range extending south into North Africa. It has an extensive breeding range from eastern Europe across central Asia to Lake Baikal. It winters in western Europe, the Mediterranean and North Africa and in scattered areas across southern Asia from Turkey to Japan.

In Britain the Pochard is a common winter visitor and a scarce breeding bird, although it increased as a resident throughout last century. About 380 pairs breed in Britain annually. Since circa 1850 the Pochard has expanded its range greatly over central and north-western Europe. Pochard begin to arrive in numbers in Britain and Ireland during September and October and leave again in March and April.

It nests on brackish and freshwater lakes and pools with plenty of emergent vegetation. The nest is placed either close to the water or on a platform on the water in dense vegetation. The nest is a shallow hollow made of reed stems or other vegetation that is lined with down.

The adult male Pochard has a long dark grey bill with a blue-grey band just in from the tip, a rich chestnut head and neck, black breast, grey back and flanks and black stern. The female is similar in size and shape to the male, but its plumage is made up of a brown head with slightly paler facial area, dark brown breast, grey-brown back and flanks and black stern. The legs of both sexes are grey.

The Pochard is a common passage migrant and winter visitor to Leicestershire and a rare breeding bird. On Swithland reservoir the Pochard is a common winter visitor and occasional breeder. The first breeding record came on the 30th May 1984, when I found a nest with seven eggs. It also bred in 1985 and 1986 and that was the last occasion that a pair of Pochard was proved to have bred in the county. The largest number of birds recorded on this water was on the 26th January 1989, when circa 600 birds were present. On the 10th February 1990, 510 birds still remained.

Ferruginous Duck *Aythya nyroca*

The Ferruginous Duck or White-eyed Pochard has a scattered breeding distribution in southern Europe. Its main breeding range is from central Europe eastwards to the Caspian Sea with more scattered breeding areas in Asia eastwards to western Mongolia. It winters in southern Europe, both North and sub-Saharan Africa, the Black and Caspian Seas, Asia Minor and from Pakistan across northern India to Burma.

This species is believed to be a rare straggler to Britain, usually in the spring and autumn. Its true status, however, remains uncertain because it is a species that is commonly kept in captivity and birds escape from time to time.

It has a liking for shallow pools, lakes and slow-flowing rivers with a lot of aquatic and emergent vegetation. The nest is a shallow hollow made of reed stems or other plant material that is lined with down and is placed in thick vegetation on or close to water.

The male Ferruginous Duck is a rich mahogany colour on the head, breast and flanks, with a slightly darker back and white undertail coverts. The sexes are similar but the male has a white eye, hence its other name. The bill is dark grey, pale near the tip with a black nail, the legs are grey. In flight it shows a distinctive broad white wing-bar, oval white belly patch and white undertail coverts.

The Ferruginous Duck is a rare vagrant to Leicestershire. A sighting has been claimed on several occasions at Swithland Reservoir but there has been only one fully authenticated record. A bird spent the time commuting between Cropston and Swithland Reservoirs during the autumn of 1990. It was noted on the 11th September, consorting with Tufted and Pochard, and on the 13th October it was seen displaying to a Pochard. It was last seen on the 2nd November 1990.

Tufted Duck *Aythya fuligula*

The Tufted Duck breeds throughout northern and central Europe and across into Asia. It can be found from Iceland south to Britain and Ireland in the west, and in a wide band across Europe and Asia to Kamchatka and south to northern Japan in the east. It winters in western and southern Europe extending southward to northern and sub-Saharan Africa and in scattered areas in southern Asia from Turkey to Japan.

It is a common winter visitor to Britain and Ireland with birds arriving in the autumn from continental Europe and Iceland. British bred birds tend to be resident. Birds from the Continent arrive in October and leave again in March and April. During this century the Tufted Duck has greatly increased its range as a breeding bird in Britain and now breeds throughout the country. Its range expansion could be firstly due to the large numbers of inland waters such as reservoirs and gravel-pits that were constructed during the late 19th century and throughout the 20th century and afford ideal habitat for the Tufted Duck. Secondly, it feeds on molluscs, especially the Zebra Mussel *Dreissnia polymorpha*, and the Tufted Duck's range expansion has followed the spread of this species through Europe, especially since the 1950s. This is probably due to the man-made waters becoming mature, enabling them to sustain a varied aquatic flora and fauna.

They nest by lowland freshwater lakes, ponds and rivers with aquatic and emergent vegetation. The nest is a shallow depression lined with plant material that is placed close to the water amongst low vegetation. Small islands are greatly favoured.

The adult male Tufted Duck can be easily distinguished by its black drooping crest, black head, neck, breast, back and stern and white flanks. The female is dark brown with slightly paler flanks and has a shorter crest. In flight they both show a broad white wing-bar and a white belly. The bill is blue-grey, slightly paler near the black tip and it has dark blue-grey legs.

The Tufted Duck is a common passage migrant and winter visitor to Leicestershire and an uncommon breeding bird. It is a common winter visitor and passage migrant to Swithland Reservoir and small numbers breed on the reservoir annually. There have been some sizeable late summer counts in recent years, the highest being 530 on the 10th August 1986, the largest count for this site, and 355 birds on the 27th July 1997. The highest winter count was 481 birds in February 1986.

Greater Scaup *Aythya marila*

The Scaup breeds on the lakes and coasts of Iceland and northern Scandinavia in Europe, eastwards across northern Siberia to Kamchatka in Asia and from Alaska to Newfoundland in North America. In winter it is generally a sea-duck, being found in bays and shallow coastal waters. It winters on the coasts of north-western Europe. In Asia it can be found from Japan southward to Taiwan and in North America on the east and west coasts.

In Britain it nests occasionally in Scotland but it is mainly a winter visitor and passage migrant arriving in October and leaving in March. Scaup still remain rare and irregular visitors inland.

It nests close to freshwater rivers and lakes on tundra or moorland close to boreal forest. The nest is a shallow depression lined with plant material and down and is placed amongst low grass or sedges.

The adult male Scaup has a green head, black breast, grey back with dark vermiculations, white flanks and black stern. The female is similar to a female Tufted Duck. It has a brown head, breast and stern and grey-brown back and flanks which are finely vermiculated. A noticeable feature is a broad white band around the base of the bill. The Scaup has a blue-grey bill with a black nail and grey legs. In flight it shows a broad white wing-bar and white belly.

The Scaup is an uncommon winter visitor and passage migrant to Leicestershire. On Swithland Reservoir it is an irregular winter visitor that is normally seen singly. A quite extraordinary number were seen on the 6th December 1950, when 28 birds were present: 8 males, 4 females and 16 immature birds. The second highest count was made on the 23rd March 1963, when 8 males and 10 females were present. The Scaup has been recorded in 33 out of the last 59 years and in every month except August.

Aythya hybrids

Care must be taken when identifying *Aythya* species because in recent years there has been a certain amount of cross-breeding by ducks of this genus. This has occurred mainly in wildfowl collections or with feral birds. D. Smallshire (in British Birds Vol. 79 No.2) suggests that over 20% of 'Scaup' seen on inland waters were in fact hybrids. When viewing a suspect bird, pay close attention to shape and colour of the bill, colour of eyes, general patterning of plumage and body shape. In recent years several *Aythya* hybrids have been noted on Swithland Reservoir. Scaup x Tufted Duck were noted in 1988 and 1989; Ferruginous Duck x Pochard in 1989 and 1994; Tufted Duck x Pochard in 1989, 1991, 1992, 1994, 1995 and 1997.

Common Eider *Somateria mollissima*

The Eider breeds on the Atlantic Coast of north-west Europe from northern France northwards to Britain, Iceland, Scandinavia and countries bordering the Baltic north to Svalbard (Spitsbergen) and Novaya Zemlya in the Arctic Ocean. Its distribution is then circumpolar as it breeds on islands and edges of the Arctic Ocean, northern Atlantic and Pacific. It can be found from Alaska to Newfoundland in North America and on the coasts of Greenland and Eastern Siberia. In winter the most northerly populations move south to winter within or just to the south of its southern breeding range. It is a maritime species and is seldom seen inland. In recent years, however, some 600 birds have been found wintering on lakes in Switzerland, mainly on Lake Constance and Lake Geneva following the colonisation of the lakes by Zebra Mussels *Dreissena polymorpha*. After the breeding season there is a large moult migration with many thousands of birds congregating in the Waddensee, south-west of Jutland in Germany.

In Britain the Eider breeds around the Scottish coast southward into England as far as Walney Island in the west and the Farne Islands in the east. In winter it can be found further south around the coasts of England and Wales.

It nests close to salt or brackish water on rocky coasts or estuaries and often near a mussel bed. The Eider duck builds her nest close to the seashore. It is a shallow depression lined with plant material and large amounts of down. On Iceland the Eider-down is still commercially farmed. The down is taken from the nest of the Eider duck. The female Eider plucks the down from her breast in order to protect the eggs and keep them warm.

The adult male Eider is a big heavy duck with a long sloping bill which is grey-olive but yellow near the base. Its plumage is largely white except for its black cap which is divided at the mid crown by a thin white stripe extending to the nape, pale green nape and black flanks and stern. The white breast has a pink suffusion and it has olive-grey legs. The female is similar to the male in bulk and has the distinctive bill shape, her bill being olive-grey with a pale tip. Like other ducks she has mottled brown upperparts but her brown flanks have dark barring.

The Eider is a rare vagrant to Leicestershire. It has been seen on Swithland Reservoir on one occasion: a female was present on the 15th December 1989. This was the eleventh county record.

Long-tailed Duck *Clangula hyemalis*

The Long-tailed Duck (or Oldsquaw, as it is known in North America) has a circumpolar distribution, breeding in the Arctic and sub-arctic zones. Its range extends from Iceland to Eastern Siberia and from Alaska to Labrador through to Greenland. In winter it is generally a sea-duck, wintering on warmer seas. It can be found southward to Washington State and South Carolina in North America and southern Japan and Korea in eastern Asia. In Europe it winters around the coasts of Iceland and Scandinavia and can also be found in the Baltic southward to Britain. It has been estimated that the Baltic holds circa 90% of Europe's wintering Long-tailed Ducks. With such large concentrations occurring in one place the largest threat to this species is pollution, particularly from oil, and its numbers have been declining in recent years.

In Britain it is a rare breeder but has nested on both Orkney and Shetland. The locals on Orkney and Shetland gave it the name 'Calloo', after the musical call they utter when flying, which can be heard at some distance. Winter visitors and passage migrants are found mainly around the coast of Scotland and the east coast of England.

It breeds on tundra with low vegetation and often adjacent to lakes or deltas. The nest is a shallow depression sparsely lined with plant material and down.

The adult male is a small duck with a stubby black bill with a pink band and elongated brown central tail feathers. In winter plumage it is largely white or pale grey with brown cheek patches, brown breast and back and elongated white scapulars. The legs are dark grey with olive tones. The female is darker than the male and lacks the long tail feathers She has a dark brown back, cap and face patch and pale brown breast. Much of the rest of the face is white and the neck and flanks are white, her bill being grey. In summer plumage both sexes become darker brown, the male retaining only white flanks and eye-patch. The female is similar but retains more white on the neck.

The Long-tailed Duck is a rare winter visitor to Leicestershire. It has been seen on three occasions at Swithland Reservoir. An immature was present between the 15th and 30th November 1969; a female from 1st to 3rd February 1981, and an adult male was present between the 18th and 20th November 1984.

Common Scoter *Melanitta nigra*

The Common Scoter breeds across northern Europe and Asia from Iceland and Britain in the west across Siberia to Kamchatka in the east. It has a very scattered and localised distribution across northern North America from Alaska to Newfoundland. During the winter months the Common Scoter is a marine duck feeding in large congregations often called 'rafts' in shallow waters close to the shore and during this period they rarely come inland. In winter it mainly feeds on bivalve molluscs such as Blue Mussels *Mytilus edulis*. It winters on both the western and eastern coasts of North America and on Asia's east coast from Kamchatka southward to Taiwan. In Europe it can be found along the Atlantic coast from Norway southward to north-west Africa.

In Britain it breeds in Scotland with about 100 pairs breeding annually and it can be found all around the coast during the winter months. The main autumn migration starts in September and the birds remain with us until April or early May. It is interesting that, from June to August, small parties can often be encountered on inland waters outside their breeding range.

It nests close to freshwater lakes or rivers on heathland and tundra. The nest is a hollow, sparsely lined with plant material and down which is usually well-hidden in low vegetation.

The male Common Scoter is a large heavy-looking duck with a long tail that is sometimes held out of the water. Its plumage is glossy black with its only colour being an orange centre on the upper mandible, the rest of the bill being black. It has black legs. The female is brown with pale cheeks that contrast with the dark brown crown and nape. The female Common Scoter is similar in patterning to the female Red-crested Pochard but the former has an all black bill.

The Common Scoter is an uncommon passage migrant and scarce winter visitor to Leicestershire. It is an irregular winter visitor and passage migrant to Swithland Reservoir, usually seen singly or in small numbers. A large number of the records are of passage birds that have occurred from March to May. In recent years, however, some of the highest counts have come in a period from June to August with 21 being present on the 12th July 1986, and 33 on the 9th August 1992. Thirty female/immature birds were noted on the 15th November 1989. These are the three largest counts for this water. The Common Scoter has been recorded in 31 out of the last 59 years and has been seen in every month.

Velvet Scoter *Melanitta fusca*

The Velvet Scoter or White-winged Scoter as it is known in America, breeds in northern Europe and Asia from Norway in the west to Kamchatka and Sakhalin in the east. In North America it can be found from Alaska and British Columbia eastwards to Manitoba. One isolated population can be found in the southern Caucasus and north- eastern Turkey. It winters on the west and east coasts of North America and from Kamchatka to southern Japan in eastern Asia. In Europe it can be found along the Atlantic coast southward to northern Spain and in parts of the Mediterranean and Black Sea. In winter it is a maritime species favouring bays and estuaries. It feeds mainly on molluscs, especially Gastropods (snails), Blue Mussels *Mytilis edulis*, cockles *Cardium* and dogwhelks *Nassa*.

In Britain it is a winter visitor in small numbers and has been thought to breed on occasions.

It breeds on forested islands and shores in the Baltic and inland close to freshwater lakes, pools and rivers in forested areas. The nest is a shallow depression lined with plant material and down that is normally well-hidden under low vegetation.

The adult male Velvet Scoter has largely all black plumage like the Common Scoter but differs in its larger size. The male also shows more orange along the edge of the bill, a white crescent immediately below the eye and white secondaries on the wing. The legs are red. The female is dark brown and lacks the contrast on the face that the female Common Scoter shows, but it usually has two pale facial patches. In flight both the male and female Velvet Scoter show distinctive white secondaries.

The Velvet Scoter is a rare winter visitor to Leicestershire. It is a rare vagrant to Swithland Reservoir and has been fully authenticated only twice. One was recorded on the 5th December 1953, and a male was seen on the 20th February 1987.

Common Goldeneye *Bucephala clangula*

The Goldeneye breeds across northern Europe and Asia from Scotland in the west to Kamchatka and Sakhalin in the east and across northern North America from Alaska to Newfoundland. In winter it can be found on both salt and fresh water. In North America it winters just to the south of its breeding range over much of the United States. In Asia it can be found in isolated pockets throughout central Asia and on the east coast from Kamchatka to Taiwan. In Europe most birds do not move as far south, wintering largely in Britain and on the coasts and in the countries of north-west Europe, although some birds migrate south reaching the Mediterranean especially in eastern Europe.

In Britain it breeds annually in Scotland with about 200 breeding pairs, mainly brought about by the use of nestboxes, and it has bred in England on a few occasions. It is a widespread winter visitor to Britain and Ireland in small well-scattered numbers.

It breeds by rivers and lakes bordering mature woodland where it generally nests in a hole in a tree, although it does take readily to nestboxes.

The adult male has a bottle-green head with a white spot at the base of its small black bill and a yellow eye. The neck, breast and flanks are white and it has a black back and stern with distinctive elongated black and white scapulars that lie over the flanks when the bird is at rest. The legs are yellowish. The female has a brown head and a grey body with a white speculum, the bill is black with an orange band near the tip. In flight both sexes show white wing panels extending from the secondaries through to the fore-wing, divided into squares by black lines.

The Goldeneye, although scarce in summer, is a fairly common winter visitor and passage migrant to Leicestershire. It is a frequent winter visitor to Swithland Reservoir. It arrives generally in early October and has departed by mid-May. The birds remain well scattered over the reservoir during the winter months. In March and April they tend to come together in pre-dispersal flocks and at this time courtship and display rituals can be seen before the birds depart. These flocks tend to contain a majority of female and immature birds with relatively few males being present. The highest counts made on the reservoir were both made in the month of March, 87 birds being present on the 17th March 1985, and 95 on the 5th March 1989.

SAWBILLS Mergellus, Mergus

Smew *Mergellus albellus*

The Smew breeds across northern Europe and Asia from Norway in the west to Kamchatka and Sakhalin in the east, although its distribution is scattered in eastern Siberia. It has a very scattered winter distribution across much of central and south- eastern Europe. It winters on the Black and Caspian Seas eastwards in small pockets across central Asia to the coasts of Japan and eastern China. The largest wintering concentrations in Europe are at Szczecin Lagoon on the Polish Baltic and at Ijsselmeer in the Netherlands, where a combined total of circa 25,000 birds has been counted in recent years.

In Britain it is a local winter visitor mainly to southern England.

It breeds by lakes, pools and rivers bordering on mature woodland and forest, where it nests in a hole in a tree, very frequently the old nest hole of a Black Woodpecker *Drycopus martius*. Like the Goldeneye, it takes readily to nestboxes.

The Smew is a small duck, with a short dark grey bill. The adult male is very white in appearance, with a short crest, small black eye patch, a black stripe on its nape and two on its breast, narrow grey vermiculations on its flanks, grey stern and a black centre to the back. The legs are slate grey. The male is sometimes given the name the 'White Nun'. The female and immature birds go by the name 'Red heads'. The female is slightly smaller than the male. It has a chestnut forehead and crown, white cheeks and throat and grey body. In flight both sexes show large white oval wing patches and white bellies.

The Smew is an uncommon winter visitor to Leicestershire whose numbers fluctuate from year to year. It is an uncommon winter visitor to Swithland Reservoir that usually occurs in ones or twos. The largest
numbe

r recorded at Swithland Reservoir was on the 12th February 1956, when nine birds were present. The Smew has been seen in 29 out of the last 59 years and all the records are in a period from October to April.

Red-breasted Merganser *Mergus serrator*

The Red-breasted Merganser breeds across northern Europe, Asia and North America. It breeds from Iceland and Britain and Ireland in the west across Siberia to Kamchatka and northern Japan in the east. It also occurs throughout northern North America from Alaska to Newfoundland and across to Greenland. It winters on the west and east coasts of North America and the eastern Coast of Asia from Kamchatka southward to Taiwan and also on the Black and Caspian Seas and a few areas in central western Asia. In Europe it winters mainly along the Atlantic coast south into the Mediterranean.

In Britain it breeds in Scotland and Ireland and is increasing as a breeding species in north-west England and North Wales. In winter it can be found all around our coast but is more frequent in the west. It differs from the Goosander in having a preference for salt-water. Wintering birds arrive in Britain during September and October and leave again in April or early May.

The nest is a shallow hollow lined with plant material and down which is placed under dense cover or in cavities between boulders close to rivers, lakes and estuaries that are surrounded mainly by woodland. It feeds mainly on small fish including salmon and trout *Salmo* fry, Brook Lamprey *Lampetra planeri* and Eel *Anguilla anguilla*.

The adult male Red-breasted Merganser has a bottle green head and upper neck with a shaggy crest, and long thin red bill. There is a white neck band, black-streaked brown breast, black and white patches on the sides of the lower breast, black back with white scapulars and grey vermiculated flanks and stern. The legs are red. The female has a brown head with a small shaggy crest, grey body and white secondaries. The brown head and upper neck merge into the grey and do not show the sharp border that the female Goosander does. In flight the male shows white wing panels across the inner wing divided by black lines, and a white belly. The female Red-breasted Merganser does not have so much white on the inner wing, but it also is divided by a black line which the female Goosander does not show.

The Red-breasted Merganser is a scarce winter visitor and passage migrant to Leicestershire. It is a rare winter visitor to Swithland Reservoir that is not recorded every year. Like the Smew, it is encountered normally in ones and twos. The largest number recorded was three males in eclipse on the 25th September 1977. An unusual spring record came when a pair were present on the 15th May 1993. The first record I have for the reservoir was a male on the 30th April 1946, and it has been recorded on 22 occasions since, all the records falling in a period from September to May.

Goosander *Mergus merganser*

The Goosander (or Common Merganser as it is known in North America) has a similar distribution to the Red-breasted Merganser, breeding mainly in northern Europe from Iceland and Britain, across northern Asia to Kamchatka and Sakhalin and in North America from Alaska to Newfoundland. There is one isolated population in the uplands of Pamir and Tibet. It winters throughout the central United States, on the coast of eastern Asia from Kamchatka southward to Taiwan and in scattered areas across central Asia including the Caspian and Black Seas. In Europe it winters mainly in central-western Europe but it can be found in isolated pockets southward to the Mediterranean.

In Britain the Goosander breeds in Scotland and northern England and its range appears to be extending. Most British bred birds tend to be sedentary. In winter there are large immigrations of birds to our shores that originate from northern Europe and Asia. They start arriving in October and leave again in March and April.

The name given to the Merganser family, 'sawbills', refers to the serrated edge to the bill which enables them to keep a hold on slippery fish, which is their basic diet. Like the Red-breasted Merganser, the Goosander feeds on small fish especially the young of salmon and trout *Salmo*, Pike *Esox lucius* and Miller's Thumb *Cottus gobio*, etc.

It breeds by fast flowing streams and lakes that are normally lined by woodland and generally nests in a hole in a tree. It differs in habitat from the Red-breasted Merganser in that in winter it prefers freshwater streams and lakes.

The adult male Goosander is a large duck with a bottle-green head and upper neck. The head has a mane on the nape making the head look large. It has a long thin red hooked bill, white breast and flanks that have a pink suffusion, black upper back and grey stern. The female has a rich brown head with a crest, clearly divided from the white throat and breast, a grey body and white secondaries. In flight the male shows white across the inner wing and a white belly. The female has a white panel on the inner wing and grey fore-wing and she too shows a white belly. In flight both Goosander and Red-breasted Merganser can look rather similar to the larger grebes and divers with their long outstretched necks.

The Goosander is a fairly common winter visitor to Leicestershire in varying numbers. It is an irregular winter visitor to Swithland Reservoir which is seen in most years, but normally only in small parties or even singly. 1972 was an exceptional year for sightings and, on the 20th January, 31 birds were present on the water while 45 flew overhead. This was the largest recorded number seen at the reservoir. In February of that year there were still 44 birds present. The previous best year had been 1947 when 23 birds were recorded on the 25th January. The Goosander has been seen in 43 out of the last 59 years and all have been in a period from October to May.

STIFF-TAILS Oxyura

Ruddy Duck *Oxyura jamaicensis*

The Ruddy Duck is a native of central North America and central and western South America. The Canadian and northern United States population migrate south to the Gulf States, California and Mexico to winter.

It breeds on reed-fringed lakes and pools. The nest is a floating platform of reeds and sedge stems made into a shallow cup that is generally placed in shallow water in reed- swamp vegetation.

The male in breeding plumage is an attractive thick-set little duck, with a long tail which is often held upright especially during display, hence the name Stiff-tail. The crown, hindneck and tail are black and the cheeks, chin and undertail coverts are white, the rest of the body being a deep chestnut. It has dark slate-grey legs. The most striking feature, however, about this little duck is its bright pale blue bill. The female has generally dark brown, finely barred plumage with a dark crown and pale cheeks which are bisected by a horizontal dark bar.

In Britain the Ruddy Duck first escaped in 1953 and first started to breed in the feral state in the West Midlands in 1960 and from there it spread and was first seen on Swithland Reservoir in 1967. The species first bred on Swithland reservoir in 1973 and it has bred in most years since, with four broods being seen in 1989 and 1992. During the winter large flocks were often recorded with 224 birds being present on the 22nd November 1983; 245 on 26th February 1992, and 270 on the 6th March 1993, the last being the largest recorded number on this water. The Ruddy Duck is an uncommon winter visitor and uncommon breeding bird in Leicestershire. Since 1993 the numbers at Swithland Reservoir have started to fall and flocks now rarely exceed 100 birds. The British breeding population was around 600 breeding pairs in the early 1990s.

The Ruddy Duck has now spread to the Continent where they have started to breed with the endangered White-headed Duck. It appears that the hybrid offspring can breed and it is thought that inter-breeding may well make the White-headed Duck extinct. In the mid-1990s the joint conservation body WeBs decided to cull the Ruddy Duck population at certain sites in Britain to safeguard the future of the White-headed Duck.

White-headed Duck *Oxyura leucocephala*

In Europe the White-headed Duck breeds in small numbers in Southern Spain, Romania, north-east Greece, Russia and a re-introduction programme is under way in Hungary. A small population also occurs in northern Africa mainly in Tunisia although it may still breed in Algeria. In Asia it can be found in small numbers in central Turkey but the main bulk of the bird's population is in Kazakstan. The Spanish and North African populations are mainly sedentary or only partial migrants. Asian birds are more migratory wintering in Turkey, Azerbaijan, Pakistan and northern India. The western Mediterranean population has risen in recent years and could now be has high as 2,000 birds, whereas the eastern population, which was the bird's stronghold, is falling and could now be as low as 10,000 birds.

It breeds on small shallow fresh water lakes and brackish lagoons fringed with reeds. The nest is a floating platform of reed stems and other vegetation made into a shallow cup and sparsely lined with down. It is built in shallow water in dense reed swamp vegetation. It often uses the old nest of other waterfowl like the Coot.

The adult male in breeding plumage has a large rounded white head with a small black cap and a large pale blue bill, noticeably swollen near the base. The body is chestnut with fine dark vermiculations on the back and flanks. It has a black collar which merges into the chestnut breast and the belly and undertail coverts are buff. The legs are grey. The bird is larger than the Ruddy Duck and has a more hunched appearance. The female White-headed Duck looks similar to the female Ruddy Duck but it is larger in size and has a swollen base to the bill. It has white cheeks which show a sharp contrast against the dark cap and horizontal cheek stripe. The breast, back and flanks are dark brown with fine dark barring.

The White headed Duck has been seen on Swithland Reservoir on two occasions - a male was seen on the 21st February 1981, and another male in breeding plumage between the 4th and 12th April 1982. This species has not yet been accepted onto the British list, but as it is so rare in captivity it does not seem likely these birds were escapes.

N.B. Since writing the above account I have received some information from Dr. B. Hughes, Head of Threatened Species for the Wildfowl and Wetland Trust at Slimbridge. He reports that the photographs I sent him of the bird I saw at Swithland Reservoir in April 1982 were undoubtedly of a male Ruddy Duck x White-headed Duck hybrid. After some discussion and taking into account the birds plumage and display it was thought that this bird might be a second generation three quarter White-headed Duck x Ruddy Duck F_2 hybrid and could be one of the first ever recorded. The earliest record of a first generation Ruddy Duck x White-headed Duck F_1 hybrid came from Farmwood Pool, Cheshire on the 14th December, 1980. It was subsequently seen at Blithfield Reservoir in Staffordshire from the 24th December, 1980, until at least the 4th January 1981. It was later observed at Chew Valley Lake, Avon on the 28th February, 1981, and Belvide Reservoir, Staffordshire on the 5th March, 1982. It is also believed that the 1981 Swithland record could refer to a hybrid bird. These birds are thought to have been the progeny of some young White-headed Ducks which escaped from the Slimbridge wildfowl collection a few years previously. Ruddy Duck x White-headed Duck hybrids were first bred in captivity by the Wildfowl and Wetland Trust in 1988 and the first hybrids recorded among the wild White-headed Duck population in Spain did not take place until 1991.

KITES, HARRIERS, HAWKS, BUZZARDS, EAGLES Accipitridae

When reading through the history of British birds of prey you begin to wonder how they managed to survive. Throughout the 19th century when Britain was at the pinnacle of achievement, influence around the globe and sizeable wealth, gamekeepers slaughtered our raptors to the verge of extinction. Even at the beginning of the enlightened 20th century this still continued. Most raptors got a respite from persecution during the two World Wars 1914-18 and 1939-45 when the gamekeepers went off to war. Many birds of prey made slight recoveries during those two periods. Between 1955 and 1970 many of our hawks and falcons suffered the effects of chlorinated hydrocarbon pesticides that had been used in agriculture, but since their ban, birds of prey have shown their resilience by making an astonishing recovery. Today raptors are probably more numerous and widespread than they have been in the last 200 years. In the past twenty or so years reintroduction programmes have been successful for the White-tailed Eagle and Red Kite and the first Osprey introduction is well under way at Rutland Water. For the first time Man is giving something back to these magnificent creatures. We surely owe them that! It would be wonderful to see a White-tailed Eagle on the Charnwood Forest again, and hopefully many people would be able to appreciate one of nature's wonderful spectacles. Let us hope they do not end up like the last two on Charnwood that were shot in 1840 and 1879.

My first memories of large birds of prey started when I was eleven, seeing an Osprey fishing at Swithland Reservoir. Four years later I visited Perthshire in Scotland and on an outing to Ben-y-Vrackie I saw my first Golden Eagles. A pair were first noted doing aerial display together and then one was seen to take a rabbit and carry it off in its talons. The other bird was spotted by four Ravens who started to mob it, each bird taking its turn to dive at the eagle's wings. The eagle seemed unimpressed by the antagonism and drifted effortlessly away towards where I was standing. I lay down in the heather and this huge bird drifted low over my head. That day I also saw my first Hen Harrier quartering over an area of moorland and my first Peregrine. It was a real red-letter day for me, especially considering that I had grown up in Leicestershire in the late 1950s and 1960s when any raptor other than a Kestrel was a rare sight.

Over the succeeding years I have had the privilege of watching some of the world's finest raptors, Gyr Falcon, White-tailed Eagle, White-bellied Sea-Eagle, Wedge-tailed Eagle, Bald Eagle, Andean Condor and Secretarybird. Last year I had one unexpected treat while walking in the suburbs of Torremolinos in Southern Spain early one May morning. I glanced in the air and noticed a buzzard. Looking at it through my binoculars I identified it as a Honey Buzzard. As I watched it started to rise, effortlessly circling on the thermals and suddenly it was surrounded by several hundred more buzzards gliding on outstretched wings, a magnificent sight. To see large numbers of birds on migration is always exciting, but none more so than large birds of prey.

European Honey Buzzard *Pernis apivorus*

The Honey Buzzard breeds across Europe and into Asia where it occurs in Western Siberia to the upper reaches of the Ob River. It winters in Africa south of the Sahara.

It is a rare breeding bird in Britain with about 55 breeding pairs mainly in south-east England and Scotland. It arrives in Europe in May and departs again towards the end of August and September.

It derives its name from the fact that it breaks into bees' and wasps' nests, not to get honey but to feed on the larvae. It is a woodland bird breeding in tall trees in coniferous and broadleaf woodland with adjacent open areas including parkland. It may use the old nest of such species as Carrion Crow and add to the nest using twigs and sticks, often ones that are still in leaf, and it has a shallow cup on top.

It is distinguished from the Buzzard in having a pigeon-like head, a longer tail, black trailing edge to the wing and three dark bars on the tail. When flying its wings are held almost level with a slight downcurve towards the wing tips. It has a black bill and yellow legs.

It is a rare vagrant to Leicestershire with eight records this century and all since 1976. A Honey Buzzard was observed flying with two Buzzards over Swithland Reservoir and Buddon Hill on the 21st August 1983. Unfortunately this record was not submitted to the Leicestershire and Rutland Rarities Committee and so must go down as not fully authenticated. This is one of the few unsubstantiated records I have left in this book but looking at the date and the fact that it was seen with two Buzzards must minimise the chance of misidentification.

From the 20th September through into early October, 2000, Honey Buzzards moved through Britain in large numbers. This movement was mainly concentrated on eastern England but a few birds were recorded as far west as Wales and northward into Scotland. A weather system with strong south-easterly winds is thought to have pushed the birds westwards as they migrated south from Scandinavia. This was the largest influx of Honey Buzzards ever recorded in Britain and probably involved over 1000 birds. The largest numbers recorded in Leicestershire were 18 at Beacon Hill on the 23rd September, nine at the same site on the 25th September, and 29 at Twycross on the 25th September, 2000. Three birds were recorded together over Swithland Reservoir on the 25th September, 2000. At the time of writing, all these records have yet to go before the Leicestershire and Rutland Rarities Committee.

Marsh Harrier *Circus aeruginosus*

The Marsh Harrier has a scattered breeding distribution across central and southern Europe, and it breeds in a band across central Asia reaching northern Japan. It winters as far south as west and east Africa and from India throughout much of South East Asia. It migrates from August to October and return passage takes place in April. Occasionally birds remain in eastern England throughout the winter. At one time the Marsh Harrier had a more widespread distribution across Europe but the drainage of marshlands and persecution have taken a heavy toll.

It became extinct as a breeding bird in Britain towards the end of the 19th century but re-established itself in Norfolk in 1920. There were 16-17 breeding pairs in 1977 and since then the numbers have been rising steadily. Currently there are 131 breeding pairs in Britain. Its main stronghold in Britain is the eastern counties of England.

Its breeding grounds include swamps, marshes, floodplains and reedbeds. It nests on the ground often in shallow water where it makes a large mound of sticks and reeds lined with finer material.

Marsh Harriers can often be seen gliding just above the reeds with the wings held in a shallow V, and when hunting they quarter the ground in distinctive fashion looking for prey. It is a large bird of prey with a long tail and long broad wings. The male has grey wings, black wing tips, grey tail and brown body from below and from above it shows a brown back and some wing coverts, grey wings and tail and black wing tips. The female generally looks dark brown with a buff head and shoulders. It has a black bill, yellow cere and yellow legs.

The Marsh Harrier is a scarce passage migrant in Leicestershire. It has been seen at Swithland Reservoir on four occasions: one on 13th August 1967, a female on the 12th May 1970, a female or immature on the 28th August 1978 and a female or immature on the 24th August, 2000.

Hen Harrier *Circus cyaneus*

The Hen Harrier or Marsh Hawk (as it is named in America) breeds across Europe and Siberia eastwards to Kamchatka and Sakhalin and over much of northern and central North America. It winters in southern Europe, southern Asia including India, China and Japan and in the southern United States and Central South America.

British-bred birds tend to be sedentary but we have an influx of birds from north-east Europe from September to April. These birds are either passage migrants or winter visitors. The Hen Harrier had been wiped out as a breeding bird on mainland Britain by 1900 largely due to human persecution. Only a few pairs remained in Northern Ireland, Orkney and Shetland. From 1940 the species started to recolonise mainland Britain starting with Scotland and now it nests in both England and Wales. In 1997 there were 630 breeding pairs in Britain.

Its breeding habitat is wide open spaces with low vegetation such as steppe grassland, moorland, heathland, sand dunes and upland areas. The nest is a low pile of sticks, heather and other vegetation lined with finer material on dry ground, and a larger structure in wet areas.

Hen Harriers quarter the ground when hunting and hold their wings in a V similar to the Marsh Harrier. The male Hen Harrier has blue-grey upperparts, head and neck, white belly and rump with contrasting black wing tips. The female is brown-streaked, with a dark barred tail (hence the name 'ringtail') and white rump. In flight the male shows a dark trailing edge to its underwing. The female underneath is barred across the primaries and secondaries. This barring becomes ill defined and dark near the body. The bill is black and it has a yellow cere and legs.

The Hen Harrier is a scarce winter visitor to Leicestershire. There have been two records from the Swithland area. A female flew over Buddon Wood on the 17th November 1989, and a ringtail was seen over Swithland Reservoir on the 1st November 1998.

Northern Goshawk *Accipiter gentilis*

The Goshawk is a widespread species breeding throughout Europe and northern Asia reaching Kamchatka and Japan in the east and it also occurs in Asia Minor and an isolated population in southern China. Its range also extends across northern North America. It is a partial migrant with northerly breeding birds moving southward in winter, mainly wintering within the bird's breeding range, although it winters outside its breeding range in south-east China and central North America.

The Goshawk bred sporadically in Britain during the 19th century but it was probably persecuted and remained a rare bird. A few pairs bred in Sussex in 1938, but regular breeding did not get under way until 1968 and by 1975 there were about 27 breeding pairs in Britain and at present there are as many as 347 breeding pairs.

The Goshawk is a bird of woodlands, it appears to be adaptable to what is available and even nests in city parks in some areas of Europe. The nest, usually high up in the fork of a tree, is a loose structure of sticks and twigs that is often lined with twigs still bearing leaves and pine needles. Like the Sparrowhawk it suffered massive declines in western Europe in the 1950s and 1960s due to the use of chlorinated hydrocarbon pesticides and mercury as a seed dressing in agriculture. After the banning of those substances in the 1970s their population rose dramatically.

The male Goshawk is a lot smaller than the female. The male is not a lot bigger than a large female Sparrowhawk but the female is the size of a Buzzard. The male Goshawk is bluish grey above with white underparts that are closely barred, and it has white supercilium. The female is similar but with grey-brown upperparts. In flight it differs from the Sparrowhawk in having longer wings with a more pronounced S shaped trailing edge to the wing, a deep barrel-chest, white fluffy undertail coverts and proportionally shorter but broader tail. The bill is black and the cere and legs yellow.

The Goshawk is a rare vagrant to Leicestershire that is probably under-recorded due to confusion with the Sparrowhawk. A good view is essential for identification but so often only brief views are obtained before they disappear. The Goshawk has been fully authenticated only once in the Swithland area. A bird was seen around Buddon during 1951. In recent years many observers have had brief views of what they believe to be Goshawks at Swithland Reservoir and the keepers have reported their presence but no satisfactory proof has been obtained.

Eurasian Sparrowhawk *Accipiter nisus*

The Sparrowhawk breeds throughout Europe reaching North Africa and through northern and central Asia as far as Kamchatka and Japan with an isolated population in the Himalayas. The most northerly breeding populations move south in the winter, some reaching North Africa, and it can be found wintering across southern Asia.

British birds are resident but start to disperse from their breeding areas in August. A certain amount of immigration from continental Europe takes place in September. Birds remain with us throughout the winter, returning again in April. Like so many birds of prey this species was persecuted throughout the 19th century and the first half of the 20th century. It was only with the onset of the 1939-45 war that the Sparrowhawk got some respite from persecution and its numbers started to rise. In 1955 a sudden decline was noticed throughout Britain and it almost disappeared as a breeding species in southern and eastern England. The cause was found to be chlorinated hydrocarbon pesticides used in agriculture, which killed adult birds and made their eggshells thinner, the eggs either cracking or failing to hatch. Organochlorine pesticides were eventually banned. A dramatic increase was seen in the British population from 1970 to 1998 and the numbers rose by 162%. Britain now has one of the highest densities of Sparrowhawks in Europe with 348 breeding pairs per 50km square.

The Sparrowhawk breeds in many woodland types and is one of the most common birds of prey in Europe. It nests in the fork of a tree occasionally building on the old nest of another species. The nest is a loose structure of twigs and like the Goshawk it lines the cup with fine twigs still bearing leaves.

The male Sparrowhawk is small. It has a blue-grey head and back, a white patch on the nape and a dark barred tail; the underparts are rufous with dark rufous barring. The female is larger with a browner back and the underparts are white with dark barring. The bill is blue-black and it has yellow cere and legs. Their flight is often low when hunting. They have several fast wingbeats and a glide and often work up the sides of hedges and quickly pounce on their unsuspecting prey.

The Sparrowhawk is a common resident breeding bird in Leicestershire. It is a common resident at Swithland Reservoir. It was recorded sporadically in the 1960s and early 1970s but the recovery here did not get under way until 1976. The first breeding record after the slump came in 1979 when a pair raised four young. They now breed around the margins of the reservoir or close by in most years. A good time to see Sparrowhawks is when they are performing their aerial display in late February to early May: Four birds were recorded 27th April 1994, and five birds were seen on the 21st April 1996.

Common Buzzard *Buteo buteo*

The Buzzard breeds throughout Europe and across central Asia reaching Sakhalin and Japan in the east. The northern European population will move south as far as the Mediterranean in winter. The subspecies the Steppe Buzzard, breeding in eastern Europe and Siberia, is completely migratory, wintering in east Africa. Other Asian populations winter as far south as India and south-east Asia.

The Buzzard is a resident in Britain and ringing studies have shown that British-bred birds seldom move far from their breeding areas. The Buzzard was wiped out in many areas of Britain by gamekeepers during the 19th century. Their numbers started to increase with the onset of the First World War and this continued until 1954. There was a sudden decline in 1954 due to the onset of myxomatosis in Rabbits *Oryctolagus cuniculus* and also the use of pesticides. In recent years their numbers have started to recover.

The Buzzard will breed in many habitats but generally likes woodland and forested areas with open areas in which to feed. It nests in trees and on cliffs. The nest is a large structure of sticks and twigs with a cup that is lined with various bits of greenery.

The Buzzard is a variable species but generally glides with wings held in a shallow V. The birds are generally brown-backed with whitish underparts with heavy dark streaking. The bill is black and it has a yellow cere and legs. Birds in flight sometimes show dark carpal patches and a dark terminal band to the tail and there is a variable amount of barring across the primaries, secondaries and tail, depending upon the bird.

The Buzzard is an uncommon visitor and scarce breeding bird in Leicestershire. It bred in several areas of Leicestershire in the early part of the 19th century and it last bred in the Rutland area in 1827. Re-colonisation started again in Leicestershire in 1993 when a pair bred in the Belvoir area and it has bred or attempted to breed in every year since. The Buzzard is an uncommon visitor to Swithland Reservoir that is almost becoming annual. It has been recorded in nine out of the last ten years. Most of the records fall in a period from April to May and July to September with the largest number of records coming in August. It has been seen in every month from February to October. Nearly all the records refer to single birds. Two birds, however, were present on the 8th April 1996, and the 2nd July, 2000.

Rough-legged Buzzard *Buteo lagopus*

The Rough-legged Buzzard breeds in the Arctic and Subarctic zone around the globe from Norway to Kamchatka and Alaska to Newfoundland. It winters across central Europe and Asia from Britain in the west to northern Japan in the east and across the central United States. In winter it moves southward and the European population can reach the Mediterranean and North Africa. Birds start to move in late August but much depends on the weather. If the snowfall is heavy and there is little food birds will vacate an area quickly but if plenty of food is available it might be October before they reach central Europe.

It is a scarce passage migrant and winter visitor to the British Isles in varying numbers.

It prefers open ground, generally treeless tundra areas, moorland, heathland and subalpine birch forest. It nests on cliff ledges in trees or on hummocks. The nest is a heap of small twigs and the cup is lined with moss, grass and other green vegetation. Its numbers are governed by its prey and in good vole *Microtus* and lemming *Lemmus* years when large numbers of fledglings survive it can be numerous.

The Rough-legged Buzzard is so called because it has feathered tarsi which are characteristic. It is slightly larger than the Buzzard, but like the Buzzard it soars with its wings held in a shallow V. When hunting it can often be seen to hover. It can always be identified from the similar Common Buzzard in having a white tail with a dark sub-terminal band and quite often it shows a black belly patch. The bill is dark and it has a yellow cere and feet.

The Rough-legged Buzzard is a rare vagrant to Leicestershire. It has been recorded at Swithland Reservoir on four occasions. The first was in 1925 and that was the second county record this century. The other records also refer to single birds that were seen on the 25th October 1946, 16th February 1974, and 22nd September 1988.

Osprey *Pandion haliaetus*

The Osprey is a cosmopolitan bird of prey which breeds across northern Europe with scattered colonies elsewhere in Europe as far south as the Mediterranean. It also breeds across northern Asia reaching Kamchatka and Japan and south-east Asia from China to New Guinea , North America and Australia. They winter in Central and South America, Africa, India and south-east Asia. The main migration periods are August and September with birds returning to their breeding sites in April and May. It became extinct in many parts of Europe during the 19th century and the early part of the 20th century due to persecution and collectors.

The Osprey became extinct as a breeding bird in Britain in 1916 and started to re-colonise Britain in 1954 when a pair bred in Scotland but it was not until 1959 that they bred successfully and they have done so ever since. In 1997 there were 99 breeding pairs of Osprey in Scotland.

Ospreys in northern Europe nest generally in the tops of tall trees and in the Mediterranean on cliffs although they have been known to use electricity power pylons. The nest is a large structure of sticks and twigs and the cup is lined with fine plant material. They nest close to lakes, rivers or the sea because they catch and eat only fish.

The Osprey has white underparts with a brown band across its lower neck. It has a white crown, brown eye-stripe and dark brown upperparts. The bill is black; it has a blue cere and blue-grey feet. It hovers over the water before plunging feet first to take fish. In the air it can look a very pale long-winged raptor with barring across the primaries and secondaries.

It is a scarce passage migrant in Leicestershire. During 1996 eight juvenile birds were introduced to Rutland Water from Scotland and since then another 32 birds have been released in the area in the hope that they might colonise. It appears that the young Ospreys return to the area in which they were bred, so bringing young birds to the area before they can fly imprints Rutland Water into their brains as home. In 1999 one of the first young birds released at Rutland Water returned there and the first breeding of Ospreys in central England for more than 150 years took place at Rutland Water in March 2001. Four male Ospreys from the introduction scheme arrived back at Rutland Water. One of these birds paired with an un-ringed female, probably of Scottish origin and they laid three eggs. The first chick hatched on June 6th, 36 days after nesting started.

The Osprey is an uncommon passage migrant to Swithland Reservoir that is not recorded every year. The records occur in a period from April to September with the majority of sightings coming in May. The most notable occurrence of Osprey at Swithland happened in 1967. A bird arrived on the 3rd May and remained throughout the month. Another bird joined it on the 30th May but unfortunately they both left on the 3rd June. At that time it was a very unusual sight and many birdwatchers took the opportunity to watch these marvellous raptors. The Osprey has been recorded at Swithland Reservoir on 14 occasions since 1967.

FALCONS Falconidae

Common Kestrel *Falco tinnunculus*

The Kestrel breeds throughout Europe and large parts of Asia and Africa. The northerly breeding birds are migratory and move out with the onset of snow. In Europe the northern populations winter in central and southern Europe and Africa. In Asia birds winter from Asia Minor through to India and eastwards to southern China. In Europe it nests from the tundra in the Arctic to the more arid lands of the Mediterranean.

In Britain there is a certain amount of movement of northern birds from Scotland and northern England. The southern birds tend to be resident. The numbers of Kestrel will fluctuate with the availability of prey. This is most noticeable in the most northerly breeding birds. Their numbers rise and fall depending on the availability of voles *Microtus* and lemmings *Lemmus*. Some of the recent declines throughout Europe could have been brought about by more intensive agricultural practices which make it more difficult for the birds to find mice *Mus* and voles. The Kestrel is one of the most frequently seen birds of prey and can often be seen hovering over the verges of roads and motorways and it was its method of hunting that gave it the name 'wind-hover'. It prefers open areas in which it can hunt.

It usually nests in a hole in a tree or crevice in a rock face or building where it makes a shallow scrape.

The male has a chestnut back with black spotting, black primaries, blue grey head, and tail that is black tipped. The underparts are buff with black spotting and it has yellow legs and feet, blue-black bill and yellow-green cere. The female is similar in size and has a browner back and tail that is distinctly barred. The underparts are pale brown with heavy streaking. In flight all falcons show pointed wings.

The Kestrel is a fairly common resident breeding bird in Leicestershire. It is a frequent sight at Swithland Reservoir and a common resident that breeds in the grounds or in the surrounding area annually.

Red-footed Falcon *Falco vespertinus*

The Red-footed Falcon breeds in central eastern Europe and across central Asia to Lena River in Central Siberia. It winters in semi-arid areas of south-western Africa. Autumn migration starts at the end of August and continues through into October. Return passage is mainly from April to May.

It is seen annually in Britain with usually less than fifteen occurrences, most being late spring sightings from May to June. It is much more scarce in the autumn. Like the Kestrel it hovers and may take voles

Microtus, young birds, lizards *Lacerta* or frogs *Pelobates*, but it is mainly insectivorous. It often catches prey like dragonflies *Odonata* in a similar fashion to the Hobby.

It is a lowland species, its main habitat being large open areas with scattered trees; steppe grassland with patches of woodland; agricultural land with trees and woodland on the edges of rivers. It breeds generally in colonies and is gregarious in its habits. It often takes over old Rook's nests when breeding colonially but will use the old nest of other corvids when nesting alone.

The adult male is slate-grey all over with the exception of chestnut undertail coverts, lower belly and thighs. It has a bright orange cere and legs. The female has a rusty brown crown and underparts and a dark-barred grey back and tail. Its legs and cere are similar to the male's.

The Red-footed Falcon is a rare vagrant to Leicestershire that has been seen on five occasions. An immature male was seen at Rothley Sand Pit between the 18th and 23rd June 1956. During its stay it fed on young Sand Martins that had been exposed due to the sand bank collapsing in heavy rain. In the latter part of its stay it spent long periods away from the pit and it was thought to have been hawking insects over the adjacent Swithland Estate. This was the 2nd county record.

Merlin *Falco columbarius*

The Merlin or Pigeon Hawk (as it is known in North America) breeds across northern Europe, Asia and North America. It winters throughout much of Europe southward to North Africa and in Asia Minor eastward to Iraq and northern India and also in Korea, southern Japan and south-east China. The North American population winter in the southern United States south to northern South America. Birds start to leave their breeding grounds towards the end of August and passage continues into October. Return migration takes place in April and May.

In Britain the Merlin is often associated with grouse moors where it breeds among heather on the ground. At present there is something in the region of 1300 breeding pairs. Outside Britain it breeds mainly in trees using old crows' nests and occasionally it nests on cliff ledges. On the ground the nest consists of a small depression lined with small pieces of vegetation.

It breeds on upland moorland, open mountain areas, scrub birch forest, open coniferous forest, sand dunes etc. They do not like dense woodland probably because they take their prey, which is mainly small birds in the air while in swift low flight.

The Merlin is the smallest European Falcon. The adult male has blue-grey upperparts with a barred and black-tipped tail. Its underparts are rusty brown with dark streaking and it has yellow legs, blue-black bill and yellow cere. The Female has dark brown upperparts with narrow buff bands across the dark tail and the underparts are pale buff with heavy dark streaking.

The Merlin is a scarce passage migrant and winter visitor to Leicestershire. It has been seen at Swithland Reservoir on three occasions: a female was seen on the 20th February 1955; another female was recorded on the 23rd January 1983, and a male was seen on the 29th October 1995.

Eurasian Hobby *Falco subbuteo*

The Hobby breeds across Europe southward as far as northern Africa and across Asia reaching Kamchatka and northern Japan in the east. Sometimes birds even venture into the Arctic Circle to breed. The Hobby winters in the southern part of the African continent, northern India and Burma through to southern China. Birds start to leave their breeding areas from the end of August and all have departed by mid-October. Return passage is from mid-April to May.

Due to collectors and gamekeepers there was a decrease in numbers in Britain during the 19th century and even by 1970 there were only about 100 breeding pairs. In the last 25 years, however, its range has expanded and its numbers have risen dramatically in England. In Britain the Hobby is restricted to England and a few areas in Wales as a breeding species and at present there are 624 breeding pairs.

It is a very swift species with long pointed wings and short tail and it takes all its food on the wing. It is mainly insectivorous but will take birds such as swallows and even swifts. On its visits to Swithland Reservoir it often feeds on dragonflies and damselflies *Odonata* and at dusk on several occasions it has been seen to take bats *Chiroptera*.

It often breeds in old corvid nests but will use nests of other species. It nests in hedgerow trees or coppices adjacent to open areas of grassland or agricultural land. It also likes open forest, and heathland and moorland as long as they contain scattered groups of trees.

Its upperparts are slate grey but it does show white cheeks and throat and dark moustachial stripes. The underparts are pale buff with dark streaking and its thighs and undertail coverts are a rich reddish; the bill is blueish and it has a yellow cere and legs.

In Leicestershire the Hobby is an uncommon summer migrant that breeds in small numbers. The first proved breeding in recent times came in 1953 and then it did not breed again until 1974. It has been proved to breed in every year since except for 1985. In 1985 a bird was seen carrying food on several occasions at Swithland Reservoir. The highest number of confirmed breeding pairs in the county was 7 in 1988. The Hobby is an uncommon passage migrant at Swithland Reservoir that has probably bred in the local neighbourhood. The first recent record came on the 5th June 1967. All the records fall in a period from April to October and it has been recorded during every month within that time. The earliest spring record came on the 12th April 1992, and the last autumn record was an adult with three juveniles on the 2nd October 1994. The largest number recorded at any one time was 5 birds on the 17th May 1998. Birds were thought to have bred in the area during 1988.

Peregrine Falcon *Falco peregrinus*

The Peregrine Falcon is a cosmopolitan bird breeding on every continent except Antarctica and it breeds throughout Europe. The southern and western birds appear to be sedentary while the northerly breeding birds migrate as far as southern Africa. African breeding birds are resident. Northern Asian breeding birds winter in south-east Asia; it is resident in India China and Australia. Birds breeding in northern North America winter in central and southern North America and throughout Central South America. A small population occurs in the tip of South America.

Like so many birds of prey their numbers were decimated by organochlorine pesticides and in 1962 only 68 pairs reared young in Britain. In the last two decades the fortunes of the Peregrine have been turned around in Britain and by 1997 there were 1,185 breeding pairs.

They nest generally on cliff ledges either along the coast or inland. At inland sites they often use quarries, the nest normally a shallow depression with little or no material. They breed occasionally in trees in old corvid nests.

The male is often called by the name tiercel and he is smaller than the female and she goes by the name falcon. The Peregrine is a large strong falcon with pointed wings and a broad wing base. In a stoop it has been recorded travelling at 100mph but this speed is probably rare. Its prey is mainly birds that it kills on the wing, generally in a stoop. It feeds on many species but it can take large birds like Grey Heron, goose, pigeon, duck, gull and grouse down to the small Goldcrest. The adult Peregrine's upperparts are slate grey with a darker crown and it has a white throat and cheek patch divided by a broad dark moustachial stripe. The underparts are white with the lower breast, belly and undertail coverts being barred. The bill is blue-grey, with a yellow cere and it has yellow legs.

The Peregrine is a scarce passage migrant and winter visitor to Leicestershire that has started to breed in recent years. They first bred in Leicestershire on the Charnwood Forest in 1994 when a pair raised two young. In 1995 two pairs bred on the Charnwood Forest raising five young. A single pair have bred each year since although no nest was found in 1996, but two juveniles were found with a male at the breeding site. The Peregrine is an uncommon visitor to Swithland Reservoir, mainly in winter although in recent years it has been recorded during every month. The first recent record came on the 31st October 1982, and it has been recorded in 16 out of the last 18 years. It has become a regular winter visitor over the last twelve years. In a period from July to December 1994, Peregrines were seen quite frequently and at least four individuals were noted. From July to December 1995, at least three individuals were recorded regularly.

PARTRIDGES and PHEASANTS Phasianidae

Chukar *Alectoris chukar*

The Chukar breeds in the extreme south east of Europe and across central Asia to north-east China. It was introduced into North America and New Zealand. It is a bird of arid and semi-arid lands that have sparse vegetation.

The nest is a shallow depression sparsely lined with plant material. It is very similar to the Red-legged Partridge but lacks the black streaking on the neck and it has a larger cream throat patch.

During the mid-1980s this species was introduced into Leicestershire. Introductions continued over several years. Several Chukar interbred with Red-legged Partridge and their hybrids were widely recorded. By 1994 it became illegal to release these birds into the country and by 1998 no hybrid or pure bred birds were recorded. There is one record of pure bred Chukar at Swithland Reservoir, a covey of 11 birds being noted on the 4th February 1989.

Red-legged Partridge *Alectoris rufa*

The Red-legged Partridge or French Partridge is restricted to south-western Europe breeding in Spain, Portugal, France, north-west Italy and Britain. Its natural habitat is rocky hillsides but it also occurs on lowland agricultural land, grassland, vineyards and olive groves. The nest is a shallow depression sparsely lined with plant material.

It is an introduced species in Britain that was first released here in 1673 but it did not start to colonise until 1790 when it took hold in Suffolk. This was not, however, the last introduction and many more releases were made.

The Red-legged Partridge has a brown back, grey rump and central tail and reddish outer tail feathers. It has a white throat surrounded by a black band with black streaking on the lower neck. The upper breast is grey and the belly and undertail coverts are brown, the flanks being grey-barred with black, red and white. The bill and legs are red.

The Red-legged Partridge is a fairly common resident breeding bird in Leicestershire. It is a reasonably common resident in the fields adjacent to Swithland Reservoir and it breeds within the reservoir grounds. During 1980 ten nests were recorded from the inflow end of the reservoir. The largest covey to be recorded was 25 birds on the 14th October 1976.

Grey Partridge *Perdix perdix*

The Grey Partridge breeds across Europe south of the Arctic Circle and it is also found across central Asia to south-western Siberia and Asia Minor. Introduced birds can be found in North America.

British birds tend to be resident but some birds in the east of its range are partial migrants. Over the last half century the Grey Partridge has been decreasing in numbers in Britain. Between 1970 and 1998 the British population dropped by around 82% and this is causing concern for its long-term future. The reasons for this decline are not fully understood but the changes in farming practice must have had an effect. Large areas of agricultural land have been turned over to mono-cultures which are heavily sprayed with chemicals. They have very few hedges and small numbers of insects. This must obviously have an effect on their food supply and cut down the amount of suitable breeding habitat.

It is a bird of mixed farmland, open scrub and areas of grassland. The nest is a shallow scrape sparsely lined with dead leaves and grass.

The Grey Partridge has an orange face, brown upperparts with fine vermiculations, and brown wings with light and dark streaking. Its underparts are grey, again finely vermiculated and it has a dark brown belly-patch and chestnut bars on the flanks. The legs and bill are blue-grey. It flies only a few metres above the ground but in flight it shows chestnut outer tail feathers.

The Common Partridge is a fairly common resident breeding bird in Leicestershire that is declining in most areas. Formerly a common bird on adjacent farmland and around the more open edges of Swithland Reservoir, it probably bred in the grounds from time to time, but now its numbers have declined. I have two records of large coveys: 10 birds were noted at the reservoir during the late summer of 1984 and circa 20 birds were seen in the area on the 27th August 1986.

Common Pheasant *Phasianus colchicus*

The Pheasant is a native of southern Asia, being found in Georgia, Armenia, Azerbaijan and on the western border of the Caspian Sea. Its range stretches through the northern Himalayas to south-east Asia and northwards to Japan. It is a widely introduced species, now being found throughout central Europe and North America.

The Pheasant appears to have been popular with the Romans and they are thought to have introduced it over much of central Europe. Although the Romans could have brought the Pheasant to Britain it is the Normans who are credited with introducing the birds. The feral population probably spread across Britain during the 1700s, although the first wild breeding probably took place two hundred years earlier. In Britain birds that are bred in captivity are still released in many areas annually.

The Pheasant is a bird of woodland and scrub. In western Europe it can be found on agricultural land and mixed farmland. The nest is a shallow scrape that is unlined or sparsely lined with vegetation.

Although several races have been introduced, the male Pheasant with which most of us are familiar has a dark head with a green sheen, ear tufts and large red wattles on the face and a white collar. The body is a rich brown that is dark-barred and spotted buff. It has a grey rump and a long brown tail with fine dark barring. It has a dusky-yellow bill and grey-brown legs. The female is similar in size and shape to the male but is plainer brown with buff feather edgings and dark spotting.

The Pheasant is a common resident breeding bird in Leicestershire. It is also a common resident breeding bird at Swithland Reservoir. Formerly large numbers of captive bred birds were released here annually for shooting. The largest count made at the reservoir was of 100 birds on the 2nd September 1986. Albino birds have occasionally been noted. Singles albinos were seen in the area during 1946-47 and in 1982.

RAILS and CRAKES Rallidae

Water Rail *Rallus aquaticus*
The Water Rail breeds throughout Europe south of the Arctic Circle and its range extends southwards to North Africa. It is also found through much of central Asia reaching Sakhalin and northern Japan in the east. It is resident mainly in the western and southern part of Europe but a certain amount of movement does take place in winter from the northern and eastern parts of its range. The central Asian population winter in south-east Asia.

The Water Rail breeds in small numbers throughout the British Isles but breeding is often hard to prove because of its elusive nature. Large numbers visit our shores each year to winter. They arrive from September to October and leave again in March and April. If the weather on the continent is particularly cold large influxes can take place. As already mentioned birds can be very difficult to see and the only way you know they are present is by their call which sounds like a piglet being strangled.

It is usually found in thick marsh and aquatic vegetation on the edges of lakes, ponds and rivers or in well-vegetated ditches. The nest is usually placed in dense vegetation. It is an open cup of dead reed blades and stems and other marsh plants.

The Water Rail is long-necked and sleek looking and its upperparts are warm brown streaked black. Its face, neck and upper breast are blue-grey and its flanks and belly are heavily barred black and white. The undertail coverts are whiter than the Spotted Crake. The red bill is long and slightly decurved and it has long flesh-brown legs.

The Water Rail is an uncommon winter visitor to Leicestershire that has been proved to breed on occasions. Over the past 21 years it has been an annual winter visitor to Swithland Reservoir with normally one or two birds being present. Occasionally more birds are recorded and as many as 5 birds were present on the 24th November 1985, and it was believed 4 birds were present between 22nd September and 6th December 1988. The Water Rail has been recorded at Swithland during every month. It has been proved to breed on one occasion when an adult with two young were seen on the south side of the reservoir on the 15th July 1947. Birds were also present during the breeding season in 1970, 1981 and 1989.

Corncrake *Crex crex*
The Corncrake or Land Rail breeds across central Europe and through central Asia as far as Lake Baikal in Central Siberia. It spends the winter on the savannahs of east Africa. Birds arrive in Europe in April and early May and leave again during September and October.

The Corncrake started to decline in Britain towards the end of the 19th century and its decrease continued right through the 20th century. A survey carried out in Britain during 1978 put the total population at 650 breeding pairs. At present the breeding population has remained fairly stable since 1978 and stands at 641 pairs. The reason for this species' decline is almost certainly to do with the mechanisation of farming and earlier mowing dates.

It is a bird that likes grassland: meadows, marshes, moorland fringes or lake sides. The nest is a shallow depression lined with grass or dead leaves placed in dense vegetation.

The Corncrake is about the same size as a Water Rail but appears to be a stockier bird. The bill is small and flesh-coloured and its legs are flesh brown. The back is buff-brown streaked black-brown and its wings are chestnut. The face, supercilium, throat and upper breast are grey and its flanks and lower breast are chestnut with white barring. The Corncrake often gives its presence away only by its continuous rasping call 'crex-crex'.

Towards the end of the last century it was widely distributed and a not uncommon breeding summer visitor to Leicestershire with odd birds staying through the winter. The last time it is thought to have bred in Leicestershire was around 1947 and 1948 and since that time it has been only a rare passage migrant that was last recorded in the county in June 1982. It probably bred at Swithland Reservoir in the early part of this century but the only records I have were both in 1946. A very early bird was heard calling on the 30th March and another was recorded on the 29th April.

Common Moorhen *Gallinula chloropus*

The Moorhen is found throughout Europe with other populations occurring in Asia eastwards to Japan, much of Africa, south-eastern North America throughout Central South America and in the unforested areas of northern and central South America. A certain amount of migration does take place in North America, northern Asia and eastern and northern Europe, areas that generally have freezing conditions during the winter. It generally winters within its southerly and, in the case of Europe, westerly breeding range.

The Moorhen is a common resident in Britain and Ireland and these two countries hold 70% of the European population. A certain amount of immigration does take place from continental Europe during the autumn.

It is a common species being found on freshwater lakes, ponds, rivers and streams that have emergent and aquatic vegetation along their edges. The nest is placed on partially submerged branches over water or in emergent vegetation. It makes a bulky cup nest of dead reed blades, sticks, grass, and other vegetation.

The adult Moorhen has slate blue-grey plumage with slightly browner wings. It has a white line across the flanks and white undertail coverts. It has long green toes and legs. On the forehead there is a red frontal shield, it has a red base to the bill and a yellow tip.

The Moorhen is a common resident breeding bird in Leicestershire. It is also a common resident and breeding bird at Swithland Reservoir. In recent years the numbers breeding on Buddon Brook have dropped dramatically. This could be due to human disturbance but American Mink *Lutreola vison* could be having an effect. The two largest counts for the reservoir were 64 on 5th September 1993, and 73 on the 1st October 1989.

Eurasian Coot *Fulica atra*

The Coot breeds throughout much of central and southern Europe southward to North Africa. It breeds across central Asia reaching Sakhalin and Japan in the east and also in scattered populations in Asia Minor. Other populations occur throughout the Indian subcontinent on the islands in south-east Asia, Australia and New Zealand. It is resident in western Europe, India and Australia. The eastern European population and the birds breeding across central Asia migrate during the winter months from the onset of freezing conditions. Most European and western Asian birds winter within its western and southern breeding range. The eastern Asian birds winter in Indo China and south-east China. Migration takes place from late August through to the end of November and return passage starts at the end of February and continues on into April.

The Coot is a common and widespread resident breeding species in Britain, with its numbers being augmented in the autumn by birds from continental Europe.

It can be found on most areas of open freshwater including lakes, reservoirs, ponds, rivers and streams that have an abundance of emergent and aquatic vegetation. The nest is bulky, with a shallow cup made of dead reed blades, grass, stems and other vegetation often built on submerged or partially submerged branches.

The adult Coot is a thick-set short-tailed bird with a charcoal grey body. On its forehead is a white frontal shield: hence the phrase "as bald as a coot". It has a white bill and red eye. Its legs are yellow-green with large lobed feet similar to those of a grebe.

It is a fairly common resident breeding bird in Leicestershire given the right habitat and its numbers are swollen during the winter months with birds from the continent. It is a common resident breeding bird on Swithland reservoir with large numbers of winter visitors occurring on occasions. 25 pairs were recorded in 1943. Breeding very much depends on the water level and when the water level is high over a dozen pairs nest annually at this water. Some large counts have been made at the reservoir but I am listing only those over three hundred. 350 birds were recorded in early October 1973; 380 on the 26th July 1975, and 361 on the 11th October 1998.

WADERS Charadriiformes

Swithland Reservoir is not a good place for waders! It has mature reedswamp and woodland margins and when the reservoir is full the dam provides the only place for most waders to alight. In the 1970s the water levels were very low and this culminated in the reservoir being drained in 1976. During this period large numbers of waders were recorded. After making the last comments about Swithland's unsuitability for waders, to state then that 31 species have been recorded at the site almost appears to be a contradiction. Waders of one sort or another can be seen throughout every month of the year. During the winter Woodcock can be found in the woodlands and the inflow and outflow streams generally host one or two Green Sandpipers. One winter evening back in February 1991, while bird ringing along the Buddon Brook a few hundred yards from the reservoir boundary, I caught a Snipe, Jack Snipe and Woodcock at the same time in the mist nets. It was an experience being able to study these secretive birds side by side and probably quite unique. During the summer months Lapwing were a once-frequent sight over adjacent pastureland and the dam is the favourite feeding place for the odd Little Ringed Plover. Early spring is the best time to see Common Sandpipers as they make brief but regular visits to the reservoir. As a young birdwatcher at Swithland Reservoir I would get excited during passage periods to see waders and although not easy to identify they held a special mystique. The wild cries of the Whimbrel, Curlew and Greenshank held promises of distant northern lands I knew little or nothing about.

During October 1973 I saw two extremely rare birds for Britain, a Sharp-tailed Sandpiper and a Buff-breasted Sandpiper standing side by side in a sewage-washed field at Shotton in what was then Flintshire. The Sharp-tailed Sandpiper breeds in eastern Siberia and winters in Australia and New Zealand and the Buff-breasted Sandpiper breeds on the Arctic tundra of North America and winters on grasslands of Argentina. Both are little-known species but this occurrence shows the cosmopolitan nature of wading birds.

As the years have gone by I have been fortunate enough to see waders all around the world. I have been on Arctic tundra and heard the tittering calls of the Whimbrel and the constant whistles of the Golden Plover and sat by a peat pool and had several Red-necked Phalaropes picking insects delicately off the water several inches away from my feet. These are privileges indeed. One of my most precious memories happened one morning at about 1000 metres on Mount Njulla in northern Sweden as I had a family party of Dotterels feeding happily a metre away. Suddenly the parents became agitated and crouched down and a dark shadow crossed the ground in front of me. On looking up I saw a Rough-legged Buzzard gliding effortlessly overhead. To see sheer multitudes of waders flying along the shoreline of the Wash on a winter's evening as the tide turns, and see the clouds of Knot and Dunlin twisting and turning and looking for all the world like smoke blown by the wind is an amazing spectacle.

Some waders can be quite unusual to look at and while birdwatching at Miranda on the Firth of Thames on the North Island of New Zealand in November 1993, I found one such bird. I was searching through the mass of waders gathered at high tide which included thousands of Bar-tailed Godwit, several hundred Knot and Turnstone with a few Curlew Sandpiper, Sharp-tailed Sandpiper, Red-necked Stint and one New Zealand Dotterel when I found 20 Wrybill feeding. The Wrybill is similar in some respects to a Ringed Plover and I was fortunate enough to see them before they moved south on spring passage to the South Island where they breed on stony and shingle river beds. These Wrybill were in breeding plumage, with grey upperparts, white foreheads bordered by a black bar and white underparts with a black breast band. However, the most unusual aspect about these birds is their sideways-bent bill in which the tip bends to the right. They are a real oddity in the birding world but the bill enables them to feed on prey like mayfly larvae which cling to the underside of stones and which other birds would be unable to reach. The second unusual waders were found while birdwatching along the shoreline of Nimes Laguna in southern Patagonia in Argentina in November 1999. On the shoreline of the lake were several White-rumped Sandpipers and a few Baird's Sandpipers but very few other waders. We were walking on dry ground away from the lake when my wife drew my attention to two little birds no bigger than larks feeding on the ground six feet away. They were almost unnoticeable with their cryptic coloration. They were a pair of Least Seedsnipe. They had very short yellow bills and small yellow legs, their upperparts were scaly and a mixture of browns and the lower underparts were white. The female had a small white throat patch and a heavily streaked upper breast. The male also had a small white throat patch, but with a grey face and neck bordered by black. Both those waders were highly developed to live in certain habitats and I have yet to see the mythical Spoon-billed Sandpiper with its extraordinary spatulate bill!

In recent years I have seen Ruddy Turnstone and Whimbrel on six continents and Curlew Sandpiper and Grey Plover on five. Wader movements can be very quick and they cover enormous distances. I was at Cairns in Queensland, north-eastern Australia, in mid-August 1997, watching the waders gather along the Esplanade. As the tide came in I was surprised to see so many northern species. From the high Arctic there were 40 Great Knot, 50 Bar-tailed Godwit, 24 Whimbrel, 3 Curlew Sandpiper, 24 Sharp-tailed Sandpiper, 6 Pacific Golden Plover and 2 Red-necked Stint. From slightly further south came 40 Grey-tailed Tattler, 50 Far Eastern Curlew, 10 Black-tailed Godwit and 2 Greenshank and some of the assembled species were still in their fine summer dress.

A similar thing happened while birdwatching near Cape Town, South Africa, where in late August and early September of 1996 I saw flocks of northerly breeding waders. I know some non-breeding birds remain throughout the summer in South Africa but these numbers were too large. Among the waders I saw were 100 Curlew Sandpiper, 30 Marsh Sandpiper, 20 Whimbrel, 20 Little Stint, 20 Terek Sandpiper, 12 Grey Plover, 30 Greenshank, Wood Sandpiper and Common Sandpiper. Most of them would have made the journey from Arctic Europe and Siberia within a month.

I had an amusing occurrence in May 1988, while visiting Ontario in Canada. A friend and I went to an area called Stoney Point. This area was good for waders and among the assembled Short-billed Dowitchers, Greater and Lesser Yellowlegs, Hudsonian Godwits, Wilson's Phalaropes and the numerous American sandpipers was one solitary Curlew Sandpiper. Shortly after the bird had been discovered I became aware that it was not only the Brits who have twitchers!

To watch waders anywhere in the world will always bring to me a feeling of excitement and happy memories and you are never quite sure what may turn up. But, whether rare or common, I shall never tire of seeing the nomads of the shoreline.

OYSTERCATCHERS Haematopodidae

Eurasian Oystercatcher *Haematopus ostralegus*

The Oystercatcher or 'Sea-pie' as it is sometimes known, breeds around the coastline of Europe and inland along river valleys or on the edges of lakes. It breeds more extensively in central eastern Europe eastwards to the Ob River in western Siberia. Other populations also occur in eastern Asia in Kamchatka southward into China. The northern breeding population moves south in the winter and travels as far as Africa.

In Britain it is a resident species that can be found throughout the year although severe periods of cold weather will cause the birds to move. They breed commonly in Scotland and can be found in good numbers in northern England, Wales and Ireland although they are less frequent in eastern and southern England.

It breeds on sea coasts and inland on the shores of freshwater lakes and rivers and also in grass meadows close to water. The nest is a shallow depression that is either unlined or sparsely lined with small stones or vegetation. In winter it is generally found on sea coast, on tidal mudflats and saltmarsh.

The Oystercatcher is an unmistakable large black and white wader with a long straight red/orange bill, pink legs and red eye-ring. In summer plumage its head, neck, chest and upperparts are black and the underparts white. In flight it displays a distinctive white wing-bar and white rump extending onto the lower back. In winter plumage they have a white chinstrap.

In Leicestershire the Oystercatcher is an uncommon passage migrant and scarce breeder. The first breeding record came in 1970 when a pair successfully reared three young at Wanlip Gravel Pits and since 1978 it has been a regular breeder at Rutland Water. The first record I have for Swithland Reservoir is 16th August 1961, and there have been 11 records since. All the records have been of single birds except when two birds were present on the 26th November 1992. Seven of the records were seen in a period from August to December, three in May and one in March. The last record was of a single bird seen on the 4th and 5th June, 2000. This is an unusual date but it is interesting to note that a pair raised one young at Quorn Lodge Borrow Pit earlier that year.

AVOCETS Recurvirostridae

Pied Avocet *Recurvirostra avosetta*

The Avocet has a patchy breeding distribution in central and southern Europe across central Asia and through east Africa to the Cape. The northerly breeding populations move south to the Mediterranean, Africa and southern Asia to winter.

It became extinct as a breeding species in Britain around the middle of the 19th century and did not breed again until the 1940s. The main re-colonisation however did not start until 1947 in Suffolk when four or five pairs bred on Havergate Island and four pairs at Minsmere. The Avocet was given protection by the R.S.P.B. and has become a conservation success story with colonies establishing themselves at several sites in Norfolk and Suffolk. In 1972 the population was 135 breeding pairs. By 1997 this had risen to about 654 breeding pairs.

This species tends to be a colonial nester and favours brackish lagoons and saltmarsh. Its nest is a shallow scrape usually unlined or only sparsely lined with dead vegetation.

The Avocet is an elegant bird with bold black and white plumage. The upper head, nape, sides of mantle, central wing coverts and primaries are black and the rest of the plumage is white; it has a long dark upcurved bill and long pale blue legs.

The Avocet is a rare passage migrant to Leicestershire that has been seen on two occasions at Swithland Reservoir. Two birds were present on the 13th April 1995, and a single bird was seen on the 26th October 1996. It is interesting to note that a pair tried to breed at Rutland Water in May 1996, laying four eggs but, unfortunately, they were unsuccessful. A pair did however breed successfully at the Welney Wildfowl and Wetland Centre on the Ouse Washes in Norfolk that year and these two occurrences are the first records of inland breeding in Britain. The Avocets have bred every year at Welney since then and in 1999 twenty-one pairs reared around 35 chicks.

PLOVERS Charadriidae

Little Ringed Plover *Charadrius dubius*

The Little Ringed Plover breeds across Europe and throughout much of Asia eastwards to Japan. Its range extends southward through India and it even nests in New Guinea. It is absent only from the far north of Europe and Asia. It winters in Africa and south-east Asia. In winter it is only the more northerly breeding populations that migrate. In India and south-east Asia birds tend to be resident.

The Little Ringed Plover first bred in Britain in 1938 and now has colonised most of eastern England as far north as Durham and as far west as the Severn Estuary and Cheshire. It is a summer visitor to our shores arriving towards the end of March and leaving again by September and October.

It is an inland species that breeds on bare gravel or sand at the edges of freshwater rivers, lakes, gravel pits and reservoirs. Its nest is a shallow depression, unlined or sparsely lined with small stones and plant material.

The Little Ringed Plover is a small plover with brown upperparts and white underparts. The adult has black head markings and breast band. It can be distinguished from the Ringed Plover by a yellow eye-ring, dark bill and paler grey-brown legs. In flight it lacks the prominent wing bar of the Ringed Plover.

The Little Ringed Plover was first recorded in Leicestershire in 1948 and it first bred in the county at Hemington Sand Pit in 1954. It is an uncommon passage migrant and breeding bird in the county. At Swithland Reservoir it is an uncommon and irregular breeder and an uncommon but regular passage migrant. The first record came for the reservoir when two birds were present from the 9th to the 24th July 1965, and it first bred here in 1972. Two pairs bred in 1973. Often the water is too high to allow the birds to breed and in recent years birds have been breeding in the granite quarry on Buddon and use the reservoir for feeding. There have been two notable counts for this water. On the 15th July 1995, 16 birds were present and on the 17th July 1996, 12 birds were recorded.

Common Ringed Plover *Charadrius hiaticula*

The Ringed Plover breeds in the high Arctic in eastern Canada, Greenland and across northern Siberia in Asia. In Europe it can be found around the northern coasts of western Europe. In autumn the most northerly breeding birds move south to the Mediterranean and Africa, some birds wintering as far south as the Cape.

In Britain the Ringed Plover breeds all around our coastline and less frequently inland in England, Wales and southern Scotland, though it is much more plentiful in northern Scotland. In recent years this species has suffered as a direct result of human disturbance of the shoreline especially in England and Wales. The Ringed Plover is resident in southern Britain. Large numbers of birds move through the country from as far afield as Greenland, Iceland and Scandinavia from mid-August to mid-September and return passage starts again in April and continues into May.

It nests on tundra or on stony, muddy and sandy shorelines by the side of salt, brackish and fresh water. The nest is a shallow scrape sparsely lined with pebbles, pieces of plant material or debris.

The adult Ringed Plover is slightly larger than the Little Ringed Plover. It has similar brown upperparts, white underparts, black head markings and breast band. It differs in having an orange-based black bill and bright orange legs. In flight it shows a prominent white wing bar.

The Ringed Plover is a rare breeding bird in Leicestershire but a regular passage migrant. They first bred in the county in 1965 at Wanlip Gravel Pits. This species is an irregular passage migrant to Swithland Reservoir that was first recorded on the 15th March 1944, and has been seen on eight occasions since. There are two notable counts: 8 were present on the 14th August 1974, and 11 were recorded on the 9th September 1974.

Killdeer *Charadrius vociferus*

The Killdeer breeds across North America and winters in the southern United States, Central and South America. The northern North American population start to move southwards from July to November and return from February to April.

The Killdeer is the American counterpart of our Lapwing. It breeds on pastureland and agricultural land and can be found by fresh or salt water. The nest is a shallow depression either unlined or sparsely lined with debris, small stones or pieces of plant material.

It derives its name from the loud 'Kill-dee' call that often draws your attention to its presence. The Killdeer resembles a very large Ringed Plover with brown upperparts and white underparts. It has a double black breast-band, dark face mask, orange eye-ring and dark bill and legs. In flight it shows a white wing-bar, a rufous rump and a long graduated tail.

The Killdeer is a rare vagrant to the British Isles. There has been one occurrence at Swithland Reservoir, a bird being present from the 2nd of November until the 19th November 1975. A bird had also been at Eyebrook Reservoir from the 28th September, until the 19th October 1975, and it was considered that these records referred to the same bird and this constituted the 19th British record. It is interesting to note that the only other Killdeer to be seen in Britain in 1975 was seen in Thorn Moors, Humberside, from the 29th to 30th November and it makes one wonder whether this too was the same individual.

European Golden Plover *Pluvialis apricaria*

The Golden Plover breeds across northern Europe and Asia into Central Siberia. It winters across Europe reaching the Mediterranean and North Africa.

In Britain it breeds on upland areas throughout Scotland and Wales. In England it is restricted to Dartmoor, the Pennine moorlands and the fells of the Lake District. One of its old names was the 'whistler' and I can understand why, having spent time camping in upland areas in northern Europe. Birds keep you awake day and night with their monotonous one note call. It is a common passage migrant and winter visitor to many lowland areas of Britain.

The Golden Plover breeds on upland moorland, heath and tundra. Its nest is a shallow depression lined with varying amounts of plant material. It winters on lowland pastureland and agricultural land.

It is a medium-sized wader with a small dark bill, dark legs and a large dark eye. The Golden Plover in breeding plumage is a handsome bird with golden brown upperparts and black underparts bordered by white in the northern race *P. a. altifrons*. The nominate southern race *P.a. apricaria* tends to show less black on the neck and face. In winter plumage the black is replaced by a mottled golden brown breast and white belly.

In Leicestershire the Golden Plover is a common passage migrant and winter visitor. Birds start to arrive in numbers towards the end of September and leave again by April. It can often be found associating with flocks of Lapwing in the Soar and Welland Valleys. In December 1998, a flock of 4,000 birds was noted at Enderby Pool while 3,500 were at EyeBrook Reservoir. It is rarely recorded at Swithland Reservoir and this is possibly because it is so common in other areas in the county that the odd bird at this site is of little consequence. The largest count I have for Swithland Reservoir was on the 26th February 1983, when 12 birds flew over.

Grey Plover *Pluvialis squatarola*

The Grey Plover, or Black-bellied Plover as it is known in North America, breeds on arctic tundra discontinuously around the globe but not in Europe. It winters on the coast of North and South America, western Europe, Africa, Southern and south-east Asia and Australia.

In Britain it prefers seashore, saltmarsh and estuary in winter and can be found in appreciable numbers around the coast. Unlike the Golden Plover it is not so frequent inland, especially in Britain. Return passage takes place through Britain mainly in May. It appears that a large number of males winter in western Europe and the females move southward into Africa.

The Grey Plover breeds on lowland tundra. Its nest is a shallow depression lined with a few pieces of lichen or small stones. The adults leave their Arctic breeding grounds in late July and all have left by September, whereas the young do not start to move until September, all of them having departed by October.

In size and shape the Grey Plover is not unlike the Golden Plover. In breeding plumage it has a dark speckled grey back, white forehead and sides of neck, mostly black underparts and white undertail coverts. Its summer plumage gave rise to its other name the Silver Plover. In winter it has whitish underparts and a grey back. Like the Golden Plover it has a small dark bill, dark legs and a large dark eye. In flight the white wingbar and black axillaries or 'armpits' are diagnostic.

In Leicestershire this species is a scarce passage migrant and winter visitor. It has been recorded on nine occasions at Swithland Reservoir since the first sighting on the 27th December 1969. All the records have been of single birds that were seen in a period from mid-September to May. The most recent sighting was of a single bird on the 10th and 11th May, 2000.

Northern Lapwing *Vanellus vanellus*

The Lapwing or Green Plover is a common breeding bird over much of Europe and across central Asia eastwards to the Sea of Japan. In Asia it winters in Asia Minor, Pakistan and northern India and south-east China. In winter the northerly and easterly European breeding populations move south and west reaching the Mediterranean and North Africa.

In Britain it is still a fairly common species although its numbers have fallen dramatically. Between 1970 and 1998 it decreased by more than 52% and this is a real cause for concern. This decline has almost certainly been brought about by changes in farming practice. The British population is augmented in the autumn by immigrants from Europe. Large movements of Lapwings take place during prolonged periods of cold weather and flocks can be seen moving in a generally south-westerly direction where they reach Ireland, France and Spain.

The Lapwing breeds on grassland, saltmarsh, moorland and heath. The nest is a shallow depression lined with varying amounts of vegetation.

The Lapwing is a large plump plover which at a distance looks black and white. It has a black and white face and long wispy crest with purple-shot green upperparts, a black collar and white underparts with buff undertail coverts. The bill is fairly small and its legs are pink in colour. In flight it is a very striking bird with broad rounded wings. It looks generally dark above, contrasting markedly with its white underparts. The call of the Lapwing gave rise to its country name of 'Peewit' and at one time its eggs were considered a delicacy.

In Leicestershire it is a fairly common breeder and an abundant winter visitor. In winter flocks of over 1,000 birds are frequent and huge flocks can occasionally be encountered. Circa 8,000 were recorded in the Shepshed/Belton area in January 1990, and 7,000 at Eye Brook Reservoir in early December the same year. Several pairs of Lapwing bred regularly in the fields adjacent to Swithland Reservoir and in February and March their aerial display flights were quite a feature. The last record I have of breeding in this area came in 1993. If the water levels are low post-breeding flocks numbering a hundred or more birds are a frequent sight in late summer and early autumn.

SANDPIPERS, STINTS, GODWITS, CURLEWS, SNIPE, PHALAROPES Scolopacidae

Red Knot *Calidris canutus*

The Red Knot is a high Arctic breeding species with a scattered distribution around the globe. The nearest breeding colonies to Britain are in Greenland and Svalbard (Spitsbergen). They winter as far south as southern South America, South Africa, Australia and New Zealand.

Many thousands of Knot visit Britain on passage and many will remain throughout the winter. The adult birds leave the breeding grounds in late July followed by the young in the latter part of August. Ringing studies have shown that the majority of the young birds winter further south than the adults. Most birds winter on tidal mudflats and estuaries and they are only occasionally met with inland. Spring migration happens from late May to early June.

They breed on barren tundra, stony plateaux containing Mountain Avens *Dryas octopetala* and marshy ground generally in close proximity to water. The nest is a shallow depression sparsely lined with lichens and other plant material.

The Knot is a medium-sized wader that is rather short-legged. In breeding plumage it has chestnut red underparts and its upperparts are a mixture of chestnut and black with some white feather edgings. It has a short straight dark bill and its legs are olive green. In winter plumage the upperparts are grey while the underparts are white with grey mottling on the breast and flanks. In flight it shows a narrow white wing bar and a pale barred rump.

In Leicestershire it is a scarce passage migrant and rare winter visitor. The Knot has been recorded at Swithland Reservoir on eight occasions since the first record of three birds on the 2nd February 1944. The only other occasion when more than one bird was recorded was on the 14th November 1959, when nine birds were present. The last record I have was of a single bird on the 10th September, 2000. All the records fall in a period from September to March.

Sanderling *Calidris alba*

The Sanderling, like the Knot, is a high Arctic breeding species with a circumpolar scattered distribution. The nearest breeding site to Britain is Svalbard (Spitsbergen). It winters in the tropics and temperate zone and can be found around the coasts of South America, Africa and Australia. The adults leave the breeding grounds from mid-July and all are gone by mid-August; their young leave in late August and early September. The return migration takes place from the end of March to late May.

In Britain it is a common winter visitor and passage migrant that favours coastal sandy beaches. It is uncommon inland except on passage. Birds can often be found on the shoreline just where the waves break and they run up and down the beach in synchronisation with the waves breaking.

They breed on barren coastal tundra and stony lichen-covered tundra, especially areas with Mountain Avens *Dryas octopetala* and Purple Saxifrage *Saxifraga oppositifolia*. The nest is a shallow depression lined with willow *Salix* leaves. This species has unusual breeding behaviour. The female will often lay two clutches simultaneously. The male will incubate one while she takes care of the other.

The Sanderling is about the same size as a Dunlin with a short dark bill and dark legs. The adult in breeding plumage has a rufous breast and neck intermixed with dark streaking; the rest of the underparts are white. The upperparts are a mixture of rufous, black and white feathering. In winter plumage the upperparts are pale grey and the underparts white. In flight it shows dark wings with a pronounced white wing-bar.

The Sanderling is a scarce passage migrant in Leicestershire. It has been recorded on eight occasions at Swithland Reservoir since the first record on the 30th January 1954, an interesting record because it is the only winter sighting. Of the other records five were in May, two in July and one in September. All the records were of single birds, the exceptions being that four were present on the 13th and 14th May 1973, and two on the 23rd May 1994.

Little Stint *Calidris minuta*

The Little Stint breeds on Arctic tundra in Europe and northern Siberia. The adult birds leave the breeding grounds in late July; the young birds leave by late August. On passage and in winter the Little Stint can be found on coastal beaches, mudflats and estuaries and inland on the shores of lakes, reservoirs and rivers. Winter birds reach South Africa and southern India.

In Britain the Little Stint is generally a passage migrant arriving in late August and early September and most will have passed through by October although occasionally birds can be seen during the winter months. Return passage takes place from April to June but it is more uncommon during this period as most birds migrate well to the east of Britain.

It breeds on low-lying tundra with Reindeer Moss *Cladonia* and areas covered in dwarf willows *Salix*. The nest is a shallow scrape lined with dead leaves and grass. It is a polygamous species in which both males and females will have several partners. Males and females will simultaneously incubate clutches and continue looking after the resulting progeny.

The Little Stint is a small wader which is about the same size as a House Sparrow. It has a small, fine, straight dark bill and dark legs. In breeding plumage the upper breast, head and upperparts are rufous with intermixed dark feathering with white edges to some feathers which are lost with wear; the rest of the underparts are white. In winter plumage it has grey upperparts and white underparts. In flight it shows a narrow white wing bar and grey outer tail feathers.

In Leicestershire it is uncommon on autumn passage, rare in winter and very rare on spring migration. The Little Stint was first recorded at Swithland Reservoir on 7th October 1961, and has been seen on three occasions since. Three of the sightings were in the autumn, in September and October, and one was a spring record, a bird being present from 20th to 27th May 1973. The only occasion when more than one bird was present was on 21st September 1996, when 15 birds were recorded. This occurrence was part of a massive influx of mainly juvenile birds into the country during the autumn of 1996.

Pectoral Sandpiper *Calidris melanotos*

The Pectoral Sandpiper breeds on arctic tundra in North America and eastern Siberia. It winters across central South America, with smaller numbers wintering in south-eastern Australia and New Zealand.

In Britain the Pectoral Sandpiper has become an annual passage migrant with over 50 birds being recorded annually. Most of the records are in the autumn but spring records do occur occasionally.

The Pectoral Sandpiper breeds on arctic grass and lichen tundra. The nest is a shallow depression lined with leaves and grass. Adults leave the breeding grounds towards the end of June and their young leave in early August. The majority of juvenile birds remain in North America during September and October and it is these birds that get caught in severe westerly gales, some ending up in western Europe.

The Pectoral Sandpiper is larger than a Dunlin with a long yellow-based, slightly decurved bill and long yellowish legs. The chest and upper breast are heavily streaked, the streaking ending in a neat abrupt line where it meets the white underparts. The upperparts are dark with rufous and pale feathers intermixed and it has a little dark cap with a white supercilium. In flight it shows a faint wing-bar.

The Pectoral Sandpiper is a rare vagrant to Leicestershire that has been recorded on 20 occasions, most of the records coming from Eye Brook Reservoir and Rutland Water. There is one record for Swithland Reservoir, an adult being present on the 15th September 1996, and this was the 19th county record.

Curlew Sandpiper *Calidris ferruginea*

The Curlew Sandpiper is a high arctic breeding species which breeds entirely in Siberia on tundra. Part of the population migrates south-west to Europe on its way to winter in Africa. Other birds winter in India and Australia.

In the British Isles it is a passage migrant in varying numbers. In some years it can be very plentiful and in others very scarce.

The Curlew Sandpiper breeds on coastal tundra, its nest is a shallow depression placed in low-growing vegetation. The adults leave the breeding grounds in July and August, the males leaving first because they take no part in incubation or rearing the young. The adults gather to the south of the breeding area to moult. The young birds start migrating in August and September. Return passage takes place in April and May. On migration it can be found on coasts and marshes and inland it frequents reservoir margins.

The Curlew Sandpiper is slightly larger in size than the Dunlin with longer dark legs and long decurved bill. In summer plumage it has rich chestnut red underparts and black upperparts with mixed chestnut and white feathering. In winter plumage it has grey upperparts and white underparts and shows a white supercilium, the juveniles being generally buffer in colour. In flight it shows a distinct wing-bar and a white rump.

In Leicestershire it is an uncommon autumn passage migrant that is not seen every year and it is very rare on spring migration. The Curlew Sandpiper is a rare autumn passage migrant to Swithland Reservoir that has been seen on five occasions since it was first recorded on the 3rd September 1944. All the records are of single birds except one, eight birds being recorded flying over the reservoir on the 3rd September 1998. There is one August record but all the other birds were recorded in September. One bird stayed from the 24th September to the 1st October 1969.

Dunlin *Calidris alpina*

The Dunlin or Red-backed Sandpiper breeds in north-western Europe across northern Siberia with a scattered distribution in North America through to Greenland. They do not migrate as far as other species, wintering in Europe, North America and west Africa.

The Dunlin breeds on upland moorland in northern England, Wales and Scotland but some birds will breed on saltmarsh at sea level. In winter and on passage it is an abundant bird of mudflats sandbanks, saltmarsh and estuaries. The main passage periods are from mid-July to late September and return passage from March to the end of May.

It is an arctic and alpine breeding species nesting on moorland, saltmarsh and tundra. The nest is a shallow depression lined with leaves and grass.

The Dunlin is a similar size to a Starling with small dark legs and long slightly decurved bill. In summer plumage the adult has blackish upperparts with chestnut feather edgings, white throat with black streaking and diagnostic black belly area; the rest of the underparts are white. In winter plumage the adult is grey-brown above and white below with grey flecking on the upper breast. In flight the Dunlin shows a slight white wing-bar and a dark centred tail with grey outer tail feathers

In Leicestershire it is a common passage migrant and winter visitor, although in spring it is uncommon. The Dunlin is an uncommon passage migrant and winter visitor to Swithland Reservoir that is not recorded every year. The first record I have was of 6 birds between November and December 1943. Most of the records fall within a period from August to February but there are two late spring records, one on the 31st May 1991, and one on the 4th June 1995. Unprecedented numbers were present just prior to the reservoir being completely drained in 1976. 40 birds were present in November 1975, rising to 50 on the 13th December 1975, and 30 were present throughout January and February 1976.

Ruff *Philomachus pugnax*

The Ruff breeds from central Europe to the Arctic and across Arctic Siberia. It winters in southern Europe and Africa, India and southern Australia. In some areas of western Europe it is resident.

In Britain the Ruff is a regular passage migrant and a winter visitor in small numbers. It became almost extinct as a breeding species in the early 19th century due largely to the fens being drained, and to hunting. Odd pairs sporadically bred in England until 1922. It did not breed again until 1963 when it was found on the Ouse Washes and it bred in small numbers regularly until recently when it has become a more sporadic breeder once again. In 1980 there were 11 pairs breeding in Britain but none nested in 1997. In winter and on migration the Ruff can be found on mudflats, shallow pools, reservoir margins and agricultural land. The main migration period is late June to September and return passage takes place from February to May.

The Ruff breeds in lush grassland, on open boggy ground in amongst taiga forest and on tundra. The nest is a shallow depression lined with grass and other plant material. At the begining of the breeding season up to thirty males gather together at a display ground called a 'lek', show off their finery and engage in ritual combat to impress visiting females which stand on the edges of the display ground. The Ruff's previous scientific name which is no longer used was *machetes* which is Greek for warrior. *Pugnax* is Latin for pugnacious and that sums up the male birds quite well. The females will mate with an attractive male and then leave to raise their brood. As soon as the mating period has taken place the male Ruff moult and depart on migration.

The male Ruff is quite a lot bigger than the female and she goes by a separate name, Reeve. The breeding males are quite extraordinary in appearance. They have a slightly decurved orange bill and bare warty skin around the face. On the head are plumes that can be erected and around the neck is a ruff that is fanned during display. The ruff and head plumes can be barred or plain and can range between black, purple, rufous or white and over 38 different combinations have been noted. The rest of the upperparts are mottled grey-brown with dark-centred feathers and the underparts are white with varying amounts of dark on the breast. Its legs are long and orange in colour. The Reeve is drab by comparison, with a grey brown back with black-centred feathers giving a scaled appearance. The neck, flanks and breast are greyish with black spotting. In winter plumage the sexes are similar except for size. Both have greyish upperparts with black centred feathers and white underparts with a grey wash around the neck and upper breast, the leg colour is variable yellow, orange or flesh. In flight the Ruff shows a narrow white wing-bar, a white oval patch on each side of the rump and the feet project well beyond the tail.

In Leicestershire it is an uncommon passage migrant and winter visitor. The Ruff has been seen at Swithland Reservoir on seven occasions since it was first recorded between the 23rd August and 13th September 1944. Of the eight records, seven were in autumn and fall in a period from late July to September. The other is a winter record, two birds being present on the 14th February 1976. The only occasion when more than two birds were present was on the 7th September 1994, when six birds were recorded.

Jack Snipe *Lymnocryptes minimus*

The Jack Snipe breeds in bogs amongst taiga forest and in wet Alder *Alnus* and willow *Salix* scrub in northern Europe and Asia. The nest is a deep hollow sparsely lined with grass and leaves. It is a passage migrant over much of Europe and winters as far south as the Mediterranean and North Africa and India. The main passage period is late and takes place from September to October. The birds return in late March and April.

It is a regular passage migrant and winter visitor to Britain. In winter it can be found on the edges of streams and rivers, waterlogged flood meadows and the waterlogged edges of ponds and reservoirs.

The Jack Snipe is a lot smaller than the Snipe with a much shorter bill. Several birds I have caught for ringing had a bill length of 41mm whereas the last Snipe's bill I measured was 70mm. It has a similar plumage to the Snipe with dark brown upperparts and bold buff back stripes. In good light the back shows a purple or green sheen. The head is dark with buff stripes but it has a dark crown. It also shows a dark-streaked brown breast and white underparts; the short legs are olive green in coloration. If you are fortunate enough to see a Jack Snipe on the ground you will notice the unique springing action of its body as it feeds. When flushed it rises sharply and silently when almost trodden on, with a rather wavering but direct flight, but after a short distance it drops back to the ground and into cover.

In Leicestershire the Jack Snipe is an uncommon winter visitor and passage migrant. It has been recorded on nine occasions at Swithland Reservoir but this is almost certainly because it is under-recorded. As most of the grounds and margins are private it is hard to record this species because you generally flush the bird before you know it is present. All the records except one were of single birds and fall in a period from November to March. There is one record of two birds being present on the 7th November 1982. The latest sighting was of a single bird seen on the 19th March, 2000.

Common Snipe *Gallinago gallinago*

The Snipe breeds across northern and central Europe and across northern Asia and North America. It winters in the southern United States and Central South America, Central Africa, Asia Minor, India and south-east Asia. In Europe it winters south to the Mediterranean and North Africa. The eastern and northern European populations move south and west in the winter while the western European population is resident.

It breeds in small numbers throughout Britain and Ireland and the numbers are augmented in the autumn by passage birds and winter visitors. The main influx into Britain takes place from the end of September and continues through to November. Return passage starts again in March and has finished by the end of April. In many areas it has disappeared and no longer can the drumming display flight of the Snipe be heard over marshy fields in the spring. The Snipe's breeding population appears to have collapsed in Britain between 1970 and 1998 with their numbers dropping by 74%.

The Snipe breeds on wet flood-meadows, and in swampy areas around lakes, marshes and bogs. The nest is a shallow depression lined with grass.

The Snipe is a medium-sized wader with a very long bill and shortish olive green legs. The head and upperparts are dark brown with buff striping and the upper breast is brown with dark streaks. The belly is white but the flanks have some dark barring. When flushed the Snipe gives a hoarse grating call and its zigzag flight takes it rapidly away.

In Leicestershire the Snipe is a common but declining passage migrant and winter visitor and it is becoming a very rare breeding bird. It is hard to believe now that during the mid-1970s it was still a common winter visitor and I remember a flock of between 30 and 40 birds feeding on flood-meadows in the Wreake Valley. During 1975 a friend and I ringed over one hundred birds in that area. Out of that number one bird had been ringed in Sweden only forty-four days previously and another was found dying of the cold in the same area almost ten years later. The Snipe is a frequent winter visitor to Swithland Reservoir in small numbers and is certainly under-recorded. It would almost certainly have bred within the reservoir's boundaries until 30 years ago and I have one record of breeding near the reservoir in 1975. It also bred on the nearby Buddon Brook Meadows until 1975. The largest single count I have for Swithland was 30 in October 1959.

Eurasian Woodcock *Scolopax rusticola*

The Woodcock breeds across Europe and central Asia eastwards to Japan with a separate population in the Himalayas. It moves south in winter as far as the Mediterranean and occasionally North Africa in Europe and it also winters in India and south-east Asia.

In Britain it is a widespread breeding species except in south-west England, Pembroke and Anglesey and some of the Scottish Isles. Woodcock often give their presence away in the breeding season by their roding display flights at dawn and dusk that start in late February and sometimes continue on into August. The British population's numbers are augmented by passage birds and winter visitors. Birds can arrive from the continent as early as September but the main bulk of Woodcock arrive in October and November. Return migration starts in March and continues through April. During the evening Woodcock leave the woodlands and feed in marshy meadows, wet ditches etc. The Woodcock is a bird under serious decline down by 70% between 1970 and 1998, and the population in 1998 was only a fifth of the 1980 total.

It breeds in both broadleaf woodland and in coniferous woodland that has a deciduous understorey. It generally prefers moist woodland with plenty of leaf litter. The nest is a shallow depression lined with dead leaves or other vegetation.

The Woodcock is a large wader and similar in size to a pigeon, with a large dark eye, long bill and short flesh-coloured legs. Its upperparts are a mixture of browns, buff and chestnut that affords superb camouflage and it has transverse barring on its head and nape. The underparts are pale with prominent barring on flanks and breast.

In Leicestershire it has declined as a breeding species and is an uncommon winter visitor. The reason for its sharp decline could be the lack of wet pastureland in which to feed and suitable undisturbed breeding woodlands. The Woodcock is a frequent visitor and occasional breeder at Swithland Reservoir. The Swithland Reservoir and Buddon Wood complex was one of the best sites in the county to witness the Woodcock's roding display flights and in May 1962, as many as six birds were recorded. The Woodcock has been proved breeding on two occasions in the area. An adult bird with young was noted in 1968 and a nest with four eggs was found near the Pumping Station in 1970. Birds probably nested within the grounds quite frequently but the Woodcock is a very secretive species and the nests or young are found only by chance. The last time birds were recorded roding in the area was in 1995. In winter a bird can generally be found near springs that rise in the woodland adjacent to the overflow channel. The highest counts that have been recorded were five birds adjacent to the reservoir on the 8th December 1945, and seven were shot near the reservoir in February 1945. As with the Snipe and Jack Snipe this is a very retiring species and probably even harder to see because of its crepuscular habits and therefore its status is hard to ascertain.

Black-tailed Godwit *Limosa limosa*

The Black-tailed Godwit breeds in Iceland and a band across central Europe and Asia east to the Yenisei River. Its range continues but is very fragmented over the rest of central and northern Asia but populations do reach the Sea of Japan and eastern Siberia. In winter it moves south as far as the Mediterranean and North Africa. The eastern population winters in southern Asia and Australia.

In Britain the Black-tailed Godwit became extinct as a breeding bird at the beginning of the 19th century probably due to the draining of the fens. It has bred sporadically in several areas in England and Scotland this century, but since 1952 it has re-colonised one site, the Ouse Washes in East Anglia, on a regular basis. The British population at present is 47 breeding pairs. To the rest of Britain this species is a winter visitor and passage migrant. Birds reach Britain in July but migration continues until October. Return passage takes place from February to April.

The Black-tailed Godwit has three distinct sub-species of which two can be found in Europe. The sub-species *L. l. islandica* breeds in Iceland on moorland and sub-arctic tundra and *L. l. limosa* breeds on lowland grassland and moorland across central Europe. The nest is a shallow depression substantially lined with grass and other plant material.

The Black-tailed Godwit is a large wader. In breeding plumage its long almost straight bill has an orange base, turning pinkish in winter. Its legs are very long and blue grey in colour. The head, neck and chest are rufous and the rest of the underparts are white with dark barring across the flanks. The upperparts are grey-black with intermixed chestnut feathering. In winter plumage its upperparts are grey and the head shows a white supercilium. The breast and foreneck have a grey wash but the rest of the underparts are white. In flight the Black-tailed Godwit shows diagnostic patterning: the dark wings show a broad white wing-bar, it has a square white rump patch and a black tail and the legs trail well behind the tail.

In Leicestershire the Black-tailed Godwit is a rare winter visitor and uncommon passage migrant. The first record for Swithland Reservoir was on the 13th September 1944, and prior to this the only Leicestershire records appear to be one shot at Cropston Reservoir in 1887 and one obtained at Saddington Reservoir in 1897. Since this time there have been seven more records and all were in a period from July to mid-October. Two birds were present on the 15th July 1972, and four flew round the reservoir on the 18th August 1984. The largest count for this water came on 2nd July, 2000, when 11 birds were seen in flight here. All the other records refer to single birds.

Bar-tailed Godwit *Limosa lapponica*

The Bar-tailed Godwit breeds in northern Europe across Siberia and Alaska. There are two distinct races, the nominate race *L. l. lapponica* breeding in northern Europe and western Siberia and *L. l. baueri* in eastern Siberia and Alaska. The western race winters in western Europe and Africa, while the eastern race winters in Indonesia, Australia and New Zealand.

In Britain it is a passage migrant and winter visitor, although some non-breeding birds remain throughout the summer. The adults arrive in July and August and the young from August to October. Return passage starts in April but birds do not reach the breeding grounds until late May.

It breeds on tundra in the high Arctic and in the subarctic zone among scattered low scrub and trees. Its nest is a shallow depression lined with plant material. It winters on estuaries and mudflats and only occasionally comes inland on passage.

The Bar-tailed Godwit has shorter legs than the Black-tailed Godwit and they are dark grey. The bill is not as long as the Black-tailed Godwit's and is more upcurved. In the breeding season it is dark and during the winter months it shows a pinkish base. In breeding plumage the whole underparts are dark chestnut in the male. The female is paler with washed cinnamon on the breast and a white belly. The upperparts are black in the male with intermixed chestnut white and grey feathering. The female is similar but generally paler. In flight they both show dark wings and a white rump extending in a wedge up the lower back and a black and white barred tail. Only the toes project slightly beyond the tail.

In Leicestershire the Bar-tailed Godwit is an uncommon passage migrant and a rare winter visitor. It is a rare visitor to Swithland Reservoir that has been seen on four occasions since five were recorded on the 27th April 1973. Two birds were present the following day. Three of the records were in the spring in April and May and two were in the Autumn in October and November. On the 3rd November 1984, a flock of circa 35 birds flew over the reservoir in a westerly direction. This was a most extraordinary record and is one of the largest flocks ever recorded in the county. All the other records at Swithland refer to single birds.

Whimbrel *Numenius phaeopus*

The Whimbrel or Hudsonian Curlew breeds across northern Europe with fragmented distribution across Siberia and North America. Birds winter south around the coasts of South America, Africa, India, Australia and New Zealand. The Whimbrel has four races, the nominate race *N. p. phaeopus* breeding in Iceland and northern Europe and having a white rump and back. The North American race *N. p. hudsonicus* has a uniform brown rump and back. The other two races are intermediate between the two. The main passage is from July to October and, like so many northerly breeding waders, the adults move from the breeding grounds well before the young. Return passage takes place from April to June.

In Britain the Whimbrel breeds in the Shetland Isles and the Outer Hebrides with sporadic breeding in northern Scotland. About 530 pairs breed annually of which 90% nest on Shetland. The Whimbrel is a common passage migrant over much of the country.

The Whimbrel nests on moorland and wet tundra. The nest is a shallow hollow sparsely lined with vegetation. In late summer its diet changes from insects and worms and they start to eat the berries of Cloudberry *Rubus chamaemorus* and Crowberry *Empetrum nigrum* etc.

It is smaller and shorter in the leg than the Curlew with a shorter down-curved bill that has more of a kink near the tip. The bill is dark becoming pale flesh near the base and it has blue-grey legs. The head of the Whimbrel is its most distinctive feature. It has two dark crown stripes bordered by buff supercilium and a central crown stripe with a dark stripe through the eye. Its upperparts are brown with dark feather centres and pale edges. The neck, breast and flanks are streaked brown but the belly is white.

In Leicestershire the Whimbrel is an uncommon passage visitor. On clear spring nights in April and May you can occasionally hear their tittering trill as they pass overhead heading northwards. I have thirteen records for Swithland Reservoir and all fall in a period from mid-April to early September and they have been seen in every month through that period. Two birds were present on the 15th June 1977, and the 28th August 1985, and four birds were seen on the 28th July 1977. The rest of the sightings were of single birds and none apparently stayed more than a day.

Eurasian Curlew *Numenius arquata*

The Curlew breeds across central and northern Europe and central Asia reaching the upper Amur River on the border of north-eastern China. It winters mainly on the coasts of western and southern Europe, Africa and southern Asia eastwards to Japan.

In Britain there are as many as 35,500 breeding pairs. It is a scarce breeder in central and south-east England. In winter it is found generally on coasts and mudflats. It starts to gather on the coasts in late July and passage continues until November. Return passage takes place from March to May.

It breeds in grass meadows, arable fields, heathland and moorland. The nest is a shallow hollow lined with grass and other vegetation and with a few feathers.

The Curlew is a large wader with long blue-grey legs and long decurved bill that shows pink at the base of the lower mandible. It is generally dark brown and buff all over with heavy streaking on the breast and flanks. The undertail coverts tend to be white. In flight it shows dark primaries and a white rump and lower back and the tail is barred.

In Leicestershire the Curlew is an uncommon passage migrant and scarce winter visitor usually in small numbers. It is also a scarce and irregular breeder in the county with no more than one or two pairs breeding in a good year. At Swithland Reservoir it is an irregular visitor and birds do not stay for any length of time. The records are in the periods from February to April and July to November. There have been two flocks recorded: 27 were present on the 14th November 1965, and 200 seen flying over the reservoir on the 8th August 1979. This remains the largest flock ever recorded in the county.

Spotted Redshank *Tringa erythropus*

The Spotted or Dusky Redshank breeds across northern Europe and Siberia. It migrates across Europe and Asia and winters on either fresh or salt water marshes in the Mediterranean, Africa and southern Asia. It is a regular passage migrant to Britain with the first birds arriving in July but larger numbers arrive in August and September. Some birds remain in southern England to spend the winter. Return passage starts in March and continues through to May.

It breeds on tundra with small bushes and wet boggy areas amongst birch *Betula* or conifers. The nest is a shallow scrape sparsely lined with grass leaves and a few feathers. The females leave the males to rear the young and move from the breeding grounds in mid-June. The males start to migrate in late July and the young leave in August.

The Spotted Redshank has longer red legs than the Redshank and a longer, finer bill that has a red base to the lower mandible. In breeding plumage the whole body is black with small amounts of white barring on the flanks and tail and the back has white flecking. In winter plumage it has grey upperparts and around the head it shows a black eye-stripe and white supercilium. The underparts are white with a greyish wash on the sides of the breast. In flight it shows dark wings and barred tail with a white cigar-shaped patch on the back. The feet project beyond the tail.

In Leicestershire the Spotted Redshank is an uncommon passage migrant in the autumn and scarce in the spring. It has been recorded at Swithland Reservoir on nine occasions since its first appearance on the 2nd October 1950. All the records were in the autumn between late August and early October. Five of the sightings were of single birds and on the other five occasions two birds were present together.

Common Redshank *Tringa totanus*

The Redshank breeds throughout much of Europe. It can be found in parts of Scandinavia and Iceland and in central southern Europe it has a scattered distribution, breeding down to the Mediterranean and into north-west Africa. Its range extends across central Asia discontinuously to the Sea of Japan. Other populations can be found in northern India and Tibet and in parts of Asia Minor. It winters mainly on the coasts in western Europe, Africa, India and in parts of south-east Asia.

In Britain the Redshank is resident, but large numbers pass through the country on their annual migration and we get an immigration of birds from Europe which winter on our shores. Between the years 1865 and 1925 it expanded its range and greatly increased in numbers until it bred in every county except Cornwall and Pembroke. Between 1970 and 1998, however, there has been a different story and its population has collapsed by 60%. Currently there are 32,100 breeding pairs in Britain. Autumn passage begins in July and continues through to October. Return migration starts in March and continues through April.

It breeds on wet meadows, freshwater marshes, moorland and saltmarsh. The nest is a shallow depression lined with grass and other plant material that is hidden in dense vegetation.

The Redshank is a medium-sized wader with bright red legs, white eye-ring and red base to its bill. In summer its upperparts are brown with dark barring and speckling. Its neck and upper breast are brown and heavily streaked. The streaking extends down onto the flanks, the rest of the underparts being white. In winter plumage it is grey-brown above which extends onto the neck and breast. The rest of the underparts are white with a small amount of barring on the flanks and undertail coverts. The Redshank is very distinctive in flight showing a broad white trailing area to the wing, pointed white rump and lower back, and black and white barred tail. The rest of its upper surface is dark producing a sharp contrasting wing pattern.

In Leicestershire it is a common passage migrant, scarce winter visitor and a scarce breeding bird. It now breeds in the county only in small numbers, probably no more than six pairs annually. This species has greatly declined in the county over the last thirty years. The Redshank is a regular visitor to the reservoir in small numbers. It bred for several years at Swithland Sewage Farm and birds would commute to the reservoir to feed. It has been proved to breed at the reservoir on one occasion when a nest with 4 eggs was found on the 18th May 1946. Breeding has been suspected on many more occasions especially during the 1970s in the years 1972,1973,1974 and 1976. On all occasions display and territorial behaviour were noted. Occasionally birds have been seen during the winter months. One bird was present on the 10th January

1972, one to three birds were present in January and February 1976, and a single bird was seen on the 20th February 1977. The largest single Redshank count I have for the water was 5 on the 8th August 1974.

Common Greenshank *Tringa nebularia*

The Greenshank breeds in a wide band across northern Europe and Asia reaching Kamchatka in the east. It winters in Africa, India, south-east Asia and Australia.

In Britain it is an uncommon breeding bird in northern Scotland with about 1,350 breeding pairs. Our population is not as migratory as the continental birds and they mainly winter in western England and Ireland. The first migrants appear in Britain in late July and continue to move through until October. Return passage takes place in March and April although birds are not as numerous as in the autumn.

It breeds in open clearings of boggy moorland and heathland among taiga forest and birch *Betula*. The nest is a shallow scrape that is sparsely lined with vegetation and debris. In winter it can be found on mudflats and coastal lagoons and inland on the shores of lakes.

The Greenshank is slightly larger than the Redshank with long greenish legs and a long upcurved bill with a greenish base. In breeding plumage it has grey upperparts with some dark centred feathers with light edgings on the mantle and especially on the tertials and scapulars. It has faint streaking on the head and hindneck and heavy dark streaking on the breast that continues in some measure onto the flanks, the rest of the underparts being white. In winter plumage the Greenshank looks grey above and white below and the head, neck and upper breast are white with a grey wash. In flight it shows fairly dark wings with a white rump and lower back and a pale, slightly barred tail.

In Leicestershire the Greenshank is an uncommon but regular passage migrant in the autumn in varying numbers and scarce spring passage migrant. On Swithland Reservoir it is an uncommon passage migrant that is almost annual in its occurrence. I have several spring records. Two were present on the 27th April, and again between 19th and 22nd May 1973, one on the 20th May 1992, and two on 1st May 1998. The earliest 'autumn' record I have was one on the 12th July 1972, and the largest number present at any one time has been 6 which were recorded on the 6th, 7th and 16th August 1974.

Green Sandpiper *Tringa ochropus*

The Green Sandpiper breeds across northern Europe and Asia reaching the Sea of Japan in the east. It winters in western Europe, Africa, India and south-east Asia. The adults begin to migrate in June, and the young leave the breeding grounds in July and August. Return passage takes place from March to May.

In Britain it is a common passage migrant and occasional winter visitor. On two occasions it has bred in Britain, in Westmorland in 1917 and in Inverness-shire in 1959.

It breeds in wet coniferous and Alder *Alnus* woodland, usually in a tree in an old thrush's nest or squirrel *Sciurus* drey etc.

The Green Sandpiper has a dark greenish-brown back with fine speckling and a pale brown streaked head and neck. The underparts are white with a heavily streaked upper breast. It has a long dark straight bill, a short white supercilium that does not go behind the eye and short green legs. In winter plumage the head and breast are less heavily streaked and the back is more uniform. In flight it shows dark wings and back and a white rump with a black and white barred tail. When seen settled this species often bobs its rear end. In winter it is often found on the sides of ditches and streams and the muddy shores of lakes and reservoirs.

In Leicestershire the Green Sandpiper is a common passage migrant and scarce winter visitor. At Swithland Reservoir it is an almost annual passage migrant in small numbers and birds occasionally stay throughout the winter, favouring the inflow and outflow streams. It has been recorded during every month. Maximum counts include 9 on the 22nd August 1972, and the 6th and 7th September 1990, and 15 on the 30th August 1990. Interesting winter counts are 5 on the 29th October 1986, and 29th October 1991; 3 on the 6th December 1988 and 22nd January 1989.

Wood Sandpiper *Tringa glareola*

The Wood Sandpiper breeds across northern Europe and Asia reaching Kamchatka in the east. It winters in Africa, India, south-east Asia and Australia. The adults start to migrate from the middle of June and the young from the middle of July. Migration finishes in September. Return passage starts in April and continues in May. During passage it likes the freshwater margins of lakes, lagoons and reservoirs and also flooded meadows.

In Britain it is a regular passage migrant through the eastern half of England. It is far more frequent on autumn passage than spring. It has bred once in England, in Northumberland in 1853. In 1959 it bred in Sutherland and in 1960 in Inverness-shire. Since that time between 10 and 15 pairs have bred regularly in Scotland.

It breeds in open forested areas with wet heathland and bogs and also in scrubby tundra. The nest is a shallow depression lined with small amounts of grass and leaves, hidden in dense herbage. Like the Green Sandpiper it occasionally nests in trees in old thrushes' nests.

The Wood Sandpiper has longer legs than the Green Sandpiper and they are greenish yellow in colour; otherwise it is similar in many ways. Its back is grey-brown with heavy pale speckling. The head, neck and breast have brown and white streaking with small amounts of barring on the flanks and the rest of the underparts are white. The head shows a prominent white supercilium that extends over the eye and a dark eye-stripe. The bill is long and straight with a greenish base. In winter plumage the streaking becomes fainter and the back is a more uniform brown. In flight it shows a similar pattern to the Green Sandpiper except the tail is more finely barred and it shows a pale underwing.

The Wood Sandpiper is a scarce passage migrant to Leicestershire. It was first recorded at Swithland Reservoir in May 1923, and this was the first county record. Since then it has been recorded on seven occasions at Swithland Reservoir. All the records fall in a period between July and October with the exception of two May records. The last spring record was on the 11th May 1973. All the records were of single birds except on the 23rd and 25th August 1970, and 31st July 1979, when 3 birds were present.

Common Sandpiper *Actitis hypoleucos*

The Common Sandpiper breeds in a wide band across central and northern Europe with scattered populations throughout much of the south. It also occurs throughout northern and central Asia reaching Kamchatka and Japan in the east. It winters south through Africa, India, south-east Asia and Australia.

In Britain it is a common passage migrant and it breeds mainly in Scotland, Wales, Ireland and north-western England. Passage takes place from July and continues until October. Return passage is generally from April to May. Occasionally a few birds will remain to winter in Britain.

It nests by the sides of fast flowing rivers, the edges of pools and lakes and in certain coastal habitats. The nest is a shallow depression that is often concealed by vegetation, sparsely lined with debris and plant material. On migration it mainly favours fresh water and can often be seen on the shores of lakes, reservoirs and rivers.

The Common Sandpiper has greenish or yellowish short legs and a short straight bill. It has a crouched stance and the bird's rear is continually bobbed up and down. In breeding plumage the upperparts are greenish-brown with dark feather-centres and a noticeably long barred tail. The head is paler brown and there is a white supercilium and dark eye-stripe. The neck and upper breast are streaked brown and the remainder of the underparts are white. In winter plumage the back becomes a more even brown and the gorget disappears, leaving two brown neck patches. In flight it shows a conspicuous white wing bar, it has a fluttering flight low over the water and the wings are almost arched.

The Common Sandpiper is a common passage migrant and rare winter visitor to Leicestershire. It is an annual passage migrant at Swithland Reservoir in small numbers and rarely birds remain through the winter. It has been recorded in every month of the year. A single bird wintered from October to March in 1972-1973 and in 1973-1974 and one was recorded between the 9th and 23rd December 1984. There were 8 present on the 14th September 1974; 11 on the 30 July 1987, and 9 on the 9th September 1989.

Ruddy Turnstone *Arenaria interpres*

The Turnstone breeds around the coast of Scandinavia and northern Europe and on the Arctic coasts of Asia and North America. In winter it migrates to southern latitudes and can be found on the shores of South America, Africa, India, south-east Asia and Australia.

In Britain it is a common passage migrant and winter visitor around our coasts and birds can be seen throughout every month of the year with the main concentration being from mid-July to May. Passage takes place from July to mid-September and return migration from late April until June.

It breeds on stony and pebbly shorelines on the edge of tundra. The nest is a shallow scrape lined with varying amounts of vegetation.

The Turnstone is a thick-set wader with a small bill and bright orange legs. The adult male in breeding plumage has a striking black and white head, neck and breast pattern. The rest of the upperparts are a mixture of bright chestnut scapulars and wing coverts and black striping over the back and wings. The underparts are white. The female is duller in summer. In winter plumage the upperparts are grey-brown and the black and white head and breast pattern is replaced by dull grey-brown with a darker lower breast. In flight they are a very striking black and white showing a dark tail, white rump, central back and wing-bar.

The Turnstone is an uncommon passage migrant to Leicestershire. It has been recorded on Swithland Reservoir on three occasions. One was recorded in July 1940, another on the 28th July 1994, and two on the 18th May 1997.

Red-necked Phalarope *Phalaropus lobatus*

The Red-necked Phalarope breeds across northern Europe, Asia and North America. In winter large concentrations gather mainly at sea off west Africa, Arabia, Peru and the East Indies. Migration takes place as early as the end of June for the females. The males follow in late July and the young in August and September. Return passage takes place from April to June. European birds move across Europe to the Black and Caspian Seas where they mass together before moving to the wintering grounds.

The Red-necked Phalarope is a rare breeding bird in Britain with only 38 breeding pairs in 1997, most of which were on Shetland. Occasionally it has bred at one site on mainland northern Scotland and also on Orkney and the Hebrides. For the rest of the country it is an uncommon passage migrant that is more frequent in the autumn than the spring.

It breeds close to small freshwater bog pools in the birch *Betula* zone and on tundra. The nest is a small depression lined with grass and stems. The female, unlike most species has the brighter plumage and takes no part in caring for the young or in the initial incubation. They procure their food by picking it from the water surface. It is often mosquito larvae on the breeding grounds and, during the winter, sea-plankton.

The Red-necked Phalarope is a small dainty wader with a fine bill and short grey legs, the feet of which are lobate. It is a very energetic wader that swims constantly and can often be very approachable. In breeding plumage the female has a slate-grey crown, cheeks, rear neck, mantle and lower breast. The slate-grey back has buff fringes to the feathers. It has a white throat, white spot above the eye and white lower underparts. There is a dark chestnut band starting at the rear of the eye and extending down the neck to form a collar underneath the white throat. The male is similar but less richly coloured. In winter plumage it is grey above with white feather edgings and white below with a darker nape and hind neck and a black eye patch. In flight it shows a white wing-bar and white sides to the rump.

The Red-necked Phalarope is a rare vagrant to Leicestershire. It has been recorded on two occasions at Swithland Reservoir. Two juveniles were recorded on the 6th and 7th September 1992 and this was the 15th county record. Another juvenile was seen for a few hours on the 5th September 1995, before being eaten by a Pike *Esox lucius*.

Red Phalarope *Phalaropus fulicarius*

The Red Phalarope or Grey Phalarope breeds on the edge of the Arctic Ocean around the globe. The Red Phalarope is the only wader whose migration routes are entirely over water. They winter off the coast of west and south Africa and Chile. At sea they feed in plankton-rich areas and small parties may gather around whales where they probably take parasites from the animals' backs.

In Britain it is mainly seen in autumn from late September to November when storm driven birds are forced ashore.

It breeds near the coast on marshy tundra and prefers areas with sedges, grass and moss on the edges of small pools. The nest is usually a shallow depression lined with vegetation. Once the eggs have been laid the female leaves the male. Like the Red-necked Phalarope the female has the brighter plumage, the male incubating the eggs and tending the young. When the breeding season is finished they move back to the sea.

The Red Phalarope is the same size as a Dunlin with a thicker bill than the Red-necked Phalarope that is yellow at the base. Its legs are yellow-brown and it has lobed toes. The breeding female has brown feathering around the bill extending over the crown and down the rear of the neck. Its cheeks are white and the whole foreneck and underparts are a rich chestnut. The upperparts are brownish black with buff feather-edgings. The male is similar in patterning but paler, especially on the breast and around the head. In winter plumage it has a white forehead, a black nape and a black eye patch. The back is pearl grey and the underparts are white. In flight it shows a pronounced white wing bar.

In Leicestershire it is a rare vagrant. One of the most severe storms ever to hit Britain in living memory struck on October 15th 1987. The following day around 100 birds were recorded in the Midlands and south-east England. Two first-winter birds were found at Swithland Reservoir on the 17th October. One was eaten by a Pike *Esox lucius* and the second bird remained throughout the following day. This record is the only one for the reservoir.

SKUAS Stercorariidae

Great Skua *Stercorarius skua*

The Great Skua breeds in the north Atlantic on Iceland, Scotland, the Faeroes, Shetland, Orkney and the Hebrides and there has been a recent range expansion to northern Norway, Svalbard (Spitsbergen), Jan Mayen and northern Russia. It winters in the north and south Atlantic south to at least Brazil in South America and the Gulf of Guinea in West Africa.

It nests not far from the coast in grass or heather and usually near a seabird colony. The nest is a shallow depression that is lined with grass and other vegetation.

The Great Skua is endemic to northern Europe and nearly half of its population breeds in Scotland and its northern islands with 8,500 breeding pairs. In 1861 it was almost extinct in Scotland, with only nine breeding pairs on Shetland, due to human persecution. It is a regular passage migrant along our coasts. The Great Skua or Bonxie (as it is known to the locals in the Shetlands) feeds on eggs, young birds and fish and by parasitising other seabirds.

The adult Great Skua is a large dark-brown gull-like bird similar in size to a Herring Gull that is mottled and streaked buff with a dark cap. The most distinguishing features, however, are the light patches at the base of its primaries that are clearly visible in flight. It has a heavy hooked black bill and black legs.

The Great Skua is a rare vagrant to Leicestershire. It has been recorded at Swithland Reservoir on one occasion. An adult was found at Swithland Reservoir in foggy conditions on the 18th September 1992, and was still present the following morning. This was the 17th county record.

Parasitic Skua *Stercorarius parasiticus*

The Parasitic or Arctic Skua is a high Arctic breeding species, breeding across North America (in America they go by the name Jaeger) to Greenland and across northern Asia southward to Kamchatka. In Europe it breeds in Iceland and around the coast of Scandinavia, reaching northern Scotland in the south.

It nests on coastal moorland and tundra. The nest is a shallow scrape sparsely lined with vegetation.

In Scotland there are about 3,200 breeding pairs. They are piratical in their habits, harrying and chasing gulls and terns in order to rob them of a meal. Like its larger relative the Great Skua, it is a common passage migrant around the coast of Britain. This species winters in the southern oceans around the coasts of Africa, South America and Australia.

The Parasitic Skua has two colour forms. The dark morph is dark brown all over except for its pale wing patches. The pale morph is grey on the mantle with a black cap, white neck with yellow suffusion forming a collar and a white breast and belly. The pale morph also has pale patches at the base of the primaries. The adult Parasitic Skua has reasonably long pointed central tail feathers although in juvenile birds they are stunted. The bill and legs are black.

It is a rare passage migrant to Leicestershire's inland waters. It has been recorded on two occasions at Swithland. A pale phase bird was present on the 12th November 1985, and a dark phase juvenile on the 11th August 1993.

Four dark phase skuas flew south-east over the reservoir on the 4th October 1992, and although they were not positively identified, the observer considered them to be Parasitic Skuas.

GULLS Laridae

Most people will be aware of what they term 'seagulls' in their towns and villages and of the large massed flightings of these birds which can be seen towards dusk and at dawn passing overhead. The term 'seagull', however, is not a correct one and these days is very misleading as only the Kittiwake is an exclusively maritime species as far as Europe is concerned.

Over the last century there has been a population explosion among the *Larus* gulls world-wide and this has probably come about as a result of their exploitation of new food sources as well as a decreased amount of egg collecting by man for food at breeding colonies. As their numbers increased it led to their moving inland to investigate the rich food sources of rubbish tips, sewage farms, arable and pastureland, in addition to the food thrown out by people in urban areas. The large numbers of gulls required safe roosting sites that would be relatively free from predators and these they found on the many reservoirs.

As many as fifteen thousand gulls have been seen at peak roosting times on Swithland Reservoir. The winter gull roost generally starts in early autumn and tails off by March. With so many gulls coming in to roost it had to be likely that rarer species would be found amongst the massed throng. Many birdwatchers now watch roosts and with more comprehensive field guides and the sorting out of taxonomic status of the species many interesting records have been obtained.

Mediterranean Gull *Larus melanocephalus*

The Mediterranean Gull is confined as a breeding species to Europe and is a resident of south-eastern Europe, breeding mainly on islands in the Aegean and Black Seas. It has bred sporadically northwards to Holland including Britain. Most birds breed near the coast on lagoons, marshes or deltas. The nest is a shallow scrape lined with grass and a few feathers.

The Mediterranean Gull is a scarce visitor to Britain and Ireland that first bred in Britain in 1968 and has bred regularly since 1976.

This species is similar to the Little Gull and Black-headed Gull in having a dark hood in breeding plumage. The hood is more extensive than the Black-headed Gull's, extending down the nape. The adult in summer plumage has a black hood, pale grey mantle and white underparts, tail and primaries. It has a heavy red bill that droops down towards the tip, and red legs. It is more like a Common Gull in size. In winter it loses most of its black hood but retains a dark area around and behind the eye and a dark streaked nape. This species reaches its adult plumage in its third year.

The Mediterranean Gull is an uncommon passage migrant and winter visitor to Leicestershire. The first county record came in 1980 but it was not until the early evening of 2nd November 1987, that one was recorded at Swithland. Since this initial sighting it has become almost annual in occurrence with most records falling between October and April. Eight individuals were present between October and December 1988. Six were first-winter birds, one was a second-winter and the other an adult. This constituted the largest number of sightings over a two-month period. Three birds were recorded on both 2nd November and 3rd December 1988, and they are the highest counts for any one day. In total there have been some 46 individuals recorded since 1987.

Little Gull *Larus minutus*

The Little Gull breeds in north-eastern Europe and in two populations in Asia, the first in Western Siberia and the second from Lake Baikal north-eastwards into Eastern Siberia, with a small population in Canada where it first bred in 1962. The European population winters as far south as north-west Africa.

The Little Gull is mainly a passage migrant and winter visitor to Britain and Ireland although it has bred in Britain. Birds can be seen on passage from April to May and August to October. In autumn its migration tends to have a westerly bias.

It breeds on inland marshes in small colonies often with other gull or tern species. The nest is a mound of plant stems and other aquatic vegetation with a cup in wet habitat, or a scrape lined with grass, sedge or reeds on drier ground.

The Little Gull is the world's smallest gull. It is smaller than the Black-headed Gull and has a more buoyant flight that is more reminiscent of a tern, with which it often associates. The adult in summer plumage has a black hood, pale grey mantle, white underparts and tail and it has a dark red bill and red legs. The best identification feature for the older birds is their dark underwing coverts that are noticeable in flight. Although it is a small gull it does not attain its adult plumage until the third year. The adults have a dark hood which extends further down the nape than the Black-headed Gull but lack the white leading edge to the wing of that species. In winter they lose most of their black hood, retaining a dark crown and black ear-spot. Care should be taken when identifying juvenile birds because they show a dark 'W' on the top surface of the wing, not unlike a juvenile Kittiwake.

The Little Gull is an uncommon passage migrant and rare winter visitor to Leicestershire. The first county record came from Belgrave in 1868. It has been recorded on Swithland Reservoir in twenty-two years and in every month except January. They have become almost annual over the past few years but only in small numbers. They are often observed on spring passage in association with tern species. The first possible record was in 1950, but the first authenticated record came in 1956. The largest numbers recorded were five adults and two immatures on 1st May 1984, and seven adults and six immatures on the 23rd April 1988.

Black-headed Gull *Larus ridibundus*

The Black-headed Gull breeds throughout much of Europe and across central Asia reaching Kamchatka and Sakhalin in the east. It winters over much of central and southern Europe southward to West Africa and also throughout the Mediterranean to the Red and Caspian Seas and the Persian Gulf. In eastern Asia it winters from Kamchatka southward along the coast to Malaysia and Borneo. Some birds also winter off the coast of eastern North America.

It is resident, even if it does not necessarily breed, over most of Britain. During the late autumn and winter months large immigrations of birds move into Britain. These birds originate mainly from the Baltic and Low Countries (see notes in ringing report).

It breeds in colonies on marshes, small islands in lagoons, moorland and on coastal shingle beaches. The nest is a shallow hollow, lined with grass and other vegetation. On wet ground it will make a mound of vegetation with a cup.

The Black-headed Gull is a small gull that takes two years to reach adult plumage. The adult in summer plumage has a brown hood with a grey mantle and black tipped primaries and white underparts and tail. It has a dark red bill and red legs. When flying it is easily identified by the white leading edge to the upper wing and dark trailing edge to the primaries. In the winter the head becomes white leaving a dark ear-spot.

It is the most common and frequently seen gull in Leicestershire and can be seen throughout the year although its numbers are much reduced during the summer months. It is a great opportunist and cosmopolitan in its feeding habits. Birds can be found in the centre of our cities, towns, parks, playing fields, farmland and any large area of open water. It also has the distinction of being the only gull species to have bred in the county. It first bred in Leicestershire in 1946 and has bred irregularly since, where the right conditions prevail. It is quite surprising that it did not breed at Rutland Water until 1999, given the large number of terns and waterfowl that have bred there in the last twenty-five years. Of the gull species that roost on Swithland it is by far the most numerous. Birds can be seen on Swithland Reservoir in varying numbers throughout the year. On those sultry hot days of mid-summer when the flying ants take to the wing, mixed flocks of Starlings and Black-headed Gulls appear from nowhere to take advantage of a feast and can be seen hawking for these insects over town and village. The number of Black-headed Gulls that roost on Swithland has risen from 4,500 in 1953 to a count of 13,000 on 8th November 1987. This figure remains the highest number recorded for this water. Since that period the total numbers of Black-headed Gulls roosting on the reservoir appear to be falling slightly. In his book on Victorian natural history, 'The Vertebrate Animals of Leicestershire and Rutland' published in 1889, the author Montague Browne has this species noted as a rare straggler with only five occurrences in Leicestershire.

Ring-billed Gull *Larus delawarensis*

This species is a transatlantic vagrant from North America. It breeds on the Great Lakes and Prairies and also in the mid-west states in the U.S.A. and Canada. It winters from the Great Lakes southward, including California, Mexico and Cuba.

It breeds mainly on islands in lakes or rivers where it nests generally on the ground, although it has been known to use trees. The nest is usually a scrape sparsely lined with vegetation, feathers and debris.

The adult Ring-billed Gull is similar in many respects to the Common Gull. It has a white head, neck, underparts and tail but it is a thicker-set bird than the Common Gull with an appreciably heavier yellow bill that has a broad band around it, yellowish legs, lighter grey mantle, smaller wing mirrors and a pale iris.

It was first recorded in Britain in March 1973, and since then it has been identified on many hundreds of occasions and has become annual in its occurrence. The first two county records came from Swithland Reservoir: an adult on 30th December 1988, and a bird in second-winter plumage on 28th November 1989.

Common Gull *Larus canus*

The Common Gull breeds in northern Europe across northern Asia reaching Kamchatka and Sakhalin in the east and in north-western North America. It winters on the coasts of western and eastern Europe with some birds reaching North Africa. In North America it winters along the west coast from Alaska south to California and in eastern Asia along the east coast from Kamchatka south to southern China.

In Britain it is common in its main breeding areas of Scotland and north-western Ireland. It is a fairly common passage migrant and winter visitor throughout Britain and Ireland. Its feeding habits are different from some of the other gull species as it has a preference for pastureland including upland pastures. In December 1963, the number roosting inland in Britain was 124,000.

It breeds on islands in lakes, marshes, bogs, moorland, grassy slopes, sand dunes and beaches. The nest is a shallow cup made with seaweed or other vegetation. Although it usually nests near water it sometimes breeds well inland away from the sea or lakes.

The Common Gull or Mew Gull is like a small Herring Gull with a yellowish-green bill and a less aggressive expression, looking almost gentle in comparison. The adult has a white head and body and tail, a grey mantle with dark wing-tips which show large white mirrors, and greenish yellow legs. This plumage is attained in its third year.

It is a common winter visitor and passage migrant to Leicestershire from August to April. In 1973 the population of the Swithland roost was 450 birds. Circa 600 birds were present at the roost on 15th January, 2000. This appears to be the largest number recorded and is far fewer than on the Eye-Brook Reservoir where as many as 26,000 have roosted on occasions and well into the thousands on a more regular basis.

Lesser Black-backed Gull *Larus fuscus*

The Lesser Black-backed Gull breeds along the coastline of western Europe including Iceland northward from northern Spain. Its range extends eastward from northern Norway to the Taimyr Peninsula in central Siberia. It winters from Britain southward to the coast of Spain and Portugal down to north-west Africa.

It is a breeding bird, winter visitor and passage migrant to Britain and Ireland. It breeds around the coast with the highest density being in western Scotland and northern Ireland and about 20,000 pairs breed inland. In Britain there are an estimated 83,000 breeding pairs which is about a third of the entire world population of this species. B.T.O. enquiries have shown that in 1949 only 300 birds wintered in Britain yet by 1964 this figure had risen to 7,000 on inland waters in England alone.

It nests on islets, cliff tops and inland on moors and bogs. The nest is usually a large heap of vegetation including grass and seaweed with a central cup. Occasionally, however, it will use a shallow scrape that is lined with vegetation.

The Lesser Black-backed Gull that attains its adult plumage in its fourth year, has a dark grey mantle and the wings show only small white mirrors on the primaries. It has a white head, neck and underparts, the bill is yellow with a red spot near the tip of the lower mandible and it has yellow legs. Several races do occur and it is worth looking for them: *L. f. graellsii* could be confused with a dark-mantled Herring Gull having a slate grey mantle. This race has a western European distribution. *L. f. fuscus* is most likely to be confused with a Great Black-backed Gull with a black mantle but differing from the aforementioned in leg colour and with only one white spot on the first feather of the wingtip. This race breeds around the Baltic. *L. f. intermedius* is, as its name suggests, intermediate in mantle colour between the above two races and breeds in southern Norway, Denmark and on the west coast of Sweden.

The Lesser Black-backed Gull is a common passage migrant and winter visitor to Leicestershire. It is a regular winter visitor to Swithland Reservoir and it joins the gull roost in varying numbers. The highest count recorded was 670 on the 18th February 1999. The summer roost of Lesser Black-backed Gulls on Swithland Reservoir has been very interesting. It started in 1959 when 300 birds were present and there has been a steady increase since. By September 1966, the number had risen to 4,000 birds, the maximum figure ever recorded here. The roost has been known to start in May with a hundred or so birds and rise to a couple of thousand by September. Numbers of this species summering here do tend to fluctuate from year to year.

Herring Gull *Larus argentatus*

The Herring Gull breeds around the coasts of northern Europe, Asia and North America and winters south over much of North America, Europe and Asia.

The Herring Gull is the familiar gull of the British coastline. The British population appears to be sedentary but these are augmented by passage birds and winter visitors from northern Europe.

It nests on cliffs and islands. In Scotland it also breeds on lochs and moorland areas. The nest is a large heap made of seaweed, grass and other vegetation with a cupped centre.

The adult Herring Gull is a large gull with a white body and pearl-grey mantle. The legs are flesh-coloured and the bill yellow with a red spot near the tip of the lower mandible. The outer primaries are black and show white "mirrors". Most of the larger gulls take four years to attain their adult plumage and the sub-adult birds are various shades of mottled-browns and greys.

The Herring Gull is a common winter visitor to Leicestershire, but uncommon during other seasons. The winter roost at Swithland contains several hundreds of these birds. On 5th January 1986, 1,000 were recorded and circa 1,300 on 2nd February 1996. These are the largest counts for this water.

Yellow-legged Gull *Larus michahellis*

The Yellow-legged Gull breeds in the Mediterranean basin north along the Atlantic coast of Spain to southern France. It winters from Holland southwards to north-west Africa.

In the breeding season it favours rugged cliffs, stacks and islets but it will also breed on beaches and at salinas.

Formerly thought to have been a race of the Herring Gull with longer wings, more black on the outer primaries, smaller white mirrors and yellow legs, it has now been given specific status by some authorities.

It is an uncommon autumn passage migrant to Leicestershire and is rare during other seasons. It has been seen on Swithland Reservoir in every year since an adult was first recorded on the 29th October 1987. This was also a new county record. Seven adults were present on the 21st August 1991, and this remains the largest number recorded at any one time on this water. All of the sightings have been in a period from the end of July to February.

Caspian Gull *Larus cachinnans*

This species occurs from the Black Sea eastwards into the Ukraine and southern Russia to the Caspian Sea. It winters in the eastern Mediterranean, Red Sea, Persian Gulf and north-west India.

Like the previous species this was thought to have been a race of the Herring Gull and at another time was considered to be the nominate race of the Yellow-legged Gull. It differs from the Yellow-legged Gull in having a paler mantle, larger spots on the primary tips, more like those of a Herring Gull, and longer legs.

The Caspian Gull is a rare passage migrant and winter visitor to Leicestershire, but it might be several years before its overall status is fully known. In October 1996, an adult Caspian Gull was recorded for the first time in the county at Rutland Water. Since then there have been four records at Swithland Reservoir: an adult on 19th December 1998; a third-winter bird in the gull roost during March 1999, and a first-winter bird on 11th November. Two birds, an adult and a third-winter bird were both seen on 9th, 16th and 24th December 2000 and this is the only period when more than one bird was recorded.

Since there is still a lot of debate concerning the specific status of the last three species, their classification might change in the future. At the moment I have kept them separated as individual species because their plumage differences enable specific identification.

Iceland Gull *Larus glaucoides*

The Iceland Gull breeds in Greenland and Arctic America and winters in the north Atlantic. It breeds in small colonies on rocky islands or cliffs and generally on an area of sheltered coastline such as a fjord. The nest is a substantial structure made of grass and moss with a large cup.

The Iceland Gull is a rare winter visitor to Britain and Ireland.

It is slightly smaller than the Herring Gull and differs in having white primaries, or dirty white in immature plumages. In all its four plumages it is very similar to the larger Glaucous Gull but has a more rounded head, shorter bill, long primary projection and a red eye-ring in the adult. The adult winter Iceland Gull has a pale grey mantle with white primary tips and brown-streaked head and neck and white underparts. The bill is yellow with green tones and it has a small red spot near the tip of the lower mandible. The legs are flesh coloured. First-winter birds are coffee-coloured with faint barring, by the second winter their plumage becomes slightly paler and it has less barring, third winter birds are similar to adults but have paler wings and are very white-looking birds at a distance.

It is a rare winter visitor to Leicestershire. The first authenticated record for Swithland Reservoir came on the 18th January 1971, and it has been recorded on eight occasions since. Both immature and adult birds have been recorded and all have been seen during the winter months in a period stretching from the beginning of December to the end of March.

Glaucous Gull *Larus hyperboreus*

The Glaucous Gull or Burgomaster, a name given by sailors in Arctic waters because of its predatory habits, breeds predominantly north of the Arctic Circle and is circumpolar. In winter birds wander into the north Atlantic and north Pacific, some reaching Britain.

It is an uncommon visitor to Britain and Ireland being seen mainly from October to April. The nest is a large heap of seaweed, moss and vegetation with a central bowl.

As already stated this species is very similar to the previous species but somewhat larger with a yellow eye-ring in the adult and a short primary projection. The adult Glaucous Gull in winter has a pale grey mantle with white primary tips, white underparts and the head and neck have varying amounts of brown streaking. The bill is yellow with a red spot near the tip of the lower mandible and it has pale flesh-coloured legs. Like the Iceland Gull the Glaucous Gull is a four-year gull that has four distinct plumages. In all its plumages it is very similar to the smaller Iceland Gull.

The Glaucous Gull is a rare winter visitor to Leicestershire. This species has been seen at Swithland Reservoir on eleven occasions since it was first recorded on the 2nd February 1978. Most of the birds have been immature but occasionally adults have occurred. All the records have come during the winter period when they are generally spotted coming into the gull roost. All the records fall in a period from late December to early March. Two birds were present on the 9th February 1986, and this remains the only occasion when more than one individual was present.

Great Black-backed Gull *Larus marinus*

This huge predatory gull breeds around the coast of northern Europe, Greenland and eastern North America. It winters in the north Atlantic and over much of Europe as far south as North Africa.

In Britain it breeds in Scotland and Ireland and along the west coast of England and Wales. There is a migration of birds into Britain that generally begins in August. It moves south during the autumn with some birds wintering in the Mediterranean region.

It breeds on islands and on the tops of stacks mainly close to the sea and it tends to be more solitary than other gulls. Occasionally birds nest inland on lakes or moorland. Its nest is a large mound of seaweed, debris, sticks and plant material with a large cup in the centre.

The Great Black-backed Gull differs from the dark races of the Lesser Black-backed Gull in its larger size, flesh-coloured legs and larger white mirrors on the tips of the primaries. The adult has a dark grey-black mantle with large white spots on the primary tips, a white head, neck and underparts and at close range a red eye-ring can be noticed. It has a large yellow bill with a red spot near the tip of the lower mandible. Like all the other large gulls it does not attain its adult plumage until the fourth year.

The Great Black-backed Gull is a frequent winter visitor to Leicestershire in small numbers and uncommon during other seasons. It is the largest gull species to visit Swithland. The numbers roosting at Swithland are generally fairly small. In 1973 the winter roost held sixteen birds, but 60 were present in February 1981, and January 1986. The highest count for the site came on the 2nd February 1996, when circa 120 were present.

Black-legged Kittiwake *Rissa tridactyla*

The Kittiwake takes its name from its call. It is the most pelagic of the European gulls and breeds on precipitous cliffs in the north Atlantic and Pacific. The Kittiwake is a colonial nester that will occasionally breed on buildings close to the coast. The compact nest of seaweed, mud and grass is hollowed out to form a depression for the eggs. It is placed on a ledge normally many hundreds of metres up from the ground or sea. The Kittiwake winters at sea in the north Atlantic and north Pacific. During the winter they move out a long way from shore into open water where they feed on crustaceans and surface-swimming fish.

This species attains its adult plumage in its third year. The adult is slightly larger than a Black-headed gull. It has a white head and body with a grey mantle; the wingtips are solid black and give the impression of having been dipped in ink; the legs are black and its bill yellow. The first-winter birds have a black W on the upper surface of the wing and a black tip to the tail, black half collar and ear spot.

The Kittiwake is a scarce passage migrant or storm-driven bird to Leicestershire. It has been seen in 22 of the last 60 years at Swithland Reservoir but normally only one or two birds are present at any given time. There was an exceptional flock of 89 birds present on the 12th March 1998, and circa 40 the following day. All the birds were adults. Large numbers were reported at the same time throughout the Midland region. They appear to have been grounded by a stationary weather front across central England. A similar occurrence happened on the 14th March 1992, when 65 birds were present.

TERNS Sterninae

Sandwich Tern *Sterna sandvicensis*

The Sandwich Tern breeds in north-western Europe, on the Black and Caspian Seas and in a few areas in the Mediterranean. In North America it breeds on the Atlantic coast down to the Gulf of Mexico and the Caribbean. It winters on the coast of South America and the European birds move south to Africa as far as the Cape.

At present there are about 14,000 breeding pairs in Britain. Migration starts in August and continues on throughout September. It is the first tern to return, arriving back mainly in March and by April most birds have returned.

They generally breed on low-lying areas of coast with lagoons, sand dunes, or sandy beaches. It breeds in colonies and the nest is a shallow scrape that might be sparsely lined with any available material.

The Sandwich Tern is a large tern with short dark legs, a short forked tail and a long dark bill that has a yellow tip. The adult in breeding plumage has a shaggy black cap and pearl-grey mantle. The rest of the body is white. In winter plumage the forehead and crown are white leaving a black facial mask.

The Sandwich Tern is a scarce passage migrant to Leicestershire. It has been recorded on Swithland Reservoir on 13 occasions. There have been four April records and one in late June, but the majority of records fall in a period from July until early October. Most records are of single birds but the numbers of note were: 3 birds on the 10th September 1956, and 29th April 1984. 6 birds were recorded on the 20th September 1995, and this is the largest count for this species at this water.

Common Tern *Sterna hirundo*

The Common Tern breeds across Europe from the Arctic Circle to the Mediterranean and across much of central Asia reaching Kamchatka and Sakhalin in the east and also in eastern North America. It winters around the coasts of Africa, eastern Australia and eastern South America.

The Common Tern is a summer visitor breeding throughout the British Isles except south and central Wales and western England. It arrives in late April and most have left by October. Passage takes place at the end of April and continues through May. Return passage is from the end of July until October.

It breeds on coasts and inland and nests on headlands, beaches, islets in gravel pits or lagoons and shingle on the edges of rivers etc. Its nest is a shallow scrape that is sometimes lined with debris or plant material.

The Common Tern has an orange-red bill with a black tip and red legs. It has a black cap in summer plumage, a grey mantle and whitewashed grey underparts. At rest the wings are longer than the tail. In winter the forehead becomes white and the bill dark. In flight it shows a white forked tail and for this reason it was sometimes given the name 'sea swallow'. It differs from the Arctic Tern in flight in having a dark wedge on the upper surface of the inner primaries, and a broad diffuse band along the trailing edge of the primaries on the underwing. Only the inner primaries are translucent. The Common Tern is very similar to the Arctic Tern and in past years they were often lumped together as Commic Terns and so precise records have been obtained only in the last few years.

It is a regular passage migrant through Leicestershire in varying numbers and a localised breeder. It first bred in 1979 when two pairs bred at Cossington Gravel Pits and one pair bred at Rutland Water. The Common Tern is a frequent passage migrant at Swithland Reservoir, both in the spring and autumn, but normally only in small numbers. Notable counts were 29 on 2nd May 1983, and 32 on 19th August 1990.

The earliest record is of 2 birds on 27th March 1989, and the latest record was of a juvenile with an injured wing which arrived on the 7th August and left on the 6th October 1989. In 1993 two pairs bred for the first time at Swithland on the rafts on the northern side of the reservoir and two chicks were hatched. In 1994 three pairs bred and raised seven young; 1995 four pairs bred, two pairs failed, four young were raised; 1996 two pairs bred and raised five young; 1997 four pairs bred and raised five young; 1998 four pairs bred raising at least five young; 1999 two pairs bred and raised seven young.; and in 2000 two pairs also bred.

Arctic Tern *Sterna paradisaea*

The Arctic Tern is a circumpolar breeder in the Arctic and sub-Arctic zones. It breeds in northern Britain, Scandinavia, Siberia, North America and Greenland. It has the longest migration of any bird. Each winter it migrates south as far as the Antarctic pack ice where it feeds on concentrations of fish and plankton. The eastern North American population cross the Atlantic and join birds from west Siberia and Europe before starting their migration southward. Their migration takes them along the European coast to West Africa. From there some fly back across the Atlantic to Argentina, South America before heading southward to Antarctica. Others continue on to the Cape and then onward to Antarctica.

In Britain it breeds locally in Scotland, northern England and north Wales. Odd pairs breed in Norfolk and sporadically elsewhere among colonies of Common Terns. The Arctic Tern arrives later than the Common Tern and is often not seen before May. Birds can still be moving through as late as June. Return migration starts in July and continues on into October. In autumn birds are less frequently seen inland.

The Arctic Tern nests generally on the coast using islets, shingle beaches, marsh or tundra and it often breeds in small colonies. Its nest is a shallow scrape that is sometimes sparsely lined with debris or plant material.

The Arctic Tern is very similar to the Common Tern in all its plumages. Adults differ in having a completely dark red bill, greyer body, longer tail streamers that extend beyond the wings when the bird is at rest and shorter legs. In flight all the primaries are translucent and it shows a narrow distinct black band on the trailing edge of the primaries from below.

In Leicestershire it is a frequent spring passage migrant in varying numbers and a scarce autumn passage migrant. It is a frequent spring passage migrant at Swithland Reservoir, normally being seen from the last week in April until early June. It is only very occasionally recorded in the autumn. The earliest spring record was one on the 7th April 1991, and the latest is 5 on the 7th June 1975. The first autumn record was of 2 birds on the 11th August 1989, and last autumn record was a juvenile between 19th and 26th October 1983. Several large counts have been recorded: 60 on 30th April 1978, 71 on 5th May 1987, and 105 on 2nd May 1998.

Little Tern *Sterna albifrons*

The Little Tern is a very widespread species with a scattered distribution. It has many subspecies and some authorities class the Least Tern *S. antillarum* from North America and Saunders's Tern *S. saundersi* from the Red Sea and Indian Ocean as separate species. The Little Tern breeds throughout Europe, south-east Asia and northern and eastern Australia. The European population winters off the coast of central Africa and some reach South Africa.

It is well distributed around the coasts of Britain and the current population is about 2,400 breeding pairs. The Little Tern arrives in April and May. They depart again in July and passage continues until October.

It nests on low-lying coasts on shingle or sand beaches and inland along rivers on gravel deposits. The nest is a shallow scrape that is sparsely lined with small pebbles or pieces of plant material.

The Little Tern is our smallest tern, about half the size of the Arctic and Common Terns. The adult in breeding plumage has a yellow bill with a black tip, and small yellow legs. It has a white forehead, black lores, black cap, grey mantle and white underparts. In winter the bill becomes black and it has more extensive white on the forehead. In flight the outer primaries are dark from above and it has a very fast wing action. It often hovers looking for prey before plunging into the water.

The Little Tern is a scarce passage migrant in Leicestershire. It has been recorded at Swithland Reservoir on nine occasions since it was first noted on the 29th August 1950. There have been six spring records, the earliest being two birds on the 19th April 1976, and the latest two birds on the 19th June 1977. It has been seen on four occasions during autumn passage. The earliest record was of two birds on the 21st July 1975, and the latest record was again of two birds on the 28th September 1969. Single birds were recorded on four occasions and two birds were recorded on six occasions.

Black Tern *Chlidonias niger*

The Black Tern breeds in central and southern Europe and in Asia across western Siberia as far as the Yenisei River, and throughout much of central North America. The European and Asian populations winter off the west coast of Africa and the American birds move down to central and north-western South America.

In Britain the Black Tern is a passage migrant arriving in April and May and moving back through on return passage in August and September. It bred regularly in Britain before 1850 and only sporadically after until about 1858. It has bred on occasions in the 20th century, the first being on the Ouse Washes in 1966 when two pairs bred.

The Black Tern breeds on slow-moving rivers, freshwater marshes and lakes with plenty of aquatic vegetation. The nest is normally a floating platform of aquatic vegetation in shallow water although occasionally it will nest on dry land where it makes a scrape that it lines with small amounts of plant material.

The adult in breeding plumage has a black bill and dark reddish-tinged legs, grey wings and tail, a black head, neck and breast and white undertail coverts. In winter plumage the black is replaced by white leaving only a black cap and a dark breast patch. In flight it shows a small forked tail and fairly uniform grey upper surface to wings, back and tail.

In Leicestershire the Black Tern is an uncommon passage migrant in spring and autumn. It is almost annual in small numbers at Swithland Reservoir with the majority of spring passage taking place in May. Most autumn passage happens during August and September. The earliest spring record came on 13th April 1980, and the last on 19th June 1983. The earliest autumn record was of two adults on the 14th July 1987, and the last, a very late bird, remained until the 6th November 1967. Large numbers appear occasionally on spring passage. On the 10th May 1959, 34 birds were present and on the 22nd May 1959, 33 birds were recorded. On the 1st May 1968, 30 birds were recorded and on the 9th May 1968, from 30-40 birds were present. Although these large counts occurred within a few days of each other they refer to different birds. On spring passage birds sometimes stop for only a few hours. The largest autumn count was of 13 birds on 31st August 1990.

White-winged Tern *Chlidonias leucopterus*

The White-winged Tern, or White-winged Black Tern as it was formerly known, breeds in eastern Europe and across central Asia discontinuously as far as China. The European and western Asian birds winter on inland lakes and rivers in central and southern Africa. The eastern Asian birds winter in south-east Asia and Australia.

It is a rare migrant to Britain with about 15 occurrences annually. In spring birds are seen mainly in May and June and on autumn passage in August and September. Over two-thirds of the records are in the autumn.

Like the Black Tern it breeds on freshwater marshes, lakes, rivers and flooded grassland. Its nest is normally a floating raft of plant material and water weed.

The White-winged Tern is very similar to the Black Tern but differs in breeding plumage in having a darker grey back, white wing coverts and longer red legs. In flight it shows a white rump and tail and black underwing coverts and the paler wings contrast markedly with the dark back. In winter plumage it has a pale grey mantle and white underparts, rump and tail. It shows slight streaking on the head and a dark ear spot.

The White-winged Tern is a rare vagrant to Leicestershire. There has been one record at Swithland Reservoir, a juvenile being present in the company of ten Black Terns on the afternoon of the 21st September 1991. This was the ninth county record.

AUKS Alcidae

Little Auk *Alle alle*

The Little Auk or Dovekie is only the size of a Starling. It breeds in the high Arctic on the coast of Greenland, on Svalbard (Spitsbergen) as far as Severnaya Zemlya which lies off the coast of Siberia. A few pairs nest on Grimsey off the north coast of Iceland. In winter they move into the north Atlantic and numbers can move into the North Sea.

It is a regular winter visitor to northern and eastern coasts of Britain and occasionally birds are swept well inland by storms and gales.

There are thought to be about 12 million breeding pairs and they feed mainly on crustaceans. They breed in holes between boulders on scree slopes or in crevices on cliffs.

The Little Auk is a small short-necked bird with a very short bill. In breeding plumage it has a black neck, head and back, white streaks down the wing and a white trailing edge to the secondaries. The belly and undertail coverts are white and in winter the throat and foreneck become white. It has a very fast whirring flight.

The Little Auk is a rare vagrant to Leicestershire. A bird was seen at Swithland Reservoir on the 10th November 1957. Over the following two days single birds were found dead at Grace Dieu and Beacon Hill.

Atlantic Puffin *Fratercula arctica*

The Atlantic Puffin breeds on rocky coasts around the north Atlantic. It breeds as far south as Maine in the U.S.A. and Brittany in France to Labrador, Greenland and Novaya Zemlya in the north. It breeds in north-western Europe around the coasts of Iceland and Norway. They spend the winter far out at sea.

In Britain it breeds in scattered colonies around the coasts of Scotland, Ireland, Wales and western England. It breeds in north-eastern England as far south as Flamborough Head and Bempton Cliffs in north Yorkshire. Birds return to the breeding sites in April and have all departed by mid-September. They nest generally in burrows on steep grassy slopes on the tops of sea cliffs or islands.

In summer plumage the Puffin is unmistakable with a brightly coloured large bill (from where they got their name 'Sea Parrot'), white cheeks, black crown, collar and back, white underparts and orange legs. In winter plumage the bill becomes darker and the cheeks become dusky grey.

The Puffin is a rare vagrant to Leicestershire. A bird was caught at Shelthorpe, Loughborough, on the 22nd May 1951, and released at Swithland Reservoir the next day, 23rd May. This was the first county record.

SANDGROUSE Pteroclididae

Pallas's Sandgrouse *Syrrhaptes paradoxus*

The Pallas's Sandgrouse is a bird of the Steppes of southern Asia. It breeds from the shores of the Caspian Sea to China. It can be found on arid open plains and uplands up to 2,500 metres. The nest is a shallow scrape on the ground.

It is a rare vagrant to Britain that has been seen only on six occasions (involving seven birds) since 1909. Prior to this period irruptions were noted on twelve occasions with large influxes taking place in 1863 and 1888. It was proved to breed in Britain on two occasions in 1888 and once in 1889. The reasons for the bird's large-scale movements are not fully understood, but if their numbers are high and heavy snow and ice cover the Steppes this could account for their large westerly movements.

The Pallas's Sandgrouse is slightly smaller than a Wood Pigeon with a small bill, short feathered legs, long needle tail and elongated outer primary. Its overall colour is beige with black crescents on a white band forming a collar across its breast and black bars and spots across the back and wings. The head and neck are grey with an orange chin and cheeks and a black band across its belly. The female is similar to the male but has spots and speckling on the crown, hindneck and mantle. The orange chin is separated from the grey upper breast by a black necklace and it lacks the white collar and black crescents of the male and it has a browner belly patch.

The Pallas's Sandgrouse is a rare vagrant to Leicestershire. Three other occurrences were recorded in Leicestershire during 1888 apart from the birds at Swithland and these remain the only records for the county. A flock of 12 birds was seen between Swithland and Buddon Wood in early June, 1888. This is the area that the reservoir now occupies.

PIGEONS and DOVES Columbidae

Stock Dove *Columba oenas*

The Stock Dove breeds throughout Europe except Iceland and its range extends into North Africa. In Asia it occurs as far east as west Siberia and as far south as Turkey. The western European population tends to be resident but the birds from Fenno-Scandinavia, eastern Europe and Asia are migratory. It winters in southern and south-west Europe, North Africa and in the northern part of the Middle East. Passage takes place from mid-September and continues through October. Return migration starts in February and is normally completed by early April.

The Stock Dove breeds throughout Britain but is absent from the northern Scottish Islands. Between 1970 and 1998 the British population has increased by 140%. The expansion in the bird's range started in the early 19th century when it spread from south-east England. It first bred in Scotland about 1856 and in Ireland about 1877. It did decrease from the mid-1950s and early 1960s due to the use of chemical seed-dressing in agriculture.

It breeds generally in holes in trees although it has been known to use rabbit burrows or holes in buildings. It is a woodland species that is generally associated with broadleaf woodland that has adjacent cultivated land, where it feeds on weed seeds. It also requires a good supply of drinking water.

The Stock Dove is generally a grey bird that shows a green neck patch. It is smaller and shorter-tailed than the Wood Pigeon. In flight it shows a dark tail band, and the black trailing edge to the wing contrasts markedly with paler grey greater and median wing coverts. The bill is yellow with a red base and the legs are red.

The Stock Dove is a common resident breeding bird in Leicestershire. It is also a common breeding resident at Swithland Reservoir. For many years birds have bred underneath the railway bridges that cross the reservoir and in holes in the cliff adjacent to the overflow channel. It also bred in a Kestrel nestbox in the waterworks grounds during 1986. Two large winter flocks have been recorded at the reservoir. 40 birds were recorded on the 7th December 1969, and 105 were noted on the 27th February 1990.

Common Wood Pigeon *Columba palumbus*

The Wood Pigeon breeds throughout Europe except Iceland (where it has bred occasionally). In Asia it occurs east to western Siberia and south to Turkey and also North Africa. The western European populations appear to be sedentary but the Fenno-Scandinavian and eastern European birds are migratory and most winter in Britain, France, Portugal and Spain. Autumn migration takes place in September and October and return passage in March and April.

The Wood Pigeon is a common resident throughout Britain that has expanded markedly in range and numbers during the 19th century. Its numbers increased by 201% between 1970 and 1998.

It builds a small stick platform nest usually in trees and bushes. It occurs primarily in woodland but has adapted to Man's changes on our environment and can now be found on arable farmland, parks and in urban areas.

The adult Wood Pigeon is a large grey pigeon with a pinkish breast and long tail. Its most diagnostic feature is the white patch on the side of its neck (absent in juveniles). In flight it shows a large white transverse bar across each wing and a black band across the tip of the tail, bordered by a blue-grey subterminal band. The bill is yellow with a red base and white area extending over the nostrils and its legs are red.

The Wood Pigeon is an abundant resident breeding bird in Leicestershire. It is a common resident breeding bird at Swithland Reservoir that can occur in very large numbers. The largest number recorded for the reservoir was 1,250 birds on the 6th November 1993. A mixed flock of Wood Pigeon and Stock Dove were seen in the Swithland area in November and December 1951, and contained 3,000 birds, but no specific numbers were recorded.

Eurasian Collared Dove *Streptopelia decaocto*

The Collared Dove breeds throughout Europe and across southern Asia including India (where this species has its origins) and China, Korea and Japan where it has been introduced. Before 1900 this bird did not breed in Europe in any great numbers and this century has seen one of the most amazing colonisations of a continent by any bird species. It spread from Turkey, moving north-westwards colonising the Balkans by 1928, and breeding in Hungary c.1930, Austria 1943, Poland 1943, Germany 1946, Italy 1947, Switzerland c.1952, France 1952 and Britain in 1955. Since 1955 it has colonised Ireland, the Iberian Peninsula and parts of Fenno-Scandinavia and it even bred in Iceland in 1971!

In recent years it has become a common garden bird in Britain where it feeds on grain and seed put out on bird tables. In the period from 1970 to 1998 its numbers rose in Britain by a staggering 782 %.

It is a bird associated with trees and scrub where it builds a stick platform on which to lay its eggs. It often feeds on cultivated land and large numbers often congregate around grain silos and farmyards.

The adult Collared Dove is a medium sized bird with a long tail, a small dark bill and red legs. It is generally a buff bird that is paler on the head and underparts. It has a black half collar that is white edged just below the nape. In flight it shows white-tipped outer tail feathers and blue-grey greater and primary coverts.

The Collared Dove is a common resident breeding bird in Leicestershire. It was first seen in Leicestershire on the 12th May 1961, when a bird was recorded at Ratby. It was first confirmed breeding at Stoneygate in Leicester in 1965 although it probably bred prior to this but went unrecorded. The Collared Dove was first recorded at Swithland Reservoir in the spring of 1971 but it probably occurred prior to this period because it was already well established in the county at this time. It is now seen quite frequently at the reservoir and almost certainly breeds in the grounds.

European Turtle Dove *Streptopelia turtur*

The Turtle Dove breeds throughout central and southern Europe, North Africa and Asia east to western Siberia and south to Kazakhstan. The Turtle Dove is mainly migratory except possibly for some of the North African birds. It winters in a band across North Africa in a semi-arid zone from Senegal to Ethiopia and southward to northern Ghana and central Sudan. Autumn migration takes place from late July through to October and return passage occurs in April and May.

In Britain the Turtle Dove breeds in England and Wales becoming more infrequent in the west. A few pairs breed in eastern Ireland and southern Scotland. In England its most important food source appears to be the Common Fumitory, *Fumaria officinalis*. It increased its breeding range in Britain before 1865, spreading into Wales and northern England. Between 1970 and 1998, however, this species has undergone a marked decline in Britain and its population has dropped by 77%. There are several possible reasons why this as occurred. The recent trend of grubbing up hedges has destroyed many breeding sites and the greater use of herbicides in agriculture leaves fewer weed seeds on which birds can feed. Also the hunting pressure on this species abroad has been immense with many thousands of birds being slaughtered annually. Since the early 1970s there has been a severe drought in its wintering quarters in the Sahelian and Sudanese areas of Africa which has cut down on its food and water supply and must obviously have taken a heavy toll on this species.

It likes open country with scattered trees, scrubland, old hedgerows, orchards and gardens. Like many pigeons and doves it constructs a fine stick platform on which to lay its eggs.

The adult Turtle Dove is a small slim dove that has a blue grey head, rump and edge to the folded wing, a rich orange-brown mantle with black-centred feathers and a black and white patch on the side of its neck. Its breast is pinkish and its lower belly and undertail coverts are white. It has a small black bill and red legs. In flight the outer tail feathers are broadly tipped white, edged by a black subterminal band and it shows a blue grey band across the centre of the wing.

The Turtle Dove is an uncommon migrant breeding bird in Leicestershire. This species was fairly common at Swithland Reservoir during the summer months 30 or more years ago and it bred annually in the reservoir grounds. During a bird survey carried out on 7th June 1981 nine purring or singing males were recorded. As already stated there has been a marked decline in this species' numbers in recent years and it is doubtful if it now still breeds, although a bird was recorded collecting nesting material in 1987. The last positive breeding record however came in 1985. The earliest date for the Turtle Dove to be recorded at Swithland Reservoir was the 3rd May 1998, and the last autumn sighting came on the 9th September 1967.

CUCKOOS Cuculidae

Common Cuckoo *Cuculus canorus*

The Cuckoo breeds throughout Europe, north-west Africa and most of northern and central Asia. Most European and western Asian birds winter in Africa south of the Sahara and the eastern Asian population winter in south-east Asia. The Cuckoo migrates south from the end of July through to September. The adults usually leave a month before the juveniles and they return in the spring in April and May.

It breeds throughout the British Isles but over the last 30 years has been declining. This is probably due to the more intensive farming methods and the use of herbicides and pesticides that would almost certainly have killed the large hairy caterpillars which are the Cuckoo's main food source.

It breeds from shrub tundra in the Arctic through most habitat types except high barren mountains, dense tracts of forest and built-up urban areas. The Cuckoo lays its eggs in other birds' nests and when the young Cuckoo hatches it throws the host species' eggs out of the nest and then the single Cuckoo is reared by its host foster parents. The Cuckoo has been known to have over 100 host species in Europe but each individual female will lay her eggs in only one species' nests.

The adult male Cuckoo has long pointed wings and a long rounded tail and in flight it can often be mistaken for a small falcon. It has a slate-grey upper breast, throat, head, back, wings and tail. The tail has white barring on the outer feathers. The belly and undertail coverts are white with fine dark barring. The bill is dark with a yellow base and it has a yellow eye, orbital ring and feet. The female grey morph is similar to the male but has a buff wash and barring on the upper breast. The female brown morph has rufous upperparts with dark barring and is not unlike the juvenile.

The Cuckoo is a fairly common breeding summer migrant to Leicestershire and a regular but uncommon breeding bird at Swithland Reservoir that has declined in recent years. It has been known to parasitize Reed Warblers and Dunnocks within reservoir grounds. The earliest spring record was on the 13th April 1988, and the last autumn record was a very late juvenile on the 12th October 1992.

OWLS Strigiformes

Owls can be found on every continent with the exception of Antarctica. They occur over a wide range of habitats from Arctic tundra to desert regions. The 174 species of owl feed on a wide variety of prey including invertebrates, amphibians, fish, birds and mammals. Although owls are widely distributed and not uncommon they are more often heard than seen.

My first encounter with an owl came when I was about six years of age. Two of my father's work colleagues stood at the front door of our house holding a Barn Owl that had just been hit by a car near Rothley. It was put in a cardboard box and placed in the kitchen. It looked in perfect condition as I bent over it and I remember gently stroking its soft plumage. Unfortunately by morning it was dead. It had obviously suffered internal injuries. That Barn Owl remains the first and last wild Barn Owl I have ever seen in Leicestershire.

Over the years my contact with owls has been minimal, but on the few occasions when I have come across them it has left me with some wonderful memories. I recall one instance in northern Norway when I crawled several yards over barren tundra to get close views of a male Snowy Owl that was being mobbed by a pair of Arctic Skuas. On another occasion while on a night safari in Hawange National Park in Zimbabwe, a Milky Eagle Owl was caught in the beam of our spotlight on a low branch directly above us. This huge owl sat motionless except for an occasional blink that showed off its extraordinary pink eyelids that looked for all the world as though they had just been painted with eye shadow!

This May a dream came true when I was able to visit northern Finland. In several areas around Oulu I was taken and shown the owls of the Taiga! In three days we had views of an amazing seven species. My wife Pamela was not relishing an exclusive birding trip, but so as not to seem a complete novice, several weeks before our departure she had decided to do her homework and gen up on the owls she was likely to see, using the new Collins Bird Guide. The descriptions of their individual face patterns captured her imagination. Suddenly she was making me aware of new names for these birds that she had gleaned from her hours of study.

The first full day in Finland saw us out early and, close to the hotel, we found a Short-eared Owl quartering a grassy field. Later in the day we were taken to see an "Astonished Owl" known to me as a Tengmalm's Owl. It stuck its head out of its nest hole on hearing our noisy approach. Its pale facial disc bordered by black, and startling yellow eyes, made it quite a sight. It peered unimpressed at us for a few minutes and looked to me more like a "Dozy Owl". After its brief stir it retreated back into its dark nest chamber. Our next stop was to visit the nest site of the "Deceptively Gentle Owl" or Ural Owl. This large pale owl made its presence known to us as soon as we arrived in the area and sat quite high up in a spruce making harsh barking noises. It had a plain brown facial disc and noticeable yellow bill and it glared at us through piercing black eyes. It is called "deceptively gentle" because if you get too close to its nest it will attack and probably take your head off! We kept a healthy distance!

Next morning we were up early and headed off into the forest to find what Pamela referred to as "Austere Owl". To me it was the Pygmy Owl, Europe's smallest owl, only slightly smaller than a Starling. We carefully peered into its nest hole and this tiny little owl looked back at us with glowing yellow eyes and its brown face showed distinctive white eye-brows. We quietly retreated from the area and headed back to our vehicle. After a hearty breakfast we set off again into the forest. This time we were after what I considered the greatest prize of them all - Pamela's "Stately Owl". After a two hour hike we reached our goal. Sitting on an old Goshawk's nest about one hundred metres away and about four metres up in a spruce sat the enormous Great Grey Owl. This magnificent bird slowly turned its head and stared straight at us. Its large grey disc was finely lined with dark concentric rings. In the centre of this large round head were two small yellow eyes with white feathering forming an "x" in the centre of its facial disc above its noticeably yellow bill. We savoured the moment but had to leave after a few minutes. Later on in the day we visited an area of trees on the edge of a small lake. Here in another spruce about four metres from the ground sat a Long-eared Owl on her nest. All that was visible above the rim of the nest from our vantage point was its long white-edged "ears" and part of its head!

On the third day of our trip Pamela was fully in the swing of owl watching and made it known to our guide that she would like to see "Grim Owl". Two hours later our vehicle stopped in an area of open woodland. After a five minute walk we found "Grim Owl" sitting on the top-most point of a spruce. It glared at us with its yellow eyes set in a white face broadly bordered in black. The Hawk Owl balanced precariously on the top of the tree using its long tail to balance itself. Again we did not go too close to this bird because Hawk Owls have a reputation for being fearless and aggressive near their nest and so ended our brief encounter. You cannot help but be impressed when you come in close proximity to such wonderful birds and I felt as though I had just experienced the feast after the famine.

Barn Owl *Tyto alba*

The Barn Owl is a very cosmopolitan species that breeds on six continents and it is absent only from Antarctica. It is found in central and southern Europe and in southern Asia. It is absent from large areas of northern Europe and Asia because it is a species that suffers from extremely cold weather and the winters in these areas are too severe. The Barn Owl is generally sedentary throughout Europe although occasional birds have been known to make movements of over 1000km.

It can be found over most of the British Isles but in Scotland the population is very sparse. The Barn Owl has been declining steadily in Britain since the 19th century but the decline has been particularly sharp over the past half century. There are probably a variety of reasons for this. Over much of the country there has been a change from pastureland and hedgerows to large open cereal fields. This has obviously had a marked effect leaving smaller tracts of land for the birds to hunt over. They are also thought to have succumbed, as many birds of prey did, to organochlorine pesticides in the late 1950s and early 1960s and hard winters like those in 1947 and 1963 had a massive effect on an already dwindling population. In recent times the Barn Owl has suffered on the roads. Large numbers trying to hunt on some of the only decent grassland available-the grass verge-have been killed by cars.

It is generally a bird of open country and favours rank grassland, moorland, scrubland, marshland and parkland. It feeds mainly on small rodents up to the size of a rat but it will also take birds, insects and reptiles. It nests in holes in trees, cavities in cliffs and old buildings, barns etc.

The adult Barn Owl of the nominate race *T. a. alba*, found in Britain, has a heart-shaped white facial disc with black eyes and white underparts. Its upperparts are a mixture of buff-brown and grey with white and dark spotting. In flight it can look almost white and its legs are often dangling.

The Barn Owl is now an uncommon or scarce breeding resident in Leicestershire. It was frequent at Swithland Reservoir in the 1940s and bred in an old tree, only a few hundred yards from the reservoir grounds, in 1945 and 46. Since 1947 it has been recorded on only three occasions. A bird was seen in 1965 and another heard calling on the 22nd October 1968, then it was not recorded until the 29th May 1992, when a bird was seen near the waterworks grounds. A weak bird of the dark-breasted race *T. a. guttata* was recorded being attacked by crows at the reservoir on the 11th April 1995. It was considered to be an escape or an illegally released bird.

Little Owl *Athene noctua*

The Little Owl breeds across central and southern Europe, North Africa, the Middle East and across central Asia from Turkey to China.

Several attempts were made to introduce the Little Owl into the British Isles but it was not until 1879 that they first started to breed in Kent. They then increased rapidly until the 1930s and spread throughout England and Wales and into the borders of Scotland by 1958. There has been a steady decrease in the birds' numbers since the 1940s due probably to a succession of severe winters in the early decades followed by the use of organochlorine pesticides in agriculture which probably caused the population to crash between 1955 and the early 1960s. Since this time the changes in agricultural practices with large areas of land used for growing cereal crops and rape have done away with much breeding and hunting habitat. The Little Owl can often be observed during daylight hours sitting on fence or telephone posts or on its favourite perch in certain trees.

It can be found in a wide range of habitats including olive groves, open Cork Oak woodland, parkland, hedgerows adjacent to pastureland and arid semi-desert regions. The Little Owl is mainly sedentary, it nests generally in holes in trees or cavities in rocks and has even been known to use old rabbit burrows.

It is a small owl with greyish brown upperparts that are spotted white on the head and spotted and barred on the back and tail. The underparts are white streaked brown and the bill and eyes are yellow. It has an undulating flight and shows small but broad rounded wings.

The Little Owl is a fairly common breeding bird in Leicestershire. It is a resident in small numbers at Swithland Reservoir breeding occasionally in the hedgerows of adjacent fields. It was recorded quite frequently throughout the 1970s and was proved breeding at the reservoir in 1970. In recent years it has become much scarcer and the records have become more infrequent although four birds were noted in the area in February 1990. Two adults were also recorded in July 2000, and they were seen with two juveniles on the 29th July 2000.

Tawny Owl *Strix aluco*

The Tawny Owl breeds across central and southern Europe and its range extends slightly into North Africa. In Asia it has a patchy distribution breeding across to western Siberia and in fragmented areas in central Asia. It has a larger population in China and Korea.

In Britain it breeds throughout England, Scotland and Wales but is absent from Ireland. The Tawny Owl is a sedentary species that is very territorial. Between 1970 and 1998 the British population declined by 30%. Its numbers also fell markedly during the 19th century due to persecution.

It is a bird that favours deciduous woodland but can also be found in mixed and coniferous woodland, farmland with scattered trees, parkland etc. It is a highly adaptable species and even nests in urban areas. It nests normally in a hole or cavity in a tree but will on occasions nest in buildings and on rock ledges.

It is a medium-sized owl whose plumage varies in ground colour from rufous-brown to grey-brown, the rufous-brown birds being generally found in Britain. Its upperparts are rich rufous brown with dark mottling and barring and it shows white tips to the secondaries and two pale crown stripes. The facial disc is plain brown and it has a yellow bill and black eyes. The underparts are pale brown with dark streaking and it has feathered legs.

The Tawny Owl is a fairly common breeding bird in Leicestershire. It is also a fairly common breeding resident at Swithland Reservoir but because of its nocturnal habits it is rarely seen. It is a species that is often vocal throughout the year and that is the easiest way of ascertaining its numbers. If you listen for several bird species' excited calls and follow the hullabaloo you often come upon the Tawny Owl being mobbed.

Long-eared Owl *Asio otus*

The Long-eared Owl breeds throughout Europe, central Asia and North America with scattered populations in north and eastern Africa. It is absent from much of the Arctic but in the winter the northern populations move south reaching Mexico in North America and northern India and China in Asia. Its autumn passage can start as early as September and continues through to December with the number of moving birds peaking in October. Spring passage normally occurs from March to May.

It is found throughout the British Isles but is thinly distributed in England and Wales with only small numbers being found in south-west England and southern Wales. Its breeding population appears stronger in Scotland and Ireland. The Long-eared Owl's numbers have declined in England, Wales and in some parts of Scotland throughout the 20th century. The reasons for the decline are not fully understood but it could have something to do with competition from the Tawny Owl. In Ireland where the Tawny Owl is absent the Long-eared Owl population appears to have remained static. In some years the northern and eastern counties of Britain can have their numbers augmented by large numbers of birds from continental Europe. In winter in a good feeding habitat birds can often be found in a communal roost.

It is a bird of coniferous and broadleaf woodland but it can also be found in coppices, moorland with groups or lines of trees parkland, marshes and steppe. It usually makes its nest from an old Crow, Magpie or Jay nest but it has been known to use old squirrel dreys. Like so many birds of prey its numbers are linked closely to the amount and availability of prey and in good rodent years its population can rise dramatically.

The Long-eared Owl is slightly smaller than the Tawny Owl. It has streaked grey-brown upperparts with vermiculations and a brown finely barred tail. Its underparts are brown and heavily streaked with arrow shaped markings. Its facial disc is brown and it has orange irises and a dark bill. When alert the bird shows two erect ear-tufts which can be folded down when the bird is at rest. In flight it is very similar to the Short-eared Owl but it has more streaking on the belly and whiter wing tips.

It is a rare breeding bird in Leicestershire and a scarce winter visitor. It is a vagrant to Swithland Reservoir that has been recorded on one occasion, two birds being noted on Brazil Island during November 1943.

Short-eared Owl *Asio flammeus*

The Short-eared Owl is a widespread species breeding in northern and central Europe across northern and central Asia reaching Kamchatka and Sakhalin in the east and throughout northern North America. There is a resident population in southern South America. It winters in southern and central Europe, north-west Africa and central Africa south of the Sahara, the Indian subcontinent and south-east Asia northward to Japan and the United States of America southward to Mexico.

It is a thinly distributed species in Britain, breeding in Scotland, northern England and north Wales although it nests sporadically in East Anglia and southern Wales. It first bred in Ireland in 1959 and has bred on a few occasions since. It is a winter visitor throughout much of Britain and coastal Ireland. Birds arrive in southern England, Wales and Ireland from northern Britain and continental Europe in September and October and leave again from March to early May. It is a species whose population has marked fluctuations depending upon the availability of small rodents. In Britain nearly 50% of its diet is made up of the Short-tailed Vole *Microtus agrestis* and when they have a good year the owl's population rises dramatically. The Short-eared Owl has declined as a breeding bird throughout central Europe probably as a result of habitat loss, the important Russian population has declined by 50% and this is particularly worrying.

It is a bird of open country and can be found on moorland, heath, tundra, grassland, saltmarsh, bog, marsh and young conifer plantations. It nests on the ground among the cover of young trees, grass, heather and reeds.

The Short-eared Owl can often be seen hunting during the day. Its flight is slow and it often glides and quarters the ground showing a white trailing edge to its long wings and a boldly barred tail. The adult Short-eared Owl has a round head and buff facial disc and black markings around its yellow eyes. The upperparts are buff-yellow, heavily streaked and barred dark. The throat and upper chest are similar and the rest of the underparts are white, streaked dark. It has a black bill and feathered legs. The male is smaller than the female.

The Short-eared Owl is an uncommon winter visitor to Leicestershire. It is a vagrant to Swithland Reservoir that has been recorded on one occasion. A bird was noted on the northern side of the reservoir hunting over the reed bed and the adjacent pastureland in October 1974.

NIGHTJARS Caprimulgidae

European Nightjar *Caprimulgus europaeus*

The Nightjar breeds across much of Europe, through central Asia as far as China and into North Africa. All the Nightjar populations winter in Africa south of the Sahara. Its autumn migration takes place from August to September and it returns in the spring from late April and May.

In Britain it occurs in England, Wales and Ireland but generally it is a localised breeding bird. It bred in several areas in Scotland at the beginning of this century but its range is decreasing and it now breeds only in the south-west. Its range has decreased over much of Britain since the end of the 19th century but this decline has been marked since 1930. In recent years there seems to have been a slight recovery but it still occupies less than 50% of the territory it did in the early 1970s. The reasons for the decline are not known but habitat destruction and disturbance must have an effect. The widespread use of insecticides and the overall changing landscape of our country must also affect a species that feeds on insects.

It is a bird of open woodland and forest edges. It also occurs on heathland and heather moorland with scattered pines. It usually likes a dry sandy soil. It breeds on the ground making a shallow scrape in which to lay its eggs. The Nightjar is a crepuscular and nocturnal species and so it is difficult to find. The easiest way of seeing one is finding a calling male. On its breeding grounds it makes a mechanical monotonous "chrr", usually given from a branch, alternatively at dusk they fly about giving a "ku-ik, ku-ik" call and these birds are easily observed.

The Nightjar has a cryptic plumage of greys, browns and buffs with bars streaks and vermiculations that blends effortlessly into a background of dead leaves and branches. In flight it shows a long tail and wings with white corners to its tail and white wing patches.

The Nightjar is a scarce passage migrant to Leicestershire that once bred regularly in several areas of the county. It bred on the Charnwood Forest in areas like Bradgate Park, Bardon Hill and Benscliffe Wood, breeding at the latter site regularly until 1962 and then probably not again until 1978, 1979 and 1982. It bred on Buddon Wood shortly after it was felled, from 1947 until 1950 and then it probably bred again in 1963. It has been recorded twice at Swithland Reservoir. One bird was seen on the 19th May, 1965, and another came hawking around a moth light on the edge of the overflow channel on the 28th July, 1978.

SWIFTS Apodidae

Common Swift *Apus apus*

The Swift breeds throughout Europe from the Arctic to the Mediterranean and across central Asia as far as northern China. There is also a small population in North Africa. It is a migratory species wintering in Africa south of the Sahara although small numbers occasionally winter in northern India.

It can be found in most villages, towns and cities in Britain, however, it is more uncommon on the west coast of Ireland and Scotland where wet and windy conditions prevail. The autumn migration takes place from July to September with only occasional birds remaining into October. They return in spring at the end of April and May.

It is a colonial species breeding in holes and crevices and on ledges in buildings and cliff faces or in caves and occasionally in cavities in trees. Its breeding is closely associated with buildings. Unfortunately modern construction methods leave very few cavities for the birds to exploit and in some areas its numbers are dwindling.

The Swift has unusual habits. During periods of very cold wet weather when adult birds cannot catch insects to feed their brood the young become torpid and their body metabolism shuts down which gives them a better chance of survival. Young birds will migrate almost as soon as they leave the nest. This was illustrated amazingly by a young bird ringed in the nest at Oxford which three days after fledging reached an area near Madrid, a distance of about 1,300km. Swifts can also live for many years. A bird that was caught at Swithland Reservoir in June 1977, was killed by a car on the streets of Leicester in May 1987, it must have been at least 11 years of age.

In Arabia it was known by the name Hadji or Pilgrim that noted its transient passage through that land at certain times of the year. It is also the heraldic Martlet that showed the bearer had served as a pilgrim crusader. During aerial displays on their breeding grounds they fly after each other loudly screaming. Old village churches are often nesting sites. They can also be seen in large numbers feeding and screaming before frontal systems that bring storms. Because of their behaviour they were considered harbingers of evil and so gained the name 'devil birds'.

There was an extremely cold and windy spell of weather in late June and early July 1978, and the Swifts were flying extremely close to the ground in order to procure insects. A friend and I caught over 400 Swifts in the Wreake Valley in a few days during that period. On handling the birds we noticed large balls of insects about a centimetre in diameter inside their gapes. This was obviously food for young birds.

Swifts only come to earth to breed. They spend most of their lives in the air. They sleep and have even been known to mate while on the wing. The oldest known Swift lived to be about 16 years old and it is estimated it travelled 4,000,000 miles in its lifetime.

The Swift has a small bill and legs, long narrow scythe-shaped wings, short slightly forked tail and blackish plumage.

It is a common migrant breeding species in Leicestershire and a common summer visitor to Swithland Reservoir that uses the area for feeding and can occasionally be seen in very large numbers. The earliest spring record was of a single bird on the 1st April 1976. This was exceptionally early, the next earliest date being the 19th April 1959. The latest recorded autumn birds were two on the 15th September 1994, and one on the 18th September 1992. As already stated large numbers occasionally occur and the highest counts were circa 1,000 on the 8th and 15th June 1997; circa 1,600 on the 9th July 1990, and circa 3,000 on the 12th July 1989.

Alpine Swift *Apus melba*

The Alpine Swift breeds in southern Europe through Asia Minor to western Pakistan and it also occurs in North Africa. It is resident or a partial migrant in certain areas in southern and eastern Africa including Madagascar, western Arabia and India. Like so many swifts it suffers from cold weather and the lack of availability of insects and this has some bearing on its range. The European population is believed to winter in southern and eastern Africa. Birds migrate in the autumn from mid-September to mid-October and they return in the spring in late March and April.

The Alpine Swift occurs annually in Britain and most records come from southern and eastern England. It has been recorded from early March through to November with most records coming from April to June and from mid-September to early October.

It nests colonially in crevices and ledges on cliff faces, both in mountainous areas and on sea coasts. It also occasionally uses tree cavities and in recent times it has started to breed on tall buildings.

The Alpine Swift is a very large swift with long scythe-shaped wings and a short forked tail. It has brown upperparts and a white throat and belly that is divided by a brown breast band. The rest of the underparts are brown. It has a slower wing action and looks more sluggish in flight than the Common Swift.

It is a rare vagrant to Leicestershire and has been recorded at Swithland Reservoir on one occasion. A bird was present on the 13th April 1942 and this was the first county record.

KINGFISHERS Alcedinidae

Common Kingfisher *Alcedo atthis*

The Kingfisher breeds throughout central and southern Europe with small populations in North Africa It has a patchy distribution across central Asia reaching Japan in the east. It also occurs in southern Asia in India and across south-east Asia reaching China and New Guinea in the south. It is a bird that suffers badly in severe winters and cannot stand freezing conditions. For this reason the eastern European and central Asian birds are migratory. The population found in western Europe is only partially migratory, depending on the severity of the winter. If the weather remains mild then the birds will not move. The birds in central Asia move south into south-east Asia and India and the eastern European birds move to southern and south western Europe.

The Kingfisher breeds throughout most of the British Isles but it becomes more uncommon the further north one goes in Scotland and is absent from the far north. All most people see of the Kingfisher is its iridescent blue back as it vanishes into the distance. If you recognise the shrill call of this bird it often helps you to get good views of what to most people is a retiring species. Kingfishers sit above the stream or lake on overhanging branches waiting for their prey, but will also hover, and when they spot a small fish they plunge into the water head-first with lightning speed. They normally return to the fishing branch in order to devour their prey.

It is a bird that inhabits freshwater streams, rivers, lakes, ponds, canals and even coastal lagoons, estuaries and bays. It nests generally in vertical banks over water, excavating a hole and nest chamber usually in clay or sand.

The Kingfisher is a small-bodied big-headed bird with a long bill. It has a bluish green crown and wings and tail with a cobalt-blue back and rump. The underparts and ear coverts are a rich chestnut orange and the throat and neck patch are white. It has small red legs and its bill is black with varying amounts of orange-red at the base of the lower mandible depending upon the sex.

The Kingfisher is an uncommon resident breeding bird in Leicestershire. Its numbers can be severely diminished during bad winters like those in 1947, 1963 and 1982 and it can take several years for its numbers to recover. It is a not infrequent visitor to the reservoir and it bred in 1979 near Brazil Island on the central section of the reservoir. It has always been frequent along the Buddon Brook and one or two pairs breed on the quieter stretches most years. Birds move between the Buddon Brook and the reservoir grounds and they enjoy fishing in the two cooling ponds adjacent to the brook at the rear of the pumping station. In 1990 I was bird ringing along the hedges on the Buddon Brook meadows close to the reservoir grounds and from the 23rd April, to the 1st May, I caught two male and two female birds. At this time of year their courtship chasing often takes them quite a little way from the water.

HOOPOES Upupidae

Eurasian Hoopoe *Upupa epops*

The Hoopoe breeds across central and southern Europe and through central Asia to China and eastern Siberia. These populations are mainly migratory, moving to Africa south of the Sahara and south-east Asia to winter. Small numbers are resident or remain to winter in southern Spain and North Africa. Other races of the Hoopoe are resident in India and south-east Asia and sub-Saharan Africa although the last race is considered a separate species by some authorities. It migrates in autumn from August until October and returns in the spring in April and May.

The Hoopoe is a regular but scarce visitor to the British Isles and a very rare breeding bird. It is recorded most frequently in the spring and these birds are probably migrants that have overshot their destination and ended up in Britain. The vast majority of records come from southern England.

It is a bird of warm climates and likes open countryside with old trees and sparse ground cover that enables it to feed. The Hoopoe does not like areas of intensive agriculture but it is at home in orchards, olive groves, vineyards, old pastureland and parkland. It nests in cavities in trees, stone walls or buildings and it also nest in banks.

In recent years there has been a steady decline in its numbers throughout Europe. This could be due to the widespread use of insecticides and the changes in agricultural practice with the taking out of old hedges and trees. These measures will obviously affect the amount of insects available for the bird to feed on.

The Hoopoe is unmistakable with pinkish-brown head, neck, upper back and breast and a long slender slightly decurved bill. It has a long crest which when flattened is pinkish-brown and black but when erect forms a comb of feathers right over the crown, each feather being pinkish-brown with a black tip. The lower back, wings and tail are barred black and white and it shows white undertail coverts. It has fairly small dark legs. It has a very jerky, slightly undulating flight and shows broad black and white barred rounded wings, a white rump and a black tail with a single white bar across the centre.

The Hoopoe is a rare vagrant to Leicestershire. It has been recorded at Swithland Reservoir on one occasion, a bird being seen in flight in the early morning of the 4th August 1991.

WOODPECKERS Picidae

The Green and Great Spotted Woodpeckers are fairly common birds in Leicestershire. Around Quorn the Lesser Spotted Woodpecker was not uncommon, but in recent years its numbers have declined. The Great Spotted Woodpecker occasionally came to our garden to feed on peanuts and fat, especially during March. I had not seen either the Green Woodpecker or the Lesser Spotted Woodpecker in our garden at Quorn until the time I caught them in a mist net while bird ringing. We would probably be astonished if we knew what birds had gone unrecorded in our gardens! Woodpeckers tend to be elusive, but if you recognise their calls you might be surprised how many you could record on a birdwatching outing to the right habitat. Britain has only one other native species of woodpecker and that is the Wryneck. It is now a very rare visitor to Leicestershire and I have only ever seen one in the county. One summer's day in July 1963, I was walking with my father on the footpath across Tom Long's Meadow in Quorn, when my father pointed out a Wryneck calling from the top most branches of a dead tree. Over the last 20 years this species has declined greatly in Britain, and has been lost as a breeding species in England. It still, however, retains a foothold in Scotland.

It was not until late April 1973 that I had my first experience of other European woodpeckers, while walking on Mount Olympus in Greece. Firstly, I came across a Black Woodpecker calling loudly in the forest several hundred metres below, but at that time I was unaware of what it was! Its call was amplified and reverberated around the mountainside. I realised it was something new and I thrilled with excitement and anticipation. Eventually the culprit showed itself and flew from the trees before disappearing into the thick canopy below. Unfortunately my only recollection is of a large black crow-sized bird! I have been fortunate though, over the years, to see the Black Woodpecker on many occasions. The last time was in May, 2000, in northern Finland when I was able to stand within a few feet of a Black Woodpecker's nest hole and watch the jet black male with its crimson crown come to feed its three large young. Meanwhile, back on that day in April 1973, on Mount Olympus, I left the party I was with and walked along a path leading slowly uphill. On the side of the track a few metres away was the stump of a tree and at its base a woodpecker was busy feeding. It was unaware of my presence. It was a large woodpecker slightly bigger than the Great Spotted Woodpecker but it looked more like a giant Lesser Spotted with its black and white barred back and red crown. It was a White-backed Woodpecker and to this day it remains the only one I have ever seen.

With the exception of the Wryneck, British woodpeckers are not generally regarded as being migratory, although occasionally Great Spotted Woodpeckers from the continent do make it to our shores. Britain has only one other species of woodpecker on its list and surprisingly it is an American species – the Yellow-bellied Sapsucker. It was seen on Tresco in the Isles of Scilly in September 1975. Sapsuckers feed on insects and as their name suggests, on sap, which they obtain by drilling a series of holes either horizontally or vertically into the tree and wait for the sap to gather in them. The only epitaph the Tresco bird left was a series of characteristic holes drilled in Tresco's trees that would be a constant reminder to all future birdwatchers of what they had missed! Our own Great Spotted Woodpecker could be considered to be part way to becoming a sapsucker as it will on occasions drill numerous holes in lime trees to obtain sap. Some Small-leaved Limes in Swithland Wood are peppered with holes where this species has been at work.

Some species of North American woodpecker move southward in the autumn to escape the severe northern winters, returning again in spring. I witnessed woodpecker migration in May 1988, at Point Pelee, Ontario, Canada. Point Pelee is a spit of land extending out into Lake Erie. Over the years it has gained a reputation for being a migration 'hot spot'. Very early one May morning I was standing on the tip of the spit watching birds migrating northward. One of the first birds I noticed was a Northern Flicker flying in low over the lake. It alighted in the first trees it came to and after a few minutes rest it flew back out over the water the way it had just come. It must have been a sucker for punishment, but strange as it might seem reverse migration is not that infrequent and this bird might have kept going right back to the United States. During the time I spent at Point Pelee we also saw Yellow-bellied Sapsuckers, Red-bellied Woodpeckers and Red-headed Woodpeckers arrive to join the resident Downy, Hairy and large Pileated Woodpeckers.

Some woodpeckers are also gregarious and this is particularly true of two North American species. On visiting the Laguna Mountains in southern California in September 1995, I saw many Acorn Woodpeckers and it was not uncommon to see half a dozen or more birds in close proximity. These birds, slightly smaller than a Great Spotted Woodpecker, showed black upperparts with a small amount of white on the base of the primaries. They also have a white rump, white face and underparts, and a black chin and breast band, and varying amounts of red on the crown depending on the sex. Some of the birds could be seen catching insects in mid-air with their sallies from a branch, in a fashion not unlike that of our flycatchers. It was also a very vocal species. My main memory of these birds is finding their larder that consisted of thousands of holes drilled in a tree trunk, each containing a single acorn. The cache is collected over many years by a group of woodpeckers and it is closely defended. The Acorn Woodpecker lives in groups with several breeding males, usually only one or two breeding females and up to ten non-breeding birds or helpers. At times one or more females will lay in a single nest and the group will incubate and care for the young.

Another communal woodpecker was seen on my visit to Texas in late April 1998. Jones State Forest lies 45 miles to the north of Houston. I left Houston very early in the morning so as not to get caught up in traffic. I arrived at the forest at daybreak and strolled among the pines on that bright spring morning listening to the bird song. I soon found my first woodpecker which was the large Pileated Woodpecker, with its striking black and white neck pattern and red crested crown. I also quickly found the Red-headed Woodpecker with its white underparts and black and white upperparts. The head and neck of this bird looks for all the world as though it had been dipped in a pot of bright red paint. After about one hour I found my prize, the endangered Red-cockaded Woodpecker! It is a small woodpecker, with a black and white barred back, black crown, and white underparts, streaked black on the flanks. It gets its name from a small red streak lying just behind the male's eye but this is seldom visible in the field. This species lives in clans containing up to nine birds. It bores its nest hole and roosting chamber in large living pines affected by heart-wood disease caused by a fungus. The bird then chips out resin wells around the holes, and the slightly poisonous resin oozes out to coat the trunk of the tree acting as protection against predators such as snakes. The small clan of woodpeckers lives closely together. Only the dominant male courts and pairs with the female but other members of the clan take part in incubating and feeding the young.

In my travels I have been fortunate to see many amazing woodpeckers from the large Crimson-crested Woodpecker in the tropical forests of Venezuela to the Himalayan Flameback that I found in Royal Chitwan National Park in Nepal. Sometimes you find woodpeckers when you are not expecting them. I was seeking shelter under a palm tree on an island off Singapore during a heavy rain shower when a Common Flameback came and settled on the trunk of the palm next to me. It too was sheltering from the rain! This bird was really beautiful with a red cap and crest, black and white face and neck markings, golden-olive mantle, and bright red rump. It waited motionless on the tree until the rain had stopped and then went on its way.

November 1999, saw me birdwatching in the Southern Beech Forest of Torres Del Paine National Park in southern Chile. While out walking with my wife I came across an area containing particularly old trees, and I stopped and carefully checked the trunks and branches of the trees. I was looking for the large Magellanic Woodpecker. A few months previously I had been watching 'The Life of Birds' introduced by David Attenborough on television. One of the programmes had shown him in these southern woodlands also looking for Magellanic Woodpeckers. I remembered how he had taken a stone and knocked it rhythmically against the trunk of a tree. A pair of woodpeckers responded to this and flew in close to where he was standing, thinking that they were protecting their territory. Anyway, given a similar situation I thought I would try this approach! I found a large stone and a slightly hollow tree trunk and started to hit it rhythmically. Nothing happened! I tried again for about five minutes and then threw the stone away in disgust. We left the area and walked on for about an hour before deciding to stop for lunch. We found a log under the canopy of some old trees and ate our snack. Just as I was finishing Pamela drew my attention to a movement on a tree trunk about fifty metres away. I quickly got my binoculars trained on it and I glimpsed the bird's head peering round the trunk. It had a large bill with red feathering at the base and a black head with a very large curled crest. It was a female Magellanic Woodpecker! No sooner had I seen it, than it was gone. I was so frustrated. We walked on for another hour and then we retraced our tracks heading back to our hotel. I thought I would never see these woodpeckers properly. We reached the last section of old Beech Forest before the track opened out onto grassland. I spotted a movement low down on a tree stump. It was a male Magellanic Woodpecker. It was feeding on the stump by removing bark with its bill to get at insects. It was a large woodpecker slightly larger than a Jackdaw, with a crested head that was wholly red. The rest of the body was black with the exception of white wing patches. We watched the bird for several minutes and then it flew onto the tree above my head and started to drum. Its drumming was a rhythmical double blow. After a few seconds a female flew into the tree to join him and we had marvellous views of them both. One thing I learnt from this day is that knocking a stone on a tree stump is no substitute for the real thing!

European Green Woodpecker *Picus viridis*

The Green Woodpecker is found throughout central and southern Europe and occurs through into Asia reaching as far as the western shore of the Caspian Sea. Its northern range is governed by the severity of the winter weather. Due to its habit of feeding on the ground it finds it very difficult to procure food in snow and prolonged severe frost. This species has a tendency to remain faithful to one site and few long distance movements have been recorded from ringing studies.

In Britain it is generally distributed throughout England and Wales. It is more thinly distributed in Scotland and is absent from the far north, the Isles and Ireland. It colonised Scotland only in the early 1950s and has continued its spread northwards. It suffers badly during prolonged hard winters when its numbers decline significantly.

The Green Woodpecker is a bird of open and scattered woodland, parkland, old pasture, orchards, commons and gardens. Like other woodpeckers it nests in a hole in a tree and I have noticed that in England it has a tendency to nest in Ash trees. It does not drum as frequently as the other two British species of woodpecker but makes its presence known by its loud laughing call that earned it the name 'Yaffle'. More often than not you come across this species feeding on grassy areas where it procures its staple food, the ant, with the aid of its extremely long tongue. On being disturbed it will rise with a slow undulating flight showing off its yellow rump as it departs.

The Green Woodpecker is the largest British Woodpecker. The adult has a red crown, a black mask around the eye and black moustachial stripe which is red centred in the male and is wholly black in the female. The upperparts are olive green and the underparts are paler with a yellow grey wash and slight barring on the flanks. The outer webs of the primaries and outer tail feathers are barred black and white. The large grey bill is dagger-like in appearance and the bird has grey feet that have two toes facing forward and two back, which aid it in climbing trees.

The Green Woodpecker is a fairly common resident breeding bird in Leicestershire. It is a resident in small numbers at Swithland Reservoir with one or two pairs breeding annually either within the reservoir grounds or in the adjacent farmland hedgerow trees. Over the years the reservoir has been one of the best areas within the county to see this species. It can often be seen on the grass areas on the dam or around the adjacent cooling ponds. Before the Red Wood Ant *Formica rufa* was lost from Buddon Wood prior to the wartime clear-felling, this species was even more plentiful than it is today.

Great Spotted Woodpecker *Dendrocopos major*

The Great Spotted Woodpecker occurs throughout Europe with the exception of Iceland and Ireland and its range extends just into North Africa. It occurs eastwards through central Asia as far as Japan and southwards into China across to north-east India. During the late summer if there is a shortage of pine and spruce cones in the taiga, northern populations erupt and movements of several hundred kilometres have been recorded with a few stray birds reaching Ireland.

It is the most frequent woodpecker in the British Isles and can be found throughout mainland England, Wales and Scotland but is absent as a breeding bird in Ireland and many of our surrounding islands. The British population declined in the first part of the 19th century and it became extinct as a breeding bird in Scotland and northern England. Towards the end of the 19th century in about 1890 its population suddenly increased dramatically and it re-colonised northern England and most of Scotland by the 1950s. The population of the Great Spotted Woodpecker has shown an upward trend during the latter part of the 1990s in sharp contrast to its smaller cousin the Lesser Spotted Woodpecker that is in a steep decline.

It is a bird of both coniferous and deciduous woodland and can be found in parks and gardens. In the spring they often make their presence known by their repetitive territorial drumming. Like the other British woodpeckers their nest is a hole made in the trunk of a tree in soft or decaying wood. In winter and early spring they will come to feed at garden bird tables and I have known them to be very partial to Almond nuts, fat and peanuts.

The Great Spotted is about the same size as a Blackbird with basically black and white plumage and a striking red vent and undertail coverts. It can be told from the much smaller Lesser Spotted by its large white oval shoulder patch that is obvious at some distance. The sexes are also easy to tell apart. The male has a red bar on the nape that is absent in the female but young birds can be confusing because they show a red crown. It has a fairly long dark dagger-like bill and greyish legs.

The Great Spotted Woodpecker is a fairly common resident breeding bird in Leicestershire. It is also fairly common at Swithland Reservoir and can be found in all the areas containing mature trees. It breeds annually in the reservoir grounds and in the adjacent woodlands.

Lesser Spotted Woodpecker *Dendrocopos minor*

The Lesser Spotted Woodpecker occurs throughout Europe and southward just reaching North Africa. Its range continues across central Asia reaching Kamchatka and parts of Japan. Like the Great Spotted Woodpecker the northern populations can be partially migratory moving in the late summer or early autumn.

In Britain it is found throughout England and Wales but it is absent from Scotland, Ireland and the offshore Islands. It can be found in mixed and deciduous woodland, parkland, orchards and gardens. The best way of finding this species is by listening for its call or its weak drumming in early spring. Between 1970 and 1998 the Lesser Spotted Woodpecker population in Britain went into serious decline and fell by 42%. The losses have mainly been in the last decade and followed an overall increase in numbers between 1976 and 1984, probably brought about by the large amounts of dead timber due to Dutch Elm disease. The reasons for the fall are not clear but it is interesting that it should come about with the massive increase in Sparrowhawk numbers. A small woodpecker feeding or drumming on the top-most dead branches of a tree, which is their habit, would be an easy target for a Sparrowhawk. Although the Lesser Spotted Woodpecker has a wide distribution the density in its population is still not very high and half a dozen birds killed in any parish would probably exterminate the species in that area.

The bird itself is slightly smaller than a House Sparrow, with a black back which is finely barred white, and white underparts with fine black streaking on the flanks. The male has a red cap whereas the female's cap is black. Both sexes have white cheeks with a dark bar extending across the face. The bill on this small woodpecker is small and fine.

The Lesser Spotted Woodpecker is now going from a fairly common resident breeding bird in Leicestershire to an uncommon breeding resident. Swithland Reservoir and the surrounding area was once one of the strongholds for this species in the county and although it is still recorded annually it is not as frequent as it once was. In the local area it appears to be a bird of Alder Carr woodland and it is most commonly found in the Alder *Alnus* trees which line the edges of the Buddon Brook, the wetter areas of Buddon Wood and the reservoir margins. It often makes its nest hole in the Alder but it has been known to breed high up in a few of the larger poplars *Populus* in the area. A decade ago it was not an uncommon breeding bird in the reservoir grounds or along the Buddon Brook and Buddon Wood.

PASSERIFORMES

LARKS Alaudidae

Common Skylark *Alauda arvensis*

The Skylark breeds throughout Europe and into North Africa and it also occurs throughout central Asia reaching Kamchatka and Japan. The northern populations are migratory but the southern breeding birds tend to make only localised movements. The northern birds winter south to North Africa, the Middle East, northern India and China. It has been introduced to parts of Australia, New Zealand and Vancouver Island in Canada.

The Skylark breeds throughout Britain and Ireland. British bred birds tend to be resident but cold weather movements do take place. These movements often have a westerly bias and large numbers head for Ireland in severe weather. Large numbers of immigrants move along our east coast during the autumn. Some will pass straight through and smaller numbers will remain to winter. Between 1970 and 1998 the Skylark population in Britain has fallen dramatically and is down by 52%. This is almost certainly due to agricultural changes that leave few areas for the birds to breed and feed in the intensive farming that is now practised.

The Skylark likes large open areas and can be found on grassland, arable ground, heathland, moorland and saltmarsh. They breed on the ground in a small depression and generally have a fine grass-lined nest. The bird is probably best known for its song that can be heard most regularly from February onwards when birds start to think about breeding and taking a mate. The song can be given from a perch such as a fence post but often it can be heard while the bird is at a great height and can be almost out of sight hanging in the air on trembling wings.

The Skylark has brown grey upperparts with dark streaking, its underparts are white with a buffish suffusion on the breast and it has dark streaking and spotting on the upper breast. The head has a small crest that can be held erect by the male. It has a fairly small dark bill and flesh-brown legs. In flight it shows a dark-centred tail with contrasting white outer tail feathers and white trailing edges to the wings.

The Skylark is a common resident breeding bird in Leicestershire that is undergoing a steady decline. At one time many pairs nested in the fields adjacent to Swithland Reservoir but over recent years their numbers have been greatly reduced. One of the major changes that have occurred in farming in this area over the last few decades is from pastureland to arable and with arable crops has come the added use of insecticides which make the ground unsuitable for sustaining the larks. During periods of prolonged cold weather the open aspect of the reservoir has enabled birdwatchers to see large movements of this species as birds head westward. Some years a heavy passage of larks takes place over the reservoir during October.

SWALLOWS and MARTINS Hirundinidae

Sand Martin *Riparia riparia*

The Sand Martin or Bank Swallow breeds throughout Europe reaching the Arctic Circle, North America and Asia, breeding in Asia as far south as northern India and China. It winters in Africa south of the Sahara, South America, India and south-east Asia.

It is a summer visitor that occurs throughout Britain and Ireland. It is one of the earliest summer migrants to arrive appearing in numbers towards the end of March. Return passage starts towards the end of August and most birds have left the country by October.

The European Sand Martins winter in the Sahel region of Africa just south of the Sahara. A drought in this area in 1968-69 is thought to have brought about a population crash throughout Europe and probably over three quarters of the British population was lost. Another bad winter happened in 1983-84 and its numbers dropped to about 10% of those in the mid 1960s but despite these setbacks there has been a slight recovery in the last decade.

It is a bird that is associated with water and feeds on insects low over reservoirs, lakes, rivers and marshes. They are great opportunists and breed in holes that they excavate in vertical sand or earth banks and so their nests often can be found at gravel pits, sand pits and in river banks. They nest communally and so many hundred birds can be at one colony.

The Sand Martin is a small swallow with brown upperparts and a small forked tail. The underparts are white except for a well defined brown breast band.

The Sand Martin is a fairly common summer migrant breeding bird in Leicestershire. Birds can be seen at Swithland Reservoir from March onwards. The earliest sightings are of single birds on the 6th March 1983, and on the 10th March 1992. The highest numbers are often recorded at the beginning of April and 1,500 birds were noted feeding over the reservoir on the 13th April 1966. This is the largest count made at this site. Other large counts were 500+ on the 5th April 1989, and 300 on the 2nd April 1994. The largest autumn count recorded was of circa 100 birds on the 15th September 1997, and the latest autumn sightings were of single birds on the 6th October 1983, and the 10th October 1993. At one time large numbers of Sand Martins could be seen feeding over the reservoir throughout the summer months and this was almost certainly due to the birds that bred annually at Rothley Sand Pit but over the past two decades their numbers have dwindled and this is reflected in the smaller numbers feeding over the reservoir. In 1947 Rothley Sand Pit held 1,000 breeding pairs. By 1970 only 500 breeding pairs remained and by 1986 there were 40 pairs of which only 10 were successful.

Eurasian Crag Martin *Ptyonoprogne rupestris*

The Crag Martin breeds across southern Europe and parts of North Africa and its range extends eastwards into Asia through Turkey to the Himalayas and on into China. Most of the Mediterranean birds are resident but the more northern European populations migrate southward, some reaching Senegal and Ethiopia and some Asian birds wintering in peninsular India and parts of China.

It is a bird of mountains, sea cliffs, gorges and rock outcrops. It nests on vertical cliffs up to 2500m in Europe and up to 4000m in the Himalayas. The nest is a mud cup that is stuck to a vertical wall and not unlike that of the Swallow.

The Crag Martin is slightly larger than the Sand Martin with grey-tinged brown upperparts and buff-washed underparts becoming darker brown towards the vent and it has characteristic black underwing coverts. The tail is only slightly forked and when fanned it shows a series of white spots near the tip.

The Crag Martin is a rare vagrant to Britain. A single bird was seen at Swithland Reservoir on the 17th April 1999. This constituted the first county record and the fifth British record.

Barn Swallow *Hirundo rustica*

The Barn Swallow breeds across Europe, Asia and North America being absent only from the far north and south-east Asia. It winters in Africa south of the Sahara, South America and peninsular India and south-east Asia.

It is a widespread summer visitor that occurs throughout Britain and Ireland. Birds arrive in Britain towards the end of March but the largest proportion of the population does not arrive until April or May. Return migration starts in late August and large flocks come together prior to their departure. All but a few birds have left the country by the end of October.

Ringing studies have shown that British birds winter mainly in South Africa and most German birds winter in Zaire. The central European population appears to winter in central Africa in the equatorial forest.

The bird feeds almost entirely on aerial insects which it catches over open country, especially areas of lowland grassland and water. They build their mud cup nest generally on a beam in open buildings such as barns and outhouses but they will nest under bridges or in natural caves and crevices.

Like so many species the Swallow is in decline almost certainly due to agricultural changes and the widespread use of insecticides. When I was a child the local farms around Quorn had a great deal of pastureland which held many cattle, sheep and the accompanying manure heaps were good for insects. These were ideal hunting areas for swallows and the associated barns and milking parlours were good nesting sites. In the late 1960s and early 1970s most of the local farms went over to large scale cereal growing. These crops required spraying and this with the added loss of livestock resulted in fewer insects on which the birds could feed. Also most of the old barns, sheds and milking parlours were pulled down because they had become redundant and so the birds lost their nesting sites. This pattern was mirrored throughout much of the lowland country of central and eastern England and the resulting population decrease among the Swallows was probably far greater than currently estimated.

The Swallow with its steel blue upperparts and long tail streamers is one of Britain's best known birds. It has a rich chestnut forehead and throat and a blue breast band, the rest of the underparts being off-white. The tail is deeply forked and the outer tail feathers have white windows in them. It has a small dark bill and short dark legs.

The Swallow is a common summer migrant breeding bird in Leicestershire, a common passage migrant and is becoming a scarce breeding bird at Swithland Reservoir. Pairs bred in the reservoir grounds most years and as many as three pairs bred successfully in 1980. It normally arrives at the reservoir in early April. The earliest records for the site were a single bird on the 15th March 1989, and another on the 23rd March 1983. The two largest counts for the reservoir were circa 500 on the 24th April 1989, and circa 500 on the 3rd May 1987. The highest autumn count was 90 birds on the 4th September 1993, and the two latest records were a single bird on the 24th October 1964, and four birds on the 10th November 1967.

Common House Martin *Delichon urbica*

The House Martin breeds throughout Europe south to North Africa and across central Asia to Japan and China. It winters in Africa south of the Sahara, parts of India and south-east Asia.

It is a summer visitor occurring throughout Britain and Ireland. Most birds arrive in Britain during April and May and return migration starts in August and all but a few stragglers have left by the end of October.

Like the Swallow it tends to feed over open country and water but during the breeding season it is most frequently met with around man-made structures, especially houses, where it nests under the eaves and soffit boards. It makes a cup nest of wet mud that is generally stuck to a vertical wall and an overhang leaving a small hole at the top as an entrance. Natural nest sites include both sea and inland cliffs, trees and caves. It is often a colonial nester and in some areas in Europe over 1000 nests have been recorded in a single colony. If the weather conditions are favourable they will have two broods and sometimes even three and young can still be in the nest in early October.

Although most authorities recognise this species has large fluctuations in its population very few appear to recognise there is widespread and ongoing decline. My own observations over the years lead me to believe that this species has declined significantly, particularly in the villages around Swithland Reservoir. Twenty years ago the House Martin was a common breeding bird in Quorn with many houses supporting nests. Today there is only a small remnant of that population left. In late August through to October mixed flocks of Swallows and House Martins could be seen perched on telephone wires or sunning themselves on rooftops and on cold days large numbers would feed low over the local gardens, but unfortunately these are sights of the past. The reasons why their numbers have fallen are not clear but certainly the cleaning up of the countryside and to some extent our villages must have had an effect. It must become increasingly difficult for breeding birds to find muddy puddles from which to get nesting material. People are not willing to put up with the mess and few encourage the birds to breed and also there is a shortage of insects brought about by new farming methods.

The House Martin has blue-black upperparts with a characteristic white rump and a forked tail, its underparts are white and it has a small dark bill and white feathered feet.

The House Martin is a common and widespread summer breeding bird in Leicestershire. It is a common passage migrant and summer visitor to Swithland Reservoir. The earliest spring migrant was seen on the 27th March 1994, and other early dates were a single bird on the 7th April 1952, and three birds on 7th April 1991. The largest number recorded over the water in spring was 2,000+ on the 24th May 1987, and the largest autumn count was circa 800 on the 15th September 1997. The three latest autumn records were all of single birds seen on 25th October 1964, the 29th October 1967, and the 2nd November 1987.

PIPITS and WAGTAILS Motacillidae

Tree Pipit *Anthus trivialis*

The Tree Pipit breeds throughout most of Europe, being absent only from Iceland, and a large part of the Iberian Peninsula. Its range extends across central Asia beyond Lake Baikal. It winters mainly in India and central and eastern Africa.

It is a summer visitor to Britain breeding throughout England, Scotland and Wales although it is a scarce breeding bird in Ireland. The first birds arrive in Britain in April and passage continues throughout May. They depart again in August and most have left our shores by the end of September.

Between 1970 and 1998 the Tree Pipit population has decreased in Britain by 62% and in Leicestershire it is probably higher than that. The reasons for the sudden decline in Leicestershire are not clear but fewer insects and greater disturbance on many of its breeding sites, especially by dogs, cannot help and of course long distance migrants face many hazards from an ever-changing environment.

It is a bird of woodland edges, bushy scrubland, open conifer and deciduous woodland and heathland with scattered trees. It makes a grass cup nest that is usually well concealed under vegetation on the ground. The male announces his presence with a song flight that he makes from the top of a tree or bush. He flies upwards calling and then parachutes down back to his lofty perch.

The pipits are not unlike wagtails in their structure but most have brown streaked backs, buff and white underparts with various amounts of dark streaking. The Tree Pipit is slightly larger than the Meadow Pipit with more distinct facial markings and less pronounced markings on the back and finer streaking on the flanks. The rump is plain. The bill is more robust than that of the Meadow Pipit and it has long pink legs and the hind claw is short and curved.

The Tree Pipit is a summer visitor that is now an uncommon breeding bird in Leicestershire. It is hard to believe that half a century ago it was a very common breeding bird in the county and it even bred in some of the larger gardens in Quorn. It has now become an infrequent passage migrant to Swithland Reservoir although during the 1950s it bred within the grounds especially near Kinchley Field Quarry. Numerous pairs bred on Buddon Wood and it was such a common species that it was certainly under-recorded in the area. The earliest spring record was on the 10th April 1980, and the last sighting for the year was the 7th September 1996. The highest count I could find for the reservoir was five birds that were seen on the 17th April 1983.

Meadow Pipit *Anthus pratensis*

The Meadow Pipit breeds in eastern Greenland, across northern and central Europe into western Siberia. The northern breeding birds move southward in the autumn and winter into southern Europe, North Africa and the Middle East. Birds tend to be resident or partial migrants in central western Europe.

The Meadow Pipit breeds throughout the British Isles and some birds will remain throughout the winter. Large numbers of birds pass through Britain on passage from northern Europe during September and October. From early March until May birds move back through the country and some of these will be locally bred birds returning to spend the summer.

It is a bird of open areas such as upland moorland, rough grassland, heathland, tundra, saltmarsh and open forest or new plantations. Like the Tree Pipit it makes a grass cup nest that is hidden under any low growing vegetation. It also makes a similar song flight to the Tree Pipit but it has a tendency to start its display flight from the ground, rise up into the sky singing and parachute down normally back onto the ground.

As previously stated the Meadow Pipit is very similar to the Tree Pipit. It differs, however, in having more prominent streaking on the back and bolder streaks on the flanks and its face is not so well marked. The bill is fine and it has pink legs, the hind claw being long and only slightly curved.

In Leicestershire the Meadow Pipit is locally a fairly common breeding bird, and a frequent passage migrant and winter visitor. It is a fairly frequent passage migrant and winter visitor to Swithland Reservoir in small numbers and it can often be recorded passing over the reservoir. Only rarely are large numbers present and I can find only three records that are of note. The highest recorded number was 100+ birds on adjacent fields on the 1st April 1967. 75 birds were present in the waterworks grounds during the first few months of 1980 and 19 birds were recorded on the reservoir shoreline on the 22nd December 1996.

Rock Pipit *Anthus petrosus*

The Rock Pipit breeds around the coasts of Scandinavia, Britain and Ireland and northern and north-west France. The northern European population moves southward in autumn and winters along the western seaboard of Europe reaching North Africa.

In Britain it is well distributed and breeds around the coast of Wales, Scotland and England although it is absent along the east coast from northern Kent to south Yorkshire. It is mainly a resident in Britain although partial movements do take place and birds start to move from September onwards. Northern birds of the race *A. p. littoralis* can be found on the east and south coasts from October to early April.

It is a bird of rocky coastlines and short grassy areas that can be found above cliffs and areas adjacent to the shoreline. It makes a cup nest of grass and seaweed in a hole or crevice in a cliff or concealed in rank vegetation.

The Rock Pipit of the race *A. p. petrosus* which is found in Britain is slightly larger on average than the Tree Pipit. It is generally a dark looking bird with grey-brown upperparts and faint dark streaking and the rump and some of the upper mantle can have olive tones. It has a white throat and dark malar stripes but the rest of the underparts are grey-buff with dark streaking on the breast and flanks. When in flight it shows characteristic grey outer tail-feathers. It has a fairly long dark bill and dark legs.

The Rock Pipit is a scarce winter visitor and passage migrant to Leicestershire. It is a rare winter visitor and passage migrant to Swithland Reservoir that has been recorded on eleven occasions. The first Rock Pipit was recorded at the reservoir on the 21st March 1964. Nine of the records were seen in a period from late September to early December with five of the sightings coming in October. The other two records came in March. Two individuals were present at the reservoir on the 15th October 1989. All the other occurrences were of single birds and they made only brief visits with only one bird staying for two days.

N.B. In the mid-1980s the British Ornithologists' Union Records Committee decided to split the Water Pipit *Anthus spinoletta* into three distinct species. These are Water Pipit *Anthus spinoletta*, Rock Pipit *Anthus petrosus* and Buff-bellied Pipit *Anthus rubescens*. Of the eleven records of Rock Pipit *Anthus petrosus* that have been seen at Swithland Reservoir, four of the records were seen prior to the split and cannot with absolute certainty be assigned to that species although it is more than likely that they were.

Water/Rock Pipit

A bird flew over Swithland Reservoir calling on the 8th November 1998 but it could not be specifically assigned to either species.

Yellow Wagtail *Motacilla flava*

The Yellow Wagtail breeds throughout much of Europe southward to North Africa and across central and northern Asia reaching Alaska and Kamchatka and southwards into northern China. Some of the more southerly breeding populations are resident but it is mainly a migrant wintering in Africa south of the Sahara, the Indian subcontinent and south-east Asia. The Yellow Wagtail may have as many as eighteen distinct subspecies and these can be told apart by the colour of the head and head pattern. The head colour ranges from yellow in *M. f. lutea*, a bird from south-west Siberia, to blue-grey in *M. f. flava* from central Europe. The head is dark grey in *M. f. thunbergi*, which is found in Fenno-Scandinavia, and the black-headed *M. f. feldegg* occurs in the Balkans and Turkey.

The race that occurs in Britain and along the coast of north-western Europe from Germany to northern France is called *M. f. flavissima* and it has a largely yellow head. It is found throughout much of England and Wales although it is scarce in the extreme south west of England. Its range has been much reduced in Scotland this century. It formerly bred as far north as Aberdeen but now it is absent from much of the northern and central part of the country. In Ireland there were two large breeding groups, one at Lough Neagh and another on the edge of Mayo and Galway. Both colonies had died out by 1941 and now it is only a sporadic breeder in that country. The first Yellow Wagtails arrive in Britain in March but the main bulk of the birds arrive in April. They leave again in September and all but a few have left by early October.

In Britain the Yellow Wagtail's population has fallen between 1970 and 1998 by 13% and in some areas of the country by 30% in five years between 1994 and 1998. In Leicestershire its decline is probably greater. As with other birds whose numbers have declined significantly several factors could be responsible. Agricultural intensification has not helped this species with the ploughing up of old pastureland and draining of flood meadows and marsh. This has done away with many of the birds' breeding and feeding areas. Also the numbers of livestock have been drastically cut in central and eastern England over the past two decades. This, combined with the general use of insecticides will almost certainly have meant fewer insects on which the birds can feed. The Yellow Wagtail is also a long distance migrant and the growing desertification of areas bordering the Sahara and droughts that frequently take place in the Sahel region might mean that the birds have to make longer flights without food and this could have an enormous effect on the birds' population.

It is a bird of open country that can be found in pastureland, mixed farmland, water meadows, marshes and bogs. They build a grass cup nest on the ground usually in tall herbage.

The adult male Yellow Wagtail *M. f. flavissima* has yellow underparts and a yellow face. The crown, mantle and back are olive green which contrasts with the darker wing feathers which are pale edged, giving the bird two distinct wingbars. The central area of the tail is black and it has white outer tail feathers that are noticeable in flight. It has a fine black bill and long dark legs. The female's back and mantle are similar to the male but the underparts and head are drab in comparison.

The Yellow Wagtail is now an uncommon breeding bird in Leicestershire although it is still a fairly common passage migrant. It was once a common breeding bird in the fields adjacent to Swithland Reservoir and bred close to, if not actually in, the reservoir grounds. It was also a common passage migrant and many birds could be seen in the area during late March and April. The last breeding record came in 1990 and it is doubtful if it still breeds in the area. The number of birds on passage has fallen dramatically over the past few years. The earliest returning migrant was seen at the Reservoir on the 11th March 1970, and the last sighting in autumn was of three birds on the 26th September 1971.

The nominate Blue-headed Wagtail *M. f. flava* which breeds across central Europe to the Urals and which occasionally breeds in Britain has been seen in the area twice. One was seen close to the reservoir on the 18th May 1946, and a bird was seen at the reservoir from the 21st to the 23rd April 1973. The Blue-headed Wagtail is an uncommon passage migrant to Leicestershire that has bred on one occasion in 1944 at Croft.

Grey Wagtail *Motacilla cinerea*

The Grey Wagtail has two separate populations. The first can be found in central and southern Europe eastwards through Turkey to Iran and southwards to the Azores , Madeira and the Canary Islands and to north-west Africa. The birds in the south-west are resident or partial migrants, whereas the northern and easterly populations are wholly migratory, wintering in southern Europe, North Africa, the Middle East and eastern Africa. The other distinct population which is largely migratory occurs from the Urals eastward through to Kamchatka and south to Japan and northern China. These birds winter throughout the Indian subcontinent and south-east Asia.

The Grey Wagtail is found throughout Britain and Ireland, although it is more sparsely distributed in eastern England. British birds tend to be resident although some localised movements do take place and a certain amount of passage takes place along the coasts in September.

The Grey Wagtail has been expanding its range since about 1850 and it colonised many areas of northern Europe in the early part of the twentieth century. The expansion is still continuing and it could be linked to milder winters. This species is particularly susceptible to severe winter weather and large drops in numbers do occur after a severe winter.

The Grey Wagtail is a bird of stony fast-flowing streams bordered by trees and it can be found in upland and lowland areas. It also occurs near any fast flowing water including waterfalls, reservoir overflow channels, mill races and canal locks. They usually nest in a crevice or hole in both brickwork and rocks or in tangled roots on banks close to the water.

The male Grey Wagtail is a handsome bird with bright lemon-yellow underparts and a black bib in breeding plumage. Its head, back and mantle are slate grey and its wings are black with pale edgings to its tertials. It has a white superciliary stripe and a white moustachial stripe bordering the bib. While it is feeding it constantly bobs its long white- edged black tail and if it rises it has an undulating flight that shows off its green-yellow rump and a white wing bar. In summer it has a dark slender bill and pale brown legs that are shorter than those of either the Yellow or Pied Wagtail. The female is similar to the male but her plumage is drab by comparison.

The Grey Wagtail is a scarce breeding bird and an uncommon passage migrant and winter visitor to Leicestershire. It is a resident at Swithland Reservoir in small numbers. It breeds in the locality most years, generally near the dam and along the Buddon Brook, and has bred within the reservoir grounds on several occasions. A nest with five eggs was found in the waterworks grounds on 16th May 1978. The best place to see the Grey Wagtail is along the dam and overflow channel and they often feed at the bottom of the channel where it joins the Buddon Brook. Most often only a single bird is met with but on occasions a family party can be seen in the vicinity of the overflow. The highest numbers recorded were six birds on the 25th and 26th August 1996, and a similar number on the 6th August 1999, and judging by the dates these were probably adults with their young. Breeding has taken place more frequently during recent years.

Pied/ White Wagtail *Motacilla alba*

The White Wagtail breeds throughout Europe and in the south it reaches north-west Africa. In the east it is found over much of Asia reaching Alaska and Kamchatka in the north and Taiwan and China in the south. It is a resident in western Europe and on the southern edge of its range. Over most of its range, however, it is a migrant wintering in northern and central Africa, the Middle East across to the Indian subcontinent and eastward to Cambodia.

The White wagtail has eleven subspecies across its range but only two occur in Britain. The Pied Wagtail *M. a. yarrellii* breeds throughout Britain and Ireland and also on Europe's western seaboard from Denmark southward to northern France. The nominate White Wagtail *M. a. alba* occasionally breeds in Britain, mainly in Shetland, but it is most frequently met with as a passage migrant which occurs from March to May and August through to October. The Pied Wagtail is mainly resident in Britain although some movements do take place especially among upland and northerly breeding birds. Some Pied Wagtails move southward reaching Portugal and even Morocco.

It occurs over a variety of habitats but generally it favours areas close to water. One of its old country names is 'Peggy Dishwasher' because it enjoys feeding close to the edge of water and its rapid runs and quivering tail make this bird a delight to watch. It can be found on the shorelines of lakes, reservoirs, ponds, rivers and streams, but it also feeds on short grassland and can be found in parks and gardens and on playing fields. It is a very adaptable species and often frequents built up areas. It likes sewage works, farmyards and school playgrounds and in recent years it has taken to feeding, breeding and roosting on large flat roofs. It nests in holes in buildings or crevices among rocks, tangled roots on the banks of streams and recently on ledges and in holes found on external metalwork that adorns many flat roofs.

During the late summer and early autumn birds start to congregate together to roost and this continues throughout the winter months. Often roosts can take place in the centre of our towns and cities, probably because inner-city areas are a few degrees warmer than elsewhere. During January 1983, a roost at Vaughan Way and St Peter's Lane, Leicester, held 400-500 birds and there were 125 birds roosting in the centre of Loughborough at the end of February the same year.

The male Pied Wagtail *M. a. yarrellii* has a black crown, mantle, back and tail, the last of which has white outer feathers. The wings are largely black with white edgings to many feathers forming, two prominent wingbars and forehead and cheeks are white. The throat and upper breast are black in summer and it has some black on the flanks. The rest of the underparts are white. It has a small fine black bill and black legs. The female is dark grey on the back and has a dark rump. The male White Wagtail *M. a. alba* differs from the above in having a pale grey mantle and rump and there is a clean demarcation between the black of the nape and the grey back. The black throat and bib are also clearly defined.

The Pied Wagtail *M. a. yarrellii* is a common resident breeding bird in Leicestershire. It is a resident in small numbers at Swithland Reservoir and can often be found feeding along the dam and on the overflow. It breeds within the grounds most years and two pairs bred in 1978 and 1980. Occasionally birds roost in small numbers in the Bulrush *Typha latifolia* on the edge of the reservoir. 20 birds were noted going to roost on the 26th October 1963. The largest count I have for the site is of 41 birds feeding on the margins of the reservoir on the 16th September 1995.

Birds showing characteristics of the nominate White Wagtail *M. a. alba* have been recorded on nine occasions. Six of the records were between late March and early June and three from mid-September to early October. Some birds have stayed several days and eight of the records refer to single birds; two birds were present on the 4th April 1986.

WAXWINGS Bombycillidae

Bohemian Waxwing *Bombycilla garrulus*

The Waxwing breeds in the boreal forest of Europe and Asia and its range extend from the Atlantic coast of northern Norway to the Pacific coast at Kamchatka. In North America it breeds from Alaska through to Manitoba. The population of the Waxwing fluctuates greatly from year to year and in some years large irruptions take place. This phenomenon probably comes about when its numbers are very high and the berry crop fails. During irruptions birds can be found well outside their normal winter range.

In Britain the Waxwing is an almost annual visitor especially to the east coast, but usually it occurs only in small numbers. Most birds start to arrive in early October and leave again in March and only a few are left by early April. Occasionally, however, large invasions take place involving many hundreds of birds and then they can be found throughout the country. In recent times there have been two large invasions: in 1965-66 and 1995-96.

On its breeding grounds it favours mainly old pine and spruce forest with hanging lichens and moss and during the summer it feeds mainly on insects. It usually nests several feet up in a conifer. The nest is a cup of grass, conifer twigs and reindeer moss. In the winter it vacates the most northerly parts of its range and moves southward, changing its diet from insects to berries, especially the fruit of Rowan and Hawthorn.

In silhouette the Waxwing is not unlike a Starling in size and shape but it has a pronounced crest. Its general overall colour is pink-brown with a paler belly and chestnut undertail coverts. There is a thin black mask extending through the eye to its forehead and a small black bib. It has a grey rump and small dark tail with a yellow tip. The wings are well marked with two white bars on the wing and yellow and white edges to the primaries and it has red waxy projections from its secondaries from which it gets its name. It has a dark bill and short dark legs.

The Waxwing is a rare or scarce winter visitor to Leicestershire that does not occur every year. It has been recorded twice in the vicinity of Swithland Reservoir. Six birds were found feeding on Hawthorn berries near Rabbits Bridge on the 14th November 1965, and one was seen in the pumping station grounds on the 28th March 1971.

DIPPERS Cinclidae

White-throated Dipper *Cinclus cinclus*

The Dipper has a patchy breeding distribution throughout Europe reaching North Africa in the south. It also has a patchy distribution in central Asia occurring in the Urals and from Afghanistan to the Himalayas and central China. It is generally resident through much of its range but after breeding and in winter partial movements do take place especially during severe weather. The most northerly breeding birds or those at altitude will move only when the water freezes.

The British race *C. c. gularis* differs from continental birds in having a brown belly. In Britain it can be found over much of mainland Scotland, Wales and Ireland. It occurs in western and northern England but is absent from central parts and the south-east. Over recent years its numbers have dropped in some areas of Britain due to large numbers of conifers being planted close to breeding streams and rivers. The trees make the water more acidic which kills off the invertebrates on which the Dipper lives. In the winter occasional vagrants of the nominate race *C. c. cinclus* occur in Britain from Scandinavia. These normally arrive in October and November and can be differentiated from our native birds in having a black belly.

The Dipper is a bird of boulder-strewn fast flowing shallow streams where it feeds generally on invertebrates taken while the bird is submerged from the stony stream bed. It makes a large domed nest like a huge Wren's nest and which it positions in a hole or on a ledge under a bridge, waterfall or rock face or among tree roots exposed on river and stream banks.

The Dipper is like a very large plump- bellied Wren with short wings and small tail which is often cocked. Its head, beak and legs are thrush-like in appearance. Its head is dark brown that merges into black on its back, wings and tail. Its throat and upper breast are white, and it has a brown belly, which becomes black towards the undertail coverts. It has a fast whirring flight that is usually low just above the water's surface. It can often be seen sitting on a boulder in the middle of a stream bobbing occasionally.

The Dipper is a rare vagrant to Leicestershire that has been recorded on nine occasions. Both British and continental birds have been recorded. It has been recorded once at Swithland Reservoir. A bird was seen along the overflow channel at the end of March 1974. Unfortunately the record was not fully authenticated by the Leicestershire Rarities Committee.

WRENS Troglodytidae

Winter Wren *Troglodytes troglodytes*

The Wren breeds throughout most of Europe southward to North Africa and the Middle East. It occurs in a thin band across central Asia from Afghanistan through the Himalayas and northern China to Taiwan and Japan and northward to Kamchatka. From there its range continues through the Aleutian and Pribilof Islands and into Alaska. In North America its range lies mainly in southern Canada and along the western coast. In Europe it is only the northern and eastern birds that are migratory. They move to central and southern Europe to winter and movements of 2,500 km have been recorded. In Asia little is known about its movements although some are known to winter in south-east China. The North American birds winter in the southern and eastern states of the U.S.A. The Winter Wren is the only member of a large genus of North and South American birds to be found in Europe and Asia.

It is a common resident that occurs throughout Britain and Ireland. It is one of the most widely distributed species and can even be found on quite barren northerly islands and where populations have been isolated for many years sub-species have developed. This is the case on Shetland, St Kilda and the Outer Hebrides. The Wren's numbers fluctuate greatly especially after severe winters and winters like 1963 can decimate its population. Given mild winters their numbers soon bounce back and after a series of mild winters the Wren becomes possibly Britain's commonest species. A bird I ringed in Quorn lived to be nearly 5 years and 6 months old, which is quite an age for a small bird.

The Wren can be found in all kinds of woodland, scrubland, heathland and moorland and in any sort of rank vegetation. It can also be found in upland and mountainous areas with rocks and scree. Its Latin name *troglodytes* means cave dweller and refers to its habits of foraging in and out of holes and crevices in search of insects. The nest is a domed structure of dead leaves and moss that can be found wedged in branches, bramble thickets or in holes and crevices.

The Wren is a small brown bird with longish legs and a small tail that is often held cocked. Its upperparts are rich brown with fine dark barring across its wings and tail and its underparts are paler grey-brown with a slight amount of barring on the flanks and undertail coverts. For its size the bill is fairly long and slightly decurved and it has fairly long robust brown legs. For such a small bird its song and call are very loud and they often give this tiny bird's presence away.

The Wren is an abundant resident breeding bird in Leicestershire. It is also a common bird on the margins of Swithland Reservoir and can be found in every habitat around the margins. It has a healthy breeding population in the reservoir grounds and while survey work was being undertaken eight pairs were found breeding in 1978, nine pairs in 1979 and twelve pairs in 1980.

ACCENTORS Prunellidae

Dunnock *Prunella modularis*

The Dunnock or Hedge Sparrow breeds in western and northern Europe with a scattered distribution in the Balkans. In Asia it is thinly distributed in Turkey with larger populations occurring eastward into Iran through to the Crimea and further north extending to the Ural Mountains. In much of western and southern Europe and southern Asia it is a resident or partial migrant. In northern and central Europe across into northern Asia it is totally migratory with birds moving to southern Europe and parts of the Middle East to winter.

The Dunnock is a resident throughout Britain and Ireland. Most native birds are sedentary although migrating birds are noticed along our east coasts in autumn and spring and these birds are probably of Continental origin. It appears to have colonised the outer Hebrides and Orkney in the latter part of the 19th century. In the period from 1970 to 1998 the British population has declined by 21%. Some authorities have thought that this has come about by agricultural changes. The nests of Dunnocks are, however, easily found and I personally wonder what effect the predations by Magpie and Grey Squirrel are having on them and some of our other common garden birds.

It is a bird of woodland, scrubland, hedgerows, parks and gardens etc. In some cases the Dunnock has been found to be polygamous and the female will often mate with two or more males. They make a cup nest of twigs, moss and grass that is placed a few feet up in a hedge or bush.

The Dunnock has a rich brown back with dark streaking, its tail is brown and it has brown streaking on its flanks. Its head, throat and breast are blue-grey with brown streaking on the crown and ear coverts. It has a thin dark bill and brown legs.

The Dunnock is an abundant resident breeding bird in Leicestershire. It is a common breeding bird around the margins of Swithland Reservoir that can be seen throughout the year. During the years when detailed survey work was being carried out 15 pairs were found breeding in 1978, seven pairs in 1979 and nine pairs in 1980.

CHATS and THRUSHES Turdidae

The severe cold winters of my childhood are largely a thing of the past, but I can remember those days vividly. I would stand looking out of our living room window. The trees and bushes in the garden would be glistening with a heavy white haw-frost. Along the borders Redwings could be seen shuffling the dead leaves, their feathers all puffed out trying to remain warm. They were always a regular sight in the garden during extremely cold weather, when they were driven from the pasturelands and hedgerows in order to find warmth and food in the woodland that bordered our garden. Their nasal calls and the sound of rustling leaf litter remains a fond childhood memory. Fieldfares, on the other hand, were rare in the garden and throughout the time I lived in Quorn I can only remember them coming to feed during two winters, both after a heavy snowfall. During February 1979 we had Fieldfare, Redwing, Mistle Thrush, Song Thrush and Blackbird all feeding on the lawn on apples, and that remains the only occasion when all five common thrushes were present together in our garden.

Apart from the sighting of a Ring Ouzel in October 1962 at Groby and a female Black Redstart at the beginning of April 1969 at Swithland Reservoir, I had not had any experience of unusual chats or thrushes. This was to change in March 1972 when I visited Majorca and encountered my first Blue Rock Thrush, Black-eared Wheatear and Bluethroat. After that period I saw many species of thrush and chat in Europe. One bird I will never forget was my first male Rock Thrush that was seen during a heavy fall of migrants on Corfu in 1979. The Rock Thrush or Rufous-tailed Rock Thrush is a beautiful bird with blue grey upperparts and throat, a white centre to the back, and orange underparts and tail. In May 1999 Pamela and I were travelling around the Costa del Sol in southern Spain. We spent one day at Mijas, a small village frequented by tourists. Towards evening most of the tourists had left and we searched for a restaurant. We found one with a spectacular view looking from the escarpment on which Mijas is situated right down to the coast several miles away. As we ordered our food the waiter opened the large windows that folded back on each other leaving us with an unobstructed panoramic view. In the scrub and grassland below flocks of Goldfinch and Serin were feeding along with a Melodious Warbler. In the air a single Honey Buzzard drifted over and small flocks of House Martins with a few Crag Martins and one Red-rumped Swallow were flying up and down along the escarpment at window height. On a fence below I noticed a male Black Wheatear carrying food. It flew into a wall just below us. Throughout our meal we were given the pleasure of watching a pair of Black Wheatears coming backward and forward to their nest site. As the evening fell a Nightingale struck up with its melodic song in the scrub below. This made the perfect end to the day!

The Isles of Scilly have a reputation for being one of the best places in Britain to see rare and vagrant birds. October is the best month and during that period the islands play host to several hundred birdwatchers. Vagrant birds from North America and Eastern Asia can be present on this granite archipelago at the same time. My first holiday to the Isles of Scilly was in October 1985 which coincided with one of the largest influxes of American birds into Britain. In one week I saw six species of American landbirds, the smallest being the Northern Parula which is only 11 cm. in

length and weighs between 6 and 8 grams, and the largest the Yellow-billed Cuckoo
at 30 cm. Unfortunately most American cuckoos do not survive long once they have
reached our shores. After my first excursion I made annual trips to the Isles of Scilly
for several years. 1987 was a vintage year and again I saw six American landbirds
including Britain's first Philadelphia Vireo. The only other Philadelphia Vireo to
have reached Europe was seen in Ireland two years previously. I saw some unusual
thrushes that year, the first being an Eye-browed Thrush on October 12th at
Longstone on St Mary's which had been recorded in the country on only ten
occasions. It was feeding on blackberries in the company of Redwings. It was similar
to the Redwing in size, with a grey head and throat, white supercilium, rufous-orange
chest and flanks and grey-brown back. This species breeds in eastern Siberia and
winters in south-east Asia. The next time I would see this species would be at Sungei
Buloh Nature Reserve in Singapore in December 1996. On the 13th October another
very rare thrush appeared on St Mary's. This was a Swainson's Thrush and it too was
found at Longstone. The Swainson's Thrush is like a small Song Thrush with
spotting on the throat but little or no spotting on the flanks. This species breeds
across northern North America and winters in South America as far south as
northern Argentina. It had been recorded in Britain on only a dozen occasions. It is
thought that deep low-pressure systems gather up migrating birds travelling down
the eastern seaboard of North America and deposit them on our shores. That might
answer one question, but the other has to be, "How did the eastern Asian bird get
there?" We may never fully understand the complex mysteries of migration. Two
days later the majority of birdwatchers raced from St Mary's to St Agnes with the
news that Britain's third Hermit Thrush had been found. When I reached the area
where it had been seen last I found several hundred birdwatchers surrounding an old
grass tennis court with a small amount of scrub and bushes forming a backdrop – the
bird had apparently disappeared into the bushes! Minutes became hours but we stood
transfixed to the spot. It was like being at Wimbledon on a wet day with nothing
happening! That evening most of us went to our guest houses miserable. The bird
finally re-appeared on the 16th October when we had brief views of this elusive little
thrush. It is very like the Swainson's Thrush but has heavier spotting on the breast
and a rusty rump and tail. This species breeds across northern North America and
winters throughout central South America reaching El Salvador. I have seen this
species on several occasions since on its breeding grounds in Canada, and even there
good views are difficult to obtain! Birds can often be located singing from the
topmost branches of a spruce or pine but just as you get yourself into a position to get
a decent look they will inevitably drop into cover. Some people might think that the
naming of birds is a random affair, but as far as this species is concerned it was
'Hermit by name and Hermit by nature'.

In the springtime large numbers of American birds are on the move. Many
species have spent the winter in South America and are returning to North America
to breed. During late April and early May 1998 I was in Texas. While there I visited
High Island on the coast of the Gulf of Mexico. There are two woodlands in the area,
Boy Scout Woods and Smith Oaks. Both have become renowned for the migrant
birds that drop into them during passage periods, especially after inclement weather.
When I was there the woods were full of birds, many of which were brightly coloured
like the red Summer and Scarlet Tanagers and Northern Cardinals which stand out

against the green foliage. Twenty or more species of Wood Warbler can be seen in a single morning and all are in their handsome summer dress. They vary in colour, being a mixture of either yellow, green, blue-grey, chestnut, orange, brown or black and white. There were also Rose-breasted Grosbeaks, Grey Catbirds, cuckoos, vireos, flycatchers and thrushes. Under the trees many Swainson's Thrushes were grubbing about and mixed with them was the occasional Grey-cheeked Thrush, Veery or the larger Wood Thrush. Within a few days most of these birds will have moved on to their breeding grounds further north. The small Grey-cheeked Thrush breeds in north-eastern Siberia and throughout Alaska and northern Canada. They still had many miles to travel. One of the most amazing birds I saw in the woods was the small Ruby-throated Hummingbird. It is only 8-9 cm. in length and each year it migrates from central South America into North America reaching northwards as far as southern Canada. The Ruby-throated Hummingbird actually flies non-stop 620 miles (1,000 km) across the Gulf of Mexico. To achieve this it doubles its weight before migrating which acts as fuel for its long flight, an amazing feat for one so small.

In April 1992 I was trekking in the Annapurna Sanctuary in the foothills of the Himalayas. Several days were spent walking along the sides of fast-flowing, boulder-strewn mountain streams and rivers that meandered through thickly wooded valleys. As I walked through the area eagles and vultures were occasionally seen soaring overhead while the forest reverberated with the mocking laughing calls of the White-crested Laughingthrush. In the forest I was occasionally fortunate enough to see a Red-billed Blue Magpie, Green Magpie, Himalayan Barbet or Hoary Barbwing. Birds, however, were easier to see along the rivers. Brown Dippers were sitting on the stones in the middle of the river and as I approached they would fly away, wings whirring low over the water. Occasionally I would round a bend in the river and get brief views of the large grey and white Crested Kingfisher sitting motionless on stones either in or on the edge of the water. Two chats were particularly common along the streams and rivers and like the previous two species they could be seen sitting on stones in the water or at the water's edge. The first was the Plumbeous Water Redstart. The male was slate-blue with a fiery red tail and it would sit on rocks either fanning or wagging its tail slowly up and down. The female was quite different, being grey-brown with white in the tail. The other chat species was the larger White-capped Water Redstart. It flitted from stone to stone and occasionally made fly-catching sallies. It had a white crown, black back, wings, throat and upper breast, and chestnut underparts and tail that had a black terminal band. The Blue Whistling Thrush was also frequent being seen in pairs or singly along the river banks. It is a very large thrush with a yellow bill and blue-black plumage and pale blue spangling on its head, mantle and upper breast. On the last evening of the trek we camped above Pokhara and I left the camp and walked along a small stream that was at the base of a heavily wooded valley. I soon found myself looking at a dainty bird sitting on a stone in the middle of the stream. It had a thin straight bill, white forehead, grey cap and mantle, white rump and black and white wings and a long forked black and white barred tail that it moved gracefully up and down. Its throat and cheeks were black and its underparts white and it had small flesh-coloured legs. It was a Slaty-backed Forktail! These are unusual birds in the chat family and their behaviour is not unlike the much smaller Pied Wagtail. I walked further on down the valley and saw several more and then I came across another species of forktail. This was an energetic bird that also swayed its tail up and down. It was the Spotted Forktail that had a large white forehead, black nape, black finely spotted white mantle, black and white wings, white rump and a long black and white barred forked tail. Its throat and upper breast were black and the rest of the underparts white. Like the Slaty-backed Forktail it also had a fine dark bill and flesh-coloured legs. As I watched the bird another joined it. Together they were erratic almost nervous in their behaviour and yet graceful. After a short time they both flew off upstream. The Himalayan chats and thrushes were certainly something special and the forktails will remain some of my favourite birds.

European Robin *Erithacus rubecula*

The Robin breeds throughout much of Europe and southward into North Africa. In Asia its range extends through Turkey and Iran to the Crimea and the northern extent of its range lies to the east of the Urals. The Robin can also be found on the Azores, Madeira and the Canary Islands. In the southern and western part of its range it is resident or partially migratory, the males being more sedentary than the females. The northern and eastern birds are totally migratory with birds wintering in western Europe south to the Mediterranean and North Africa. Birds start to move in September and return passage takes place in April.

The Robin is a common resident throughout Britain and Ireland although some movements do take place, especially among first-year birds and they have been known to travel as far afield as southern Spain. In autumn and spring passage migrants pass through the country and these are most frequent on the east coast.

Robins can be found in woodland, mixed farmland, parkland, and gardens. It is a very territorial species and, if a rival male wanders onto another male's territory, fights have been known to ensue with the intruder sometimes being killed. The Robin is a very vocal bird and it has two different songs, one in the spring when it is breeding and the other in the autumn when most birds are silent which is more melancholy in nature. It can be heard singing throughout the night, especially near street lights during the spring and summer and it can often be mistaken for its relative the Nightingale. It often nests in a hole, either in a wall, a tree or bank and quite often it will pick a man-made object that is left lying around the garden.

The adult Robin or Redbreast is surely one of our best-known birds and every gardener's companion. Its head, back and tail are brown with olive tones and it has a bright orange breast that extends over its forehead and round its eye. This is bordered on each side by a blue-grey wash. The underparts are off-white and it has browner flanks and undertail coverts. It has a very upright stance with brown legs, a large dark eye and thin dark bill.

The Robin is an abundant resident breeding bird in Leicestershire. It is a common resident breeding bird at Swithland Reservoir that can be found throughout the grounds. During the years when survey work was being carried out two pairs were found breeding in 1979 and four pairs in 1980. The largest number to be recorded at this site was circa 80 on the 4th November 1998, and the observer thought they showed characteristics of the continental race. This could well have been the case considering there had been a large influx of birds into the country at that time.

Common Nightingale *Luscinia megarhynchos*

The Nightingale breeds in central and southern Europe and southward into North Africa, its range extending eastward through northern Turkey into Iran as far as Mongolia. Its main wintering area lies in a band across central Africa from Senegal to Uganda. Birds return to Europe from late March through to early May and autumn passage takes place from late July and continues until the end of September.

In Britain the Nightingale breeds south of a line stretching from the Severn Estuary to the Humber Estuary, mainly in south-east England although it breeds occasionally in south Wales. Because the Nightingale is on the edge of its range in Britain its population has gone through many fluctuations over the years and at present it appears to be decreasing. During 1999 there were 4,407 singing males recorded in Britain. This could, however, be due to changes in woodland management especially with regard to coppicing.

In Britain it is a bird of damp woodlands with associated streams and pools and it likes especially areas that have been coppiced. It can also be found in thick Blackthorn *Prunus spinosa* and Hawthorn *Crataegus* hedges, overgrown gardens and small spinneys. The nest is made of dead leaves, usually oak *Quercus*, and it is normally situated on or near the ground in tall herbage which is often Stinging Nettles *Urtica dioica*. The Nightingale is a very skulking bird and not easily observed although it makes its presence known by its rich melodic song, which it sings both day and night from when it arrives in late April until early June when the first young hatch.

The Nightingale is slightly larger than a Robin, with brown upperparts and a bright chestnut tail, the underparts being dirty white with a buff suffusion on the upper breast. It has flesh brown legs, dark bill and like the Robin it has a large dark eye, with a noticeable white eye ring.

The Nightingale is an uncommon breeding bird in Leicestershire. It has been recorded twice at Swithland Reservoir on the 9th May 1954 and the 29th May 1992. Neither bird was recorded subsequently and they were probably passage migrants. It is interesting to note that during the late 1940s and early 1950s it bred regularly on the Charnwood Forest.

Black Redstart *Phoenicurus ochruros*

The Black Redstart breeds through central and southern Europe southward into north west Africa. It occurs eastward through Turkey and parts of the Middle East into Iran with a scattered distribution across to central Asia, the Himalayas, western China and northern Mongolia. It winters in northern Africa, the Sudan, Ethiopia and the Somali Peninsula, through Arabia to the Indian subcontinent and Indo-China. The birds in south-western Europe are resident or partial migrants.

The Black Redstart was a very rare and sporadic breeder in Britain prior to 1939 but since then it has bred regularly in small numbers. It appears to have colonised south-east England during the second world war when it took advantage of ideal nesting habitat brought about by bombing. Since then its numbers have risen gradually to 99 breeding pairs in 1997. It is a summer and winter visitor to Britain with a scattered distribution in England and Wales. Birds arrive from March until May and they start to depart again in September with only a handful remaining past the end of November. A few birds remain to winter in southern England and south Wales.

It is a bird of cliffs and rocky or boulder-strewn country, either in mountains, on coasts or along rivers, but it will also breed in ruined buildings and in England it has taken a liking to power stations. The nest site is either a crevice or hole in rocks or a building and the cup nest is also built on ledges.

The male Black Redstart has slate grey upperparts, a contrasting bold white wing patch and a dark-centred tail with bright rusty-orange edges and rusty-orange rump. It has a black face, throat and belly with paler undertail coverts, the eastern races having varying amounts of rusty orange on their bellies. It has a small dark bill and black legs. The female is grey-brown all over but has a similar rufous rump and tail.

The Black Redstart is a scarce passage migrant and winter visitor to Leicestershire and a rare breeding bird. It was first thought to have bred at a power station on the Aylestone Road in Leicester in 1971 but breeding was not confirmed until 1974 when a pair bred in railway sidings at Great Central Street, Leicester. It has been proved to breed in five years since then in 1975, 1979, 1988, 1993, and 1997. It is a rare passage migrant to Swithland Reservoir that has been recorded on four occasions. A single bird was recorded on the 13th June 1964; a female from the 7th-9th April 1969, and another female on the 23rd April 1973. A pair were seen on the 28th March 1974.

Common Redstart *Phoenicurus phoenicurus*

The Redstart breeds across continental Europe and southward with small populations in North Africa. In south-west Asia it breeds in Turkey, Iran, into the Caucasus and in northern Asia it is found across Siberia to Lake Baikal. It winters just south of the Sahara from Senegal and the Gambia eastward to Eritrea and southward to Uganda.

The Redstart is distributed throughout mainland Britain but its numbers are low in central and south-east England and it is a scarce breeding bird in Ireland. Birds arrive in Britain from early April until the end of May and depart again towards the end of August, most birds having gone by mid-October. The Redstart's population has decreased markedly over much of northern and central Europe between 1970 and 1990. The reasons for the decline are probably the droughts on its wintering grounds in the Sahel region of Africa and modern forestry methods that leave it with very few nesting sites. In the last decade there has been a recovery in its population in parts of Britain although it has not recovered in eastern England and it remains a scarce breeding bird in Leicestershire.

The Redstart can be found in open woodland and on the edges of forest and generally prefers broad-leaved trees. It can however also be found in parkland and large gardens and old pine forest. It nests generally in holes in trees but it will also use holes in buildings and dry-stone walls and adapts readily to open-fronted nestboxes.

The adult male Redstart has a white forehead, grey crown, mantle and back with browner wings and a rufous rump and tail. Its face and throat are black and its breast and belly are orange, which becomes paler on the flanks and undertail coverts. It has an upright stance and a dark bill and black legs. The female is brown with paler underparts that show a slight orange wash and it has a rufous tail and rump.

The Redstart is an uncommon breeding bird and passage migrant in Leicestershire. Until the 1980s it bred in many places on the Charnwood Forest. It is an uncommon passage migrant at Swithland Reservoir that has been recorded in the grounds on nine occasions. Six were spring records and were seen in a period from April to May, the earliest record being on the 9th April 1966. The three autumn records were seen in August and early September with the latest sighting coming on the 8th September 1987.

Whinchat *Saxicola rubetra*

The Whinchat breeds throughout much of Europe, although it has a scattered distribution in western Europe and the Mediterranean and is absent from much of the Iberian Peninsula. In Asia it occurs east to the Ural Mountains and into western Siberia and in the south it can be found in eastern Turkey through to northern Iran and north into the Caucasus. It winters in Africa south of the Sahara from Senegal in the west to the Sudan in the east and southward through Uganda to Zambia.

In Britain it is fairly well distributed above a line from the Severn to the Humber but it is only sparsely distributed throughout the rest of England and localised and scarce in Ireland. It arrives in Britain during April and May and departs from mid-August to September. Since the mid-1950s its population has crashed in Britain and the low countries of Europe by 50% and this has almost certainly been caused by changes in agricultural practice.

It is a bird of rank vegetation and likes meadows, upland grassland, heathland, open areas within woodland, low scrub and young plantations. It makes a grass-cup nest that is well hidden in vegetation.

The male Whinchat is a lively little bird that often perches on fences or tall herbage. It has an upright stance and it often flicks its tail. It has dark cheeks bordered by a white supercilium and a white line from the beak to lower neck. It has a brown crown, back and rump that is heavily streaked black and its wings are dark with brown feather edgings and white on the scapulars and primary coverts. It has a short black tail with white basal feathers that are visible in flight. The throat and upper breast are rufous ochre becoming pale off-white on the flanks, lower belly and undertail coverts. Its bill and legs are black. The female is generally duller, lacks the white on the wing and has a buff supercilium.

The Whinchat is an uncommon passage migrant and rare breeding bird in Leicestershire. It was formerly a common breeding bird in Leicestershire that bred regularly on the Charnwood Forest in suitable areas such as Bradgate Park. It is a rare passage migrant and summer visitor to Swithland Reservoir that has been recorded on four occasions and all but one of the sightings was made on the verges of the railway line. All the records were of single birds. One was recorded from the 7th to the 15th July 1969, and the others were seen on 29th July 1972; 20th May 1973, and the 7th May 1983.

Common Stonechat *Saxicola torquata*

The Stonechat has a large and fragmented range, breeding in western and southern Europe southward into North Africa with isolated populations occurring throughout the African continent south of the Sahara. In Asia it occurs through Turkey and into the Caucasus and in the north its range extends to the east of the Ural Mountains throughout Siberia and it reaches Japan on the Pacific Coast. In the south its range extends to the northern edge of Indo-China. It winters in southern China, Indo-China, the Indian subcontinent, Arabia, central East Africa and north-west Africa. Severe winter weather determines the extent of the Stonechat's movements over much of its range, and Asian and eastern European birds are long distance migrants. Within this huge range there are something like 25 subspecies and some authorities regard some of the races as separate species.

In Britain the Stonechat is locally quite common, breeding on the western coast, becoming less frequent inland, but it has become absent from much of central and eastern England. It is still a well distributed breeding bird in Ireland. Some British birds are sedentary and others make partial migrations, either remaining in the country or moving south into south-west Europe during the winter. Birds in Britain have been known to suffer heavy mortality during bad winters like 1962-63 and their population took a long time to recover. The Stonechat has also suffered, like so many species, through agricultural changes that leave very few areas of rough ground on which the birds can breed and its population has fallen by about two-thirds in the last thirty years.

The Stonechat in Britain is a bird of coastal rocky rough grassland, heather moorland and heathland where it is especially associated with gorse and other areas of rough uncultivated land. The nest is an untidy cup of grass and moss that is built on or near the ground in deep vegetation, often at the base of a bush. Like the Whinchat the Stonechat perches conspicuously on the top of vegetation. It has an upright stance and regularly flicks its tail and when it becomes nervous it makes a "tak-tak" call like two stones being knocked together, from which it derives its name.

The male Stonechat is a handsome bird with a black head and throat, white neck and wing patch and very dark almost black upperparts and tail. It shows a rich orange breast that becomes paler on the lower belly and undertail coverts. It has black legs and a small black bill. In flight it shows a small white rump. The female is a browner, heavily streaked bird that lacks the rich colour and sharp contrast of the male.

The Stonechat is now an uncommon passage migrant and winter visitor to Leicestershire. One of the best places to see this species on the Charnwood Forest is on Bradgate Park, especially on the wall near the margins of Cropston Reservoir. It is a rare visitor to Swithland Reservoir that has been recorded on two occasions. A female was seen near the reservoir on the 20th January 1945, and an unsexed bird was seen at the reservoir on the 22nd March 1996.

Northern Wheatear *Oenanthe oenanthe*

The Wheatear breeds throughout Europe reaching as far south as northern Africa. It occurs through northern and central Asia to Alaska, eastern northern Canada and coastal Greenland. It winters in Africa south of the Sahara from Senegal to Ethiopia and south-east to Tanzania.

The Wheatear breeds throughout Britain and Ireland although only sporadic breeding takes place in central and south-east England. The first birds arrive in Britain towards the end of March with the main movement taking place in April and numbers tail off into May. They depart again in September and October with a few stragglers still being found into November. Large numbers of passage migrants pass through the country each year, with some birds heading northward into Scandinavia, Iceland and Greenland. It was once far more widespread in England but it started to decline at the start of the 20th century and this decline has continued to a greater or lesser extent throughout the century. The main reasons for this appear to be agricultural changes and afforestation with the loss of chalk downland and heathland and, during the 1950s myxomatosis among rabbits. In recent years the severe droughts in 1972 and 1983 in the Sahel region of Africa where the Wheatear winters have almost certainly caused high mortality and consequently fewer birds return to Europe in the spring.

It is a bird of open country that likes upland grassland, chalk downland, heathland, moorland, alpine grassland, coastal grassland and arctic tundra. It nests in rabbit burrows, holes in dry-stone walls and natural holes and crevices in rocks and holes among boulders on scree.

The Wheatear is just slightly bigger than a Robin but it has a similar upright posture and an alert attitude. The adult male has a grey crown and mantle, a white supercilium, black mask, wings and tip to tail. The throat and upper breast are yellow-buff and the rest of the underparts are white. It has black legs and bill. In flight it shows a distinctive white rump and mostly white base to the tail. The female has more brown tones and lacks the black mask.

The Wheatear is an uncommon passage migrant and a very rare breeding bird in Leicestershire. The first breeding record this century came at North Luffenham in 1972. It also bred at Rutland Water in 1974 and Desford in 1979. It is an irregular passage migrant to Swithland reservoir with the earliest spring record coming on the 9th April 1980, and the latest autumn sighting on the 18th September 1987.

Ring Ouzel *Turdus torquatus*

The Ring Ouzel breeds in Scandinavia and the upland areas of Britain. It also occurs sparingly in Ireland, Brittany and Belgium in western Europe. In southern Europe it is found mainly in the mountain ranges: the Pyrenees, Alps and the Carpathians. In Asia it occurs in Turkey and the Caucasus eastwards to Kara Kum. It winters in Southern Spain, Greece, north-west Africa, southern Turkey and Iran.

In Britain it can be found throughout much of Wales and Scotland . In England it occurs on Dartmoor in the south-west, the Pennines from Derbyshire northwards and the upland areas of the north such as the Lake District and the Yorkshire moors. The Ring Ouzel can be seen on passage over much of Britain. It arrives in mid-March and passage continues into May. Birds start their return movement towards the end of August and stragglers can still be around as late as November. It is not only British birds that can be seen at these times as numbers of birds from Scandinavia also pass through the country especially on the east coast. In Britain its population appears to be declining but it is difficult to find a reason, unless it is disturbance caused by more people using its upland breeding areas for recreational activities.

The Ring Ouzel is a bird of mountains and upland moorland. It is a bird of alpine meadows, small valleys with mountain streams, boulder-strewn hillsides, heath and moorland. In Britain it normally makes its large cup nest of grass, leaves and stalks of heather, on the ground in Heather *Calluna vulgaris*, Bracken *Pteridium aquilinum*, grass or on rock ledges.

The male Ring Ouzel is very similar in size, shape and colour to a male Blackbird but it differs in having a white crescent-shaped gorget across its breast and white edgings to its wing feathers, a yellow bill with a dark tip and brown legs. The female is similar to the male but browner and the breast marking is not so bold but she still retains the pale feather edgings so prominent in this species.

The Ring Ouzel is a scarce spring and rare autumn passage migrant in Leicestershire. During the 19th century it bred on the Charnwood Forest in the Whitwick area. There has been one record at Swithland Reservoir, a very late bird being recorded on the 7th November 1976.

Common Blackbird *Turdus merula*

The Blackbird breeds throughout much of Europe, being absent as a breeding bird in Iceland and the very far north. Its range extends southward to north-west Africa. In northern Asia it breeds to the Ural Mountains and in the south its range extends through Turkey and the Caucasus to Iran, Iraq and Afghanistan, with a separate population occurring in south-east China. There are distinct populations in the Himalayas and the Indian sub-continent and Sri Lanka that are considered by some authorities to be separate species. It has been introduced into Australia and New Zealand. The northern and eastern populations are migratory, moving to western Europe including Iceland and reaching southward to Morocco, Egypt, Iran and Indo-China to winter.

The Blackbird breeds throughout Britain and Ireland and is resident throughout the year although some British birds move to western Europe in winter and large numbers of birds arrive in the country from Scandinavia in late September, leaving generally by the end of April. This species had increased greatly from the mid 19th century until the early 1970s, spreading into towns, cities and gardens, but it did not occur in London until the 1930s. It also spread to many of Britain's islands including Shetland by the middle of the 20th century. Between 1970 and 1998, however, its numbers have fallen in Britain by 29% and this follows a worrying trend mirrored in our other resident thrush species. On the continent, however, its numbers appear to have remained stable.

It is a bird of woodland, mixed farmland, parkland, heathland, moorland, orchards and gardens. The large cup nest of grass, roots and twigs is found normally a metre or so up in shrubs, hedgerows or small trees.

The adult male Blackbird is entirely black with an orange bill and eye-ring and dark brown legs. The female is generally dark brown with a paler streaked throat and dark streaked breast. Its bill is brown with small amounts of yellow.

The Blackbird is an abundant resident breeding bird in Leicestershire. It is a common resident breeding bird at Swithland Reservoir that can be found in all habitats around the margins. In 1978 a total of 11 pairs were found breeding in the reservoir grounds, 13 pairs in 1979 and 14 pairs in 1980. The numbers of birds around the reservoir are almost certainly augmented during the winter by birds from continental Europe.

Fieldfare *Turdus pilaris*

The Fieldfare breeds across northern and central Europe and through northern Asia into eastern Siberia. The northern and eastern populations are migratory, with birds wintering in western and southern Europe. In Asia it winters in Turkey, the Middle East through to the Caucasus, northern Iran and the Tien Shan Mountains.

Throughout much of Britain it is known as a winter visitor and a passage migrant although it bred for the first time in Britain in Orkney in 1967. Since then it has colonised the mainland and small numbers breed annually in northern Scotland and occasionally northern England. The first winter visitors and passage migrants arrive in September but large numbers are not seen until late October and November. Return movement is at its peak in March although stragglers still remain into May. In the last two centuries its range has extended southward and westward over much of central Europe and consequently its numbers have increased greatly.

During the winter months the Fieldfare can be found feeding on short grassland and newly turned over arable land, in orchards and along hedgerows where it feeds on berries and fruits. It is a large thrush that is about the same size as the Mistle Thrush and it is often seen in large flocks and quite frequently in the company of Redwing. It breeds in open areas on the edges of pine *Pinus*, spruce *Picea* and birch *Betula* woodland. It generally places its large cup nest of grass, roots and twigs from seven to nine metres up in the fork of branches close to the trunk and it can either be a solitary breeder or nest in colonies.

The sexes of the Fieldfare are similar in plumage and in winter it shows a grey head and rump with a rich chestnut back and upper wings, black primaries and tail. It has a rich yellow-buff breast with a heavily spotted throat, breast and flanks, a white belly and white undertail coverts. Its legs are dark and its bill is brown with small amounts of yellow.

It is a common winter visitor to Leicestershire that is rarely seen during the summer months. It is a common winter visitor in the area of Swithland Reservoir that is most often seen passing overhead or in the adjacent farmland. It occasionally comes into the grounds to feed on berries especially those of the Holly. The earliest record was of four birds seen flying over the reservoir on the 27th September 1997, and the last spring record was of a single bird on the 6th May 1973. The largest number recorded were 12 flocks totalling circa 1,000 birds passing over the reservoir on the 2nd November 1986.

Song Thrush *Turdus philomelos*

The Song Thrush or Throstle breeds across central and northern Europe. It is absent from Iceland, a large proportion of the Iberian Peninsula, coastal Italy and southern Greece. In southern Asia it breeds in northern Turkey to the Caucasus and northern Iran. In the north it is found in a band across central Siberia to Lake Baikal. It is resident over much of central western and southern Europe, but it is wholly migratory over northern and eastern Europe and central Asia. It winters in southern and western Europe, North Africa, the Middle East, southern Turkey, Iraq and Iran.

The Song Thrush breeds throughout Britain and Ireland and is resident throughout the year, although some British-bred birds move south to north-west France to winter. Immigrant birds from central Europe and Fenno Scandinavia move into the country from September to October to either spend the winter or pass through the country on their way further south. They start to leave again from February onwards and most have left by the end of April.

In Europe the Song Thrush population appears to be stable but in Britain its population has plummeted by 55% between 1970 and 1998. Although it is not fashionable in ornithological circles to blame predators for song bird decline it is interesting to note that the Magpie, Sparrowhawk and Grey Squirrel populations have grown enormously during the period of this bird's decline. This species is susceptible to population fluctuations due to severe winter weather but in recent years the winters have been extremely mild.

The Song Thrush is primarily a bird of woodland but it also likes mixed farmland, parkland, hedgerows and gardens. It has a neat cup nest of grass, twigs and moss with a mud lining that it builds generally in a bush, hedgerow or creeper, a couple of metres from the ground.

The Song Thrush has olive brown upperparts with a mixture of pale and dark markings around the face. It has a buff wash on its breast and flanks and a white belly and undertail coverts with dark spotting covering the whole of the underparts. It has a generally dark bill with a small amount of yellow on the lower mandible and its legs are flesh coloured. The plumages of the sexes are similar. Its song was once one of the songs most frequently heard around gardens and you can always tell the Song Thrush's song from the Blackbird's by its repetitive phrases.

The Song Thrush is a common resident breeding bird in Leicestershire. It is a common resident breeding bird at Swithland Reservoir that has declined markedly in recent years. During the survey years seven pairs were found breeding in the reservoir grounds in 1978, eight pairs in 1979 and 14 pairs in 1980.

Redwing *Turdus iliacus*

The Redwing breeds across northern Europe and Asia from Iceland to the Kolyma River in eastern Siberia. It winters in western and southern Europe reaching North Africa and in Asia, Turkey the Caucasus and northern Iran.

The Redwing was first proved breeding in Britain in 1925 when a nest was found in Sutherland, Scotland. It then bred sporadically in several localities in northern Scotland until 1966 and since then it has become an annual breeder in small numbers with sporadic breeding also taking place in England. 17 breeding pairs were recorded in Britain during 1997. Over much of Britain and Ireland, however, the Redwing is a common winter visitor and passage migrant with birds arriving in late September and October and leaving again from March onwards with only a few stragglers remaining in May. The Redwing migrates during darkness and its shrill 'zeep' call is a feature of autumn nights.

During the summer months it is a bird of woodland and can be found in birch *Betula* forest and mixed forest. It will also breed in the small willows *Salix* in the arctic and where few bushes are present it will nest on the ground among rocks. The nest is a bulky cup of grass, twigs, moss and lichen. The Redwing's song, like that of most thrushes, is melodious and for that reason it was often called the Nightingale of Norway. In winter it can often be found on old pastureland and along hedgerows where it feeds on fruits and berries, especially when it first arrives. During severe winter weather the Redwing is one of the first birds to succumb and its population can suffer very high mortality.

The Redwing is similar in size to the Song Thrush. It has brown upperparts and a buff supercilium and buff patch below the eye. The underparts are white and it has rich chestnut flanks with dark spotting on the upper breast extending onto the flanks. The bill is two-tone, the upper mandible being dark brown and the lower mandible yellow at the base with a dark tip. The legs are flesh coloured.

The Redwing is a common winter visitor to Leicestershire. It is a common winter visitor to Swithland Reservoir in varying numbers and the weather and berry crop can make a difference to how many birds remain in the area and for how long. The earliest autumn record was the 26th September 1993, and the final spring record was the 18th April 1966. There have been two large numbers recorded, 310 birds being counted flying to roost on the 17th December 1989, and circa 480 birds on the 21st October 1995.

Mistle Thrush *Turdus viscivorus*

The Mistle Thrush breeds throughout much of Europe but is absent from a large part of Norway and Iceland. It occurs southward to north west Africa and can be found across central Asia nearly reaching Lake Baikal in eastern Siberia and from there its distribution heads south-westwards to the western Himalayas. It also occurs in Turkey, the Caucasus and northern Iran. It is a resident over much of western and southern Europe. The eastern and northern populations are totally migratory with birds wintering in western and southern Europe, North Africa and the Middle East through to the Hindu Kush.

The Mistle Thrush breeds throughout Britain and Ireland and a large number of birds are sedentary although some are partial migrants and move out of the country in the autumn, reaching Ireland and France. In autumn between September and November large numbers of immigrants and passage migrants move into and through the country. The return passage takes place from February to April.

During the 19th century this species increased greatly in Britain and Ireland, breeding for the first time in Ireland at Louth in 1907 and it spread throughout most of mainland Scotland, where it was considered a rare bird at the end of the 18th Century. Between 1970 and 1998, however, its population has declined in Britain by 21%.

It is a bird of open woodland, pastureland, parkland and old grassland, hedgerows and gardens. It puts its large cup nest of grass, roots and plant stems on branches often quite close to the trunk in large trees at a height of between five and ten metres from the ground. The Mistle Thrush starts to breed in late February and it can be seen early in the year singing from the top of large trees. It sings its often distant-sounding song sometimes in appalling weather and so it was given the name Stormcock.

The Mistle Thrush is our largest resident thrush. It has grey-brown upperparts, its wings show pale feather edgings and it has a long tail that shows white outer tips. Its underparts are pale buff-white covered by large dark spots that are very heavy, almost joining on the sides of the breast. The bill is horn coloured with a slight amount of yellow on the lower mandible and its legs are pale brown with a yellow tinge.

The Mistle Thrush is a common resident breeding bird in Leicestershire. It is a common breeding bird at Swithland Reservoir in small numbers. Because it breeds so early in the year and often nests high up in trees positive proof of breeding and numbers of pairs are hard to ascertain. One pair was found breeding in the grounds in 1979. Two large counts have been made at the reservoir. 30 birds were seen on the 29th July 1991, but the highest count for the site was 65 birds on the 7th September 1997.

WARBLERS Sylviidae

Warblers live up to their name and towards the end of March the first Chiffchaffs can be heard singing their simple song in our woodlands. By late April as many as ten species will have arrived in Leicestershire and woodland, hedgerow, marsh and reedbed resound with their many varied songs. Some are simple in their melody while others like the Blackcap have a rich and varied repertoire that can equal any Nightingale. This is the essence of spring to most birdwatchers and these small birds which have returned over thousands of miles herald the re-awakening of the land that has remained dormant through winter's short days and you know that the onset of summer months and warmer days will not be long in coming.

My first trip to continental Europe came when I visited Majorca in spring 1972 and among the aromatic bushes I came to grips with many new birds, one of the most frequent of these being the handsome Sardinian Warbler, the male of which had a black head, white throat and grey body and a startling red eye. I was like a child with a new toy. I soon added Spectacled Warbler and the Marmora's Warbler. The latter species is endemic to the islands of the western Mediterranean and a real prize to any ornithologist. The Albufera Marsh provided several pairs of Moustached Warblers, which looked superficially like a Sedge Warbler with a dark cap and white supercilium, and the Fan-tailed Warbler whose high display flight and monotonous "zee-zee" song are a real feature of the marshland. It is no wonder its name has been changed to Zitting Cisticola. In nearly every damp patch the explosive song of the Cetti's Warbler could be heard but getting good views of this small brown warbler is a real achievement. The Cetti's Warbler's range has spread northwards through western Europe. It was first recorded in Britain in 1961 and first bred in 1972. Along with the Dartford Warbler it shares the distinction of being the only resident warbler in Britain although in recent years the Blackcap and Chiffchaff have been spending the winter in Britain in increasing numbers; but I shall come back to that topic latter. One of my predictions is that in the next decade the Cetti's Warbler will be seen, if not breeding, at Swithland Reservoir. Anyway I shall never forget my first continental holiday. Since then I have travelled to many countries in Europe and have been thrilled and excited at seeing many different species of warblers. Springtime in the Mediterranean is always a special time for me and I have happy memories of watching the *Sylvia* warblers in their striking breeding plumage. My favourites are the adult male Cyprus, Ruppell's, Subalpine and Orphean Warblers that I found on trips to Greece and Cyprus. I visited Rumania in 1985 and on a trip to Histria on the Black Sea coast I found an unexpected bird, the Paddyfield Warbler. At that time it was a rare bird in Europe. Since then, however, Histria has become known as one of the few sites in Europe where this eastern species breeds. So much for the highlights of springtime in Europe! What about autumn in Britain?

I remember spending some time at Gibraltar Point bird observatory in Lincolnshire on the weekend of the 20th and 21st August 1977. During the weekend there was quite a bit of passage taking place and we were catching Wheatears, Pied Flycatchers and Redstarts as well as one Wryneck. Large numbers of warblers were also moving and we ringed several Whitethroat, Lesser Whitethroat, Blackcap, Sedge Warbler, Reed Warbler and many Willow Warbler, some of which were very light in weight indicating they had probably travelled a great distance. Normally a Willow Warbler on the nesting site in Leicestershire would weigh between 9 and 10 grams but some of these birds were weighing as little as 7.4 grams, which is quite a difference in body weight for such a small bird. I was late up on the Sunday morning and did not get to the observatory at dawn. On my arrival the senior ringer met me with a bird. He handed it to me and said "What do you think this is?" It was obviously a large warbler, but very nondescript. My mind raced through all the European warblers but I could not identify it! He then put me out of my misery and shame and told me it was a first-year Barred Warbler. It is an eastern European and central Asian species that is a rare but regular passage migrant to the east coast mainly on autumn passage.

Some of the most interesting warblers turn up in the late autumn usually in October and a number of them have their origins in eastern Asia. I visited Spurn Point on the 16th October 1988, during a fall of passerines. Spurn Point is a spit of land protruding out into the mouth of the Humber Estuary and another bird observatory that is renowned for the large number of rare and unusual birds that turn up there. In some scattered Hawthorn bushes we found several Goldcrest feeding along with the odd Chiffchaff and two Yellow-browed Warblers and one Pallas's Warbler. It is amazing that the last two species ever reach our shores. The Yellow-browed Warbler is of annual occurrence in Britain in small numbers. It breeds throughout central and eastern Siberia and winters in south-east Asia. It is 10cm in length and weighs between 6 and 7 grams. It is a neat little green warbler showing a yellow supercilium, dark eye-stripe, two yellow wing-bars and pale-tipped tertials. Its underparts are dirty white. The Pallas's Warbler is also almost annual in Britain but in even smaller numbers than the Yellow-browed Warbler. It breeds in the mountains of eastern Asia and winters in the northern part of south-east Asia. It is the size of the Goldcrest, being 9cm in length and weighing 5 or 6 grams but by the time it reaches Britain it weighs only 4.8 grams. It is very similar to the previous species in looks but has a yellow crown-stripe, an even darker eye-stripe and a lemon yellow rump. I still wonder how something as small as a Pallas's Warbler can travel such an enormous distance. The next time I would come across this species was early one morning on Mount Phulchowki in Nepal. After leaving these warblers we walked on the shoreline along the spit. There was a lot of visible bird movement taking place and many Goldcrests were flying in off the sea and falling into the Sea-blite *Suaeda maritima*, some of them unable to make it to the nearby bushes, one actually flying between my legs. I have never seen birds so tired. In a bush close by we saw an Isabelline Shrike, with its sandy brown plumage and rusty red tail, making easy pickings of the small birds. In the brief time I watched it, it killed Robin, Blue Tit and the inevitable Goldcrest. The shrike probably required feeding up because it too had travelled thousands of miles from its central Asian breeding grounds. I have reminisced about only two autumn experiences with warblers but I have many more.

Even in Leicestershire interesting and unusual warblers can turn up from time to time. As a child I well remember the excitement in our household when a friend found a singing male Great Reed Warbler at Coleorton Fish Pond in May 1963. It is engraved on my mind as yet another notable dip for my Leicestershire list. This was the first Great Reed Warbler to be seen in the county and it still remains a rare visitor to Britain from central and southern Europe. In May 1980 another friend found

Leicestershire's first Savi's Warbler at gravel pits in the Wreake Valley and I was fortunate enough to watch this bird singing from the top of reeds for quite a time; its low pitched reeling call being audible at several hundred metres. It is interesting to note that the Savi's Warbler reached a peak in 1980 with between 28 and 30 pairs breeding in England and since then their numbers have declined.

Even in the midst of winter, warblers can appear. In February 1988 I went to a housing estate in Ashby where the Hume's Leaf Warbler was residing in a small hawthorn hedge. Some authorities regard the Hume's Leaf Warbler and the Yellow-browed Warbler as being conspecific and the identity of this bird has left birdwatchers divided. I personally think it was a Hume's Leaf Warbler, but whichever one it was, it had travelled an enormous distance as it should have been wintering in India or Indo-China. Even gardens can produce unusual birds and while ringing in my parents' garden at Quorn, on the 29th August 1981, I caught a Sedge Warbler which was really unusual for an overgrown garden on the edge of woodland but the surprises were not over. Four days later, on the 2nd September, I caught Leicestershire's second Marsh Warbler, followed on the 5th December by a Firecrest, which at that time was only the 11th county record. So it just pays to keep your eyes peeled.

Although I have visited West Africa in the winter and seen many of our common species on their wintering grounds, one of my most enjoyable experiences came in Singapore. I had just seen my wife off to work and decided to do some birdwatching in the Botanical Garden. Over the past few years I have got to know this area fairly well and seen many interesting species within its confines. In the sapping heat of the tropics it is good to get into the shade of trees and bushes and in some of the lower scrub a leaf warbler was feeding. It was an Arctic Warbler and to me that was quite ironic for I have missed this species by seconds in Britain and spent hours in birch forest in northern Lapland looking for them, only to find one half a world away and that really sums it up. That is the wonder of warblers!

Common Grasshopper Warbler *Locustella naevia*

The Grasshopper Warbler breeds across central Europe and through into Asia. It occurs across southern Siberia to western Mongolia and north-western China. It is believed that the western European population winter in western Africa south of the Sahara, with other populations wintering in Ethiopia and on the Indian sub-continent.

It is thinly distributed across most of Britain and Ireland although it is scarce in parts of northern Scotland. The first birds arrive in Britain in early April and movement continues on into May. Return passage takes place mainly at the end of August and only a handful of birds are left by October.

In Britain it is a bird whose population fluctuates greatly from year to year. It does not appear to be faithful to nesting sites but is a great opportunist and where conditions are right pairs will suddenly take up residence. I remember when I was a child a piece of woodland was felled next door to our house in Quorn in order to make way for new housing and in the few months that the ground remained fallow a pair of Grasshopper Warblers took up residence and bred. Between 1970 and 1998 its population has fallen in Britain by 73%. One reason for this could be the severe droughts that have affected the Sahel region of Africa but so little is known of its wintering habits that this remains an educated guess.

The Grasshopper Warbler likes tall rank vegetation and scattered bushes. It can be found on heathland and moorland, in osier beds and in thick vegetation at the edges of water and in newly planted plantations and cleared areas of woodland that have become overgrown with herbaceous vegetation. It makes a grass cup nest that is placed on or close to the ground in dense vegetation. The Grasshopper Warbler is an unobtrusive and skulking bird and when not breeding can be very difficult to see. In the breeding season the male makes its presence known by its monotonous reeling song, which is normally given from a small bush and which is at its most persistent at dusk. It often takes quite a time to pinpoint where the sound is coming from as the song gets louder or softer as the bird turns its head.

The Grasshopper Warbler is a small bird with olive-brown upperparts with dark feather- centres that form spots on the wings and streaking on the head, back and rump. It has a long graduated tail. The underparts are off-white with a buff suffusion on the flanks and across the breast. The latter may also have small amounts of streaking and the undertail coverts are streaked dark. It has flesh-pink legs and a small dark bill.

The Grasshopper Warbler is an uncommon breeding bird in Leicestershire. It is a sporadic visitor to Swithland Reservoir that has probably been overlooked because of its retiring and unobtrusive nature. It has certainly bred within a few feet of the reservoir grounds and during May 1973 singing birds were present in the north-east corner of the reservoir grounds and at Kinchley Promontory. It has, however, not been proved to nest within the grounds although it almost certainly will have done. It has been recorded at the reservoir in four years, 1956, 1973, 1975 and 1982. It bred in a spinney close to the cooling ponds in 1989 and on the Buddon Brook Meadows in 1979.

Sedge Warbler *Acrocephalus schoenobaenus*

The Sedge Warbler breeds throughout much of Europe although it is absent from Iceland, much of central Sweden and Norway, the Iberian Peninsula and southern Italy. Only scattered populations occur in the Balkans. It occurs through northern and central Asia reaching the Yenisei River in the north and the Tien Shan Mountains in the south. Smaller populations are found in south-western Asia in Turkey, the Caucasus and the Aral Sea. It is a totally migratory species wintering in Africa south of the Sahara.

It can be found throughout most of mainland Britain and Ireland and even Orkney, which it colonised in the 19th Century, and the Outer Hebrides that were populated in the 20th century. It is a summer visitor and passage migrant to Britain arriving towards the end of April and into May and leaving again in August and September with only a few stragglers remaining into October.

The numbers of Sedge Warblers in Britain have fluctuated greatly over the last thirty years and the reason for this appears to be severe droughts in west Africa where the birds winter. These prolonged periods of drought dry up the marshes along the river valleys and leave few areas for the birds to feed and they probably struggle to take on sufficient fat to migrate. The Sedge Warblers I have caught on their breeding grounds in Leicestershire weigh between 10 and 12 grams, but it has been found that prior to their departure from southern England their weight almost doubles to 20 grams, mainly as a result of feeding on plum-reed aphids *Hyalopterus pruni*, whose numbers reach a peak just at the time the birds are starting to move. This gives the birds enough fuel to reach their wintering grounds in one flight. Unfortunately the aphid numbers vary from year to year and some birds may have to cross to reedbeds in France in order to take on enough fat for migration.

It is a bird that favours thick vegetation at the edges of fresh water or in marshy ground and can often be found breeding on the edges of rivers, canals, gravel pits and reservoirs. It will occasionally breed well away from water in herbaceous vegetation along hedgerows and in scrub. Its flimsy nest is a woven cup of grass and plant stems which is normally placed in tall herbage or a bush from ground level to half a metre up.

The Sedge Warbler is a small stocky warbler with rich brown upperparts that are streaked dark on the head and wings and more diffusely streaked on its upper back. It has a plain tawny rump. It shows a large pale buff superciliary stripe. The underparts are off white with a buff suffusion on the flanks and upper breast. It has a small dark bill with a small amount of yellow or flesh colour to the base of the lower mandible and brownish legs.

The Sedge Warbler is a common breeding bird and passage migrant in Leicestershire. It is an uncommon breeding bird at Swithland Reservoir whose numbers fluctuate greatly from year to year. It was once a regular breeding bird but in recent years it has become more irregular. During the survey years three pairs were found breeding in 1979 and none was found in 1980. The earliest spring migrant was recorded on the 3rd May 1958, and the latest autumn record came on the 12th October 1969.

European Reed Warbler *Acrocephalus scirpaceus*

The Reed Warbler breeds across central and southern Europe reaching southward to north-west Africa. Small populations can be found in south-western Asia, Turkey and the Middle East and from the Caucasus through northern and central Iran. There is another population from the northern end of the Caspian Sea eastwards through the Aral Sea to the Tien Shan. It is a totally migratory species that winters in Africa south of the Sahara.

In Europe it spread significantly northwards at the end of the 19th century and this range expansion has continued throughout much of the 20th century with the Reed Warbler colonising southern Scandinavia, northern Poland and the Baltic states.

The Reed Warbler is a summer visitor and passage migrant to Britain. The highest breeding populations are in central and south-east England and it becomes more thinly distributed in northern and western England and eastern Wales. It does not breed on mainland Scotland although it bred in Shetland in 1973 and in recent times it has started to breed in Ireland, the first time being in 1935, and now several pairs breed annually. The first Reed Warblers arrive in Britain towards the end of April but the vast majority appear in May. They start to leave again in August and only a few birds remain into early October.

It is generally a bird of reedswamp vegetation on fresh or brackish water. It can be found on the edges of lakes, reservoirs, rivers and in fenland. It also breeds in Osier *Salix* beds and occasionally in cereal fields. Its main breeding site is usually in stands of Norfolk Reed *Phragmites australis* or Bulrush *Typha latifolia* where it weaves its grass cup nest around the stems of the reeds about three quarters of a metre up above standing water. They frequently draw attention to themselves by their staccato grating song that is often delivered from the top of a reed in full view. The Reed Warbler is one of the favourite hosts for the Cuckoo and it was not an uncommon sight when Cuckoos were more plentiful to find a noisy young Cuckoo filling the warblers' small nest and the adult warblers working feverishly trying to keep the huge baby fed.

The Reed Warbler has uniform brown upperparts and off-white underparts with a buff suffusion on the breast and flanks. Its bill is dark on the upper mandible and pink on the lower and its legs are generally brown-grey.

The Reed Warbler is a fairly common breeding bird and passage migrant in Leicestershire. It is a regular breeding bird at Swithland Reservoir in varying numbers. In good years as many as 20 pairs could be found breeding around the margins of the reservoir, usually in Reed Sweet-grass *Glyceria maxima* or in the Osiers *Salix viminalis*, while more recently only small numbers have bred. During the survey years only one pair were proved breeding in both 1979 and 1980. In more recent times five singing males were found in 1992. The first spring record was on the 21st April 1966, and the latest autumn sighting was of two birds on the 10th September 1988.

Lesser Whitethroat *Sylvia curruca*

The Lesser Whitethroat breeds across central and southern Europe and through a large part of central Asia reaching the Lena River in eastern Siberia in the north and across northern western China in the south. In Europe it is absent from Iceland, the Iberian Peninsula and the leg of Italy. It winters in Africa south of the Sahara in a thin band from eastern Mali to Ethiopia, across Arabia and throughout the Indian sub-continent. Within this large range there are several well-defined sub-species.

The Lesser Whitethroat is a passage migrant and summer visitor to Britain. It breeds throughout England and Wales but it is a scarce breeding bird in northern Scotland and Ireland. It bred in Ireland for the first time towards the end of the 1980s and at a similar time it also extended its range into much of Wales, northern England and Scotland. The first birds arrive in Britain towards the end of April but most do not arrive until May. They start to leave in August and heavy passage continues into early September. A few individuals, however, can still be found into early October.

The Lesser Whitethroat has been shown through ringing studies to have an unusual loop migration. In autumn birds move south-east across Europe to northern Italy and then fly along the edges of the Adriatic Sea across southern Greece to the Nile Estuary in Egypt and then on into their wintering grounds in north-east Africa. In the spring they travel further to the east moving through Israel, Jordan, Turkey and Cyprus before heading back to Britain. This species undergoes large fluctuations in its population from year to year in Britain and this could be partly due to weather conditions at the time of spring migration, as Britain lies on the western edge of its range.

It is a bird of woodland edges, open woodland with bushes, plantations and areas of scrub and it likes particularly old overgrown hedgerows. It places its grass cup nest in hawthorns, brambles and small trees from near ground level to over two metres in height. The best way of finding this species is to walk along old overgrown hedgerows in early May and listen for its short burst of rattling song.

The Lesser Whitethroat has a grey head and dark grey cheeks. Its back, wings and tail are grey-brown, with the tail showing white on the outer tail feathers. Its throat is white whilst the rest of the underparts are off-white with a buff suffusion on the flanks. It has a small dark bill and dark legs.

The Lesser Whitethroat is a fairly common breeding bird and passage migrant in Leicestershire. It is an irregular breeding bird at Swithland Reservoir and a regular but uncommon passage migrant. One nest containing five eggs was found in 1978. Five singing males were recorded on the margins on the 30th April 1992. The earliest spring record came on the 18th April 1964, and the last autumn record was of two birds on the 27th September 1992.

Common Whitethroat *Sylvia communis*

The Whitethroat breeds through central and southern Europe southward to North Africa. It is absent from most of the southern part of the Iberian Peninsula but occurs across central Asia reaching Lake Baikal and southward to Tien Shan. In south-western Asia it occurs through Turkey to the Caucasus and northern Iran. It is totally migratory, wintering in Africa south of the Sahara.

The Whitethroat is a summer visitor and passage migrant to Britain that occurs throughout mainland Britain and Ireland though it is scarce in northern Scotland. Birds arrive in Britain during mid-April and passage continues on into May. They depart again in late August and early September but stragglers remain into October.

In Britain the population declined enormously after the 1968/69 winter by as much as circa 80% and this was thought to be as a direct result of a severe drought in the Sahel region of Africa where the birds were wintering. The drought probably affected their food supply and so some birds would starve and others struggle to put on enough fat to complete their migration. Their numbers fluctuated throughout the 1970s and 1980s but generally remained low and further droughts in the 1980s did nothing to help them or their recovery. The decline was not restricted to Britain alone and many countries across central Europe suffered by varying degrees. During the late 1990s a recovery started in Britain and in the summer of 1999 they appeared quite plentiful again, especially in parts of Leicestershire.

It is a bird that likes a dry open habitat occurring in hedgerows, scrubland, woodland edges, newly planted plantations and tall herbage at the sides of roads. Its grass cup nest is placed in tall herbaceous vegetation, bramble thickets or small bushes on or near the ground. Because it nested and kept low, skulking in tall herbage, it was given the name of Nettle-creeper. In May it can be found uttering its scratchy song from the top of a hedge or in a small display flight, the bird flying upward singing and then descending again usually to the same area from which it took off or occasionally flying down to the top of an adjacent bush.

The male Whitethroat has a grey head and a brown-grey back and tail. The tail shows white outer tail feathers and the wings are dark with distinctive rusty brown fringes. It has a white throat and off-white underparts with a pink suffusion on the upper breast and flanks. The bill is dark on the upper mandible and pink on the lower mandible, the legs are flesh-coloured with a hint of yellow and the male shows a white eye ring. The female is generally duller and lacks the grey head and the pink wash on the breast.

The Whitethroat is a common breeding bird and passage migrant in Leicestershire. At Swithland Reservoir it is a regular breeding bird in small numbers and a frequent passage migrant. During the breeding bird survey, two pairs were found nesting in 1979 and three pairs in 1980. The first spring record occurred on the 18th April 1957, and the last autumn record was on the 10th October 1985.

Garden Warbler *Sylvia borin*

The Garden Warbler breeds throughout much of Europe but it has only scattered populations in Portugal, southern Spain, Italy and Greece and is absent from Iceland. It occurs through central Asia reaching the Yenisei River in central Siberia, and in south-western Asia it can be found in northern Turkey through to the Caucasus. It is a totally migratory species wintering in Africa south of the Sahara.

It is a summer visitor and passage migrant to Britain. It breeds throughout all of mainland Britain though it is sparsely distributed in northern Scotland and it bred for the first time on Orkney in 1964. It is a local breeding bird in Ireland that is found in scattered populations in the north of the country and is absent from the south. Birds arrive in Britain from mid-April and movement continues on into May. They start to leave again in August and passage carries on through October with a few birds still being seen in November.

In recent years there has been a certain amount of range expansion in northern Scotland and this species has not suffered the major decline that the Whitethroat experienced. After stating that, it did decline in the early 1970s at the time of the droughts in the Sahel but it recovered quickly, probably due to the fact that it winters further to the south outside the main drought area. This is actually shown quite well by the recovery of a Garden Warbler that was ringed at Swithland Reservoir in June 1982, and killed in Asesewa, Ghana, west Africa in February 1989.

The Garden Warbler can be found in open broadleaf and mixed woodland and at woodland edges. It can also be found in scrubby areas, young plantations and along old overgrown hedgerows. It makes a loosely-woven grass cup nest which is placed in small bushes, brambles and tall herbaceous growth close to or generally within a metre of the ground.

The Garden warbler is the archetypal "little brown job". It has olive-brown upperparts with a blue-grey wash on the neck and its underparts are off-white with a buff suffusion on the flanks. One striking feature of this bird is its large dark eye. The bill is fairly thick and small for a warbler and is largely grey although it has a flesh-coloured base to the lower mandible and the legs are dark blue-grey. The sexes are similar.

The Garden Warbler is a fairly common breeding bird and passage migrant in Leicestershire. It is a regular breeding bird at Swithland Reservoir in small numbers and a common passage migrant. During the breeding bird survey three pairs were found breeding in 1979 and six pairs in 1980. The earliest spring record came on the 22nd April 1983, and the last autumn bird was recorded on the 20th September 1985.

Blackcap *Sylvia atricapilla*

The Blackcap breeds throughout most of Europe being absent only from Iceland and much of the extreme north. It occurs southward to north-western Africa. It can be found in a small part of central Asia to the Ural Mountains and in the south-west through northern Turkey to the Caucasus and northern Iran. It is totally migratory in the northern and eastern parts of its range but it can be found throughout the year in small numbers in south-western and southern Europe. Certain populations winter in Africa south of the Sahara.

The Blackcap breeds throughout Britain and Ireland although it is sparsely distributed in northern Scotland. It apparently doubled its population in the second half of the 20th century due to more habitat being made available by recent changes in the environment. British breeding birds and passage migrants arrive in the country from mid-April to May and depart or pass through in August and September with a few stragglers remaining into October. Most of the British-bred birds winter in southern Europe and northern Africa although several ringed birds have been recovered in sub-Saharan Africa, indicating that some of our birds spend the winter there.

The Blackcap that are seen in Britain during the winter months have been found to originate in central Europe. Wintering Blackcaps have been recorded in Britain since the beginning of the 19th century but only in small numbers. Between 1945 and 1954 there was an average of 22 birds wintering annually in Britain, this had risen between 1970 and 1977 to 380 birds annually. Blackcaps have now become a fairly frequent sight at bird tables during the winter months and my thoughts wander back to the 8th February 1975 when two males and two females were present at our bird table at Quorn feeding on an old wedding cake.

The Blackcap breeds in broadleaf or mixed open woodland with undergrowth and scrub. It also occurs in parkland, large gardens and orchards. It places its woven grass cup nest in brambles, nettles or small bushes from quite close to the ground to 4-5 metres up. During the spring and early summer its rich varied melodious song can be heard in many of our woodlands and the Blackcap must surely rank as one of Britain's finest songsters.

The male Blackcap is grey-brown above with a blue grey wash on the nape and it has a jet black cap. Its underparts are a paler dirty grey with a slightly whiter throat and undertail coverts and a brown suffusion on the flanks. The bill is a dark grey-brown and the legs are blue-grey. The female and juveniles are similar to the male but have a rich rusty brown cap.

The Blackcap is a common breeding bird and passage migrant and an uncommon winter visitor to Leicestershire. It is a fairly common breeding bird and passage migrant to Swithland reservoir. During the breeding bird survey, four pairs were found breeding in 1979 and five pairs in 1980. The earliest spring migrants were seen on the 24th March 1985 and 1990, and the latest autumn records came on the 8th October 1986, when two birds were seen, and the 12th October 1995, when one was present.

Wood Warbler *Phylloscopus sibilatrix*

The Wood Warbler breeds throughout central Europe, being absent from most of the Iberian Peninsula and much of the south. It is also absent from Iceland and a large part of northern Europe. Its range extends eastwards into central Asia through the Ural Mountains to the River Ob in central Siberia. It is a totally migratory species wintering in central west Africa.

The Wood Warbler is a breeding bird and passage migrant throughout most of mainland Britain. It breeds throughout Britain, but has a more fragmented and sparse distribution on the eastern side of the country. It was first seen in Ireland during the second half of the 19th century but became regular as a breeding bird only towards the end of the 20th century, where it is restricted to the north of the country and a small part of the east coast. Its patchy distribution in Britain is largely due to the lack of forest and that is why much of eastern England and Scotland have very few pairs compared with the rest of the country.

The Wood Warbler arrives in Britain from mid-April into May and it departs again in late July and August with only a few individuals being present into September. There appears to have been a decline in England since about 1940 but it is hard to ascertain how much of this has been brought about by habitat changes and woodland destruction. It is also a species that is not site-faithful and its population fluctuates greatly from year to year, so that one year none may breed in a county like Leicestershire whereas in a good year there may be as many as ten breeding pairs.

It is a bird of mature broadleaf forest but it can occasionally be found in mixed forest. It is a species that requires a closed canopy of trees and a shady woodland floor with only small amounts of ground vegetation. It makes its domed nest out of grass and leaves. The nest is placed on the ground under a fallen branch or tree trunk or in any vegetation that is available.

The Wood Warbler is slightly larger than the Willow Warbler. It has green upperparts with darker yellow-edged feathers in the wings, a bright yellow supercilium and dark eyestripe and a bright yellow throat and upper breast, the rest of the underparts being pure white. The bill is brown with a yellow-pink base to the lower mandible and it has pale brown legs, both the sexes being similar.

The Wood Warbler is a scarce passage migrant and rare breeding bird in Leicestershire. Its main breeding sites in Leicestershire were on the Charnwood Forest, where its stronghold was Swithland Wood that had as many as six breeding pairs in some years. It also bred at the nearby Brand, Buddon Wood, Ulverscroft, Outwoods and Beacon Hill. The Wood Warbler is an irregular and scarce passage migrant to Swithland Reservoir that has been recorded on 12 occasions in the last 60 years. All the records were of birds on spring passage and probably all referred to singing males, the earliest record on the 6th April 1984, and the latest record on the 20th May 1995. It almost certainly occurs in the reservoir area on autumn passage, but being a highly arboreal species and silent at that time of year, it would be difficult to detect.

Common Chiffchaff *Phylloscopus collybita*

The Chiffchaff breeds throughout much of Europe, being absent only from Iceland and parts of the extreme south and north of the continent. Small numbers also breed in northern Africa and the Canary Isles. It breeds across northern Asia reaching eastern Siberia in the north and Lake Baikal in the more southern part of its range. It also occurs in south-west Asia in northern Turkey, the Caucasus and northern Iran. It can be found throughout the year in south-west Europe but throughout the rest of its range it is totally migratory. It winters in the southern Mediterranean, North Africa, Africa south of the Sahara, the Middle East and Arabia through southern Iran and Pakistan and across northern India.

Within this huge range there are several sub-species and just recently some of them have been split up into separate species. We shall probably end up with three new species and possibly four. These will be the Canary Island Chiffchaff *canariensis* from the Canary Isles, the Iberian Chiffchaff *brehmii* from Spain, Portugal, south western France and North Africa, the Caucasian Chiffchaff *lorenzii* which breeds in the Caucasus, eastern Turkey and Afghanistan and the Siberian Chiffchaff *tristis* which breeds from the Urals eastwards, although this has not been proposed as a full species yet.

In Britain it is the nominate *collybita* that breeds although the Iberian Chiffchaff and Siberian Chiffchaff have been recorded on passage and occasionally the latter has been known to winter. The Common Chiffchaff breeds throughout Britain and Ireland although it is sparsely distributed in northern Scotland. Over the last 150 years this species appears to have expanded its range in Ireland and in the last 50 years in northern Scotland. Most Chiffchaffs arrive in Britain in the middle of March and passage continues through April. They depart again in August with the main movement taking place in September and passage birds can still be seen through October.

Records of wintering Chiffchaffs go back to the mid-19th century and over the last 30 years they have become more frequent. They now winter regularly in small numbers in southern Ireland, Wales and England and have even been recorded as far north as southern Scotland. In Britain the main races which are found wintering are the nominate *collybita*, which breeds over much of western and central Europe, and a few of the sub-species *abietinus* which breeds in Fenno-Scandinavia east to the Urals, with occasional *tristis* which I have already mentioned. I was bird ringing in my parents' garden in Quorn on the 31st December 1997 when I caught my first wintering Chiffchaff and I caught it again the following day on New Years Day, 1998. Most British Chiffchaffs, however, winter in western France, western Iberia, North Africa and west Africa south of the Sahara.

It is a bird of mature woodland and forest that likes a fairly open canopy allowing a good shrub and herb layer to survive. It makes a domed nest out of grass and leaves that is placed in herbaceous growth or small bushes on or near the ground.

The Chiffchaff is very difficult to tell from the Willow Warbler in the field except that it has dark legs, and when it sings it tells you its name, "chiff-chaff", in its very simple song. It is a small warbler with green-brown upperparts with an indistinct buff supercilium and off-white underparts. It has a yellow or buff suffusion on the flanks. It has a brown bill with a small amount of yellow on the lower mandible and the legs are dark, almost black, both sexes being similar.

The Chiffchaff is a fairly common breeding bird in Leicestershire and a scarce to uncommon winter visitor. It is a common passage migrant at Swithland Reservoir and a regular breeding bird in small numbers. During the breeding bird survey two pairs were found breeding in 1979 and four pairs in 1980. The earliest spring record came on the 4th March 1985, and the last autumn record was on the 10th October 1993. There are three wintering records, one being seen on the 2nd December 1962; a bird remaining at the reservoir from the 5th December 1988 to the 18th January 1989, and one being present on the 7th December 1997.

Willow Warbler *Phylloscopus trochilus*

The Willow Warbler breeds throughout northern and central Europe and across central and northern Asia reaching well into eastern Siberia as far as the Chukotskiy Peninsula. In Europe it is absent from Iceland and the Mediterranean. It is totally migratory, wintering in Africa south of the Sahara. Some Willow Warblers have an exceptionally long migration, and birds summering in eastern Siberia at the easternmost extremity of their range have in excess of 12,000 kilometers to travel to their African wintering grounds.

The Willow Warbler breeds throughout Britain and Ireland and is a common passage migrant. It spread its range in the second half of the 19th century colonising the Outer Hebrides and Orkney and it has occasionally bred on Shetland in the 20th century. The first birds arrive in Britain at the end of March but most do not arrive until April. Birds start to depart again in August and most leave by the end of September with only a few passage birds remaining into early October. Between 1970 and 1998 the Willow Warbler has declined in Britain by 23%, and it is possibly a higher percentage than that in southern Britain. The reasons for this decline are unclear because this species has not been affected by the droughts in the Sahel region of Africa that have so decimated other migrants, as it winters further south. It is also interesting that this large decline has not been reflected over the rest of Europe.

Its song differs from that of the Chiffchaff in being a delightful melody falling effortlessly down the scale in short bursts. The Willow Warbler can be found in a variety of habitats from open forest and woodland to birch scrub and areas of bushes, scrub, young plantations and regenerating woodland. It makes a domed nest of leaves and grass that is placed in herbaceous vegetation on the ground. It often breeds on banks and slopes.

The Willow Warbler is slightly larger than the Chiffchaff, with olive-brown upperparts and a well defined yellow supercilium, its underparts being off-white with a yellow wash on the throat and upper breast. The bill is brown with a yellow base to the lower mandible and the legs are pale brown, the sexes being similar.

The Willow Warbler is an abundant breeding bird and passage migrant in Leicestershire. It is a regular breeding bird at Swithland Reservoir in small numbers and a common passage migrant. During the breeding bird survey one pair only was found breeding in 1979 and none in 1980. The earliest spring record was on the 21st March 1989, and the last autumn record was on the 24th September 1987. On the 27th April 1991, nineteen singing males were recorded around the margins.

Goldcrest *Regulus regulus*

The Goldcrest breeds throughout much of Europe but is absent in Iceland and much of the Mediterranean. It occurs across central Asia as far as lake Baikal and its range extends southward to Tien Shan. Within Asia there are three other fragmented populations. In the south-west it can be found in Turkey and the Caucasus and further east it breeds through the Himalayas to western China; in the far east it occurs in Manchuria across to Japan. It is only the most northerly breeding birds that are fully migratory and throughout the rest of its range only partial movements take place with most birds wintering within its breeding range or just to the south.

The Goldcrest breeds throughout Britain and Ireland. Most British-bred birds are resident with only partial movements taking place. Large immigrations of birds do take place into Britain during the autumn months, especially in September and October, from continental Europe. The Goldcrest has increased in Britain during the 19th and 20th century due to the widespread planting of conifers. It is a bird that succumbs quickly to cold weather and its population can suffer high mortality, but after a severe winter its numbers soon recover. Between 1972 and 1996 the Common Bird Census has shown that its population in Britain has fallen by 60% and there does not appear to be any reason for this. Its population throughout continental Europe appears to be relatively stable and within that time there have been very few periods of prolonged cold weather in Britain. In the last few years, however, the British population has shown a slight recovery.

The Goldcrest is a bird of coniferous forest particularly spruce *Picea* and fir *Abies* but it also occurs in mixed and occasionally broadleaf woodland. It makes a small cup nest of moss, lichen and cobwebs which it suspends near the end of a branch of a fir *Abies*, spruce *Picea*, yew *Taxus* or pine *Pinus*.

The Goldcrest is a tiny bird being olive-green above and pale buff below. Its darker wings show two prominent wingbars and it has a brilliant yellow crown stripe, bordered on each side by black, and two thin black moustachial streaks. The bill is very fine and dark and the bird has brown legs. The male differs from the female in having a bright fiery orange centre to the crown that is normally visible only during display.

The Goldcrest is a common breeding bird in Leicestershire with its numbers being augmented during the autumn by continental birds. It is a common bird at Swithland Reservoir and breeds in small numbers. Positive proof of breeding is difficult because birds breed fairly high up and the nests are difficult to locate in conifers. One nest, however, was found in 1965 and 1978. During the autumn and winter months some notable numbers have been recorded: 18 birds were seen on the 26th January 1986; 20 on the 29th September 1990, and circa 40 on the 2nd December 1997.

Firecrest *Regulus ignicapillus*

The Firecrest breeds throughout central Europe with scattered populations in southern Europe and around the Mediterranean extending into north-west Africa. In Asia there are several isolated pockets in northern Turkey. It is resident or partially migrant in the west and south of its range and totally migratory in the north and east. It winters in southern and south-west Europe, north-west Africa and southern Turkey.

The Firecrest is a breeding bird, passage migrant and winter visitor to Britain which occurs mainly in England and Wales. It first bred in southern England in 1962 and has regularly bred in south-east England since the early 1970s. Its population seems to fluctuate greatly and in 1983 an estimated 175 pairs bred which was a peak year, but in succeeding years its numbers fell again below 100 breeding pairs. At present only 60 pairs breed in Britain. It first bred in Wales in 1975. There has been a slow extending of its range in north-western Europe with Belgium, Netherlands, Denmark and Sweden all being colonised in the 20th century.

The Firecrest breeds in coniferous, mixed and broadleaf woodland and favours the last more than the Goldcrest. It makes a cup nest of lichen, moss and cobwebs, which is placed on the end of a branch, usually coniferous, but it will use broadleaf trees and ivy.

The Firecrest has brighter green upperparts than the Goldcrest and it has distinct bronze shoulder patches, a white supercilium and dark eye-stripe. Otherwise it is similar to the Goldcrest and the sexual differences are also similar to those of the Goldcrest with the male having a yellow crown stripe with a bright orange centre and the female having a largely yellow crown stripe.

The Firecrest is a rare visitor to Leicestershire. It has been recorded on six occasions at Swithland Reservoir involving seven birds. It was first recorded on the 25th February 1944. It was not recorded again until the 25th March 1985, and was recorded subsequently in 1986, 1989, 1992 and 1993. The 1992 bird was seen on the 30th October but the rest of the records were in a period from January to March. In 1989 a female was seen from the 2nd January until the 21st March and a male was noted from the 12th January until the 25th March. On several occasions both birds were seen together and the male was heard singing during March.

FLYCATCHERS Muscicapidae

Spotted Flycatcher *Muscicapa striata*

The Spotted Flycatcher breeds throughout Europe except Iceland and its range extend southward to North Africa. It occurs across central Asia to just beyond Lake Baikal and southward to Tien Shan. It can also be found in south-west Asia across northern Turkey to the Caucasus and through northern Iran. The Spotted Flycatcher is completely migratory, wintering in Africa south of the Sahara.

It is a breeding bird and passage migrant throughout Britain and Ireland, although it only occasionally breeds on the Outer Hebrides and Orkney, and is generally a passage migrant on Shetland. It does not arrive in Britain until the last week in April or early May and is one of the latest summer visitors to arrive. It leaves again in September with passage continuing on until mid-October. Between 1970 and 1998 the Spotted Flycatcher population in Britain collapsed by 68%. Although there have been some reductions in other European countries the decline has not been as great as that seen in Britain and they have fallen by only circa 25%.

It can be found in many different habitats but requires trees and bushes on which to perch. It can be found on the edge of woodland, in open broadleaf or mixed forest, parkland, churchyard, garden, farmyard and orchard. It makes a loosely woven cup nest of grass and moss that is placed on some form of ledge, either natural or artificial. It nests readily in open-fronted nestboxes.

At my parents' house in Quorn it nested regularly on the house wall, some years having two broods. In 1982 at least four adult birds were seen building the nest and then feeding the growing young. I would not have been aware of this unusual behaviour had I not ringed the individual birds.

It feeds mainly on airborne insects which it takes in short sallies from a prominent perch. After catching its prey it normally returns to the same position where it remains, occasionally flicking its tail, until another insect is spotted. The Spotted Flycatcher is a nondescript bird with an upright stance and large dark eye. Its upperparts are grey-brown and it shows a dark streaked crown and pale fringes to the secondaries, tertials and greater coverts. Its underparts are dirty white with diffused brown streaking on the throat and upper breast. It has a brown bill and short black legs and the sexes are alike.

The Spotted Flycatcher is a fairly common breeding bird and passage migrant in Leicestershire. Until a few years ago it was a common breeding bird in small numbers at Swithland Reservoir but in the last few years it has become a sporadic breeder. During the survey years, three pairs were found breeding in 1978 and six pairs in both 1979 and 1980. The earliest spring record came on the 28th April 1996, and the final autumn sighting was on the 3rd October 1999.

European Pied Flycatcher *Ficedula hypoleuca*

The Pied Flycatcher breeds across northern and central Europe with only a scattered distribution in south-west Europe as far as western North Africa. It occurs through central Asia across the Ural Mountains into western Siberia. It is a totally migratory species wintering in West Africa south of the Sahara.

It is a passage migrant and breeding bird in Britain. It breeds mostly in western and northern England, Wales and southern, central and western Scotland with only sporadic or low numbers breeding over the rest of England and northern Scotland. It is a sporadic breeder in Ireland where it first bred in 1985. It had a marked range expansion between 1940 and 1952 in which it spread into the Scottish Highlands, the west Midlands and Devon, the spread continuing but slowing over the following decade. Pied Flycatchers arrive in Britain towards the end of April and passage continues through May. They start to depart again in mid-August and birds move through until late October.

They are birds of broadleaf and mixed open woodland with plenty of old trees with holes in them for nest sites. They occasionally nest in coniferous woodland, parkland or large gardens. They nest in old woodpecker holes, natural holes in trees and take readily to nestboxes.

The adult summer male Pied Flycatcher has black upperparts with a white forehead, large white wing patch and white sides to the tail, its underparts being white. The female has brown upperparts with darker wings and tail, and a smaller white wing patch and white sides to the tail. Her underparts are white with a buff wash on the breast and flanks. They both have black bills and legs.

The Pied Flycatcher is a rare or scarce passage migrant in Leicestershire that has bred on one occasion. It bred at Broombriggs Country Park in 1996, with one pair raising two young. In 1997 five males took up territory on the adjacent Beacon Hill but unfortunately no breeding was proved. A single male took up territory in 1998 but again without success. A large number of nestboxes have been put up in the area and it seems only a matter of time before this species colonises the site. The Pied Flycatcher is an uncommon passage migrant at Swithland Reservoir that has been recorded on nine occasions. The first record was of a female that was seen on the 4th May 1951. There have been eight spring records falling in a period from the 25th April to the 29th May. All were of single birds with the exception of a pair that were present on the 25th April 1969. A singing male was present on the southern margins on the 29th May, 2000. There are two autumn records, a bird being present on the 23rd August 1973, and a first year bird being seen on the 1st October 1978.

TITS Paridae

Long-tailed Tit *Aegithalos caudatus*

The Long-tailed Tit breeds throughout much of Europe, being absent from Iceland and parts of northern Scandinavia. Its range continues across central Asia, reaching Kamchatka and Japan on the Pacific coast and north-eastern China as far south as the Yangtze River. In south-western Asia it occurs in Turkey, the Caucasus and parts of Iran. It is mainly resident although partial and irruptive movements sometimes take place.

The Long-tailed Tit breeds throughout Britain and Ireland but it is more sparsely distributed in northern Scotland and south-west Ireland. It bred on the Outer Hebrides in 1939. It does not breed on Orkney or Shetland. The British population is sedentary with only partial movements taking place, which are normally under 100km and only one continental recovery of a bird, is recorded, in Belgium. Occasionally continental birds of the northern nominate race *A. c. caudatus*, with a white head and neck, have been recorded on the east coast. It is a bird that is susceptible to large fluctuations in population especially after severe winters, which can cause declines of up to 80% but these sudden falls are soon recovered given several mild winters and good breeding success.

It is naturally a bird of broadleaf and mixed woodland which has a good understorey of bushes and shrubs but it can be found in many different habitats that have bushes and trees, including parkland, garden and farmland hedgerows. It builds an oval domed nest of moss, lichen, wool and cobwebs that is lined with an average of 1,558 small feathers. Occasionally up to 2,084 feathers have been recorded. Its nest is built either low down in brambles, in a tree fork or on the outer-most branches of a conifer, many metres up.

The Long-tailed Tit that occurs in Britain is the sub-species *A. c. rosaceus*. The adult has a dirty white head with a large black stripe extending from near the beak over the eye to the nape. Its back and tail are black with the exception of pink scapulars and rump and it has white edges to the secondaries and tertials and white edges to the outer feathers on its long graduated tail. The underparts are off-white with a pink wash on the belly and flanks, extending to the undertail coverts. It has a tiny black bill and black legs, the sexes being similar.

The Long-tailed Tit is a common resident breeding bird in Leicestershire. It is a common resident breeding bird at Swithland Reservoir and during the breeding bird survey three pairs were found breeding in 1979 after one of the last severe winters in recent times and ten pairs in 1980. In winter this species moves around in large nomadic flocks, sometimes in fairly large numbers, and I have listed the four largest. 35 birds were seen on the 5th January 1986; 37 birds on the 3rd October 1992, circa 40 birds on the 8th November 1999, and the largest was circa 50 birds on the 14th January 1996. I caught a small flock of Long-tailed Tits at Quorn on the 30th December 1974, and three of the same group were re-trapped together at the same site on the 28th December 1975.

Marsh Tit *Parus palustris*

The Marsh Tit breeds across central and southern Europe although it is absent from northern Scandinavia, Iceland and much of the Iberian Peninsula. It occurs in south-west Asia in northern Turkey and the Caucasus and across central Asia as far as the Ural Mountains. There is a second population occurring in central eastern Asia that is 2000 km away from that in the Western Palearctic. It occurs from Altai in south-east Siberia through to northern Japan and southward into Korea and eastern China. It is largely a sedentary species and very few ringed birds have been recorded travelling further than 50km.

The Marsh Tit is a resident breeding species throughout England and Wales but it occurs in southern Scotland only and is absent from Ireland. It appears to be extending its range in Scotland but elsewhere in Britain its numbers are in decline. Between 1970 and 1998 the British population has fallen by 69%. It is unclear what has caused this decline although the Marsh Tit does require large areas of deciduous trees to support each pair of birds as they have such a big territory.

As already stated it is a bird of deciduous woodland and particularly likes stands of oak *Quercus* and beech *Fagus* although it can also be found in parks and gardens. It nests in a hole in a tree or tree stump and it does not appear to make its own nest hole but may alter an existing hole to suit and seldom uses nestboxes.

Two subspecies occur in Britain, *P.p. dresseri* which occurs in north-west France and southern and central England and all of Wales and the nominate *P.p.palustris* which can be found in northern England and southern Scotland and across the majority of continental Europe. Birds often move about in pairs and at our house in Quorn they would nearly always visit the bird table together. The adult Marsh Tit has a glossy black cap, white cheeks and plain brown upperparts. Its underparts are off-white with a buff wash on the flanks and it has a small black bib. Its bill is small and dark and its legs are blue-grey, the sexes being similar.

The Marsh Tit is a fairly common resident breeding bird in Leicestershire. It is a regular breeding resident at Swithland Reservoir in small numbers that was proved breeding in 1987 and 1989. Two pairs possibly bred in 1981. In more recent years three males were holding territory in 1993 and four in 1994. During the late summer family parties are occasionally recorded and six birds were seen together on the 9th July 1986, and five on the 11th June 1991.

Willow Tit *Parus montanus*

The Willow Tit breeds across northern and central Europe but it is absent from Iceland, the Iberian Peninsula and much of Italy and Greece. It occurs throughout most of northern and central Asia reaching as far east as Kamchatka in the north and Japan in the south.

In Britain it breeds throughout England and Wales and the lowlands of southern Scotland. It does not occur in Ireland. Since about 1950 there has been a contraction of its range in Scotland where it previously bred north to Ross and Inverness. It is a sedentary species in Britain with very few ringing recoveries over 50km. In some of the northern parts of its range, however, large irruptive movements do take place from time to time. The Willow Tit increased in numbers in Britain between the mid-1960s and mid-1970s but an overall study carried out between 1970 and 1998 showed that the British population in this latter period had fallen by 63%. At present there appears to be no explanation for this. However, this species and the Marsh Tit feed in open situations on Burdock *Arctium* seeds where they would be very vulnerable to predation by Sparrowhawks.

It occurs at higher elevations than the Marsh Tit and can be found in coniferous forest and broadleaf woodland. It likes riparian woodland especially those of willow *Salix*, Alder *Alnus* and birch *Betula* and it favours the edges of gravel pits and reservoirs. It breeds in a tree or stump that is rotten so that it can excavate a nest chamber. Occasionally, however, it will nest in a cavity that is already present but will enlarge it to suit.

The Willow Tit has eleven or twelve sub-species throughout its range. The one that occurs in Britain is *P.m. kleinschmidti* that is a small dark race. The adult bird has a dull sooty black cap that extends further down the nape than that of the Marsh Tit. It has off-white cheeks and brown upperparts. In its wing it shows pale edges to the secondaries that produce a distinctive pale wing panel. The underparts are pale buff with darker brown flanks and it has a large black bib. It has a small dark bill and blue-grey legs and the sexes are similar. One of the best ways of distinguishing between the Willow Tit and the Marsh Tit is by call. The Willow Tit has a harsh "zi-zi-tchay-tchay" call whereas the Marsh Tit has an explosive "pitchu-pitchu" often followed by a "chay-chay" which is less nasal than the Willow Tit's corresponding call.

It is a common resident breeding species in Leicestershire. It is a regular breeding resident at Swithland Reservoir in small numbers that was proved breeding in 1945, 1960 (when a pair successfully raised nine young) and 1986. A group of six birds was recorded on the 30th January 1987.

Coal Tit *Parus ater*

The Coal Tit breeds throughout much of Europe being absent only from northern Scandinavia and Iceland. It occurs southward into north-west Africa. Its range extends into south-west Asia through Turkey and the Caucasus and into northern Iran and in a wide band across central Asia reaching Kamchatka and Japan in the east and southward into China.

The Coal Tit is a common resident breeding bird throughout much of Britain and Ireland except the northern Isles although it has bred on the Outer Hebrides on several occasions during the 20th century. Its range appears to have spread in Britain due to the large areas of afforestation especially in areas of northern Scotland. In Britain it tends to be a sedentary species with few ringing recoveries over 50km. In northern and eastern parts of its range irruptive movements do take place with birds moving southward in the autumn but distances travelled tend to be variable.

The Coal Tit is primarily a bird of coniferous woodland with a preference for spruce *Picea* but it can also be found in mixed and broadleaf woodland. In Britain it favours conifers and Sessile Oak *Quercus petraea* and birch *Betula* stands. It nests in a hole either in a tree, a tree stump or in tree roots. It will also use holes and crevices in rocks and walls, disused mouse holes on the ground and nestboxes.

The Coal Tit throughout its range has somewhere in the region of twenty sub-species. The race that occurs in Britain is *P. a. britannicus*. It has a black head and white cheeks and a white stripe on the nape. The rest of the upperparts are greyish with an olive tinge and the wings show two distinct white wing-bars. The underparts are dirty grey-buff with a darker wash on the flanks and it has a large black triangular bib. The bill is thin and dark and it has dark grey legs, the sexes being similar.

The Coal Tit is a common resident breeding bird in Leicestershire. It is a fairly common resident at Swithland Reservoir that breeds in small numbers. In 1985 a pair bred in a hole in the dam wall and successfully raised a brood.

Blue Tit *Parus caeruleus*

The Blue Tit breeds throughout Europe being absent only from Iceland and northern Scandinavia. Its range extends southward reaching north-west Africa and eastward into Asia as far as the Urals. It occurs also in Asia Minor, in Turkey, the Caucasus and Iran. In the 20th century it spread its range northward in Scandinavia reaching the Arctic Circle and beyond. This spread, however, could easily be halted by severe winters and cold wet summers and the species' numbers fluctuate greatly especially after a cold winter.

It is a common breeding resident throughout Britain and Ireland but it is absent from the Northern Isles except for the Outer Hebrides, which it colonised in 1963. It colonised the south-western Isles of Scilly in the 1940s. In Britain it is generally a sedentary species with very few ringing recoveries over 100km. One bird I controlled at Quorn, in March 1989, had been ringed at Sutton-on Sea, Lincolnshire in December 1987. It had travelled 117km, which is very unusual. I also ringed a Blue Tit on the 6th November 1988 at Quorn that I re-trapped there on the 3rd December 1996. This bird was nearly nine years old. Birds breeding in northern Europe move southward and westward in winter and occasionally large irruptions take place. One such movement took place in 1957 and from the end of September and through October large numbers of continental birds were recorded moving past bird observatories on the east and south coast of Britain and large numbers wintered in England, Wales, southern Scotland and eastern Ireland.

It is generally a bird of deciduous woodland but it can be found in most habitats that have trees and bushes. It is also a bird that tolerates human activity and has even adapted to life in our inner cities. The Blue Tit or Tom Tit is one of the most frequent visitors to bird tables or feeding stations. It nests in holes in trees and walls and readily takes to nestboxes.

The Blue Tit has fifteen sub-species. *P. c. obscurus* that occurs in Britain is not so well-marked as continental birds. It has a blue cap, white face and cheeks with a black eye-stripe and dark blue collar, a blue-green back and blue tail and wings. The wings show white tips to the tertials and a white wing-bar. The underparts are yellow with a greyish central belly stripe. It has a dark bill and grey-blue legs. The sexes appear similar in the field although the male generally shows brighter plumage.

The Blue Tit is an abundant resident breeding bird in Leicestershire. It is a common resident at Swithland Reservoir breeding in small numbers. Five pairs were found breeding in 1980 and one pair were found breeding in a bat box in 1993. In the winter large nomadic flocks can sometimes be seen and on the 7th October 1995 a group of 40 birds was recorded and this is the largest flock recorded at this site.

Great Tit *Parus major*

The Great Tit breeds throughout much of Europe, being absent only from Iceland and parts of northern Scandinavia. Its range extends southward into north-west Africa. It breeds over an enormous area of central and southern Asia reaching Kamchatka and Japan in the east, southward through much of south-east Asia as far as Sumatra and Java. It also occurs throughout much of peninsular India and Asia Minor. It appears to be absent only from the arid high ground of Iran, northern India and the Plateau of Mongolia including the Gobi Desert. Over this huge range there are 33 subspecies that are split into three main groups and some races are considered separate species by some authorities.

The Great Tit is a common breeding resident throughout much of Britain and Ireland, being absent only from the Northern Isles except the Outer Hebrides that it colonised in 1962. It also colonised the Isles of Scilly in south-west England in the 1920s. In the first half of the 20th century its range expanded in northern Scotland, Norway and Finland.

In Britain the Great Tit is a sedentary species with few ringing recoveries over 10km but in the north and east of its range large irruptive winter movements do take place. In the autumn of 1957 a large influx of continental birds moved into Britain, even reaching Ireland, but their numbers were only a third of the numbers of Blue Tit that accompanied them. We have ringed two adult Great Tits at Quorn, both of which were re-trapped alive at the same site over 8 1/2 years later; each bird therefore must have been at least 10+ years old. We had one unusual movement. A nestling ringed on the 5th June 1983, at Treswell Wood in Nottinghamshire, was controlled at Quorn on the 2nd November 1983, some 67km away.

The Great Tit is generally a bird of mature deciduous and mixed woodland but it is a species that has easily adapted to our changing environment and so can now be found in hedgerows, parks, orchards and gardens and even in urban areas like city parks. It is a common visitor to bird tables and feeding stations. It nests in a hole in a tree or stump or a hole in a wall and it readily uses nestboxes.

The male Great Tit that occurs in Britain, *P.m. newtoni* has a glossy black head with white cheek patches, a green back and blue-grey tail and wings, the last showing a well-defined white wing-bar. The underparts are yellow with a large black central stripe extending from the throat to the undertail coverts. It has a sturdy black bill and blue grey legs. The female differs from the male in having slightly drabber coloration and the black belly stripe is thinner with more admixed pale feathers.

The Great Tit is an abundant resident breeding bird in Leicestershire. It is a common resident at Swithland Reservoir with small numbers breeding in the grounds. During the breeding bird survey one pair was found nesting in 1979 and four pairs in 1980. In 1985 one pair actually bred in the spine of the pumping station dome.

NUTHATCHES Sittidae

Eurasian Nuthatch *Sitta europaea*

The Nuthatch breeds throughout much of central and southern Europe extending southward into north-western Africa. It is found in Asia Minor in Turkey, the Caucasus and Iran, and in a wide band across central Asia reaching Kamchatka and Japan in the east and southward into eastern China, reaching Taiwan.

It is a resident breeding bird in Britain that is found throughout England and Wales but is absent from much of Scotland and Ireland. Since the 1940s it has spread both westwards and northwards in Britain expanding its range in both England and Wales and it first bred in Scotland in 1989. It is a very sedentary species in Britain with very few ringing recoveries over 10km. Of the 62 Nuthatches we ringed in Quorn over forty years we had no recoveries and most birds remained faithful to the area with the oldest living to over 4 years and 7 months. There is a tendency for some irruptive movements to take place in the sub-species *S.e. asiatica* from eastern Europe and Russia.

It is mainly a bird of mature broadleaf woodland where it particularly favours stands of beech *Fagus* and oak *Quercus* with a shrub layer of Hazel *Corylus avellana* bushes. It can be found in small and large woodlands, both deciduous and mixed, but only rarely in pure conifers and it also has a liking for old parkland. In recent years it has taken to visiting bird tables for nuts and seed and this practice could have helped in spreading its range, giving it a regular food source during the winter months. It usually nests in a natural hole in a tree or uses an old woodpecker hole, plastering mud around the entrance hole to suit its size.

The Nuthatch is a stocky little bird with a long dagger-like bill, sturdy legs and short tail and it has the ability to climb both up or head-first down a branch or tree trunk. The male of the British and continental race *S.e. caesia* has slate-grey upperparts and it shows white-tipped black outer tail-feathers. It has a black eye-stripe, off-white throat and buff breast and belly with rich chestnut flanks and chestnut and white-spotted undertail coverts. It has a dark bill and brown legs. The female differs from the male in having paler flanks and undertail coverts.

The Nuthatch is a fairly common resident breeding bird in Leicestershire. It is a localised bird around the margins of Swithland Reservoir and breeds in small numbers within the grounds. If you walk in the grounds on an early spring morning you will almost certainly hear the bubble song and the whistle that gives away the Nuthatch's presence, otherwise it can be a species that is easily overlooked. The most recent nest to be found within the grounds was in 1996.

TREECREEPERS Certhiidae

Eurasian Treecreeper *Certhia familiaris*

The Treecreeper breeds throughout much of Europe but it is scarce in the south-west, especially the Iberian Peninsula, and it is absent from Iceland and much of northern Scandinavia. It occurs in a band across central Asia reaching Japan on the eastern seaboard and small populations occur in Asia Minor in Turkey, the Caucasus and northern Iran and another isolated population breeds in Nepal through into southern China.

The Treecreeper is a resident breeding bird throughout Britain and Ireland being absent only from Orkney and Shetland. It first bred in the Outer Hebrides in 1962. The British race *C. f. britannica* is a sedentary species with few recoveries over 20km. The northern European populations of the nominate race *C. f. familiaris* have a tendency to be irruptive and it is a partial migrant with birds moving from the most northerly parts of its range in a south-westerly direction. They have occasionally been known to reach Britain.

It is a bird of woodland and can be found almost anywhere where there are trees. In Scotland in 1905 it was found roosting in hollows it excavated or were natural in the soft bark of the Wellingtonia *Sequoiadendron giganteum*. The Wellingtonia is an introduced ornamental tree, and since 1905 this roosting habit has spread throughout the country. Roosting sites can be seen on the trunks of the Wellingtonias within the grounds of Swithland Reservoir. It generally positions its nests behind loose bark or in a crevice in a tree trunk and it will use specially made nestboxes. It often creeps up a tree like a mouse in a jerky fashion, usually spiralling up the main trunk. When it reaches the top it flies down to the base of an adjacent tree and starts again. Amazingly it can also be seen hanging upside down feeding on the undersides of branches.

The adult Treecreeper of the race *C. f. britannica* has brown upperparts with buff and white streaking and barring on the head, back and wings. It has a buff supercilium and a plainer pale brown long tail with pointed tips to the tail feathers. The underparts are white with a buff wash on the flanks and it has a thin slightly decurved bill which is brown on the upper mandible and pinkish on the lower. The legs are brown and the sexes are similar.

The Treecreeper is a common breeding resident in Leicestershire. It is a fairly common resident at Swithland Reservoir that breeds in the grounds and around the margins in small numbers. Nests were found within the grounds in 1978,1979 and 1980.

ORIOLES Oriolidae

Eurasian Golden Oriole *Oriolus oriolus*

The Golden Oriole breeds throughout central and southern Europe reaching north-west Africa. It occurs across central Asia eastward to the River Yenisei in central Siberia and southwards to northern India and it can also be found in Asia Minor. It winters in Africa south of the Sahara and in peninsular India.

It is a localised breeding bird and passage migrant to Britain and Ireland that only breeds in south-east England. During the mid to late 19th century a few pairs bred in east Kent and it did not breed regularly in its main stronghold of East Anglia until about 1967. Circa 30 pairs were found breeding in East Anglia in 1987. It has bred sporadically in ten other counties in England and once in Scotland in 1974. In 1997 there was a maximum of 24 breeding pairs in Britain. The Golden Oriole arrives in Britain in late April and May and departs again in July and August. A lot of the records in Britain will be of overshoot migrants and these are seen mainly on the south and east coasts of England.

It is a bird of open woodland that particularly likes riverine valleys and areas of woodland adjacent to water. It favours oak *Quercus* ash *Fraxinus* and poplar *Populus*. In Britain it bred during the 1970s mainly in a plantation of Black Poplar hybrids *Populus nigra* x *canadensis* and it appears that new poplar plantations have aided its spread into other areas of northern Europe. It nests high up in a tree in a fork at the end of a branch where it suspends its cup nest that is made of grass, leaves and wool.

The male Golden Oriole often gives its presence away in the spring by its clear fluting whistle and you may catch brief glimpses of this large thrush-like bird flying away from you with undulating flight. The adult male Golden Oriole is a handsome bird with a bright yellow body, black wings, central tail-feathers and lores and it has a red bill and grey legs. The adult female and immature male have green upperparts and yellow rump and the wings and tail are not as black as in the male. The underparts are off-white with fine dark streaking and it has a yellow wash on the flanks.

The Golden Oriole is a rare vagrant to Leicestershire that has been seen on about twenty occasions. It has been recorded once at Swithland Reservoir. A bird was heard calling in the grounds on the 14th May 1990, and earlier the same day a bird was heard singing in Swithland Woods about a mile away.

SHRIKES Laniidae

Great Grey Shrike *Lanius excubitor*

The Great Grey Shrike breeds across northern and central Europe and Asia and northern North America. In winter the northern populations move south, some wintering within its breeding range and others moving well to the south. In Europe it winters southward, reaching the Mediterranean, and westward to Britain. The wintering population in central Europe has been declining since the mid-1970s possibly due to the falling breeding numbers in this area and also because the northern breeding birds in Scandinavia are not moving as far south, remaining to winter in southern Fenno- Scandinavia.

It is a passage migrant and a winter visitor to Britain in small numbers, arriving in October and November and generally leaving again by April.

It is a bird of open country with bushes and scattered trees that have high vantage points. It also uses telephone or power lines and fence posts on which it can perch to look for prey. Its nest is a bulky solid structure that is made of grass and plant material based on twigs, which is placed in a tree or thorn bush.

The Great Grey Shrike has pale grey upperparts with a black mask and white supercilium. The scapulars are white and the wings are black and show a white wing patch and white tips to tertials. It has a long black rounded tail with white outer feathers. The underparts are off-white and it has a small dark hooked bill and black legs, the sexes being similar.

The Great Grey Shrike is a rare winter visitor to Leicestershire. It is a rare winter visitor to Swithland Reservoir that has been recorded on fourteen occasions. The first record came on the 25th March 1961, and it was last recorded on the 20th February 1983. All the records fall in a period from November through to the beginning of April. Several birds spent a few months in the area, one from 7th January to 19th March 1973; another from 5th November 1974, to 5th April 1975, and one from 16th November 1975 until the end of the year.

CROWS Corvidae

Eurasian Jay *Garrulus glandarius*

The Jay breeds throughout Europe, being absent only from Iceland. It occurs southward to north-west Africa and across central Asia as far as Japan and south into China and south-east Asia and then westward into the Himalayas. It can also be found in Asia Minor and parts of the Middle East. There are some 33 sub-species of the Jay throughout its range that can be put into eight major groupings.

It is a resident breeding species throughout much of Britain and Ireland, being absent only from northern Scotland and the northern Isles. The Jay has expanded its range greatly in Britain and Ireland throughout the 20th century, probably due to a lack of persecution, and the first rise in numbers was recorded after 1914 when many gamekeepers went off to the Great War. Its range expanded in northern Scotland during the 1970s due largely to afforestation and it colonised urban areas like central London from 1930.

British Jays tend to be sedentary with only a few ringing recoveries over 50km. The northern and eastern birds are partial migrants and in some years probably when the acorn *Quercus* crop fails they become eruptive. In 1983 one such movement took place with many thousands of birds moving from the continent into Britain from late September through to early November. In autumn the acorn is one of the Jay's most important food sources and they collect and store them in caches in the ground. It is estimated that a single bird could plant 3000 acorns in a single month. It is easy to see why the Jay helps so much in the spread of oak trees. An adult Jay was ringed at Quorn on the 24th July 1964, and subsequently shot at Woodhouse Eaves on the 30th October 1976, over twelve years later.

The Jay is generally a bird of broadleaf woodland that favours oak *Quercus* beech *Fagus* and Hornbeam *Carpinus* although in the north of its range it will breed in pure coniferous forest. It can also be seen in parkland, orchard, small copse and gardens where it occasionally comes to a bird table. It places its stick nest lined with roots in a tree, thorn bush or climber several metres up.

The adult Jay has a pinkish-brown body with a white throat and undertail coverts. It has black moustachial stripes and a back and white streaked crown, black tail and when it flies it shows a white rump. Its primary and outer wing coverts are blue with fine black barring and it has light-edged black primaries, black and white secondaries and chestnut on the tertials.

The Jay is a fairly common resident breeding bird in Leicestershire. It is a common resident at Swithland Reservoir that breeds in small numbers. During the autumn and winter when the leaves are falling from the trees the birds become more conspicuous and it is at this time of year when the acorn crop becomes ripe that several high counts have been made at Swithland. 16 birds were recorded on the 10th October 1982, and 17 on the 2nd November 1986.

Common Magpie *Pica pica*

The Magpie breeds throughout much of Europe, being absent only from Iceland. Its range extends southward into north-west Africa and eastward in a wide band across central Asia reaching southern Japan and China. There is an isolated population in Kamchatka and north-east Siberia and it also occurs over much of western North America.

It is a resident breeding bird throughout much of Britain and Ireland but it is absent from the far north of Scotland and the northern Isles. The Magpie was introduced into and colonised Ireland towards the end of the 17th century. It is generally a sedentary species with few ringing recoveries over 30km. It has increased greatly over much of Britain during the 20th century which is probably due to the lack of persecution particularly after the war years. There was, however, a decrease in parts of East Anglia in the late 1950s and this was attributed to the removal of hedgerows and the use of toxic chemicals. Since the mid-1960s the Magpie numbers have increased markedly especially in urban areas where they have exploited food sources put out by Man, becoming one of the twelve most frequent species to visit gardens according to the B.T.O. in 1999. Between 1970 and 1998 the British population has risen by 113%.

They often plunder the nests of songbirds, taking both eggs and young. According to many authorities in Britain this has little effect on our songbird population, but in a five- year survey of a 10 hectare suburban area in northern Germany a total of 64% of open nesters were taken and 1.3% of hole nesters and a staggering 100% of some species.

The Magpie can be found in a wide variety of habitats, from urban areas through to Arctic tundra where it is associated with Man. It occurs in open areas with belts of bushes or trees and can be found on farmland, parkland, heathland, in open woodland and in gardens. It usually builds its nest several metres up in a tree or bush and often favours those with thorns, but it is very adaptable and will on occasions nest in cover close to the ground. It makes a stick nest with a dome of thorns and constructs a bowl with mud and twigs which it then covers with grass hair and feathers. They are either gregarious, being seen in loose chattering flocks, or solitary.

The Magpie is a long- tailed black and white bird and is easily recognised by most people. When close views are obtained in good light its black plumage shows iridescent green, blue and purple colours. It has a black head, back, upper chest and undertail coverts and shows black wings while at rest with white scapulars, belly and flanks and a long black graduated tail that has a green sheen. It has short rounded wings and in flight it shows white centres to the primaries. It has a black bill and black legs. The male is slightly larger than the female and has a longer tail.

The Magpie is a common resident breeding bird in Leicestershire. It is a common resident at Swithland Reservoir breeding in small numbers.

Western Jackdaw *Corvus monedula*

The Jackdaw breeds throughout central and southern Europe southward into North Africa. Its range extends eastward across Asia in a wide band as far as central Siberia and it also breeds in Asia Minor. It is a partial migrant and migrant over much of its range but only the most northern and eastern breeding birds vacate their breeding area and move south-westward in winter. Most Jackdaws winter within the breeding range.

The Jackdaw is a resident breeding bird throughout Britain and Ireland. In Britain they vacate some northern high ground in winter and movements of this species tend to have a westerly bias but, even so, Britain's population tends to be mostly sedentary with few ringing recoveries over 100km.. Birds from northern and western Europe occasionally reach eastern Britain. During the 20th century it has expanded its range in northern Scotland and increased its numbers over much of Britain, and between 1970 and 1998 its population has risen by 148%.

The Jackdaw can often be seen feeding around livestock and sometimes perches on the backs of animals, removing parasites from their hair and skin. It can be found in many habitats but likes feeding on the ground in old pastureland and particularly likes old parkland with ancient scattered trees in which to nest. It places its stick nests in crevices, cavities and holes in cliffs, in trees and on buildings and especially favours chimneys, which it invariably blocks with its bulky stick nest. It also takes readily to nestboxes and occasionally it has an open nest in a tree or uses a disused Rabbit *Oryctolagus cuniculus* hole. It also has the reputation of being an inquisitive bird that has a liking for bright and shiny objects that it takes to adorn the nests.

The adult Jackdaw is the smallest British crow with mostly black plumage that is slightly grey on the breast. It has a grey neck and nape and its cap is dark in contrast to the nape and shows a blue sheen. It has a distinctive pale eye. The bill is black and shorter than most crows and it has black legs. The sexes are similar.

The Jackdaw is a fairly common resident breeding bird in Leicestershire. It is a common resident at Swithland Reservoir that is most frequently seen flying to and from the crow roost in Buddon Wood. One of the best places to see Jackdaws on the Charnwood Forest is Bradgate Park where they breed in the old oaks *Quercus*. There have been some large numbers recorded flying to and from the roost over Swithland Reservoir; 130 birds were seen flying to roost on the 18th March 1990, and 320 on the 1st March 1996, but the largest recorded number came on the 22nd December 1985, when circa 400 were seen leaving the roost in three separate flocks.

Rook *Corvus frugilegus*

The Rook breeds across central Europe and Asia reaching northern Mongolia and eastern Siberia southward into eastern China. Populations also occur in Altai and Asia Minor through to northern Iran. The northerly and easterly populations are migratory, wintering in central and southern Europe, Asia Minor, Afghanistan, Pakistan, Korea, southern Japan and south-east China. It has resident populations in central Europe, Asia Minor, Altai and China that are augmented in winter by northerly breeding birds. It was introduced into New Zealand.

The Rook is a common resident breeding bird throughout Britain and Ireland. In recent times it has expanded its range in northern Scotland colonising the Outer Hebrides in 1895 and Shetland in 1952. Between 1928 and 1944 the Rook population in Leicestershire increased by as much as 45% and throughout Britain by 20%. Between 1950 and the mid-1970s, however, there was a marked decline throughout Britain which wiped out the species' earlier gains and this was probably brought about by changes in agriculture and the use of insecticides and toxic seed dressings. Most British Rooks tend to be sedentary with only partial movements taking place and there are few ringing recoveries over 100km. In the autumn large numbers of immigrants from continental Europe move into Britain and they remain throughout the winter and leave in the spring.

The Rook requires mainly tall trees in which to breed but it is generally a bird of open country and large flocks can be seen feeding on arable and old pastureland in association with Jackdaws, and earthworms

Lumbricidae, beetles *Coleoptera* and other invertebrates make up a large proportion of their diet. The Rook is an early breeder and nest building can start in February with the first eggs being laid from mid to late March. They breed communally and use either conifers or broad-leaved trees. Their large stick nests can be seen in close proximity in the crowns of tall trees.

As a boy growing up in Quorn I can remember three Rookeries and all were situated in the tops of oak *Quercus* and Ash trees *Fraxinus excelsior* and one colony was close to the centre of the village. Unfortunately this disappeared in the mid-1960s. In recent years the Rook has taken to breeding lower down in hedgerows and this could possibly be due to there being fewer hedgerow trees. The elm *Ulmus* was an important breeding tree for the species in Leicestershire and most of those were destroyed by Dutch Elm disease leaving the Rooks with few nest sites.

The adult Rook has an all black glossy plumage that shows blue, purple and violet sheens depending on how the light catches it and it has a black bill and legs, the sexes being similar. It differs from the Carrion Crow in having a peaked crown and a grey-white patch of bare skin to the base of the more slender bill and its stomach appears to sag due to the looser feathering.

The Rook is an abundant resident breeding bird in Leicestershire. It is a common resident at Swithland Reservoir that is most frequently seen flying to and from the large crow roost in Buddon Wood. The largest single count was a flock of circa 600 birds flying to roost on the 24th January 1993.

Carrion Crow *Corvus corone*

The Carrion Crow has two all black subspecies that are separated by thousands of miles. The nominate *C. c. corone* breeds in western Europe, the Iberian Peninsula northwards to Britain and Denmark and eastwards to West Germany, the Czech Republic, Austria and Northern Italy. This race tends to be sedentary with only small numbers of birds moving outside the breeding range. The other all black race *C. c. orientalis* occurs to the east of the Yenisei River in central Siberia, southwards into the Tien Shan Mountains, east to Japan and Korea and north reaching the Pacific coast in eastern Siberia and Kamchatka. The northerly breeding birds are migratory, wintering mainly within its southern breeding range but some birds move further south wintering in south-east China.

In Britain the Carrion Crow is a resident breeding bird occurring from central Scotland southwards throughout England and Wales. It has increased greatly throughout Britain during the 20th century partly due to the lack of persecution by game-keepers and Britain now holds an estimated one million breeding pairs. Between 1970 and 1998 the British population rose by an estimated 120%.

It feeds mainly on invertebrates and cereal grain, but it will also eat small mammals, fish, birds and of course carrion. It is an avid nest robber and will take young birds and eggs. It is a species that has been able to adapt to Man's activity and can be seen in many urban areas. It has exploited the regular food source found on rubbish tips and can be seen scavenging on them with gulls. It has expanded its range in Scotland and the Isle of Man at the expense of the Hooded Crow *Corvus c. cornix* and it has also bred sporadically in Ireland. The Carrion Crow is sedentary in Britain with few ringing recoveries over 30km.

It is a bird of open country that requires some tall trees in which to breed. These can be found along hedgerows, in coppices or along woodland edges. It is a very territorial solitary breeder placing its large stick nest in the top of a tall tree or, if one isn't available, it will use electricity pylons.

The Carrion Crow has all black plumage with a green or violet sheen when seen in good light. It has a heavy black bill with a slightly curved culmen and black legs, the sexes being similar.

It is a common resident breeding bird in Leicestershire. It is a common resident at Swithland Reservoir breeding in small numbers. Two pairs bred in the reservoir grounds during 1979. There are two records of large numbers feeding at the reservoir and both occurred during freezing conditions: 35 were recorded on the 18th January 1985, and circa 60 on the 11th and 12th February 1986. Large numbers are recorded flying to and from the crow roost on Buddon Wood: 240 were counted on the 18th March 1990, and 300 on the 1st March 1996. These were doubtless attracted to the area by the close proximity of the Mountsorrel refuse site.

Hooded Crow *Corvus corone cornix*

The Hooded Crow is still considered a subspecies of the Carrion Crow *C. c. corone* and although their ranges and plumages are quite different, where their populations meet they do hybridise. The Hooded Crow breeds in northern Britain, Ireland and throughout Scandinavia southwards through the leg of Italy, eastwards into the Middle East and Asia Minor and north into Western Siberia reaching the Yenisei River.

The northerly breeding birds are migratory, moving south in the winter, but they winter mainly within its southern breeding range.

The Hooded Crow is a resident breeding bird in Britain and Ireland occurring in northern Scotland, the northern Isles and throughout Ireland. British and Irish birds tend to be sedentary but birds from continental Europe winter along the eastern side of Britain arriving in October and November and leaving again from mid-March to mid-April .

It favours upland areas more than the nominate Carrion Crow and can often be found on seashores where it breeds on cliffs or rock ledges.

It is generally the same size and shape as the Carrion Crow but it differs in having bicoloured plumage and a slimmer bill. It has a black head with a long black bib, black wings and tail, the rest of the plumage being grey.

It is a rare winter visitor to Leicestershire. It is a very rare winter visitor to Swithland Reservoir that has been recorded on three occasions. All the records were of single birds. One was seen on the 11th and 28th February 1986, and another on the 9th December 1993. There was one long- staying individual which was seen from the 19th November 1990 until the 16th March 1991.

Common Raven *Corvus corax*
The Raven has an enormous range, breeding throughout much of northern and southern Europe southwards into North Africa. It occurs across much of Asia from the Arctic southward to northern India and over much of northern and western North America southward to Nicaragua.

In Britain the Raven is found mainly in south-western and north-western England, Wales, Scotland and Ireland. In the first half of the 19th century it was persecuted over much of Britain and was exterminated throughout central and southern England. Since the beginning of the 20th century there has been a slow but steady expansion of its range but it has not managed to regain all the territory it lost, especially in England. More recently afforestation and changes in farming practices have brought about a decline in its numbers in certain areas of Britain, especially Scotland. The Raven is mainly sedentary in Britain although partial movements of immature birds do take place in the autumn.

It favours large areas of open country with safe nest sites like cliffs. The nest is a large mass of twigs and sticks, bound together with earth and dung, that is lined with fine plant material like roots and grass, overlaid with wool and hair and is generally placed on a cliff or in a large tree.

The Raven is the size of a Buzzard and it is the largest passerine. Its plumage is entirely black with a glossy purple-blue sheen. It has a shaggy throat and a very large, heavy black bill and black legs. In flight it shows a distinctive wedge-shaped tail. The Raven mates for life and so it is often met with in pairs. It feeds on a variety of foods but it is mainly a scavenger feeding on dead carrion such as sheep and rabbits.

The Raven is a rare vagrant to Leicestershire. In the 1820s the Raven still bred on Bradgate Park and High Sharpley but it had gone from the Charnwood Forest by the 1840s. In the period from the end of March to December 2000 several birds were again seen regularly on Charnwood Forest and two birds were actually seen displaying over Bradgate Park. During that period birds were recorded for the first time at Swithland Reservoir with one bird being present on the 26th March and two birds on 31st May, 9th July and 22nd October 2000.

STARLINGS Sturnidae

Common Starling *Sturnus vulgaris*
The Starling breeds throughout much of Europe but is absent from most of the Iberian Peninsula. It occurs in a wide band across central Asia reaching Lake Baikal and central Siberia. It also occurs in Asia Minor through Turkey and the Caucasus into Iran. It can also be found in Altai south to eastern Tien Shan and isolated populations occur eastward to the western Himalayas. The northern and eastern populations are migratory and tend to move in a south-westerly direction during the autumn. Starlings winter in south western Europe, North Africa, the Middle East, Asia Minor eastward to Pakistan and northern India. It has been introduced into North America and now occurs over much of the continent and also South Africa, New Zealand, south-east Australia and Tasmania.

The Starling is a resident breeding bird throughout Britain and Ireland. There was a marked decline and range contraction in Britain in the early 19th century and it withdrew from many western and northern areas. From 1830 it started to increase again and expanded its range throughout the whole country and this continued until the 1950s. Since the 1960s there has been a marked decline. Between 1970 and 1998 the British population has fallen by 58%. Populations have also declined over northern and eastern Europe from the 1970s and this has resulted in fewer birds wintering in Britain. The Starling appears to have suffered because of the changes in agriculture. It is a bird that feeds on invertebrates which it often gathered on pastureland around livestock but now many areas have changed to arable land. In the winter it also fed on grain and invertebrates gained by feeding on stubble fields but now very few of these remain with the autumn sowing of crops.

Until this period large numbers of birds from continental Europe poured into Britain each autumn arriving in late August and remaining throughout the winter months departing in March. Two Starlings were ringed at our garden at Quorn on the last days of December in 1962. Both were recovered in West Germany in June 1964, one at Wilster near Hamburg and the other at Greifswald on the Baltic Coast.

During the winter months huge numbers of Starlings come together in communal roosts which can number many thousands of birds and the twisting and turning flocks can look like smoke being blown about and blacken the sky. The Starling can be found in many habitats but rarely feeds under low cover. It can often be a pest in fruit-growing areas during the late summer and early autumn when large flocks can be found feeding on apples and pears. They nest in cavities and holes in buildings, cliffs and trees.

The Starling is about the same size as a Song Thrush. It has a short tail, long bill and upright stance. It is a very vocal bird having a good repertoire of chuckles and whistles and it is an excellent mimic. The adult summer Starling has a shiny black plumage with a purple, green and blue sheen, depending on how the light catches the feathers, and a small amount of buff-brown spotting which in winter becomes more pronounced. In summer the bill is yellow with a blue-grey base in the case of the male and a pink base for the female, the bill becoming black during the winter. The legs are red-brown in colour.

The Starling is an abundant resident breeding bird in Leicestershire. It was once a common resident at Swithland Reservoir that bred in good numbers but in recent years it has declined markedly. Three pairs were found breeding in 1978, four pairs in 1979 and 12 pairs in 1980. There is only one recent record of note involving numbers of birds and that was of 160 flying over the reservoir in a thirty-minute period on the 1st November 1998. Thirty years ago that number would not have been considered worth recording. It is amazing how times change.

SPARROWS Passeridae

House Sparrow *Passer domesticus*

The House Sparrow breeds throughout Europe, being absent only from Italy where a hybrid with the Spanish Sparrow *Passer hispaniolensis* occurs, commonly known as the Italian Sparrow, and also over much of Iceland where only seven pairs bred in 1987. It occurs southward into north-west Africa and eastward throughout much of central Asia as far as northern Manchuria and also through Asia Minor and the Middle East across into the Indian subcontinent and Burma. It has been introduced and occurs throughout most of North America and large areas of South America, being absent only from the tropical forests of the north. Introduced populations can also be found in south-east Africa, eastern Australia and New Zealand.

The House Sparrow is a resident breeding species throughout Britain and Ireland and most birds are sedentary with few ringing recoveries over 10km. It is a species that has found a niche alongside man and is quite at home in urban and suburban areas. It is an opportunistic feeder feeding on scraps and food put out at bird tables but it also feeds on the seeds of cereals and grasses found on local farmland or cultivated land. In Britain it breeds mainly in holes and cavities in buildings. It has declined markedly in Britain over the last few years and between 1970 and 1998 its population has declined by 58%. The reasons for this decline are not clear but it is probably due to the changes in agriculture, especially the autumn sowing of cereals that leaves few stubble fields on which birds can feed in the winter months, and also greater use of herbicides and pesticides. Another factor could be that old buildings with pan-tiled roofs have become rarer in many districts as these were favoured by the birds for breeding and now few nesting sites remain.

The adult summer male has a grey crown with rich brown sides to the head and nape. The back and wings are also rich brown streaked black and the wings show a white wing-bar. It has a brown tail. It has a large black bib and grey-white cheeks and underparts. The bill is grey and the legs are brown. The female has a brown head and nape, buff supercilium and brown, black-streaked upperparts and brown tail, the underparts and cheeks being grey-white.

The House Sparrow is an abundant resident breeding bird in Leicestershire. It was a common resident breeding bird at Swithland Reservoir but over the last decade its numbers have dropped. There are very few reports of this species over the past sixty years because it was considered so common and so there is little information on its historical status.

Eurasian Tree Sparrow *Passer montanus*

The Tree Sparrow breeds throughout central and southern Europe and throughout much of Asia reaching Japan in the east, southward through China throughout much of south east Asia reaching south to Sumatra and Java. It is absent from northern Siberia, most of the Indian subcontinent and much of the Middle East. Only the most northerly and easterly populations are migratory and most winter within its southerly breeding range. Small introduced populations occur in North America and south-eastern Australia.

The Tree Sparrow is a resident breeding bird in Britain and Ireland. It is absent from north-west Scotland, some of western Wales and much of Cornwall and large parts of western and southern Ireland. Most British birds are sedentary but occasionally partial movements do take place. It is a species that has undergone large fluctuations in population. In the first half of the 20th century the population decreased and then from the mid-1950s to 1966 numbers increased enormously with many new areas being colonised. Between 1970 and 1998 it has decreased significantly and the British population as fallen by 87%. The reasons for this decrease are not fully understood but it is almost certainly linked to agricultural changes. The sowing of autumn crops has done away with many stubble fields that were an important source of food for this species throughout the winter months and the added use of herbicides and insecticides cannot have helped. There is also a decline in other western European countries, but in Scandinavia, the Iberian Peninsula and some Mediterranean Islands it is increasing.

The Tree Sparrow occurs in open country with scattered trees and can be found on farmland, parkland, and in hedgerows. It is quite frequent around habitation and can be found in villages. It breeds communally in holes and cavities in trees and buildings and it readily takes to nestboxes. Pollarded willows and old Ash trees are favorite nesting sites and it also frequently nests in the base of old Magpie and crow nests.

The adult Tree Sparrow has a rich brown cap and nape, white cheeks and a white neck collar that nearly meets on the nape, a black cheek-patch and a small black bib. The upperparts are brown with black streaking and the wings show a white wing-bar. The bird has a brown tail. The underparts are grey-white, it has a small black bill and pale brown legs, the sexes being similar.

The Tree Sparrow was a fairly common resident in Leicestershire that has undergone a significant decline. It was a common resident at Swithland Reservoir that bred in small numbers. Over the last few years, however, it has also declined. The only records of note are of two pairs that were found breeding in 1979 and of a flock of 20 birds that was seen near Rabbits Bridge feeding with finches and buntings on the 30th March 1980.

FINCHES Fringillidae

Common Chaffinch *Fringilla coelebs*

The Chaffinch breeds throughout Europe and southward into North Africa. Its range extends eastward in a band across central Asia through western Siberia to Lake Baikal. It also occurs in Asia Minor through Turkey and the Caucasus into northern Iran. The northern and eastern populations are migratory and generally move in a south-westerly direction. In Europe most winter within the birds breeding range. It has been introduced into South Africa and New Zealand.

The Chaffinch is a resident breeding bird throughout Britain and Ireland and most British bred birds are sedentary with the majority of adults moving less than 5km. There are large autumn immigrations of birds into Britain from north-eastern Europe, mainly in September and October, and they remain through the winter and leave in March and April. In Britain the Chaffinch declined from 1950 to the early 1960s but from that time to the 1980s it has increased by as much as 20%.

The Chaffinch is one of Britain's commonest birds occurring in woodland, parkland, orchard, hedgerow and garden. It has a distinctive "pink" call that can be heard throughout the year. It usually places its compact cup nest made of moss, lichen, wool and cobwebs several metres up in the fork of a tree or bush or on the end of a branch.

The adult summer male Chaffinch has a black forehead, blue-grey crown and nape, brown mantle and green rump. The tail is dark with white outer feathers and the wings are generally black with two distinct white wing-bars. It has pinkish cheeks, breast and belly with white undertail coverts, a lead-blue bill and grey legs. The female is grey-brown above with a greenish rump and more buff feathers in the wing-bar. It has buff to off-white underparts and a greyish bill. In winter the male's plumage becomes duller.

The Chaffinch is an abundant resident breeding bird in Leicestershire. It is a common resident at Swithland Reservoir, breeding in small numbers. Eight pairs were found breeding in 1978, 11 pairs in 1979 and five pairs in 1980. The two largest recorded flocks in the area were both seen in fields near Rabbits Bridge. Between 150 and 200 birds being recorded on the 30th March 1980, and 300 on the 1st October 1988. There have been several large roosts recorded within the grounds and in the winter and autumn of 1989 birds regularly roosted there, the highest count being 147.

Brambling *Fringilla montifringilla*

The Brambling breeds throughout northern Europe and northern Asia from Norway through to Kamchatka and eastern Siberia. It winters over much of Europe through to Asia Minor in the west and Japan, Korea and south-east China in the east.

In Britain it is a sporadic breeder in northern Scotland with the first proved breeding in 1920 and in recent years it has become almost annual. Otherwise it is a winter visitor to much of Britain and Ireland arriving in September and October and departing in April and May. The numbers of birds that arrive in Britain vary greatly from year to year and much depends on the availability of food on the continent.

Many authorities call the Brambling the northern counterpart of the Chaffinch. It breeds in open conifer forest and birch *Betula*, alder *Alnus* and willow *Salix* woodland. Its nest is a cup not unlike that of a Chaffinch but larger and it is made of moss, lichen, grass, heather, birch strips and cobwebs. It is placed in the fork or near the trunk of a tree several metres up. In winter it can often be found feeding under beech *Fagus* trees on the beech masts. The call of the Brambling is quite unlike that of the Chaffinch, being a harsh nasal wheeze "tew-ehp".

The adult summer male Brambling has a glossy blue-black head and mantle, white rump, black tail and black wings which show two white wing-bars. The lesser wing coverts and upper breast are orange and it has a white lower belly and undertail coverts with dark spotting on the flanks. The bill is black in summer and the legs vary, being either flesh-brown or greyish-flesh. In winter the black of its head and back are replaced by dark-centred, brown-edged feathers and the bill becomes yellow with a dark tip. The female differs from the male in having a grey crown-stripe and cheeks bordered by dark feathering, a brown mantle with dark markings and it has a tinge of orange on the breast, lesser wing coverts and wing-bar.

The Brambling is an uncommon to fairly common irruptive winter visitor to Leicestershire. It is a regular winter visitor to Swithland Reservoir in varying numbers. The earliest autumn sighting came when two birds were seen on the 22nd October 1995, and the last spring sighting came on the 8th May 1943. The two highest counts made at the site were circa 100 on the 25th February 1998, which rose to circa 150 on the 10th April 1998.

European Greenfinch *Carduelis chloris*

The Greenfinch breeds throughout much of Europe extending southward into north-west Africa. It is absent from Iceland and parts of northern Scandinavia. In Asia its range extends eastwards to the Ural Mountains. It also occurs in parts of the Middle East bordering the Mediterranean, Turkey, the Caucasus and northern Iran and there is a separated population in Uzbekistan and Kazakhstan. It has been introduced into coastal Uruguay, north-eastern Argentina, New Zealand and south-east Australia. Throughout much of its range it is sedentary with only partial movements taking place although the extreme northern breeding birds migrate south-westwards, wintering mainly within its southern breeding range.

The Greenfinch is a common resident breeding bird throughout Britain and Ireland, being absent only from Shetland. British birds are mainly sedentary with only partial movements taking place and the vast majority of these move under 100km, although some British ringed birds have been recovered on the near continent. Since the mid-20th century the Greenfinch has moved into our towns and cities. The probable reason for this is the garden feeding of birds that started on a large scale in the 1960s with the use of seed and peanuts.

The Greenfinch population has remained stable in Britain between 1970 and 1998, falling by only 2%. In some areas of Leicestershire, however, its numbers appear to have fallen considerably compared with twenty-five years ago. From the mid-1970s and through the 1980's it was a common bird in our garden at Quorn where between fifty and a hundred birds would regularly feed on seed and peanuts. In recent years, however, it has become an uncommon visitor and only occasional birds now feed in the garden. Changes in farming practice could be having an effect because this is a species that feeds on stubble fields during the winter months and these are largely gone with the autumn planting of cereals.

It is a bird of woodland edges, scrub areas, farmland, orchards and recently parks and gardens. It often nests in conifers but will use a wide variety of bushes and trees. It places its robust, loosely constructed cup nest of twigs, moss, grass and lichen close to the trunk or in a fork of a tree or bush usually a few metres from the ground. During the winter months large numbers of birds come together to roost communally and they often use rhododendron or laurel bushes because they are evergreen.

The adult male Greenfinch has an olive-green body with a yellow suffusion on the breast and a grey wash on the face flanks and wings. It has black primaries with yellow basal feather edgings, which form a yellow wing panel, and a black forked tail with yellow base to the feathers. It has a robust pale grey-pink bill and flesh-coloured legs. The female is drabber than the male, being browner on the back with faint streaking and greenish-grey underparts.

The Greenfinch is a common resident breeding bird in Leicestershire. It is a common resident at Swithland Reservoir breeding in small numbers. Two pairs were found breeding in 1978 and three pairs in 1979. There has been a roost in the rhododendron bushes in the grounds of the reservoir for many years and the numbers of birds have fluctuated from winter to winter. Two hundred were present on the 30th November 1946.

European Goldfinch *Carduelis carduelis*

The Goldfinch breeds throughout central and southern Europe southward to North Africa. It also breeds from Turkey to the Caucasus through to Iran, Afghanistan, Tien Shan as far as north-west China. In the Middle East it occurs in countries bordering the eastern Mediterranean. It also occurs across central Asia through Western Siberia as far as the Yenisei River and a separate population can be found in western Pakistan across to the Himalayas and eastwards to Nepal. It has been introduced into several areas in the U.S.A., north-east Argentina, south-west and south-east Australia and New Zealand. The northern and eastern populations are migratory and birds generally move in a south-westerly direction in the autumn, to winter within its southern breeding range.

The Goldfinch is a resident breeding bird throughout much of Britain and Ireland but it is scarce in northern Scotland and absent as a breeding bird in the northern Isles. It decreased in Britain during the 19th century largely due to the popularity of keeping Goldfinches in cages. Its population increased throughout the second half of the 20th century largely due to laws making it illegal to catch and cage birds, and since the 1960s it has spread into northern Scotland. Many birds remain in Britain throughout the winter although some British-bred birds move onto the continent. They fly in a south-westerly direction moving into France and Spain with occasional birds reaching Morocco in north-west Africa. Movements generally take place from September to October and birds return in March and April. Some continental birds move through eastern Britain in the autumn and spring.

The Goldfinch is a bird of woodland edges, orchards, parks, groves and gardens. During the late summer numbers can often be found feeding on teasel *Dipscacus*, burdock *Arctium* and thistle *Cirsium* while in the winter they often feed in trees particularly alder *Alnus*, pine *Pinus* and birch *Betula*. It builds a closely knit, neat cup nest made of fine roots, moss, grass and cobwebs which it often places several metres up, well hidden behind leaves on the end of a branch, often in a fruit or other deciduous tree.

The adult Goldfinch has a red face, black crown and half-collar with the remainder of the head being white. It has a pale brown mantle and white rump. The wings are black with prominent white tips to the tertials and primaries and they have a distinctive broad yellow wing-bar. The tail is also black with large white spots. The underparts are white and it has pale brown flanks and a suggestion of two pale brown breast bands forming a suffusion on the upper breast. It has a long fine horn-white bill and pinkish brown legs. The sexes are similar in the field but males show more red behind the eye in the hand.

The Goldfinch is a common resident breeding bird in Leicestershire. It is a common resident at Swithland Reservoir breeding in small numbers. One pair were found breeding in 1978 and 1980. Occasionally large flocks can be found feeding in alders and birch trees on the margins of the reservoir: circa 200 were recorded on the 19th December 1964, and 100+ were seen on the 26th November and 12th December 1998, and also 4th and 5th January 1999, on this occasion feeding on burdock. During the winter months Goldfinches occasionally roost in the reservoir grounds, usually in an old Holly *Ilex* bush and 200 were recorded going to roost on the 23rd December 1979.

Eurasian Siskin *Carduelis spinus*

The Siskin breeds mainly across northern Europe with scattered populations throughout the remainder of Europe reaching the Mediterranean. It also occurs in Turkey and the Caucasus across into northern Iran. It has two separate populations in central Asia. In the west it can be found across western Siberia as far as the Yenisei River and in the east from Lake Baikal eastwards into northern Japan. The northerly and easterly populations are migratory with the western population wintering throughout Europe southward into north-west Africa and eastward into Asia Minor and the eastern population wintering in southern Japan, Korea and south-east China.

The Siskin is a resident breeding bird breeding over much of Scotland, Wales and Northern Ireland with scattered and more thinly distributed populations occurring in England and Southern Ireland. Since the mid-20th century its population has increased greatly in Britain and Ireland and it has expanded its range southward over much of the country and this is almost certainly due to the large-scale planting of conifers. Large numbers of birds winter in Britain, arriving from northern and eastern Europe in September and October, and they remain through the winter departing in April and early May. The Siskin's numbers fluctuate greatly from year to year and at times large irruptions take place.

In the mid-1960s this delightful little finch started to feed in gardens in Surrey on peanuts and fat and this habit spread throughout the country enabling birdwatchers to study this normally very arboreal species in detail. During 1989, a large irruption year, I caught and ringed 250 birds in my garden at Quorn from January through to late April. Over that period retrapped birds were seen to put on weight and many travelled long distances shortly after feeding in the garden. One bird was recovered in Northumberland, three in Scotland, one was found in southern Sweden and previously I caught a Siskin that had been ringed in Latvia. These recoveries give some indication of where wintering birds in Leicestershire are coming from. One bird was controlled in 1989 which I had ringed in 1986 showing that some birds are faithful to wintering areas.

The Siskin is a bird of coniferous forest particularly spruce *Picea* but it will also breed in fir *Abies* and pine *Pinus*. It normally places its small cup nest made of lichen covered twigs, moss, grass, cobwebs and root fibres very high up on the outer branches of a spruce or Pine. During the winter months it can most frequently be seen feeding on the seeds of alder *Alnus* and birch *Betula*.

The adult male Siskin has a black crown and chin, yellow face with green ear coverts, dark streaked olive-green mantle and yellow rump. It has black wings that show a large yellow wing-bar and a black forked tail with yellow basal feathers. The upper breast is yellow and the white belly and undertail coverts are streaked black. It has a greyish bill and flesh-brown legs. In winter its plumage becomes drabber and the black cap becomes mottled with grey feather edgings. The female is grey-green on the crown and mantle, which is dark streaked, and the rump is pale yellow, also with dark streaking. It has a pale yellow wing-bar and upper tail. The underparts are white with dark streaking and it shows a yellow wash on the upper breast.

In Leicestershire the Siskin is a fairly common to common winter visitor that is scarce but increasingly seen during the summer months. During 2000 a pair bred for the first time in Leicestershire, raising a brood of young in a cypress *Cupressus* at Newtown Linford. It is a common winter visitor at Swithland Reservoir that is occasionally seen during the summer. It has been recorded at the reservoir during every month except June. Three birds were seen on the 6th July 1997. Large numbers are occasionally recorded feeding in birch *Betula* and alder *Alnus* on the margins of the reservoir during the winter months. The largest flocks were 250 on the 23rd January 1951, and 155 on the 19th January 1986.

Common Linnet *Carduelis cannabina*

The Linnet breeds throughout much of Europe, being mainly absent from northern Scandinavia and Iceland. It occurs southward into north-west Africa. In Asia it can be found in Asia Minor across Turkey to the Caucasus and into Iran. It is also found across central western Siberia eastwards to the Yenisei River and southwards through Altai to Tien Shan. The northern and eastern populations are migratory, moving in a south-westerly direction, wintering mainly within or just to the south of its southern breeding range, while other populations are only partial migrants.

The Linnet is a resident breeding bird throughout much of Britain and Ireland. It is, however, thinly distributed in north-west Scotland and the northern Isles. It bred on Shetland for a few years from 1934 but has now disappeared and it has also gone from the Outer Hebrides. Some British-bred birds remain in the country throughout the winter while others move south-westwards into France and Spain after first crossing the English Channel into Belgium. Most birds leave Ireland in the winter, again moving south-westwards into France and Spain. Birds from northern Europe arrive in Britain during September and October and remain throughout the winter, leaving again in March and April.

The Linnet was a common and numerous species throughout much of Britain until the mid 1970s when there began a dramatic decline that is still continuing. Between 1970 and 1998 the British population has declined by 38%. This has probably been brought about by the changes in agriculture with the autumn sowing of cereals that has done away with many stubble fields on which the birds could feed. There has also been a large scale use of herbicides and insecticides which has done away with much of its food supply in the form of weed seeds and the chemicals appear to have affected its breeding success.

The Linnet is a bird of open country and it particularly likes scrub areas, heathland and woodland edges. It can also be seen in orchards, gardens and hedgerows and on agricultural land. It makes its bulky cup nest of twigs, grass, roots and moss and places it low down in a small bush or tree, a favoured bush being gorse *Ulex*. It occasionally nests close to the ground in Marram Grass *Ammophila arenaria* and rushes *Juncus* and frequently in accumulations of dead Bracken *Pteridium*.

The adult summer male Linnet has a crimson forehead and breast, greyish head and rich brown mantle. The black wings and tail have distinctive white edges to the feathers. The underparts show a white belly and undertail coverts with buff flanks. The bill is grey and the legs are brown. In winter the male loses much of its crimson coloration. The female is similar to the male but lacks the crimson patches on its head and breast and it has a streaked mantle and breast.

The Linnet is a common resident breeding bird in Leicestershire that becomes less frequent during the winter months. It was a common resident bird at Swithland Reservoir that bred in small numbers but in recent years it has declined markedly. During the breeding bird survey two pairs were found breeding in 1978 and one pair in 1979 and 1980. The largest recorded flocks were of circa 100 birds seen on the 19th September 1976 and the 17th October 1982.

Twite *Carduelis flavirostris*

In Europe the Twite, or Mountain Linnet, breeds in Britain, Ireland and Norway with small numbers in Sweden and Finland eastward onto the Kola Peninsula. In Asia it can be found in eastern Turkey, the Caucasus through to northern Iran and also on the mountains and high ground of eastern and central Asia.

The Twite of the race *C. f. pipilans* is a resident in Britain and Ireland breeding on the coast of northern and western Ireland, North Wales, the Lancashire mosses, the Lake District and parts of the Peak District and throughout much of northern Scotland, including the northern Isles. In the Outer Hebrides there is a separate race *C. f. bensonorum*. The Scottish and Irish birds are mainly sedentary although birds breeding on high ground in Scotland will move to the coast in winter. Some English birds especially those breeding in the Pennines move further afield, vacating their upland breeding grounds in autumn to winter on the east coast from Lincolnshire to northern Kent.

The Scandinavian and north-west Russian Twite of the nominate race *C. f. flavirostris* winter mainly around cities in Germany and around the coasts of southern Scandinavia, Poland and the low countries through to northern France. These birds have also been recorded on the east coast of Britain and other records have come from more central areas of Europe, from Hungary, Rumania and Spain.

The Twite has been declining in Britain since the 1970s and over the last 25 years it has declined by 41% according to the Common Bird Census. The reason for this decline is probably the deterioration of moorland habitat due to overgrazing and the changes in land use in upland areas with more land being taken for agriculture.

It is a bird of open ground which breeds on heather moorland, rocky coastal grassland, high rough pastureland and mountain scrub. It places its bulky nest of heather twigs, grass, roots and moss on or near the ground in vegetation like Heather *Calluna vulgaris* or Bilberry *Vaccinium myrtillus* but it will occasionally nest in cavities in dry stone walls. In October and November they move to sea coasts where they particularly favour the seeds of the Sea aster *Aster tripolium* and the glassworts *Salicornia sp.*. They start to return to their breeding sites in March and April.

The Twite is similar in size and shape to the Linnet but it has a longer, more deeply forked tail. The adult summer male Twite has buff-brown upperparts heavily streaked dark with a pink rump. It has dark wings that show a pale wing-bar and a dark tail that has pale feather edgings. The throat is buff-brown and the rest of the underparts are white, heavily streaked dark on the upper breast and flanks. It has brown legs and a light grey bill. The female lacks the pink rump and in winter both sexes have buffer underparts with less streaking and the bill turns yellow.

The Twite is a rare winter visitor and passage migrant to Leicestershire. It is a vagrant to Swithland Reservoir that has been recorded once, two birds being seen on the 11th March 1978.

Common Redpoll *Carduelis flammea*

The Redpoll breeds across northern Europe with small scattered populations occurring from Denmark southward as far as the Alps. It occurs throughout northern Asia right across Siberia reaching Kamchatka and Sakhalin Island in the east and its range continues across northern North America. The most northerly populations are migratory. These are mainly Asian and American birds whereas the western European birds are only partial migrants but all populations can be eruptive from time to time. Birds winter throughout much of central Europe, southern Japan, Korea and eastern China and across central North America.

The small dark subspecies of the Redpoll *C. f. cabaret* is a resident breeding bird throughout much of Britain and Ireland although it is only thinly distributed in some areas and is absent from Shetland. In Britain its numbers tend to fluctuate from year to year. In the mid 1800s *C. f. cabaret* was restricted to northern Britain, Ireland and the Alps. By the early 1900s it had started to spread in Britain, then its expansion was halted and its range contracted. From the mid-1950s its range expanded again and it spread throughout Britain and onto the continent colonising the Netherlands, Denmark, Belgium, Germany and southern Sweden by the 1970s and northern France by 1983. The reasons for its spread are probably closely linked to the conifer afforestation and before its recent fall 80% of this small sub-species population was to be found in Britain. Between 1970 and 1998, however, its numbers have declined again and the British population has fallen by 92%. This decline appears to be restricted to Britain. British birds tend to be sedentary or only partial migrants that leave Britain mainly when food is short.

Birds from Fenno-Scandinavia are larger and paler looking and are the nominate race *C. f. flammea*, often called the Mealy Redpoll. They reach Britain in October and November and remain throughout the winter, leaving from March to early May. Their numbers fluctuate greatly from year to year.

The Redpoll is a bird of scrub and woodland that occurs from prostrate willows *Salix* on Arctic Tundra through to birch *Betula* and alder *Alnus* woodland and even stands of pine *Pinus*. It places its untidy cup nest of twigs, leaf stems, roots and grass at varying heights in small bushes and trees. During the winter months it can often be found swinging upside down feeding on the seeds of birch and alder.

The adult male Redpoll *C. f. cabaret* has a crimson forehead with brown upperparts that are heavily streaked and a pinkish rump. The wings and tail are dark and it has a distinct pale wing-bar. The chin is black with varying amounts of pink on the breast and it has a buff wash and dark streaking on the flanks, the rest of the underparts being white. The upper mandible is dark and the lower yellow. The legs are dark brown. The female lacks the pink breast and rump; otherwise it looks very like the male.

The Redpoll is a fairly common winter visitor and passage migrant to Leicestershire in varying numbers and it is an uncommon breeding bird. It is a regular winter visitor and passage migrant at Swithland Reservoir with occasional birds remaining to breed. Breeding colonies were found at or near the reservoir during the period 1970 to 1973. On the 22nd June 1971, a large breeding colony was discovered in a young plantation of Norwegian Spruce *Picea abies* at Kinchley Hill Promontory and six nests were located at heights of between eight and 25 feet. Some of the young had already left their nests and were being fed by their parents. During June 1972 a large breeding colony again occupied this site. It was also proved breeding in 1975, 1979 and 1980 and display was noted in 1998. During the winter months birds can be found feeding in the birch and alders on the margins of the reservoir and occasionally large flocks can be seen: 40 were recorded in 1960 and on the 30th November 1997, and 50 were seen in the winter of 1968 and in late September 1961. A sizeable flock of 200 birds was recorded roosting in the pumping station grounds on the 13th February 1971.

N.B. Towards the end of 2000 the British Ornithologists' Union Records Committee split the Redpoll subspecies into two separate species, the Lesser Redpoll *Carduelis cabaret* and the Mealy Redpoll *Carduelis flammea*. The Lesser Redpoll has been proved to breed at Swithland in the past and has been present throughout the year. The Mealy Redpoll, however, is a winter visitor to Leicestershire that has occurred at Swithland Reservoir in small numbers. The status of both species at the site will now have to be reviewed.

Common Crossbill *Loxia curvirostra*

The Crossbill breeds in the boreal forest around the globe and it also occurs in southern areas in montane coniferous forests and more recently in conifer plantations. Scattered populations occur throughout much of Europe extending south to north-west Africa.

Scattered populations also occur throughout much of Britain and Ireland and it has expanded its range greatly since the 1920s helped by the large scale planting of conifers. They are an irruptive species and erratic in their breeding habits. After large-scale movements, if the conditions are favourable they will breed outside their normal range but they will also disappear from an area equally quickly. Irruptions have been noted in Britain since as early as 1251 and often when large immigrations are going to occur birds can be seen in the country as early as mid-June and they continue to arrive into August. These birds originate mainly from Fenno-Scandinavia and in large invasions many thousands, if not millions of birds flood into the country as happened in the last two major influxes in 1990 and 1997. These birds will very often stay throughout the winter and even remain to breed. It is a species that will breed throughout the year depending on food availability, but with a preference for nesting between January and May.

The Crossbill can be found in coniferous and mixed forest, in coniferous plantations and even in shelter belts. They are very thirsty birds and require areas of fresh water from which to drink. They have a distinctive heavy, cross-tipped bill that is highly adapted for the prising open of cones in order to get to the seed. They feed mainly on the seeds of spruce *Picea*, pine *Pinus* and larch *Larix*. The cup nest of pine twigs, grass, moss, lichen and wool is generally placed high up on the outer branches of a pine or close to the trunk in spruce.

The adult male Crossbill has crimson plumage with slightly darker wings and tail and white dark-streaked undertail-coverts. The mandibles cross near the tip and are grey-horn in colour. The bird has brown legs. The female has a mainly olive green-grey plumage, faintly streaked with a brighter yellow-green rump. The wings and forked tail are slightly darker.

The Crossbill is a rare irruptive visitor to Leicestershire and a very rare breeding bird. One of the favourite locations for Crossbills in Leicestershire was in the conifer plantation at Eye Brook Reservoir and I remember my first sightings there in the early 1960s. Two pairs bred at that locality in 1960 and it was also suspected of breeding in 1966-67. It is a rare visitor to Swithland Reservoir that has been recorded on twelve occasions. At Swithland most of the sightings come from around the pumping station grounds that hold large plantings of various species of conifer. Nearly all the records fall within a period from mid-September through to March with only one record falling outside: three birds were seen at the end of June 1997. The highest counts that were recorded are six on the 12th March 1994; seven on the 31st December 1942, and nine flying south over the reservoir on the 1st November 1992.

Eurasian Bullfinch *Pyrrhula pyrrhula*

The Bullfinch breeds throughout much of Europe but it is absent from large parts of the Iberian Peninsula and does not breed in Iceland. It occurs in a wide band across central Asia reaching Kamchatka in the north-east and southward to southern Japan, Manchuria and Korea. It can also be found in Asia Minor in Turkey and the Caucasus and a small fragmented population occurs in the Tien Shan Mountains. Throughout much of its range the Bullfinch is sedentary or only partially migratory with the northern breeding birds moving the furthest and occasionally it can be an irruptive species.

The Bullfinch breeds throughout much of Britain and Ireland being scarce only in the far north of Scotland and not breeding on Orkney or Shetland. Most British-bred Bullfinches are sedentary with few ringing recoveries over 25km. It expanded its range greatly in Britain and Ireland from the mid-1950s through to the mid-1970s. Between 1970 and 1998, however, the British population has shown a marked decline with its numbers falling by as much as 40%. It is interesting to note that the Bullfinch increased in numbers in the years that the Sparrowhawk was scarce and when their numbers recovered the Bullfinch declined dramatically. Over much of Europe its population has remained much the same with little change in range or numbers.

The Bullfinch can be found in a wide variety of habitats, garden, orchard, hedgerow, scrub, park, deciduous, mixed or coniferous woodland. In the fruit-growing areas of southern England it was considered a pest because birds would take the flower buds off the fruit trees in winter and spring, particularly pear *Pyrus*, plum *Prunus*, currant *Ribes*, cherry *Prunus* and apple *Malus*, but it is interesting to note that most damage was done in years when the ash *Fraxinus* seed crop failed. The Bullfinch makes a cup nest of grass, moss, lichen and roots that is supported by a loose platform of fine twigs that is placed in a bush or tree at varying heights.

The adult male Bullfinch has a black cap and chin, grey nape and mantle, white rump and blue-black wings and tail, the wings showing a distinctive white wing bar. The cheeks and much of the underparts are bright red merging into white on the undertail coverts. It has a small, thick-set black bill and brown legs. The female is similar in size and shape to the male but has greyish-brown underparts instead of red.

The Bullfinch is a common resident breeding bird in Leicestershire. It is a common resident at Swithland Reservoir that bred in small numbers but recently it has declined. One pair were found breeding in 1978, two pairs in 1979 and three pairs in 1980. Occasionally small flocks have been noted, the largest being 12 birds that were recorded on two occasions 13th January 1985, and 9th September 1990. 11 birds were seen together on the 5th January 1961.

Hawfinch *Coccothraustes coccothraustes*

The Hawfinch breeds over much of central and southern Europe extending southward to north-west Africa. Its range extends eastward in a thin band across central Asia to northern Japan. It also occurs in two isolated populations, in Kamchatka in eastern Siberia and in Afghanistan and the Tien Shan mountains in central Asia. It breeds in Asia Minor in northern Turkey and the Caucasus through to northern Iran. The northern and eastern populations are migratory, wintering in south-west Europe and Asia Minor, and in eastern Asia it winters in southern Japan, Korea and eastern China. It is a sedentary bird over much of central and southern Europe.

The Hawfinch is a resident breeding bird that is thinly distributed throughout much of England and Wales extending northward into southern Scotland. It has bred only once in Ireland, in Kildare in 1902. It is local in Wales and southern Scotland and it does not breed in Cornwall. Its main stronghold still appears to be in south-east England. During the mid-19th century it was restricted as a breeding bird to south-east England and the Midlands. From that time, however, it slowly spread its range and this expansion continued into the early part of the 20th century. It is an erratic species and its numbers have fluctuated in Britain throughout much of the 20th century. Since the 1963 winter it has declined markedly in Leicestershire and probably over much of Britain. During October and November a certain amount of immigration takes place, with birds arriving from north-east Europe. They probably remain throughout the winter and return in April. One of the few Continental ringing recoveries for this species came from Leicestershire. A female ringed at Stoughton Airport, Leicester, on the 20th April 1994, was recovered on the 24th April 1998, in Sokndal, Rogaland in southern Norway.

The Hawfinch is a bird of deciduous forest and it especially favours oak *Quercus* and hornbeam *Carpinus* woodland. It occurs in a wide variety of broadleaf woodland habitats, feeding on the seeds of hornbeam, beech *Fagus*, ash *Fraxinus*, elm *Ulmus* hawthorn *Crataegus* and cherry *Prunus* and it can occasionally be found in coniferous forest. It also occurs in parkland, garden and orchard. It places its bulky cup nest of twigs, roots and stems on a horizontal branch or near the trunk of a tree or bush several metres up. The best way of finding Hawfinch is to listen for their sharp explosive "tzick" call note in the early spring before the leaves have unfurled.

The Hawfinch is a large finch with a stout conical bill and short square-cut tail. The head is brown and it has thin black lores, a black line around the bill and black bib. The nape is grey and it has a dark brown back with a paler brown tail that is white tipped. The wings show a large white wing patch and distinctive blue-black inner primaries, curved at the tip. The underparts are pinkish brown that merge into white on the undertail coverts. It has a blue-grey bill and flesh-brown legs. The sexes are similar but the female shows pale edges to the secondaries. The bill becomes paler in the autumn turning to ivory-yellow.

The Hawfinch is an elusive scarce resident in Leicestershire. Throughout much of the 1940s and 1950s it was frequently recorded on Charnwood Forest especially around Quorn House Park, Swithland Wood, The Brand and in the vicinity of Swithland Church, which lies in close proximity to the reservoir. Most of these populations died out during the early 1960s and there were few records on the Charnwood Forest after that time. As already stated it is a very elusive bird that is easily overlooked. There have been two records at Swithland Reservoir. A pair with two immature birds were seen in the waterworks grounds in

August 1974, and one has to wonder whether these birds bred in the area. The latest sighting was of five birds flying over Rabbits Bridge on the 7th October 1995.

BUNTINGS Emberizidae

Snow Bunting *Plectrophenax nivalis*

The Snow Bunting is the most northerly nesting land bird, breeding around the globe on barren open tundra along the edges of the Arctic Ocean. Its range extends southward where it breeds on high mountain tops in Scandinavia and Scotland and on old volcanic lava flows in Kamchatka . Most populations are migratory, wintering across central Europe and Asia from the east coast of England in the west through to northern Japan in the east and across central North America. It is only a partial migrant in Scotland and Iceland moving from high ground in summer to lower altitudes in winter.

In Britain the Snow Bunting breeds only on the high mountain peaks of northern Scotland with the main population concentrated around the Cairngorms. The British population is circa 85 breeding pairs but its numbers fluctuate from one year to another. During the latter part of the 19th century and the beginning of the 20th century it bred quite widely on the mountains of northern Scotland from Sutherland to Perthshire including Ben Nevis, but throughout much of the 20th century it has been restricted to the Cairngorms, although in recent years its numbers have been rising. During the winter months it can be found over much of northern Scotland, the east coast of England southward to Kent and on the coast of Ireland. The number of birds wintering in Britain varies greatly from year to year. Birds arrive on the wintering grounds during October and November and depart again in March and April.

During the summer it can be found breeding on treeless rocky tundra, sea cliffs, high barren mountain tops, rocky areas adjacent to snowfields and glaciers and in Greenland it nests on nunataks, which are isolated rock peaks protruding above the icecap. It nests in holes and crevices amongst rocks and boulders and in crevices in sea cliffs among seabirds and, where available, it will breed in holes in buildings. In winter it can be found on seashores especially along shingle and sandy beaches and on saltmarsh. It also occurs on moorland and stubble fields in western Europe. In eastern Europe and across Asia it can be found on steppe grassland and in North America on the prairies.

The adult male summer Snow Bunting has a white head and underparts, black mantle, whitish rump and a black tail with white outer feathers. Much of the wing is white which contrasts with the black outer primaries, tertials, scapulars and bastard wing. The bill and legs are black. The female has a grey-brown head and a brown mantle, back and rump with varying amounts of dark streaking. Otherwise it is similar to the male. In winter both sexes have pale buff-ochre heads and upperparts with dark streaking and they have buff neck patches and flanks, the rest of the underparts being white. The wings become slightly darker and on both sexes the bill becomes yellow with a black tip.

The Snow Bunting is a rare winter visitor to Leicestershire. It is a rare vagrant to Swithland Reservoir that has been recorded once. Between 10 and 20 birds were present on the 17th January 1960.

Yellowhammer *Emberiza citrinella*

The Yellowhammer breeds throughout much of Europe but it is absent from most of the Iberian Peninsula and it does not breed in Iceland. It can be found in northern and central Asia across western Siberia eastward, reaching the Lena River and Lake Baikal in Central Siberia. The Yellowhammer was introduced into New Zealand in the second half of the 19th century it now flourishes on both islands. It is sedentary or only a partial migrant over much of its range but the most north-easterly populations are migratory and move south-westwards in the autumn. Most winter within the bird's southern breeding range except in Asia where it winters in the Caucasus and Iran and in Kazakhstan and the western Tien Shan Mountains.

The Yellowhammer is a resident breeding species throughout Britain and Ireland, being absent only from the Outer Hebrides and Shetland. Most British bred birds are sedentary with few recoveries over 50km but in the winter the upland breeding populations move to lower ground. Birds from northern Europe move south in September and October and a few reach Britain's east coast. Some probably pass straight through, while others may remain to winter. Between 1970 and 1998 the Yellowhammer population in Britain has decreased by 43%. The reasons for the decline are probably linked to the changes in agriculture, particularly the autumn planting of cereals that does away with stubble land on which the birds would have fed during the winter months. Also the large-scale use of herbicides and insecticides kills weeds and insects which would have been an important source of food.

The Yellowhammer is a bird of open woodland, scrubland, heath and moorland and it can be found on a variety of agricultural land where it particularly likes old hedgerows and rough grassland. It makes a cup nest of grass, leaves and plant stems which it places on or close to the ground in tall grass or herbage or low down in brambles, small bushes and trees. During the spring the male can be seen singing its well-known wheezy song from the top of a small tree, bush or fence post. It is often described by country folk as 'little bit of bread and no cheese'.

The summer adult male Yellowhammer has a bright yellow head and throat with small amounts of dark streaking on the crown and ear coverts. The back is chestnut, heavily streaked dark and the rump bright chestnut, the tail being dark brown. The underparts are lemon yellow with a chestnut suffusion on the upper breast and flanks and small amounts of dark flecking. The bill is grey and the legs flesh-brown. The female is similar to the male but has heavier dark streaking on the breast and flanks and darker streaking on the head. In winter the male becomes more like the female but still retains more yellow on the head.

The Yellowhammer is a common to abundant resident breeding bird in Leicestershire. It is a common resident bird at Swithland reservoir that breeds in small numbers on the margins. Over the last decade its numbers have declined. One pair was found nesting during the breeding bird survey in 1978 and 1979. During the winter months large flocks have occasionally been recorded on the adjacent farmland. The largest of these were 50 seen on the 3rd December 1967, and circa 200 on the 10th February 1988.

Common Reed Bunting *Emberiza schoeniclus*

The Reed Bunting breeds throughout much of Europe, although it is absent from Iceland and only sparsely distributed in southern Europe. It does, however, reach southward into north-west Africa where there is a small population. Its range extends eastward over much of northern and central Asia reaching northern Japan and isolated populations occur in Kamchatka and Asia Minor. Birds from central and southern Europe, the Caucasus and central southern Asia are mainly sedentary. The northern and eastern populations are migratory, wintering throughout central and southern Europe southward to north-west Africa. In Asia it winters in Turkey, the Caucasus east to Iran and in Pakistan and north-west India. In the east it can be found in southern Japan, Korea and north-west and south-east China.

The Reed Bunting is a resident breeding bird throughout Britain and Ireland that spread its range to Shetland in 1949. Most British-bred birds are sedentary and only small numbers leave the country. Some birds from northern and eastern Europe winter in Britain and others pass along the east coast heading southwards to France and Spain. Wintering and passage birds arrive from mid-September through to early November and return again mainly from March to early May. During the 1960s the Reed Bunting started to breed in drier habitats and so locally expanded its range. At about the same time it also started to feed regularly in gardens. Between 1970 and 1998, however, it has declined markedly in Britain by as much as 52%. The reasons for this decline are not fully understood but it seems likely to be linked to agricultural intensification and the drainage of wetland habitat.

The Reed Bunting can be found on the margins of lakes, rivers, gravel pits and reservoirs. It can also be seen on salt-marsh, fen and bog. It breeds in reedbeds, wet meadows, wet birch *Betula*, alder *Alnus* and willow *Salix* scrub and other tall herbage on the edges of water. Its cup nest made of grass, sedge and moss is placed on or close to the ground in sedges *Carex* and reeds *Phragmites* or a few metres up in small trees such as willows.

The adult summer male Reed Bunting has a black head and large black bib separated by a white moustachial stripe and it has a white collar across the nape. The back and wings are rich chestnut-brown heavily streaked black. It has a dark-streaked grey rump and a black tail with white margins on the outer tail feathers. The underparts are dirty-white with fine dark streaking on the flanks. The bill is grey and the legs are flesh-brown. The female is similar to the male but has a brown dark-streaked head, white and dark moustachial stripes, white throat and brown rump and heavier, dark streaking on the flanks. In winter the male looks similar to the female but he still retains some dark feathering on the head and bib.

The Reed bunting is a common resident breeding bird in Leicestershire that has recently declined in numbers. It is a common resident at Swithland Reservoir that breeds around the margins in small numbers, although in recent years it has declined. During the breeding bird survey ten pairs were found breeding in both 1978 and 1979 and seven pairs in 1980. During a bird survey carried out around the margins of the reservoir on 7th June 1981, 14 singing males were recorded. Occasionally birds can be found roosting in the Bulrush *Typha latifolia* on the reservoir margins, the highest count being 40 in January 1988. The largest number recorded at the site was 100 on the 22nd March 1973.

Corn Bunting *Miliaria calandra*

The Corn Bunting breeds across southern and central Europe southward into North Africa. In Asia it can be found throughout Turkey and the Caucasus eastwards into Iraq and Iran. A separate population occurs in northern Afghanistan north-eastwards into Kazakhstan and western China. It is a resident or partial migrant that winters mainly within its breeding range.

The Corn Bunting is a resident breeding bird in Britain and Ireland. It can be found throughout much of England but it has become scarce in the south-west since the 1930s. Its range started to contract in Wales during the 1920s and by 1945 it had disappeared from much of the country. A similar range contraction has taken place in Scotland since the 1930s and now it is restricted mainly to coastal areas. The Corn Bunting was a widespread species in Ireland at the beginning of the 20th century and could be found breeding in most counties but since that time it has declined dramatically and is now on the verge of extinction. British-bred Corn Bunting tend to be resident with very few ringing recoveries over 15km. Between 1970 and 1998 its population in Britain has declined by 85% and it is now under serious threat. This decline has not been restricted to Britain and Ireland as many other European countries in the north of the bird's range have also been affected and they have also seen populations fall markedly. The reasons for this decline appear to be linked to agricultural intensification particularly the autumn sowing of cereals, which leaves no fields of stubble on which the birds can feed during the winter months. The greater use of insecticides and herbicides has also diminished other food sources. Another major factor is that autumn-sown crops are harvested earlier, probably resulting in the destruction of many nests because the Corn Bunting is a late breeder with the eggs being laid only in June and July.

The Corn Bunting is a bird of open agricultural country that requires a few trees, bushes, fence posts or telephone wires from which to sing. The song of the Corn Bunting has often been described as the sound made by jangling keys. In areas where the birds breed the males can easily be located on their song posts. If they are watched over a period of time they can be seen to fly short distances, singing as they go, feet dangling with a fluttering flight to a nearby perch. The pair bond is not good in Corn Buntings and the males are quite often polygamous. The female regularly raises the young with little or no help from her mate. The loose untidy cup nest of grass roots and straw is placed on or near the ground in grass, crops or herbage or sometimes low down in brambles or a bush.

The Corn Bunting is heavily built and the largest European bunting. It has greyish-brown upperparts that are streaked dark. The underparts are buff-white and show dark malar stripes on the throat, fine dark streaking on the upper breast and flanks and a dark cluster of streaks on the centre of the breast that looks like a dark spot at a distance. The large bill has a grey upper mandible and yellow lower. The legs are flesh brown, both sexes having similar plumage.

The Corn Bunting was a common resident breeding bird in Leicestershire that has declined markedly in recent years. It seems hard to believe now that during the late 1970s a flock of between 30 and 40 birds roosted regularly in rank grassland on flood meadows in the Wreake Valley and they were a familiar sight during the late autumn and winter months. The Corn Bunting has been recorded on two occasions at Swithland Reservoir. Both were singing males, one being seen on the 20th April 1979, and the other recorded in 1982. The Corn Bunting almost certainly bred on farmland adjacent to the reservoir, but like so many formerly common birds it has probably been under-recorded.

5. EXOTIC SPECIES

Over the years several species of birds have been recorded at Swithland Reservoir that have clearly been escapes from captivity.

Fulvous Whistling Duck *Dendrocygna bicolor*

The Fulvous Whistling Duck is a cosmopolitan tropical species. Four birds were seen at Swithland Reservoir on 12th October 1992, and they commuted between Cropston and Swithland Reservoirs. Three were still together on 25th October and two on the 28th November. They were initially recorded at Cropston Reservoir from 30th September to 12th October.

Black Swan *Cygnus atratus*

A native of Australia. One bird was recorded at Swithland Reservoir on 19th March 2000.

South African Shelduck *Tadorna cana*

A resident of South Africa, often called the Cape Shelduck. One bird was present between the 12th and 26th September 1999. It commuted regularly between Swithland and Cropston Reservoirs.

Ringed Teal *Callonetta leucophrys*

A native of southern South America. Two males were present at Swithland Reservoir on 17th March 1992.

Chiloe Wigeon *Anas sibilatrix*

Another native of southern South America. There have been two records at Swithland Reservoir: one bird was present on 15th September 1974, and a male on the 28th April 1998.

African Yellow-bill *Anas undulata*

A resident of Africa. One bird was present at Swithland Reservoir from 17th April 1982, to the 8th January 1983, when it was shot dead.

Pintail Sp.

A bird showing characteristics of either Eaton's Pintail *Anas eatoni* or Crozet Pintail *Anas drygalskii* was seen on Swithland Reservoir on 25th November 1992. These two closely allied species are considered by some authorities to be conspecific. They are natives of Kerguelen and Crozet Islands in the Southern Ocean.

Blue-winged Teal *Anas discors*

A North American species that winters in South America. This species is a regular annual vagrant to Britain. A single bird was recorded at Swithland Reservoir on the 25th July 1985. This bird was very tame.

Falcon Sp.

A juvenile falcon considered by the observer to be either a Saker Falcon *Falco cherrug* or a Lanner Falcon *Falco biarmicus* was observed on the 24th August 1988.

Budgerigar *Melopsittacus undulatus*

A native of Australia. It has been recorded at Swithland Reservoir on two occasions. One bird was recorded on 31st July 1985, and the other between the 5th and 7th September 1991. The feathers of a Budgerigar were found under a Tawny Owl roosting tree in 1986.

Zebra Finch *Taeniopygia guttata*

Another native of Australia. One was recorded at Swithland Reservoir on 21st May 1983.

6. WILDFOWL COUNTS

Since 1947 wildfowl counts have been undertaken in Britain at sites of large waterfowl concentrations. From 1952 they were carried out under the auspices of the Wildfowl Trust. At present, WeBs which is a partnership between the British Trust for Ornithology, the Royal Society for the Protection of Birds, the Wildfowl and Wetlands Trust and the Joint Nature Conservation Committee run the scheme and publish the results. Major waters are counted on specified dates once each month from September to March. The figures collected enable ornithologists to monitor the size of waterfowl populations, trends in numbers and distribution, and to identify and monitor important sites for waterfowl.

In 1967 the counting of ducks across Europe, North Africa and parts of Asia was started by the International Waterfowl Research Bureau which has its headquarters at Slimbridge in Gloucestershire. This scheme has expanded over the years and now covers much of the Palearctic region. Since waterfowl are highly mobile and logistics difficult, international counts are only carried out twice each winter, once in November and once in January.

These two schemes enable ornithologists to monitor waterfowl populations. In Leicestershire the wildfowl counts have been undertaken by volunteers who are mainly members of the Leicestershire and Rutland Ornithological Society. The results are published each year in their Newsletter and by WeBs.

I have extracted the counts made at Swithland Reservoir of nine common species of waterfowl. These figures were taken from the Leicestershire and Rutland Ornithological Societies Annual Reports and Newsletters and cover the period from September 1960 to March 2000. The charts show all counts made during the period and where 'N/C' is shown in a column this means no count was undertaken. Each decade's monthly figures have been averaged out and the graph shows the last four decade's average monthly counts side by side.

Great Crested Grebe: Yearly Counts

	Sept	Oct	Nov	Dec	Jan	Feb	March
1960-61	28	0	0	0	20	25	30
1961-62	28	0	35	N/C	1	28	35
1962-63	N/C	N/C	N/C	N/C	N/C	N/C	N/C
1963-64	N/C	N/C	N/C	N/C	N/C	N/C	N/C
1964-65	37	6	8	N/C	3	5	12
1965-66	0	18	6	3	7	0	0
1966-67	N/C	N/C	N/C	N/C	6	10	12
1967-68	50	37	46	19	0	40	32
1968-69	16	N/C	17	N/C	3	12	8
1969-70	38	28	28	10	4	4	12
Average	28.1	14.8	20	8	5.5	15.5	17.6
1970-71	15	38	26	14	4	8	24
1971-72	N/C	44	9	12	6	10	10
1972-73	2	2	1	3	1	0	N/C
1973-74	4	N/C	4	6	5	6	8
1974-75	12	N/C	7	5	0	4	7
1975-76	11	10	21	8	2	6	6
1976-77	2	5	0	0	0	4	2
1977-78	14	9	32	11	20	5	14
1978-79	15	26	12	16	0	0	19
1979-80	11	23	23	26	1	12	23
Average	9.5	19.6	13.5	10.1	3.9	5.5	12.5
1980-81	35	34	44	49	39	55	34
1981-82	46	54	52	9	0	17	51
1982-83	32	44	42	42	19	37	27
1983-84	29	27	37	19	32	21	31
1984-85	29	42	62	75	0	0	15
1985-86	37	45	23	21	6	0	15
1986-87	25	18	30	12	0	14	14
1987-88	7	11	15	1	11	13	8
1988-89	19	21	24	5	8	16	13
1989-90	37	56	58	26	14	15	11
Average	29.6	35.2	38.7	25.9	12.9	18.8	21.9
1990-91	49	93	18	7	19	0	3
1991-92	21	40	14	1	5	4	9
1992-93	8	13	7	16	8	2	8
1993-94	12	14	5	12	12	14	8
1994-95	17	8	12	17	11	18	11
1995-96	3	9	18	4	2	2	2
1996-97	36	N/C	4	3	0	1	3
1997-98	39	33	23	7	17	7	6
1998-99	47	74	57	N/C	18	11	14
1999-2000	23	38	12	28	29	25	16
Average	25.5	35.8	17	10.5	12.1	8.4	8

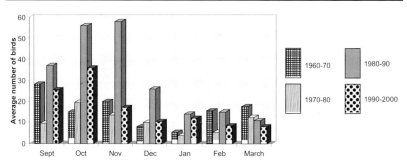

Eurasian Wigeon: Yearly Count

	Sept	Oct	Nov	Dec	Jan	Feb	March
1960-61	0	N/C	0	0	2	40	7
1961-62	0	0	4	0	10	100	20
1962-63	0	2	15	0	30	100	10
1963-64	0	3	0	3	0	0	0
1964-65	0	2	0	0	45	160	200
1965-66	0	0	0	11	50	0	0
1966-67	N/C	N/C	N/C	N/C	87	30	138
1967-68	0	0	2	0	18	250	0
1968-69	0	N/C	12	N/C	11	170	33
1969-70	0	0	1	40	0	275	370
Average	**0**	**1**	**3.8**	**6.7**	**25.3**	**112.5**	**77.8**
1970-71	0	0	6	8	21	0	33
1971-72	N/C	0	0	7	109	55	0
1972-73	0	0	0	13	37	0	N/C
1973-74	0	N/C	0	0	1	306	65
1974-75	0	N/C	12	0	6	0	0
1975-76	30	0	0	0	19	0	0
1976-77	0	28	17	85	385	182	0
1977-78	7	20	106	110	115	2	6
1978-79	0	12	25	308	42	4	25
1979-80	0	2	47	8	4	42	175
Average	**4.1**	**7.7**	**21.3**	**53.9**	**73.9**	**59.1**	**33.8**
1980-81	11	28	80	0	464	251	164
1981-82	13	68	207	20	0	496	341
1982-83	20	77	27	286	375	564	180
1983-84	0	1	69	144	0	528	30
1984-85	9	81	25	27	0	0	319
1985-86	17	28	48	12	1156	23	1
1986-87	0	13	142	182	392	1664	893
1987-88	0	9	9	29	113	270	489
1988-89	82	114	45	10	141	253	289
1989-90	15	120	18	5	194	421	160
Average	**16.7**	**53.9**	**67**	**71.5**	**283.5**	**447**	**286.6**
1990-91	38	91	8	47	452	64	10
1991-92	7	116	14	0	421	3	0
1992-93	0	2	174	163	80	24	19
1993-94	1	34	19	34	109	0	0
1994-95	160	65	343	0	105	63	0
1995-96	60	253	254	89	765	805	950
1996-97	139	N/C	26	77	0	403	346
1997-98	160	168	64	128	68	72	383
1998-99	60	270	32	N/C	122	32	3
1999-2000	93	53	57	9	3	64	0
Average	**71.8**	**116.9**	**99.1**	**60.8**	**212.5**	**153**	**171.1**

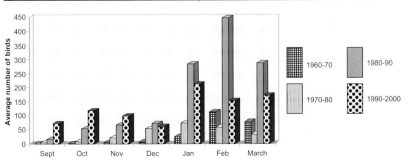

Common Teal: Yearly Counts

	Sept	Oct	Nov	Dec	Jan	Feb	March
1960-61	0	N/C	50	20	0	65	7
1961-62	0	5	35	0	120	40	60
1962-63	N/C	2	0	0	100	20	10
1963-64	5	0	0	0	0	10	0
1964-65	16	6	30	0	40	105	44
1965-66	0	10	8	55	11	0	0
1966-67	N/C	N/C	N/C	N/C	18	43	18
1967-68	0	12	22	19	2	0	4
1968-69	8	N/C	14	N/C	2	87	0
1969-70	0	14	28	12	5	24	4
Average	**3.6**	**7**	**20.8**	**13.2**	**29.8**	**39.4**	**14.7**
1970-71	33	20	25	8	22	12	16
1971-72	N/C	12	6	42	26	10	25
1972-73	15	15	42	46	9	6	N/C
1973-74	6	N/C	0	14	25	6	2
1974-75	18	N/C	24	12	32	8	0
1975-76	17	63	92	75	69	60	49
1976-77	35	265	150	325	725	170	6
1977-78	50	101	38	156	47	19	14
1978-79	19	48	23	97	115	16	8
1979-80	70	16	8	12	20	2	0
Average	**29.2**	**67.5**	**40.8**	**78.7**	**109**	**30.9**	**13.3**
1980-81	5	4	37	4	55	138	2
1981-82	32	104	111	82	54	29	8
1982-83	53	76	97	12	170	24	2
1983-84	0	7	19	12	19	57	7
1984-85	36	84	37	25	16	62	8
1985-86	11	10	16	41	178	60	36
1986-87	19	86	44	19	195	70	6
1987-88	29	31	41	111	75	20	29
1988-89	27	40	24	47	71	22	21
1989-90	23	101	98	49	39	17	0
Average	**23.5**	**54.3**	**52.4**	**40.2**	**87.2**	**49.9**	**11.9**
1990-91	197	179	84	173	285	38	16
1991-92	89	81	140	31	128	74	29
1992-93	32	35	29	32	42	0	19
1993-94	51	14	0	12	6	0	6
1994-95	92	45	55	47	6	32	0
1995-96	98	27	121	170	94	165	26
1996-97	81	N/C	168	83	0	226	40
1997-98	81	44	22	10	7	4	0
1998-99	79	52	7	N/C	6	4	0
1999-2000	92	32	2	0	45	3	2
Average	**89.2**	**56.5**	**62.8**	**62**	**61.9**	**54.6**	**13.8**

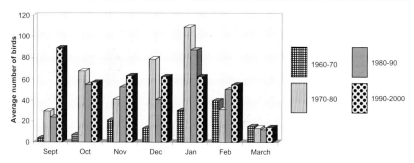

Mallard: Yearly Counts

	Sept	Oct	Nov	Dec	Jan	Feb	March
1960-61	260	N/C	400	150	60	75	40
1961-62	N/C	220	265	N/C	150	100	130
1962-63	N/C	150	60	25	400	200	50
1963-64	75	300	150	150	25	150	100
1964-65	118	230	150	N/C	313	103	44
1965-66	N/C	251	74	700	125	N/C	N/C
1966-67	N/C	N/C	N/C	N/C	350	215	158
1967-68	10	208	183	95	300	225	133
1968-69	92	N/C	192	N/C	333	415	42
1969-70	89	160	230	150	326	320	43
Average	**107.3**	**217**	**189.3**	**211.7**	**238.2**	**200.3**	**82.2**
1970-71	141	425	490	450	170	163	151
1971-72	N/C	195	189	200	256	235	44
1972-73	70	157	170	465	432	235	N/C
1973-74	36	N/C	460	335	300	255	105
1974-75	140	N/C	325	380	574	105	36
1975-76	205	250	115	375	445	195	53
1976-77	75	300	375	650	610	346	165
1977-78	723	350	430	733	355	295	58
1978-79	532	425	227	620	767	116	56
1979-80	125	345	291	145	241	56	20
Average	**227.4**	**305.9**	**307.2**	**435.3**	**415**	**200.1**	**76.4**
1980-81	119	23	191	188	272	95	32
1981-82	225	263	369	407	214	97	37
1982-83	204	273	196	84	276	179	18
1983-84	125	32	99	68	37	84	22
1984-85	568	387	171	81	208	146	19
1985-86	88	88	160	105	280	227	27
1986-87	60	163	100	79	407	101	12
1987-88	35	47	32	245	40	11	21
1988-89	95	121	44	52	40	21	19
1989-90	75	107	22	34	31	14	13
Average	**159.4**	**150.4**	**138.4**	**134.3**	**180.5**	**97.5**	**22**
1990-91	128	63	61	71	74	57	19
1991-92	68	48	142	91	37	52	41
1992-93	196	57	36	21	50	32	28
1993-94	91	27	28	31	27	27	26
1994-95	84	167	224	81	56	57	79
1995-96	106	101	111	61	68	73	53
1996-97	133	N/C	94	110	58	100	64
1997-98	113	50	104	60	40	58	61
1998-99	129	63	51	N/C	40	53	29
1999-2000	92	77	68	57	65	59	48
Average	**114**	**72.5**	**91.9**	**64.8**	**51.5**	**56.8**	**44.8**

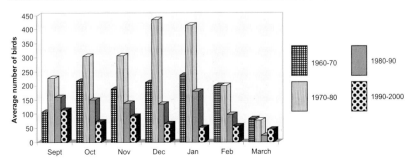

Northern Shoveler: Yearly Counts

	Sept	Oct	Nov	Dec	Jan	Feb	March
1960-61	0	0	7	10	0	2	2
1961-62	N/C	0	0	N/C	0	0	3
1962-63	0	0	0	0	6	0	0
1963-64	0	0	6	0	0	0	0
1964-65	0	0	17	0	0	1	0
1965-66	0	0	0	7	0	0	0
1966-67	N/C	N/C	N/C	N/C	2	0	0
1967-68	0	1	0	0	0	0	0
1968-69	6	N/C	8	N/C	3	0	1
1969-70	6	0	16	0	85	0	0
Average	**1.5**	**0.1**	**6**	**2.4**	**9.6**	**0.3**	**0.6**
1970-71	0	6	29	65	11	3	8
1971-72	N/C	4	74	90	38	24	0
1972-73	5	8	6	10	0	12	N/C
1973-74	17	N/C	25	6	0	16	6
1974-75	45	N/C	65	48	54	20	2
1975-76	18	27	6	27	24	18	8
1976-77	12	61	27	32	23	22	4
1977-78	20	76	45	43	18	29	24
1978-79	33	38	14	16	3	0	0
1979-80	36	18	47	3	8	4	6
Average	**20.7**	**29.7**	**33.8**	**34**	**17.9**	**14.8**	**6.4**
1980-81	12	18	11	8	17	0	28
1981-82	2	17	19	8	2	2	4
1982-83	26	28	24	2	22	4	9
1983-84	1	32	48	27	6	39	29
1984-85	2	8	61	27	68	40	3
1985-86	13	9	28	22	33	3	12
1986-87	88	81	12	3	0	3	0
1987-88	12	17	22	0	0	0	0
1988-89	56	55	0	9	1	6	14
1989-90	33	95	2	1	0	0	5
Average	**24.5**	**36**	**22.7**	**10.7**	**14.9**	**9.7**	**10.4**
1990-91	67	72	56	0	15	4	9
1991-92	120	181	39	4	2	14	12
1992-93	179	10	0	0	2	4	13
1993-94	48	65	1	0	0	0	2
1994-95	158	102	41	11	0	5	0
1995-96	74	64	104	76	0	4	0
1996-97	98	N/C	1	0	0	0	0
1997-98	116	82	17	4	0	15	2
1998-99	51	36	3	N/C	2	1	0
1999-2000	184	203	1	0	0	0	0
Average	**109.5**	**90.5**	**26.3**	**10.5**	**2.1**	**4.7**	**3.8**

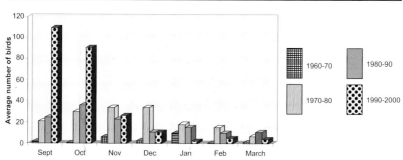

Common Pochard: Yearly Counts

	Sept	Oct	Nov	Dec	Jan	Feb	March
1960-61	0	N/C	14	50	2	0	12
1961-62	0	18	9	0	0	20	36
1962-63	0	2	20	0	0	0	30
1963-64	0	45	80	60	11	80	40
1964-65	0	8	175	0	192	186	139
1965-66	0	0	83	32	45	0	0
1966-67	N/C	N/C	N/C	N/C	54	19	31
1967-68	25	12	69	162	70	145	35
1968-69	0	N/C	27	N/C	41	197	28
1969-70	18	64	81	180	34	228	35
Average	4.8	21.3	62	60.5	44.9	87.5	38.6
1970-71	29	35	115	70	58	28	8
1971-72	N/C	60	57	66	158	146	27
1972-73	43	0	79	179	92	220	N/C
1973-74	124	N/C	90	27	31	157	40
1974-75	55	N/C	50	217	137	88	0
1975-76	65	74	56	83	108	89	14
1976-77	2	51	35	0	435	400	3
1977-78	34	65	55	129	109	110	53
1978-79	43	65	142	165	150	3	14
1979-80	49	27	35	56	8	83	8
Average	49.3	47.1	71.4	99.2	128.6	132.4	18.5
1980-81	3	21	50	53	78	55	40
1981-82	70	60	113	97	17	135	40
1982-83	27	12	34	11	59	70	40
1983-84	26	61	80	285	157	115	42
1984-85	8	24	81	0	57	67	19
1985-86	9	9	5	1	42	103	14
1986-87	35	23	29	24	21	69	39
1987-88	5	16	4	37	40	13	9
1988-89	7	11	0	29	114	5	1
1989-90	99	303	7	108	15	36	13
Average	28.9	54	40.3	64.5	60	66.8	25.7
1990-91	14	48	12	7	30	182	7
1991-92	25	167	47	6	100	102	13
1992-93	53	150	49	116	121	62	9
1993-94	31	23	6	25	50	1	6
1994-95	33	19	32	120	54	23	0
1995-96	37	130	34	27	245	335	61
1996-97	12	N/C	51	52	0	85	13
1997-98	50	15	28	33	21	21	11
1998-99	48	4	10	N/C	39	24	3
1999-2000	13	18	17	32	56	39	14
Average	31.6	63.8	28.6	46.4	71.6	87.4	13.7

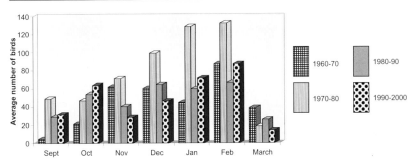

Tufted Duck: Yearly Counts

	Sept	Oct	Nov	Dec	Jan	Feb	March
1960-61	8	N/C	21	60	14	20	40
1961-62	0	9	1	0	10	40	20
1962-63	0	15	10	0	0	0	30
1963-64	5	0	4	20	0	20	10
1964-65	18	14	10	0	59	35	68
1965-66	0	8	12	17	81	0	0
1966-67	N/C	N/C	N/C	N/C	56	41	65
1967-68	32	4	34	54	180	59	22
1968-69	20	N/C	26	N/C	22	185	24
1969-70	27	25	34	60	11	200	60
Average	**12.2**	**10.7**	**16.9**	**26.3**	**43.3**	**60**	**33.9**
1970-71	31	22	35	45	45	65	116
1971-72	N/C	36	26	57	52	36	57
1972-73	25	55	89	110	105	125	N/C
1973-74	120	N/C	168	38	175	148	95
1974-75	160	N/C	88	170	319	77	63
1975-76	255	76	135	147	90	104	53
1976-77	15	38	6	4	6	57	74
1977-78	52	74	134	73	78	95	72
1978-79	79	55	65	104	75	5	85
1979-80	90	35	75	117	33	76	55
Average	**91.9**	**48.9**	**82.1**	**86.5**	**97.8**	**78.8**	**74.4**
1980-81	78	58	64	55	125	106	83
1981-82	42	32	51	18	5	63	133
1982-83	69	17	51	30	83	63	128
1983-84	90	98	66	47	28	66	55
1984-85	22	18	61	48	0	28	42
1985-86	95	46	93	126	167	481	116
1986-87	59	84	97	86	46	46	59
1987-88	103	48	50	74	57	52	49
1988-89	140	98	76	63	66	89	214
1989-90	164	114	29	101	11	38	54
Average	**86.2**	**61.3**	**63.8**	**64.8**	**58.8**	**103.2**	**93.3**
1990-91	94	54	43	29	98	196	68
1991-92	96	76	25	13	41	100	72
1992-93	140	97	28	34	57	73	62
1993-94	253	55	41	53	38	51	61
1994-95	114	45	96	169	61	58	48
1995-96	118	151	87	57	122	71	31
1996-97	301	N/C	48	50	0	61	92
1997-98	91	54	100	147	92	92	99
1998-99	110	102	60	N/C	74	50	66
1999-2000	122	81	42	33	55	53	45
Average	**143.9**	**79.4**	**57**	**65**	**63.8**	**80.5**	**64.4**

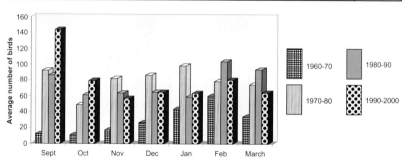

Common Goldeneye: Yearly Counts

	Sept	Oct	Nov	Dec	Jan	Feb	March
1960-61	0	0	3	3	0	6	2
1961-62	0	0	4	0	0	0	12
1962-63	0	0	3	0	0	0	4
1963-64	0	0	0	5	0	3	7
1964-65	0	0	0	0	0	7	3
1965-66	0	0	0	0	1	0	0
1966-67	N/C	N/C	N/C	N/C	15	18	6
1967-68	0	0	8	13	14	22	10
1968-69	0	N/C	5	N/C	2	20	11
1969-70	0	1	9	15	0	17	6
Average	**0**	**0.1**	**3.6**	**4.5**	**3.2**	**9.3**	**6.1**
1970-71	0	2	6	10	5	10	27
1971-72	N/C	3	8	22	22	15	9
1972-73	0	3	4	8	12	4	N/C
1973-74	0	N/C	12	9	11	29	17
1974-75	0	N/C	5	13	7	24	24
1975-76	0	1	3	5	2	4	2
1976-77	0	0	0	1	2	6	7
1977-78	0	0	2	4	4	5	21
1978-79	0	0	6	4	8	3	11
1979-80	0	0	1	9	15	18	21
Average	**0**	**1.1**	**4.7**	**8.5**	**8.8**	**11.8**	**15.4**
1980-81	2	2	14	16	20	23	32
1981-82	0	2	23	31	3	31	28
1982-83	0	4	13	12	31	43	22
1983-84	0	2	39	69	41	43	43
1984-85	0	0	17	33	19	19	87
1985-86	0	1	29	32	41	42	42
1986-87	0	2	23	25	27	39	41
1987-88	0	3	24	23	23	42	51
1988-89	1	7	34	36	41	62	60
1989-90	0	3	15	31	26	21	32
Average	**0.3**	**2.6**	**23.1**	**30.8**	**27.2**	**36.5**	**43.8**
1990-91	0	1	14	15	19	37	17
1991-92	0	0	14	11	24	32	22
1992-93	0	10	15	24	27	23	21
1993-94	0	5	17	19	21	29	22
1994-95	0	0	8	0	0	0	17
1995-96	0	0	13	20	9	24	19
1996-97	0	N/C	10	9	0	39	54
1997-98	1	6	17	35	18	61	73
1998-99	0	0	28	N/C	32	69	61
1999-2000	0	1	25	22	40	64	64
Average	**0.1**	**2.5**	**16.1**	**17.2**	**19**	**37.8**	**37**

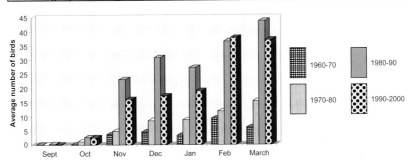

Ruddy Duck: Yearly Counts

	Sept	Oct	Nov	Dec	Jan	Feb	Mar
1980-81							
1981-82							
1982-83							
1983-84							
1984-85	12	52	51	29	6	8	76
1985-86	44	62	42	19	30	3	84
1986-87	53	61	19	0	2	66	61
1987-88	9	0	4	0	1	26	48
1988-89	42	12	1	1	0	49	55
1989-90	1	5	3	13	27	51	81
Average	26.8	32	20	10.3	11	33.8	67.5
1990-91	50	30	36	11	32	13	184
1991-92	94	118	77	1	6	171	192
1992-93	107	115	53	9	85	151	234
1993-94	49	49	31	37	65	145	127
1994-95	25	20	31	23	45	46	41
1995-96	1	12	29	28	20	73	49
1996-97	8	N/C	0	0	0	1	12
1997-98	2	9	9	4	6	41	67
1998-99	1	5	6	N/C	2	7	20
1999-2000	0	1	0	0	0	0	10
Average	33.7	39.9	27.2	12.5	26.1	64.8	93.6

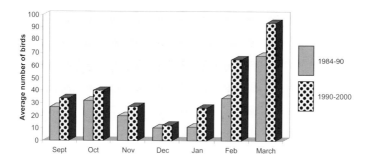

7. BIRD RINGING

Over the sixteen years from 1974 to 1989 a small amount of bird ringing was undertaken at Swithland Reservoir, although not enough to be able to break down the numbers statistically to come to any conclusion about population dynamics.

The reservoir has narrow margins and much of these can be seen from different vantage points along the roads, so that a bird ringer would often be under the watchful eye of the public and some might trespass to see what he was doing. To show one's face along the shoreline would be certain to put many waterfowl into the air to the obvious annoyance of the many local birdwatchers and during the breeding season agitate the many species of bird that breed on the margins. I have always felt that regular disturbance to the site could not really be justified.

If the area could have been worked regularly by a team of bird ringers, both the numbers of birds ringed and the species caught would have been greater and even more interesting results obtained.

There have, however, been 57 species ringed by the four ringers who have worked Swithland Reservoir sporadically. Other ringers have done work at the reservoir but their visits were brief and they were interested mainly in catching Mute Swans for a survey being carried out on the species and I have none of their figures.

The following two tables are a breakdown of the numbers of birds caught each year at Swithland Reservoir. The "p" after a number indicates "pulli" – or chicks. The two tables are followed by some interesting recoveries of birds ringed at the site or found there.

SPECIES \ YEAR	74	75	76	77	78	79	80	81	82	83	84	85	86	87	88	89	total
Little Grebe														1			1
Teal				3													3
Mallard				1													1
Sparrowhawk								5p		6p							11p
Moorhen					6	1							2				9
Coot						1											1
Little Ringed Plover			4p														4p
Green Sandpiper						2											2
Common Sandpiper	2																2
Swift	54	7	23														84
Kingfisher						2	1	1					1				5
Great Spotted Woodpecker						1											1
Lesser Spotted Woodpecker								1									1
Sand Martin		6															6
Swallow		7	1					5p									13

SPECIES \ YEAR	74	75	76	77	78	79	80	81	82	83	84	85	86	87	88	89	total
House Martin		7	15														22
Yellow Wagtail			5														5
Grey Wagtail						2											2
Pied Wagtail		3	1														4
Wren		5	1			7	3	3				6	6	25			56
Dunnock		21	7			11		2				2	6	2			51
Robin		11	4			8		3				4	4	18			52
Blackbird		20	5			16	12					19	8	5		1	86
Fieldfare												2					2
Song Thrush		7	2			1						1				1	12
Redwing						4						4					8
Mistle Thrush			1			1											2
Sedge Warbler		2	1										2				5
Reed Warbler		9						1	5	4			2	9			30
Lesser Whitethroat		2	1										1	5			9
Whitethroat		2	1	2				1	1				1	1		1	10
Garden Warbler		4				1			3				3	2		1	14
Blackcap		6	2			2							3	10		1	24
Willow Warbler		11				4		1	1				3	5			25
Chiffchaff												1	1	1			3
Goldcrest		4						1				7	1	2			15
Spotted Flycatcher		1				1							1				3
Long-tailed Tit		1	4				2					23	4	14			48
Marsh Tit		1						1				5	2	5			14
Willow Tit	1	3	1				1	1	2			2	3	3			17
Coal Tit		2	2				1							1			6
Blue Tit		4	1			13	2	7				25	44	34			130
Great Tit		3	2			6	8	2			3	8	15	14			61
Nuthatch													1				1
Treecreeper												2	2	3			7
Jay												1					1
Carrion Crow						2											2
Starling		1	3														4
Tree Sparrow		4	1	1													6
Chaffinch		6	5			1	4						15	3			34
Goldfinch		2	1														3
Siskin													1				1
Linnet		3	4														7
Lesser Redpoll		15	7										5				27
Bullfinch	2	10	2						7			4	4	9			38
Yellowhammer		2											2				4
Reed Bunting	2	14	2					1	1			12		1			33

Obviously with so few birds being ringed one would have to be very lucky indeed to hear of many of them again but we have had a few controlled or recovered. There have also been birds found here that have been ringed elsewhere and below are the notable ones.

Controlled: Trapped away from the ringing site and released with the ring intact.
Recovery: Normally denotes a bird found dead or dying away from the ringing site.

M:	Male
F:	Female
1Y:	Fledged bird in first calendar year.
2Y:	Second calendar year of life.
+:	Bird is age shown before the plus sign or older.

Mute Swan

Z 48894	1Y	01-10-81	Swithland Reservoir
One of brood of six			52° 43'N 1° 10'W
Dead		05-01-82	River Soar, near Sileby
			52° 44'N 1° 6'W

Pochard

GJ44427	2YM	03-09-81	Abberton, Colchester, Essex.
		51° 49'N	0° 50'E
Shot		01-09-87	Swithland Reservoir,
170km NW	2281 days		52° 43'N 1° 10'W

Tufted Duck

FV77310	2Y+M	29-06-83	Abberton, Colchester, Essex.
		51° 49'N	0° 50'E
Shot		01-09-87	Swithland Reservoir,
170km NW	1525 days		52° 43'N 1° 10'W

Sparrowhawk

EB65293	1Y Nestling brood of five	26-06-81	Swithland Reservoir,
		52° 43'N	1° 10'W
Found dying;injured wing		05-03-83	Hemel Hempstead, Hertfordshire
Movement 116km SE			51° 46'N 0° 28'W

Coot

GK34490	1Y	12-09-80	Staunton Harold Reservoir, Derbyshire
Found dead		15-05-86	Swithland Reservoir,
			52° 43'N 1° 10W

Black-headed Gull
EJ59962	2Y	20-12-81	Enderby, Leicestershire. 52° 35'N 1° 13'W
Freshly dead on dam part eaten		21-02-82 52° 43'N	Swithland Reservoir, 1° 10'W

Black-headed Gull
NLA 3302317	2Y+	27-02-79	Hilversum Noord, Holland Arnhem, Netherlands. 52° 13'N 5° 9'E
Freshly dead on dam part eaten.	movement 432km W	29-12-82 52° 43'N	Swithland Reservoir 1° 10'W

Black-headed Gull
KALO DKK 617912	1Y Nestling	16-06-82	Barnekold Stavns Fjord, Sanso, Denmark 55° 53'N 10° 39'E
Freshly dead part eaten		29-12-82	Swithland Reservoir, 52° 43'N 1° 10'W

Black-headed Gull
EP25740	2Y+	10-01-87	Godmanchester, Nr. Huntingdon, Cambridgeshire 52° 19'N 0° 9'W
Dead	movement 82km N.W.	08-03-90	Swithland Reservoir, 52° 43'N 1° 10'W

Black-headed Gull
	1Y Nestling	02-06-88	Klaipeda, Lithuania. 55° 42'N 21° 24'E
ring read		11-02-89	Swithland Reservoir 52° 43'N 1° 10'W

Black-headed Gull
	1Y Nestling	23-06-87	Kymi, Finland.
Found dead	Movement 1916km	03-11-89	Swithland Reservoir 52° 43'N 1° 10'W

Note: The four Black-headed Gull recoveries from abroad point to an immigration of this species from the Baltic region to over-winter in Britain. It is interesting to note that another Black-headed Gull ringed as a nestling in Klaipeda, Lithuania was found dead at Charnwood Water near Loughborough on 10th January 1991. This conclusion is strengthened by other recoveries of this species in the county.

Swift

SE 67377	1Y+	16-05-75	Swithland Reservoir, 52° 43'N 1° 10'W
Controlled		06-07-78	Queniborough Sewage Farm, Leicestershire.
	Movement 8km		52° 43'N 1° 04'W

Swift

SC82888	1Y+	19-06-77	Swithland Reservoir, 52° 43'N 1° 10'W
Controlled		30-06-78	Sinderland Sewage Farm, Cheshire.
	Movement 115km N.W.		

Swift

SC82892	1Y+	19-06-77	Swithland Reservoir 52° 43'N 1° 10'W
Freshly dead road casualty		23-05-87	Leicester.
	Movement 11km, 3625 days		52° 38'N 1° 5'W

Take note of the age of this last swift.

Robin

A199259	1Y+	04-09-81	Swithland Reservoir 52° 43'N 1° 10'W
Killed by cat		26-02-84	King's Norton, Birmingham.
	Movement 63km		52° 12'N 0° 35'W

Reed Warbler

A632421	1Y+M	19-07-80	Harold Gravel Pit, Bedfordshire.
		52° 12'N	0° 35'W
Controlled		22-05-82	Swithland Reservoir, 52° 43'N 1° 10'W
	Movement 70km		

Garden Warbler

KB09306	1Y+	09-06-82	Swithland Reservoir 52° 43'N 1° 10'W
Killed by stone being thrown at it.		27-02-89	Asesewa, Ghana.
	Movement 5149 km, Duration 2455 days		6° 23'N 0° 8'W

The first trans-Saharan recovery of this species (also in Ghana) was reported in November 1983. Since then there have been nine more birds ringed in Britain recovered in Ghana. The Swithland bird was the fifth record from Ghana. In 1998 a bird ringed at Wanlip Gravel Pits was also found in Ghana.

GLOSSARY

Adult: A bird that has reached its full plumage and sexual maturity.

Arboreal: A species that lives in trees.

Avifauna: The total bird species found in a particular region or during a given period.

Axillaries: The feathers found at the base or armpit of the wing.

Bill: The bill or beak are the jaws of a bird with a horny covering. It is made up of two parts, the upper mandible and the lower mandible.

Breeding Territory: An area that is used for the purpose of nesting and defended against intruders. This area varies in size depending on the species.

Brood: The term given to the progeny of a single clutch of eggs.

Call note: Used by birds to communicate, usually when taking part in activities such as flocking, feeding and migration and as a defence response against predators.

Cere: A soft fleshy covering at the base of some birds' bills such as pigeons and hawks. The fleshy covering is often coloured.

Colony: A group of birds nesting in close proximity. Species such as Rooks, Terns and Gulls nest in such a fashion.

Corvid: A term given to a member of the crow family *Corvidae*.

Cosmopolitan: Refers to a species with a nearly world-wide distribution.

Covert: The name given to the feathers that overlie the primaries, secondaries, tertials and tail.

Crepuscular: Refers to a bird that is active in the twilight, at dawn or dusk e.g. Woodcock and Nightjar.

Dimorphic: A species that occurs with two distinct forms or phases.

Diurnal: This term refers to a species that is active during daylight hours.

Eclipse: A post-breeding plumage found mainly in ducks. The males lose their normally colourful breeding dress and become drab similar to the females.

Exotic: A species of bird alien to the area being studied and normally referring to a bird that has escaped from captivity.

Feral: A species that was formerly kept in captivity or domesticated that has either escaped, been released or introduced and has become wild and self supporting.

Gregarious: A species that lives in groups.

Holarctic: A combination of the Palearctic and Nearctic.

Immature: In its early stages of life before becoming adult.

Invasion: In birdwatching terms this refers to a species normally short-term expansion of its range. It is also referred to as an irruption.

Juvenile: A young bird in its first full plumage after leaving the nest.

Malar: An area on the side of a bird's throat just below the bill.

Mandible: See bill.

Migration: The seasonal movement of birds between different areas. Normally it is the movement to and from breeding and wintering grounds.

Mirror: These are white spots found near the tips of the outer primaries of gulls.

Morph: See dimorphic and polymorphism.

Moult: The term used for the regular shedding and regeneration of a bird's plumage. This process normally takes place once or twice a year and as many as three times in some species.

Moustachial: Refers to the streak or line found in some birds' plumages that runs from the base of the bill and down the throat giving the bird a moustached appearance.

Nearctic Region: A zoogeographical area comprising the North American continent from the Pacific to the Atlantic southward to tropical Mexico.

Nest: The structure made by a bird in which it lays and incubates its eggs.

Palearctic Region: A zoogeographical area comprising Europe and Africa north of the Sahara and Asia north of the Himalayas.

Passerine: A bird that belongs to the order Passeriformes. These are often referred to as perching and singing birds.

Passage migrant: A bird that passes through an area normally only briefly on its migration to and from its breeding and wintering areas.

Pelagic: A bird that inhabits open seas and oceans.

Phase: See dimorphic and polymorphism.

Polymorphism: Two or more easily distinguishable morphs or phases that co-exist within a single inter-breeding population regardless of sex and age. e.g. Parasitic Skua and Snow Goose

Polygamy: A male or female that has more than one mate.

Predation: This is where one species preys on another in order to get food.

Primary feathers: These are the flight feathers and can be found from the carpal outwards along the manus.

Primary projection: This term refers to the distance between the tip of the longest tertial and the wingtip (the tip of the longest primary) on the closed wing.

Pullus: The name given to a young bird that is not full grown and cannot fly.

Roding: The display flight of the Woodcock which takes place from March to July.

Roost: The sleeping and resting place of birds. Occasionally huge numbers gather together for communal roosts e.g. gulls and Starlings.

Scapulars: The feathers above the shoulder.

Scrape: The term used for the meagre nest that is usually formed by scraping a shallow depression in the ground. Some plovers and waders frequently nest in this fashion.

Secondary feathers: The inner flight feathers that are attached to the forearm or ulna.

Sedentary: A bird that moves very little from the area where it was bred.

Speculum: A distinctive square patch of colour usually found on the secondaries. In ducks it is an iridescent patch of colour.

Superciliary: A marking above the bird's eye that is often a stripe.

Summer visitor: A bird that visits an area, normally to breed, during the summer months.

Taxonomy: The classification of life forms. To put birds into a classified order the anatomy, biochemical and physiological behaviour are all taken into account.

Tertials: The inner-most secondaries, or third row of flight feathers which have a different function and shape from the other secondaries.

Underparts: The under surface of the bird from the chin to the tip of the tail.

Upperparts: The upper surface of the bird from the forehead to the tip of the tail.

Vagrant: A bird that has wandered well outside its normal range.

Vermiculations: Fine wavy lines on a bird's plumage.

WeBs: This is a wildfowl monitoring group made up of a partnership between the British Trust for Ornithology, the Royal Society for the Protection of Birds, the Wildfowl and Wetland Trust, and the Joint Nature Conservation Committee.

Winter visitor: A bird that winters in a different area from the one in which it breeds.

Wing-bar: A term which usually refers to a pale bar across a bird's wing normally formed by pale tips to the greater or median coverts or by pale bases to the primaries and secondaries.

Wreck: A term used to describe the occasional forcing ashore of sea birds by gale force winds.

REFERENCES

BAKER, Kevin. *Warblers of Europe Asia and North Africa.* 1997. Christopher Helm, London.

BROWN, Leslie. & AMADON, Dean. *Eagles, Hawks & Falcons of the World Volumes 1 & 2.* 1968. Country Life Books, Middlesex.

BROWN, Leslie. *The New Naturalist: British Birds of Prey.* 1976. Collins, London.

BROWNE, Montague. *The Vertebrate Animals of Leicestershire and Rutland.* 1889.

B.T.O. *Field List of British Birds.* 1993. British Trust for Ornithology, Thetford, Norfolk.

B.T.O. NEWS 218: *The B.T.O.'s Danger List: Warning to Government about 40 species.* 1998. British Trust for Ornithology, Thetford, Norfolk.

B.T.O. NEWS 224: *The findings of the 29th Garden Bird Feeding Survey winter 1998/99.* 1999. British Trust for Ornithology, Thetford, Norfolk.

BURTON, John A. Edited by. Several authors. *Owls of the World, their evolution structure and ecology.* 1973. Peter Lowe, Holland.

CLEMENT, P. *Finches & Sparrows: An Identification Guide.* 1993. Christopher Helm, London.

COWARD, T.A. *Birds of the British Isles and their eggs.* 1969. Frederick Warne & Co Ltd., London.

CRAMP, S. et al. (eds.) *Handbook of the Birds of Europe, the Middle East and North Africa: 1977-1994.* 9 Volumes. Oxford University Press, Oxford.

DIAMOND, A.W., SCHREIBER, R.L., CRONKITE, W. & TORY PETERSON, R. *Save the Birds.* 1987. Houghton Mifflin Company, Boston.

FORSMAN, Dick. *The Raptors of Europe and the Middle East: A Handbook of Field Identification.* 1999. T & D Poyser, London.

GLUE, David. *The Garden Bird Book.* 1982. Macmillan, London.

GREGORY, D.G., CAMPBELL, L.H., and GIBBONS, D.W. *The State of the UK's Birds 1999.* 2000. R.S.P.B. and B.T.O. Sandy, Bedfordshire.

GRIMMETT, R, INSKIPP, C. & INSKIPP, T. *Birds of the Indian Subcontinent.* 1998. Christopher Helm, London.

HAGEMEIJER, W.J.M. & BLAIR, M.J. *The EBCC Atlas of European Breeding Birds: Their Distribution and Abundance.* 1997. Poyser, London.

HARRAP, S. *Tits, Nuthatches and Treecreepers.* 1996. Christopher Helm, London.

HARRISON, Colin. *An Atlas of the Birds of the Western Palaearctic.* 1982. Collins, Glasgow.

HARRISON, Colin. *A Field Guide to the Nests, Eggs and Nestlings of British and European Birds.* 1975. Collins, Glasgow.

HARRISON, Colin. *A Field Guide to the Nests, Eggs and Nestlings of North American Birds.* 1978. Collins, Glasgow.

HARRISON, Peter. *Seabirds, an Identification Guide.* 1985 Croom Helm, London.

HAYMAN, P, MARCHANT, A.J. & PRATER, A.H. *Shorebirds: An Identification Guide to the Waders of the World.* 1986. Croom Helm, London.

HICKLING, Ronald. *Birds in Leicestershire and Rutland.* 1978. Leicestershire and Rutland Ornithological Society, Leicester.

HOLLOM, P.A.D. *The Popular Handbook of Rarer British Birds.* Revised Second Edition 1980. H.F. & G. Witherby Ltd., London.

HOWARD, Richard, & MOORE, Alick. *A Complete Checklist of the Birds of the World.* Second edition 1994. Academic Press, London.

HUGHES, B. *Parentage of Ruddy Duck x White-headed Duck hybrids shot in Spain, 1984-1999.* 2000. Unpublished W.W.T. report. 3pp.

JOHNS, Rev. C.A. *British Birds in their Haunts.* Fifth Edition 1919. George Routledge & Sons Limited, London.

JONSSON, Lars. *Birds of Europe with North Africa and the Middle East.* 1992, Christopher Helm, London.

KEBLE MARTIN, W. *The New Concise British Flora.* 1982. Bloomsbury Books, London.

LEICESTER LITERARY AND PHILOSOPHICAL SOCIETY, ORNITHOLOGICAL SECTION. *Annual Bird Reports 1941- 1945.*

LEICESTERSHIRE AND RUTLAND ORNITHOLOGICAL SOCIETY *Annual Bird Reports 1946-2000.*

LOUGHBOROUGH NATURALISTS' CLUB. *Charnwood Forest A Changing Landscape.* 1981. Sycamore Press Limited, Melton Mowbray, Leicestershire.

LOUGHBOROUGH NATURALISTS' CLUB. Quarterly Bulletin *Heritage* 1961-2000.

MACDONALD, David, & BARRETT, Priscilla. *Collins Field Guide: Mammals of Britain and Europe.* 1993. Harper-Collins, London.

MADGE, S. & BURN, H. *Wildfowl: An Identification Guide to the Ducks, Geese and Swans of the World.* 1988. Christopher Helm, London.

MADGE, S. & BURN, H. *Crows and Jays: A Guide to the Crows, Jays and Magpies of the World.* 1994. Christopher Helm, London.

MEAD, Chris. *Bird Migration.* 1983. Country Life Books, Middlesex.

MEAD, Chris. *B.T.O. Guide sixteen, Bird Ringing.* 1974. British Trust for Ornithology, Tring, Hertfordshire.

MEAD, Chris. *The State of the Nation's Birds.* 2000. Whittet Books Ltd., Suffolk.

MONROE, Jr. Burt L. & SIBLEY, Charles G. *A World Checklist of Birds.* 1993. Yale University Press, New Haven and London.

MULLARNEY, SVENSSON, ZETTERSTROM & GRANT, *Collins Bird Guide.* 1999. Harper Collins, London.

NATIONAL GEOGRAPHIC SOCIETY, *Field Guide to the Birds of North America.* 1985. National Geographic Society, Washington.

OGILVIE, M.A. *Ducks of Britain and Europe.* 1975. T. & A.D. Poyser Ltd., Berkhamsted, Hertfordshire.

OGILVIE, M.A. *The Winter Birds.* 1976. Michael Joseph Ltd., London.

OGILVIE, M.A. *Rare Breeding Birds in the United Kingdom 1997.* 1999. British Birds 92: 389-428.

ORR, Richard & POPE, Joyce. *Mammals of Britain and Europe.* 1983. Pelham Books Ltd., London.

OWEN, Myrfyn. *Wildfowl of Europe.* 1977. Macmillan, London and The Wildfowl Trust.

PARMENTER, T. & BYERS, C. *A Guide to the Warblers of the Western Palaearctic.* 1991. Bruce Coleman Books, Uxbridge.

PARSLOW, John. *Breeding Birds of Britain and Ireland – a Historical Survey.* 1973. T.& A. D. Poyser Ltd., Berkhamsted, Hertfordshire.

PETERSON, R, MOUNTFORT, G. & HOLLOM, P.A.D. *Collins Field Guide: Birds of Britain and Europe.* Fifth Edition 1993. Harper-Collins, London.

PHILLIP'S, *Great World Atlas.* 1995. George Philip Limited, London.

RICHARDS, J. Alan. *The Birdwatchers A-Z.* 1980. David & Charles, London.

PRIMAVESI, A. L. & EVANS, P. A. *The Flora of Leicestershire.* 1988. Leicestershire Museums, Leicester.

R.S.P.B. & OTHERS, *Birds of Conservation Concern in the United Kingdom, Channel Islands and Isle of Man.*

SHARROCK J.T.R. & E. M. *Rare Birds in Britain and Ireland.* 1976. T. & A. D. Poyser Ltd., Berkhamsted, Hertfordshire.

SIMMS, Eric. *The New Naturalist: British Warblers.* 1985. Collins, London.

SIMPSON & DAY, *Field Guide to the Birds of Australia.* Fourth Edition 1994. Christopher Helm, London.

SINCLAIR, I, HOCKEY, P, TARBOTON, W, HAYMEN, P & ARLOTT, N. *Birds of Southern Africa.* 1993. New Holland, London.

STACE, Clive. *New Flora of the British Isles.* 1997, Second Edition. Cambridge University Press, Cambridge.

SVENSSON, Lars. *Identification Guide to European Passerines.* 1992, Fourth Edition. Published by the author.

TURNER, A. *A Handbook to the Swallows and Martins of the World.* 1989. Christopher Helm, London.

VINICOMBE, K. & COTTRIDGE, D.M. *Rare Birds in Britain & Ireland: A Photographic Record.* 1996. Harper-Collins, London.

WELLS, M.G. *World Bird Species Checklist.* 1998. Worldlist, Bushey, Hertfordshire.

WINKLER, H., CHRISTIE, D. & NURNEY, D. *Woodpeckers: A Guide to the Woodpeckers, Piculets and Wrynecks of the World.* 1995. Pica Press, Robertsbridge.

WIX, and others. *Bygone Quorn in Photographs.* Revised Edition 1995. The Council of the Borough of Charnwood and Quorn Parish Council. Leicestershire

COMMON AND SCIENTIFIC NAMES OF SPECIES, OTHER THAN BIRDS, MENTIONED IN THE TEXT

MAMMALS

Noctule Bat	*Nyctalus noctula*	Fallow Deer	*Dama dama*
Red Fox	*Vulpes vulpes*	Wild Boar	*Sus scrofa*
Wolf	*Canis lupus*	Grey Squirrel	*Sciurus carolinensis*
Eurasian Badger	*Meles meles*	Red Squirrel	*Sciurus vulgaris*
American Mink	*Mustela vison*	Harvest Mouse	*Micromys minutus*
Western Polecat	*Mustela putorius*	Wood Mouse	*Apodemus sylvaticus*
Stoat	*Mustela erminea*	Brown Rat	*Rattus norvegicus*
Weasel	*Mustela nivalis*	Northern Water Vole	*Arvicola terrestris*
Wildcat	*Felis silvestris*	Field Vole	*Microtus agrestis*
Roe Deer	*Capreolus capreolus*	Rabbit	*Oryctolagus cuniculus*
Red Deer	*Cervus elaphus*		

BUTTERFLIES

Purple Hairstreak	*Quercusia quercus*
White-letter Hairstreak	*Strymonidia-w-album*
Ringlet	*Aphantopus hyperantus*

DRAGONFLIES

Migrant Hawker	*Aeshna mixta*

PLANTS

Water Horsetail	*Equisetum fluviatile*	Red Campion	*Silene dioica*
Bracken	*Pteridium aquilinum*	Amphibious Bistort	*Persicaria amphibia*
Lady-fern	*Athyrium filix-femina*	Wood Dock	*Rumex sanguineus*
Male-fern	*Dryopteris filix-mas*	Golden Dock	*Rumex maritimus*
Narrow Buckler-fern	*Dryopteris carthusiana*	Perforate St. John's-wort	
Broad Buckler-fern	*Dryopteris dilatata*		*Hypericum perforatum*
Norway Spruce	*Picea abies*	Square-stalked St. John's-wort	
European Larch	*Larix deciduas*		*Hypericum tetrapterum*
Black Pine	*Pinus nigra*	Slender St. John's-wort	*Hypericum pulchrum*
Scots Pine	*Pinus sylvestris*	Lime	*Tilia x europaea*
Yew	*Taxus baccata*	Small-leaved Lime	*Tilia cordata*
Marsh-marigold	*Caltha palustris*	Sweet Violet	*Viola odorata*
Wood Anemone	*Anemone nemorosa*	Common Dog-violet	*Viola riviniana*
Goldilocks Buttercup	*Ranunculus auricomus*	White Poplar	*Populus alba*
Lesser Celandine	*Ranunculus ficaria*	Aspen	*Populus tremula*
Wych Elm	*Ulmus glabra*	Lombardy-poplar	*Populus nigra var. italica*
English Elm	*Ulmus procera*	Crack-willow	*Salix fragilis*
Common Nettle	*Urtica dioica*	White Willow	*Salix alba*
Sessile Oak	*Quercus petraea*	Cricket-bat Willow	*Salix alba Ssp.caerulea*
Pedunculate Oak	*Quercus robur*	Almond Willow	*Salix triandra*
Red Oak	*Quercus rubra*	Osier	*Salix viminalis*
Silver Birch	*Betula pendula*	Goat Willow	*Salix caprea*
Downy Birch	*Betula pubescens*	Grey Willow	*Salix cinerea*
Alder	*Alnus glutinosa*	Great Yellow-cress	*Rorippa amphibia*
Hazel	*Corylus avellana*	Large Bitter-cress	*Cardamine amara*
Greater Stitchwort	*Stellaria holostea*	Heather	*Calluna vulgaris*
Water Chickweed	*Myosoton aquaticum*	Primrose	*Primula vulgaris*
Ragged-Robin	*Lychnis flos cuculi*	Cowslip	*Primula veris*

Yellow Pimpernel	*Lysimachia nemorum*
Brookweed	*Samolus valerandi*
Black Currant	*Ribes nigrum*
Opposite-leaved Golden-saxifrage	
	Chrysosplenium oppositifolium
Alternate-leaved Golden-saxifrage	
	Chrysosplenium alternifolium
Grass-of-Parnassus	*Parnassia palustris*
Bridewort	*Spiraea salicifolia*
Meadowsweet	*Filipendula ulmaria*
Bramble	*Rubus fruticosus agg.*
Marsh Cinquefoil	*Potentilla palustris*
Wood Avens	*Geum urbanum*
Great Burnet	*Sanguisorba officinalis*
Lady's-mantle	*Alchemilla filicaulis*
	Ssp.vestita
Field-rose	*Rosa arvensis*
Rowan	*Sorbus aucuparia*
Hawthorn	*Crataegus monogyna*
Common Bird's-foot- trefoil	
	Lotus corniculatus
Greater Bird's-foot-trefoil	
	Lotus pedunculatus
Bird's-foot	*Ornithopus perpusillus*
Tufted Vetch	*Vicia cracca*
Bush Vetch	*Vicia sepium*
Meadow Vetchling	*Lathyrus pratensis*
Spiny Restharrow	*Ononis spinosa*
Zigzag Clover	*Trifolium medium*
Knotted Clover	*Trifolium striatum*
Gorse	*Ulex europaeus*
Purple Loosestrife	*Lythrum salicaria*
Great Willowherb	*Epilobium hirsutum*
Enchanter's nightshade	*Circaea lutetiana*
Holly	*Ilex aquifoluim*
Dog's Mercury	*Mercurialis perennis*
Horse Chestnut	*Aesculus hippocastanum*
Norway Maple	*Acer platanoides*
Field Maple	*Acer campestre*
Sycamore	*Acer pseudoplatanus*
Wood-sorrel	*Oxalis acetosella*
Herb-Robert	*Geranium robertianum*
Common Stork's-bill	*Erodium cicutarium*
Ivy	*Hedera helix*
Sanicle	*Sanicula europaea*
Pignut	*Conopodium majus*
Wild Angelica	*Angelica sylvestris*
Bittersweet	*Solanum dulcamara*
Water Forget-me-not	*Myosotis scorpioides*
Betony	*Stachys officinalis*
Common Hemp-nettle	*Galeopsis tetrahit*
Skullcap	*Scutellaria galericulata*
Wood Sage	*Teucruim scorodonia*
Bugle	*Ajuga reptans*
Ground-ivy	*Glechoma hederacea*
Gypsywort	*Lycopus europaeus*

Water Mint	*Mentha aquatica*
Shoreweed	*Littorella uniflora*
Ash	*Fraxinus excelsior*
Water Figwort	*Scrophularia auriculata*
Foxglove	*Digitalis purpurea*
Germander Speedwell	*Veronica chamaedrys*
Wood Speedwell	*Veronica montana*
Pink Water -Speedwell	*Veronica catenata*
Common Cow-wheat	*Melampyrum pratense*
Nettle-leaved Bellflower	*Campanula trachelium*
Harebell	*Campanula rotundifolia*
Fen Bedstraw	*Galium uliginosum*
Common Marsh- bedstraw	
	Galium palustre
Lady's Bedstraw	*Galium verum*
Elder	*Sambucus nigra*
Guelder-rose	*Viburnum opulus*
Honeysuckle	*Lonicera periclymenum*
Moschatel	*Adox moschatellina*
Common Valerian	*Valeriana officinalis*
Lesser Burdock	*Arctium minus*
Common Knapweed	*Centaurea nigra*
Sneezewort	*Achillea ptarmica*
Heath Groundsel	*Senecio sylvaticus*
Soft-rush	*Juncus effusus*
Hairy Wood-rush	*Luzula pilosa*
Great Wood-rush	*Luzula sylvatica*
Common Spike-rush	*Eleocharis palustris*
Needle Spike-rush	*Eleocharis acicularis*
Greater Tussock-sedge	*Carex paniculata*
Brown Sedge	*Carex disticha*
Remote Sedge	*Carex remota*
Lesser Pond-sedge	*Carex acutiformis*
Greater Pond-sedge	*Carex riparia*
Cyperus Sedge	*Carex pseudocyperus*
Wood Sedge	*Carex sylvatica*
Carnation Sedge	*Carex panicea*
Slender Tufted-sedge	*Carex acuta*
Wood Miller	*Milium effusum*
Rough Meadow-grass	*Poa trivialis*
Red Sweet-grass	*Glyceria maxima*
Wood Melick	*Melica uniflora*
Wavy Hair-grass	*Deschampsia flexuosa*
Red Canary-grass	*Phalaris arundinacea*
Orange Foxtail	*Alopecurus aequalis*
Hairy-brome	*Bromus ramose*
Bearded Couch	*Elymus caninus*
Branched Bur-reed	*Sparganium erectum*
Bulrush	*Typha latifolia*
Lesser Bulrush	*Typha angustifolia*
Lily-of-the valley	*Convallaria majalis*
Bluebell	*Hyacinthoides non-scripta*
Ramsons	*Allium ursinum*
Yellow Iris	*Iris pseudacorus*
Marsh Helleborine	*Epipactis palustris*
Lady's-tresses	*Spiranthes spiralis*

INDEX

"Birds are far more than robins, thrushes, and finches to brighten the suburban garden, or ducks and grouse to fill the sportsman's bag, or rare waders or warblers to be ticked off on a birdwatchers checklist. They are indicators of the environment – a sort of environmental litmus-paper."

Roger Tory Peterson (1908 - 1996)
in 'Birds', selected by Helen Exley, New York, 1994